ONE WEEK LOAN

2 0 MAR 1992
2 7 MAR 1992   2 9 NOV 1994
- 3 APR 1992   - 1 DEC 1994
- 1 MAY 1992   1 4 DEC 1994
2 8 MAR 1995
- 8 MAY 1992   1 8 JAN 1999
1 8 MAY 1992
3 0 NOV 1993
3 1 MAY 1991   6 DEC 1993
2 MAR 1992
1 3 MAR 1992   1 7 DEC 1993
14th Jan

Developments in Soviet Politics

Edited by

Stephen White
Alex Pravda
Zvi Gitelman

MACMILLAN

First published 1990

Published by
MACMILLAN EDUCATION LTD
Houndmills, Basingstoke, Hampshire RG21 2XS
and London
Companies and representatives
throughout the world

Phototypeset by Input Typesetting Ltd, London

Printed in Great Britain by Billing & Sons Ltd, Worcester

British Library Cataloguing in Publication Data
Developments in Soviet politics.
1. Soviet Union. Politics
I. White, Stephen, 1945– II. Pravda, Alex, 1947– III.
Gitelman, Zvi Y. (Zvi Yechiel), 1940–
320.947
ISBN 0–333–52742–9 (hardcover)
ISBN 0–333–52743–7 (paperback)

Contents

List of Illustrations and Maps

Illustrations

Maps

Acknowledgements

The editors and publishers wish to acknowledge with thanks permission from the following to reproduce copyright material:

Progress Publishers, Moscow, for the material in Chapter 12, from *Inogo ne dano*, edited by Yuri Afanasyev (1988).
Moskovskie novosti (1989), for data in Table 5.1.
Narodnoe khozyaistvo SSSR v 1987 g. (1989), for data in Table 9.2, and *Narodnoe khozyaistvo SSSR* (various years), for data in Table 9.1.
Kommunist (1989), for data in Table 9.2.
Goskomstat, for data in Table 10.1, from *Naselenie SSSR 1987: Statisticheskii sbornik* (1988).
Statistical Yearbook 1985/86 (New York, United Nations, 1988), for data in Table 10.2.

The publishers have made every effort to trace all copyright-holders, but if any have been inadvertently overlooked they will be pleased to make the necessary arrangement at the first opportunity.

Notes on the Contributors

Yevgeny Ambartsumov is a senior staff member of the Institute of the Economics of the World Socialist System, USSR Academy of Sciences, Moscow. He is the author of several books and of contributions to symposia including *Inogo ne dano* (1988); his articles have appeared in *Voprosy istorii, Moscow News* and elsewhere.

Mary Buckley is lecturer in Politics at the University of Edinburgh, Scotland. A graduate of Leicester and Vanderbilt Universities, her books include *Soviet Social Scientists Talking* (1986) and *Women and Ideology in the Soviet Union* (1989).

William E. Butler is Professor of Law and Director of the Centre for the Study of Socialist Legal Systems at University College London. His books include *The Soviet Union and the Law of the Sea* (1971) and *Soviet Law* (2nd edn, 1988), and he is editor or complier of *International Law and the International System* (1987), *Justice and Comparative Law* (1987) and other publications.

Alfred B. Evans, Jr, is a member of the Department of Political Science at California State University, Fresno. His articles have appeared in *Slavic Review, Soviet Studies, Coexistence*, the *Journal of Communist Studies* and elsewhere, and he has contributed to *Ideology and Soviet Politics* (1988) and other collections.

Zvi Gitelman is Professor of Political Science at the University of Michigan, Ann Arbor. A specialist in Soviet political sociology and ethnic issues, his books include *Jewish Nationality and Soviet Politics* (1972), *Public Opinion in European Socialist Systems* (coedited, 1977) and *Century of Ambivalence: Jews of Russia and the Soviet Union* (1988).

Jeffrey W. Hahn is Professor of Political Science at Villanova University, Pennsylvania. His study of political participation, *Soviet Grassroots*, appeared in 1988, and he has also contributed to *Slavic Review*, the *Journal of Communist Studies, Problems of Communism* and other publications.

Ronald J. Hill is Associate Professor of Political Science at Trinity College, Dublin. A specialist in Soviet local politics and the

xiii

CPSU, his most recent books are *The Soviet Union: Politics, Economics and Society* (2nd edn, 1989) and *Gorbachev and Perestroika* (co-edited, 1989).

Ken Jowitt is Professor of Political Science at the University of Califormia, Berkeley. A specialist in Romanian and comparative communist politics, his books include *Revolutionary Breakthroughs and National Development* (1971), *Images of Detente and the Soviet Political Order* (1977) and *The Leninist Response to National Dependency* (1978).

Nicholas Lampert is Senior Lecturer at the Centre for Russian and East European Studies, University of Birmingham, England. A graduate of Oxford and Sussex Universities, his books include *The Technical Intelligentsia and the Soviet State* (1979) and *Whistleblowing in the Soviet Union* (1985), and he is a member of the board of *Detente*.

David Mandel is a member of the Department of Political Science at the University of Montreal, Canada. His books include *Petrograd Workers and the Fall of the Old Regime* (1983) and *Petrograd Workers and the Soviet Seizure of Power* (1984); he has also contributed to *Socialist Register, Studies in Political Economy* and other publications.

Alex Pravda is a Fellow of St Antony's College, Oxford, and was formerly director of the Soviet Foreign Policy Programme at the Royal Institute of International Affairs. His books include *Czechoslovakia: the Party and the People* (with others, 1973), *Trade Unions in Communist States* (co-edited, 1987) and *Ideology and Soviet Politics* (co-edited, 1988).

Peter Rutland is a member of the Department of Government, Wesleyan University, Connecticut, and was formerly at the University of Texas, Austin. A specialist in Soviet political economy, his books include *The Myth of the Plan* (1985) and a forthcoming study on *The Politics of Industrial Stagnation in the USSR*.

Stephen White is Reader in Politics and a member of the Institute of Soviet and East European Studies at the University of Glasgow, Scotland. A graduate of Dublin, Glasgow and Oxford Universities, his most recent books are *The Bolshevik Poster* (1988), *Gorbachev and Gorbachevism* (co-edited, 1989) and *Gorbachev in Power* (1990).

John P. Willerton, Jr, is a member of the Department of Political Science at the University of Arizona, Tucson. His articles have appeared in *Studies in Comparative Communism, Soviet Studies* and other journals and professional symposia, and he is the author of a forthcoming study entitled *Patronage and Politics in the USSR*.

Glossary of Abbreviations and Terms

Advokatura	Advocacy
Apparat	Party administrative apparatus
Apparatchik	Full-time party official
Arbitrazh	Tribunal system for disputes between state enterprises
Bolshevik	Radical ('majority') faction of Russian Social Democratic Labour (later Communist) Party
CIA	Central Intelligence Agency (USA)
CMEA, Comecon	Council of Mutual Economic Assistance
CPE	Centrally planned economy
CPSU	Communist Party of the Soviet Union
Glasnost'	Openness, publicity
GNP	Gross national product
Gorkom	City party committee
Gosagroprom	State Agroindustrial Committee
Gosplan	State Planning Committee
Gospriemka	State quality control
Gossnab	State Committee on Supplies
Goszakaz	State order
INF	Intermediate-range nuclear force
Ispolkom	Executive committee of a soviet
Jurisconsult	Legal adviser to ministry, enterprise, etc.
Kadry	Cadres, staff
KGB	Committee of State Security
Khozraschet	Cost-accounting
Kolkhoz	Collective farm
Komsomol	Young Communist League
Krai	Territory
Menshevik	Moderate (minority) faction of the Russian Social Democratic Labour (later Communist) Party
NEP	New Economic Policy (1921–8)
Nomenklatura	List of party-controlled posts
Oblast'	Region, province

OECD	Organisation for Economic Cooperation and Development
Obshchestvennik	Activist
Okrug	Area, district
Perestroika	Restructuring
Plenum	Full (plenary) meeting
Podmena	Substitution, supplantation
PPO	Primary party organisation
Pravo	Law (in general sense)
Pravo kontrolya	Party's right of supervision
Raikom	District party committee
RAPO	Territorial farm management complex
RSFSR	Russian Soviet Federal Socialist Republic (Russian Republic)
SALT	Strategic arms limitation
Sblizhenie	Drawing together (of nationalities)
SDI	Strategic Defense Initiative ('Star Wars')
Sliyanie	Fusion (of nationalities)
USSR	Union of Soviet Socialist Republics
Val	Gross output
WTO	Warsaw Treaty Organisation
Zakon	(Statute) law
Zastoi	Stagnation

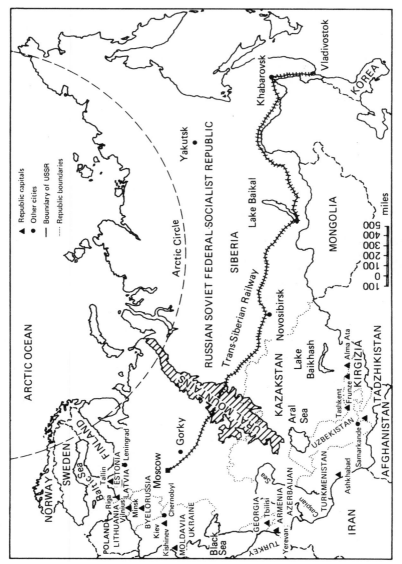

MAP 1   *The USSR*

Introduction

This is not a book about Gorbachev, nor is it simply another book about the Soviet political system. It is, we hope, the best of both: a close and analytical study of the Soviet system that takes account of the dramatic changes that have been occurring since 1985 under the Gorbachev leadership. The Gorbachev reforms, we argue, have produced a Soviet political system with new and distinctive characteristics. There is the impact of *glasnost'* or openness on all aspects of Soviet life, from history to crime, drugs and prostitution. In cultural policy there has been a greater willingness to tolerate diversity, most notably through the publication of works like Pasternak's *Doctor Zhivago* and Solzhenitsyn's *Gulag Archipelago*. There has been a sustained attempt to bring about a 'radical reform' of the Soviet economy, involving a reduction of state control and a greater role for market forces. And in political life, which is our central concern in this volume, there has been a marked if uneven shift towards 'democratisation', involving more competitive elections, greater information and accountability within the Communist Party, and moves towards a Soviet-style rule of law.

This is not, however, simply a book about the Gorbachev reforms: partly because they can be understood only in terms of what preceded them, and partly also because those reforms are incomplete, ambiguous and not necessarily permanent. As the chapters in this book make clear, for instance, there is still a difference between *glasnost'* and a free press. The media legislation that was introduced in November 1989 did nominally abolish censorship, but publications had to be 'registered' and were subject to quite severe penalties for the 'abuse' of the rights they had been given. It was in any case difficult to conceive of an end to the 'monopolisation' of the media when printing, broadcasting and other resources remained almost entirely in the hands of the state. In the economy, similarly, there were ambitious plans for a shift towards a 'fully-fledged socialist market', but government control of national income, despite these objectives, actually increased during the 1980s, and many of the most important innovations, such as the

1

cooperatives, were highly controversial and in any case made a very small contribution to the supply of goods and services.

The progress of 'democratisation' in political life was also an uneven one. The electoral process, for instance, was opened up to the mass of the population; but officials still retained substantial control over nominations, and a third of the seats in the new national legislature – the Congress of People's Deputies – were reserved for candidates from the Communist Party and other public organisations. The new Congress, in turn, raised difficult and so far unresolved issues about political authority. Did the Congress, armed with the people's mandate, have the decisive say in public policy and governmental appointments? Or was this still a matter for the CPSU, guided by its 'scientific' ideology, and qualified as a result to exercise a 'leading' or at least a dominant role in all areas of Soviet life? And could there be a genuine rule of law so long as judges remained, in the last resort, political appointees, with their decisions closely monitored by party and state officials?

The Soviet political system, as it entered the 1990s, was accordingly an uneasy amalgam of 'traditional' features, such as public ownership and the leading role of the CPSU, together with much more recent and Gorbachevian features such as *glasnost'* and democratisation. The tensions between the 'old' and the 'new', in fact, provided much of the substance of Soviet political life as the 1980s drew to a close. The leading role of the Communist Party was perhaps the clearest example. There had been no mention of the leading role in earlier Soviet constitutions until in 1977, under Leonid Brezhnev, it had been incorporated into Article 6. But how democratic was this, it began to be asked, when only a small minority of adults were members of this ruling party? In February 1990, at an historic plenum, the Central Committee agreed to abandon the party's constitutionally guaranteed leading role; but it still asserted the right to act as a 'political leader' within the wider society, and to be the only means by which the policy of *perestroika* could be made a reality. There were similar tensions between 'plan' and 'market', with some economists calling for an unapologetic embrace of commodity relations and others warning of the costs this would involve in terms of unemployment, inflation and social stability. The authorities, once again, included an unhappy mixture of both elements in their proposals for the 13th Five Year Plan, adopted in 1990, which was to cover the first half of the new decade.

Not simply, as the 1980s drew to a close, were there abstract contradictions between the logics of the 'old' and the 'new', between central management and local control, or between Leninism and popular sovereignty. The combination of these different logics within a single politico-economic system also gave rise to social tensions, some so serious that they threatened the survival of the Gorbachevian system itself. The introduction of elements of the market, for instance, led to a rapid increase in prices (as producers took advantage of scarcity conditions) and to a significant increase in poverty, particularly among pensioners (official data indicated that at least 43 million adults or 15 per cent of the total fell below the subsistence minimum). It also emerged that there were relatively high levels of unemployment or underemployment throughout the system, particularly in Central Asia. Efforts were made to improve social benefits, particularly pensions; but there was a large budgetary deficit, and there were unusually heavy demands upon it as a result of the Chernobyl nuclear explosion and the Armenian earthquake as well as health, environmental and other priorities. The miners' strikes of the summer of 1989, the most extensive in the USSR since the 1920s, showed that Soviet workers were becoming impatient for results, not just for words; and alarmingly, from the point of view of the authorities, some of them were beginning to raise overtly political demands, such as multiparty politics and the abolition of official privileges.

Apart from social tensions, the Gorbachev leadership, as it entered the 1990s, also faced perhaps the most sustained challenge that had ever been mounted to the integrity of the Soviet state itself. These nationalist pressures stemmed from a whole variety of circumstances. One of them was history: the concern of a wide range of Soviet peoples, particularly in the Baltic, for a honest account of the circumstances under which their republics had become part of the USSR. Another concern was environmental: Ukrainians, Lithuanians and others objected to the way in which their republics had become the basis of a massive energy, and in particular nuclear, industry, which was potentially unsafe and cer- tainly far larger than their own needs would have suggested. Most of all, perhaps, it was a response to the overcentralised 'command- administrative system' that Gorbachev had himself condemned, and which stifled local self-expression just as much as it obstructed popular initiatives in other parts of the Soviet system. The pressure for full independence was strongest, entering the 1990s, in the three Baltic republics, which had the most developed economies and the most recent experience of self-government. In other parts of the USSR nationalist pressures were more 'communal' in character, as in the dispute between Armenia and Azerbaijan over Nagorno- Karabakh. In all cases, however, there was pressure for a much greater degree of local decision-making in political, cultural and economic matters; and concerns of this kind extended throughout the USSR, from the Baltic and the Caucasus to the Ukraine and Russia itself, both of which formed popular fronts in the autumn of 1989.

Tensions of this kind raised in the sharpest possible way the larger purposes of *perestroika*. Gorbachev's earliest objective, as he put it to the Central Committee meeting that elected him, was the 'acceleration of socioeconomic development and the perfection of all aspects of Soviet life'. It soon became apparent that this meant, among other things, *glasnost'* in Soviet public life, a 'radical reform' of the Soviet economy, and (from early 1987) the 'democratisation' of politics. Beyond this, Gorbachev claimed to be seeking a 'qualitatively new state of Soviet society', or (as he put it to the 19th Party Conference in 1988) a 'new image' of socialism, one that was free of the abuses of the Soviet past and open to the cultural and political achievements of other civilisations. A fuller statement of his objectives, 'The socialist idea and revolutionary *perestroika*', appeared in the party newspaper *Pravda* in November 1989. Drawing upon a series of speeches he had made in the late autumn, the Soviet leader continued to insist that there could be no detailed blueprint of the kind of society he and his colleagues wished to construct, nor would it come about quickly: *perestroika* would be a 'lengthy stage in the historical development of socialism', probably extending into the twenty-first century. It would, however, avoid both the 'bureaucratic deformations' of the Soviet past and the gross inequalities of capitalism. It would draw upon the experience of other countries, including social democratic parties in Western Europe. It would be a 'genuinely democratic and self-governing social organism'. And it would involve the greatest possible cooperation between East and West to resolve their common problems. This was a certainly a different vision of the socialist future than his immediate predecessors had entertained; but it was still far from clear, entering the 1990s, that it was a sufficient or a workable statement of the longer-term purposes of the new administration, or that it would command the public support that was necessary to turn it into a reality.

The Plan of the Book

The first two chapters of this book attempt to set these and other issues within their historical and cultural context. Stephen White, in the first chapter, looks back at the Brezhnev years of 'stagnation' and then the brief general secretaryships of Yuri Andropov and Konstantin Chernenko. Gorbachev's policy agenda, he suggests,

owed something to his personal background – his relative youth
and education – but it also built upon a series of reformist speeches
in late 1984 and early 1985 which were in effect his manifesto to
the 'selectorate' that appointed him to the party leadership in March
1985. The Gorbachev policy agenda, still developing as the 1980s
moved towards their close, included a greater degree of *glasnost'*
about the Soviet past and the Soviet present together with 'democratisation' of the political system and 'radical reform' of the Soviet
economy. Alfred B. Evans, in the second of these opening chapters,
looks at the far-reaching changes in the official ideology that
accompanied and facilitated these changes. Evans argues that the
changes that have taken place in Soviet Marxism-Leninism are the
most sweeping since the 1920s, and follows through their implications for the economy, for the Soviet past, for international
relations, and for the 'alienation' that was acknowledged to exist
between the Soviet people and the system that claimed to speak in
their name.

The central chapters of the book, which follow, are devoted to
the contemporary political system and to the party and state institutions that give it shape. John P. Willerton, in the first of these
contributions, outlines the changes that have taken place in both
the membership and structure of the party leadership. The cautious
Brezhnev years had led to immobilism, as all the institutional interests of the Soviet system were accommodated within a corporatist
embrace. An attempt began under Andropov to speed up the
replacement of ageing officials by younger and better-educated
reformers; Gorbachev, in turn, was able to bring about a massive
turnover of leading officials as he consolidated his political agenda,
showing that the office of general secretary was 'still all-powerful
in the Soviet political system'. Ronald J. Hill, in his chapter on the
Communist Party, deals with the institution through which leadership policies are implemented, and which has consistently claimed
the right to direct the 'general course of Soviet development'. The
party's membership and structure were changing during the 1980s;
its place in the Soviet political system of the 1990s, however,
remained unclear, not least (as Willerton also emphasises) because
of the emergence of an elected Congress of People's Deputies as
a rival source of political authority.

In two further chapters on the state and legal system, Jeffrey W.
Hahn and William E. Butler consider the elected soviets and the
courts of law as institutions whose relative standing in the political
system has been greatly enhanced by the Gorbachev reforms. Hahn
explores the cautious electoral experiment that took place in 1987
and which led to the first partially competitive elections in modern

Soviet history in March 1989. The new state institutions that came
into being after the elections, Hahn suggests, restored the idea that
real power should belong to the soviets and their electorates, and
potentially represented a decisive shift towards a 'democratised'
political system in the future. William E. Butler's chapter explores
the implications of the reforms for the legal system more particularly. Not simply, he argues, have there been changes in official
theory, with the embracing of the notion of a 'rule of law state';
there have also been far-reaching changes in the laws themselves
and in the judicial system, reflecting the importance that Gorbachev
and other reformers attach to law as the means by which the rights
of individual citizens can be most effectively protected.

The two chapters that follow widen out this part of the book to
consider the ways in which individual citizens interact with these
central institutions of the political system. Nicholas Lampert considers the changes that have taken part in Soviet 'participation', as
old-style mobilisation gives way to a much more differentiated and
complex network of relationships. Of particular importance, he
suggests, was the developing 'informal' movement, although it continued to be regarded with suspicion by officials and members of
the ordinary public; the overall picture, despite these doubts, was
of the 'halting emergence of a new relationship between the Soviet
state and its citizens' in which changing patterns of participation
would play a vital part. Zvi Gitelman's chapter on the nationalities
complements this by focusing on the emergence of widely supported
nationalist movements throughout the USSR in the late 1980s.
Although willing to concede more scope for national self-
expression, Gorbachev proved rather reluctant to share power
within the central leadership and he had still to formulate a set of
policies which would provide a convincing answer to the challenges
that stemmed from the USSR's multiethnic composition.

We turn in the third part of the book to the making of public
policy, with particular emphasis upon the economy, social issues
and foreign and defence concerns. Peter Rutland, in his chapter on
economic management, argues that the old-style Stalinist system of
economic management had brought the USSR to the edge of a
disaster by the early 1980s but that it has proved extraordinarily
difficult to improve it. Gorbachev's reform programme included
some decentralisation of decision-making, encouragement of new
forms of ownership, and a greater emphasis upon international
economic integration. The outcome of these efforts was disappointing but there was little more that Gorbachev could do, not least
because the 'democratisation' of political life had made it easier to
oppose the unpleasant measures that appeared to be necessary.

Mary Buckley, who looks at social policy, sets out the broad framework of the Soviet welfare state in respect of employment, housing and health care, and goes on to look at some of the issues that have arisen in the 1980s such as drugs, crime and prostitution. These and other concerns, she argues, raise important dilemmas for public policy, and in particular for the notion of 'socialist social justice'. Alex Pravda, in the last of these chapters on policy formation, looks at defence and security concerns, showing that they have become an increasingly central part of the policy process in the Gorbachev years. The outcome, he suggests, will be a more 'Western' pattern of policy formation, involving a much wider range of domestic constituencies in a more openly political process.

The book concludes with a set of contrasting chapters on the future of the Soviet political system. Yevgeny Ambartsumov, a Soviet scholar who holds strongly reformist views, argues in the first of these chapters that radical reform of the economy is inconceivable without far-reaching democratisation of the political system. Indeed such reforms, he suggests, are important for their own sake, and they are beginning to take shape in the rise of the 'informal' groups and the development of more democratic forms within the ruling party, both in the USSR and elsewhere. David Mandel, in a chapter that is sympathetic towards socialism but sharply critical of the Gorbachev reforms, looks at the impact of the reforms upon the different groups of which Soviet society is composed. His argument is that *perestroika* is an 'attempt by the more farsighted members of the ruling bureaucracy to rationalise their system through the use of the market, necessarily accompanied by political liberalisation'; he points both to the limitations of the changes that have occurred and to their uncertain outcome. Finally, Ken Jowitt, building upon his earlier writings, returns to some of the issues raised in earlier chapters about the relationship between party dominance and citizen politics, asking whether the Leninist vanguard party of earliest years can transform itself into the party of politicians that is required by present circumstances. After a review of earlier attempts at reform and of the experience of other modernising nations, Jowitt suggests the most likely outcome is a strong executive presidency whose task will be the negotiation of a new relationship between the party and the society, and between the Russians and the other nationalities.

No book about contemporary Soviet politics can hope to be comprehensive, still less definitive. We have accordingly ended the volume with a selection of items that students and others may find useful if they wish to explore further, and with a detailed bibliography which includes some work that is not directly cited as well as full references for the authors whose books and articles are mentioned in earlier chapters. As the USSR entered the 1990s all kinds of future scenarios were being sketched out: at one extreme, a military coup or (rather more likely) a conservative, nationalist and probably anti-Semitic backlash emphasising order and discipline; at the other, a gradual transition towards European-style politics with a mixed economy, a multiparty system, secure civil rights and a cooperative rather than confrontational relationship with the outside world. There were 'doomsday' scenarios – famine, civil war, the collapse of public order – and scenarios that saw the emergence of strikes, nationalist movements and public demonstrations of various kinds of part of a gradual move towards 'normal politics' within the framework of Soviet socialism. We have not, in this volume, attempted to predict the future in this way; but we have, we hope, provided the informed discussion of the contemporary political system and its recent development which can alone ensure that speculation of this kind is securely grounded. Whatever the outcome, it was clear that it would be of the greatest practical as well as academic concern to the outside world as well as to the USSR and its long-suffering citizens.

PART ONE

The Historical and Cultural Context

1

A New Soviet Politics?

STEPHEN WHITE

Until quite recently there was no difficulty in identifying a 'Soviet political system'. Its central feature was a Communist Party based explicitly upon Marxism–Leninism, and organised in a highly centralised manner. The party played a 'leading role' in the society, directing the work of the elected soviets, the courts, the trade unions and all other forms of organised life. It also directed the economy, which was based upon public ownership and state planning. Its decisions were unanimous – it was, after all, a party of 'monolithic cohesion' – and its leadership's reports were greeted with 'stormy, prolonged applause', in some cases turning into an 'ovation'. The party's direction of the elected bodies of state was never challenged – indeed they too adopted their decisions unanimously and by open vote. The party's leading role was sustained, moreover, by a definition of human rights which assumed that there could be no real conflicts of interest between working people, as all of them shared the same relationship to the means of production. Those who took a different view, including nationalists and a small but active group of dissidents, were accused of anti-Soviet behaviour and whenever necessary imprisoned.

The extent to which this stereotype no longer applies is a measure of the changes in Soviet politics that have been brought about by Mikhail Gorbachev, elected General Secretary of the CPSU Central Committee in March 1985. Gorbachev himself has not hesitated to describe his programme of *perestroika* as a revolution, albeit a 'revolution without shots', and it has affected the political system perhaps more significantly than any other area of Soviet life. Gorbachev did not, to begin with, attach particular importance to political reform. In his acceptance speech, for instance, he gave more attention to the 'acceleration' of socioeconomic development, and at the 27th Party Congress in 1986 a higher rate of economic growth was the 'key to all our problems: immediate and long-term, economic and social, political and ideological, domestic and foreign'. By early 1987, however, political reform had assumed a higher place in leadership priorities, both for its own sake and for the contribution it was expected to make to social and economic progress. The Central Committee, meeting in January 1987, formally adopted a programme of 'democratisation' in all areas of Soviet public life; this policy, as promoted by the leadership and increasingly by Soviet citizens themselves, led to changes in the nature of Soviet politics which Gorbachev reasonably described as the greatest since the October revolution itself.

The reform programme, as it developed in the early years of the new administration, involved a critique of the Soviet past, and in particular of the Brezhnev and Stalin eras. It led to greater 'openness' or *glasnost'* in the Soviet media. It meant 'radical reform' of the economy, including a substantial decentralisation of management and, latterly, a deliberate move towards a 'socialist market'. Political life was transformed by the enactment of legislation which provided for the first competitive elections in modern Soviet history, and for the first-ever working parliament staffed by full-time politicians. In some ways most fundamental of all, the doctrine to which the regime was committed underwent far-reaching change: domestically there was a turn to 'socialist pluralism' in place of class-based uniformity, and internationally the Soviet leader's 'new political thinking' led to a greater emphasis than ever before upon cooperation between capitalist and socialist countries to resolve global issues such as arms control and the environment.

These were more than words, as cuts in the armed forces, defeats for party officials at the polls and the publication of an astonishing range of formerly 'anti-Soviet' writers and thinkers made clear. And yet the Gorbachev revolution, five years or more after it had been initiated, still gave rise to more questions than answers. Could party control 'from above', for instance, be reconciled with popular control 'from below'? Could a planning system coexist with different forms of property and market relations? Did *glasnost'* mean more than the exposure of Gorbachev's opponents to public criticism? Were the changes permanent, or simply another of the periodic lurches between reform and reaction that had been a feature of earlier Russian as well as Soviet history? What would be the effect on the USSR of the dramatic changes that were taking place in Eastern Europe? And could the USSR itself survive the upsurge of nationalist sentiment that Gorbachev's policies appeared to have made possible? Several years after the formation of the Gorbachev administration there was still no consensus among Western scholars (or Soviet citizens) about these matters; but it was clear that the outcome would be decisive for the understanding of Soviet-type political systems, and probably for the future shape of world politics.

The Brezhnev Inheritance

The Brezhnev era, at the time, had seemed to be something of a success story. General Secretary of the Communist Party since October 1964 and, since 1977, chairman of the Presidium of the USSR Supreme Soviet or head of state, Leonid Brezhnev had presided over a steady rise in living standards at home and an expansion of Soviet influence throughout the wider world. Under Brezhnev's leadership gross social product had doubled between 1960 and 1970 and more than trebled by 1980. Industrial production had more than quadrupled. Agricultural production had increased much more modestly (in 1981 and 1982 the harvests were so poor that the figures were simply suppressed), but the real incomes of ordinary citizens had more than doubled over the two decades and the wages paid to collective farmers had increased more than four times. Nor were these simply statistics. There were about three times as many members of the society with a higher education, for instance, as there had been on Brezhnev's accession. There were more hospital beds, more flats, more motor cars, more refrigerators, and very many more TVs. And despite the disappointments in agriculture, for which climatic conditions were at least partly to blame, there had been considerable improvements in the Soviet diet. The consumption of meat, fish and fruit per head of population was up by about half, while the consumption of potatoes and bread, the staples of earlier years, had dropped back considerably.

By the early 1980s, in parallel with these domestic changes, the USSR had begun to acquire an international influence that accorded rather more closely with the country's enormous territory, population and natural resources. Forced to back down in humiliating circumstances in the Cuban missile crisis of 1962, the USSR had since acquired a strategic capability which gave it an approximate parity with the USA by the end of the decade. The Soviet Union had one of the world's largest armies and one of its largest navies, and it stood at the head of one of the world's two major military alliances. It was the centre of one of the world's major trading blocs, CMEA or Comecon, and was an influential member of the

United Nations. Its status as a superpower had been enhanced by a series of negotiations and agreements with its major capitalist adversary, particularly SALT 1 in 1972 and its unratified successor, SALT 2, in 1979. The USSR was represented much more widely in international affairs than ever before, and it traded with many more foreign states. Its sporting achievements, its space programme and scientific prowess attracted worldwide recognition; and there was a widening network of cultural relations with the other members of the world community. The Soviet Union was 'one of the greatest world powers', the official history of Soviet foreign policy was able to boast by the early 1980s, 'without whose participation not a single international problem can be resolved'. If this was an exaggeration, it was nonetheless a pardonable one.

Leonid Brezhnev, the symbol of this developing military and politico-economic might, became increasingly the central element in the political system that underpinned it. Originally, in 1964, a 'collective leadership', it had become a leadership 'headed by comrade L. I. Brezhnev' by the early 1970s. The Politburo had been listed in alphabetical order after 1964 to emphasise its collective character, but in 1973, after KGB chairman Yuri Andropov had joined it, Brezhnev's name continued to be listed first although this was a violation of strictly alphabetical principles. In 1976, at the 25th Party Congress, Brezhnev became the party's 'universally acclaimed leader' and *vozhd'* (chief), a term previously used to describe Stalin. In 1977 he added the title of head of state and the Gold Medal of Karl Marx, the highest award of the Academy of Sciences, for his 'outstanding contribution to the development of Marxist–Leninist theory'. His seventy-fifth birthday, in December 1981, brought these tributes to a new pitch of intensity. Seven of *Pravda*'s eight pages on 19 December were wholly or partly devoted to the event; the Soviet awards, which he had himself to authorise as head of state, included a seventh Order of Lenin and a fourth Hero of the Soviet Union citation. Brezhnev's life was turned into a film, 'Story of a Communist'; his wartime exploits in the Caucasus were presented as all but the decisive turning-point of the war; and his memoirs were turned into a film, plays, mime, a popular song and a full-scale oratorio. Even a modest poem, 'To the German Komsomol', written when he was seventeen, received front-page treatment when it appeared in *Pravda* in May 1982.

Brezhnev's personal and political powers, nonetheless, were clearly failing. According to subsequent accounts, Brezhnev began to suffer serious ill-health at the end of the 1960s and in January 1976 suffered a stroke which left him very briefly clinically dead. For three months he was unable to work, as his speech and writing had been impaired, and thereafter he was constantly surrounded by doctors, with a fully-equipped ambulance following his car on trips abroad. His speech became increasingly slurred, his breathing laboured, his concentration limited. Unkind jokes began to circulate: his eyebrows, for instance, were 'Stalin's moustache at a higher level'. Perhaps most seriously of all, his grip on affairs of state became increasingly infirm. The death of Mikhail Suslov, in January 1982, seems in retrospect to have been crucial. One of the Politburo's oldest and longest-serving members with acknowledged authority in both ideology and foreign affairs, Suslov had apparently served as king-maker in 1964, declining the general secretaryship for himself and then backing Brezhnev for the position. With Suslov gone the Brezhnev leadership began to disintegrate rapidly. At the end of the same month the death was reported of Semen Tsvigun, a first deputy chairman of the KGB and a close Brezhnev associate. Rumour suggested it was a case of suicide precipitated by his impending arrest on corruption charges. At the beginning of March 1982 came the arrest of 'Boris the gypsy' and other figures from the worlds of circus and entertainment on charges of smuggling diamonds abroad, bribery and currency speculation. All were close friends of Brezhnev's daughter Galina and their arrest showed that the general secretary's authority was no longer sufficient to protect them.

Still more significantly, in May 1982 a plenary session of the CPSU Central Committee took place at which Brezhnev (according to Western press reports) was unable to secure the election of his own protege, Konstantin Chernenko, to the powerful position of Central Committee Secretary with responsibility for ideology which had become vacant with the death of Suslov. In a development widely seen as significant both at home and abroad it was the head of the KGB, Yuri Andropov, who was elected to the position, apparently with the support of the armed forces lobby. All of this suggested that Brezhnev's political authority as well as his physical health were in decline, and reports circulating in the West at this time suggested it had already been decided that he would retain the largely ceremonial state presidency, allowing another figure to be elected to the more demanding post of party leader. Brezhnev, in the event, anticipated any changes of this kind by dying suddenly on the morning of 10 November 1982, his health undermined by a two-hour stint in the reviewing box at the anniversary parade in Red Square three days earlier. *Pravda*'s obituary mourned the passing of a 'continuer of the cause of Lenin, a fervent patriot, an outstanding revolutionary and struggler for peace and communism, [and] an outstanding political and government leader of the contemporary era'.

It had widely been expected that a decent interval would elapse before a successor was named as general secretary, and indeed that a prolonged succession struggle might ensue. On 11 November, however, it was announced that Andropov was to be the chairman of the committee making arrangements for Brezhnev's funeral, and the following day it was announced that an emergency meeting of the Central Committee had elected him to the vacant general secretaryship. Andropov's main rival for the succession, Konstantin Chernenko, had the task of proposing his candidacy to the Central Committee, where it was accepted unanimously. Brezhnev was buried on 15 November, Andropov making the funeral oration, and a week later the new general secretary made his first speech as party leader to the Central Committee, a brief but effective review of Soviet foreign and domestic policy. In May 1983 it became known that Andropov had succeeded Brezhnev as chairman of the Defence Council of the USSR, the body attached to the Politburo which oversees military and security matters, and on 16 June 1983 he was elected to the vacant state presidency, thus concentrating in his hands after only seven months the same combination of posts that Brezhnev had taken almost thirteen years to accumulate. A series of changes in the membership of the Politburo and Secretariat, and at lower levels of the party and state, had meanwhile begun to put in place a coalition of reform-minded technocrats who might be expected to support both the new general secretary and the policies he intended to promote.

Andropov's own health, however, was far from certain. An elderly man (already 68 when he assumed the party leadership) with a history of heart trouble, there were persistent rumours of bad health and degenerative ailments from almost the outset of his period of office. Although a number of members of the 'Brezhnev mafia' swiftly lost their positions Andropov's rival for the general secretaryship, Konstantin Chernenko, remained prominent, making the opening speech at the June 1983 Central Committee plenum and reportedly chairing the Politburo in Andropov's absence. Andropov's effective authority in fact lasted for only a few months: he was last seen in public in August 1983 and unprecedentedly failed to attend the anniversary parade in Red Square on 7 November and then the Central Committee plenum and the Supreme Soviet session that took place the following month. It became known that Andropov was receiving kidney dialysis treatment at the Central Committee hospital near Moscow and that Mikhail Gorbachev, the youngest member of the Politburo and apparently the one most closely attuned to the general secretary's own thinking, was maintaining links between him and other members of the leadership. A series of 'interviews' and statements, and an address that was circulated to the Central Committee plenum he was unable to attend, suggested that Andropov's intellectual powers were largely unimpaired. Further changes in the Politburo and Secretariat at the December 1983 plenum indicated that his control over perhaps the most important of all the powers of a party leader, that of patronage, was scarcely diminished. Nonetheless, explanations in terms of 'colds' and 'temporary causes' began to wear thin, and it was not entirely unexpected when on 11 February 1984 the central press reported that Andropov had died two days earlier after a 'long illness'. Once again the party leadership was plunged into the search for a successor.

As before there were two principal contenders: Chernenko, whose political fortunes had revived with Andropov's illness, and Gorbachev, who was evidently Andropov's own favoured candidate for the succession. Chernenko was named on 10 February to head the funeral arrangements committee, which recent practice suggested gave good grounds for believing he would shortly be elected the new general secretary. The formal choice in fact took some time to arrange and appears to have divided the remaining Politburo members into two camps, a 'Brezhnevite' faction supporting Chernenko and composed for the most part of long-serving members of the leadership like Prime Minister Nikolai Tikhonov, Kazakh party leader Dinmukhamed Kunaev and Moscow party secretary Viktor Grishin, and an 'Andropovite' faction consisting of the younger, more reform-minded members who had joined or advanced within the leadership under the late general secretary, including Vitaly Vorotnikov, Geidar Aliev and Gorbachev himself. The choice fell finally on Chernenko, partly, it appears, because of his seniority and experience, and partly because a Gorbachev leadership would have been likely to last for an unduly lengthy period (Gorbachev at this time was just 52 and had been a full member of the Politburo for less than four years).

At all events, on 13 February 1984, four days after Andropov had died, another extraordinary meeting of the Central Committee took place at which Chernenko, proposed by Tikhonov, was elected unanimously to the vacant general secretaryship. It emerged subsequently that Gorbachev had also addressed the plenum, and unofficial reports suggested that he had been installed as a *de facto* second secretary with a power of veto, on behalf of the younger 'Andropovite' faction, over leadership decisions. Gorbachev's greater prominence was apparent in, for example, his more advanced placing in the line-up of leaders beside Andropov's coffin, in the ranking he received in pre-election speeches and on other formal party and state occasions. In turn it indicated that the Chernenko leadership was a relatively evenly-balanced coalition, containing both supporters of the late president Andropov's reforming policies and those who believed they had been pressed too far. These sharp internal divisions were sufficient in themselves to slow down the momentum of reform, quite apart from what the new general secretary might have wished, and they persisted throughout his period of office as neither side could allow the other to gain what might be a decisive advantage by changes in the membership of the Politburo or Secretariat.

The state presidency and chairmanship of the Defence Council, as well as the party leadership, had become vacant with Andropov's death. It became known later in February 1984 that Chernenko had also assumed the chairmanship of the Defence Council, and in April 1984, on Gorbachev's nomination, the first session of the newly-elected Supreme Soviet elected him to the vacant presidency. Chernenko was nevertheless, at 72, the oldest general secretary ever to have assumed this office, and he had a history of lung disease which caused difficulty in breathing. Perhaps inevitably, it was regarded as a transitional secretaryship from the outset. Two regular Central Committee plenums were held during Chernenko's period of office: the first, in April 1984, was devoted to the work of the soviets and educational reform, and the second dealt with land improvement. Neither plenum made any change in the membership of the Politburo or Secretariat or even in the membership of the Central Committee itself, and neither could be said to have initiated any major new departure in Soviet public policy (the educational reforms, which were of some importance, had been launched the previous year). A series of missed engagements suggested that Chernenko's health was already deteriorating, and official spokesmen had to admit that the general secretary was suffering from a serious cold, or perhaps worse.

Chernenko was last seen in public at the end of December 1984. He failed to meet the Greek prime minister Papandreou on his visit to Moscow in February 1985, and failed to deliver the customary eve of poll address to the Soviet people in the republican and local elections later the same month. Although he was shown voting on television on 24 February and was pictured in the central press receiving his deputy's credentials on 1 March, rumours of the general secretary's physical incapacity were strengthened rather than dispelled by his evident ill-health. Finally, on the evening of 10 March 1985, he died, the medical bulletin recording that he had expired as a result of heart failure following a deterioration in the working of his lungs and liver. The next day, with unprecedented speed, an extraordinary session of the Central Committee elected Mikhail Gorbachev as its third general secretary in three and a half years, Gromyko proposing him for the position with the evident support of the KGB, economic administrators and the 'Andropovite' faction within the leadership. Gorbachev, who had just celebrated his fifty-fourth birthday, was still the youngest member of the Politburo and apparently in robust good health, which was in itself a considerable change. As one of the earliest jokes put it: 'What support does Gorbachev have in the Kremlin?' Answer: 'None – he walks unaided'.

Gorbachev's Policy Agenda

The advent of a new general secretary has normally meant a significant change in the direction of Soviet public policy, although any change of course has usually taken some time to establish itself as the new leader gradually marginalises his opponents and coopts his supporters on to the Politburo and Secretariat. At the outset of his administration Gorbachev's objectives, and indeed his personal background, were still fairly obscure even at leading levels of the party. Gorbachev, unlike his two main rivals Grigory Romanov and Viktor Grishin, had not addressed a party congress, and he had still no published collection of writings to his name. He had made only a couple of important visits abroad, to Canada in 1983 and to the United Kingdom in late 1984, on both occasions as the head of a delegation of Soviet parliamentarians. Andrei Gromyko, proposing Gorbachev's candidacy to the Central Committee, explained what had convinced him personally that Gorbachev would be a suitable general secretary: Gorbachev, he indicated, had chaired meetings of the Politburo in Chernenko's absence and had done so 'brilliantly, without any exaggeration'. Gorbachev himself, in his acceptance speech, paid tribute to the late general secretary and then pledged himself to continue the policy of his two predecessors, which he defined as 'acceleration of socio-economic development and the perfection of all aspects of social life'. There were, however, some elements in the new general secretary's biography which suggested that this new administration would be more than a continuation of its immediate precursors.

One of those elements was Gorbachev's own background, particularly his education and more youthful generation. Gorbachev was born, according to his official biography, on 2 March 1931 to a peasant family in the Stavropol' territory in southern Russia. His father was wounded in the war and he was brought up mainly by his grandparents. He worked first as a mechanic at a machine-tractor station, and then in 1950, with the help of his local party organisation, enrolled in the Law Faculty at Moscow State University. Gorbachev was a Komsomol activist while at university, and joined the CPSU itself in 1952. He graduated in 1955, the first Soviet leader since Lenin to have received a legal training and the first to graduate from the country's premier university. The Czech communist and later dissident Zdeněk Mlynář, who was his classmate and close friend at this time, later, recalled Gorbachev's openmindedness and his enthusiasm for Hegel's dictum that the truth was 'always concrete'. His years near the front during the war, Mlynář believed, gave him appreciation of the human suffering it had meant, and he was ready even in 1952 to take issue with the purges (Lenin, he pointed out, had at least allowed his Menshevik opponents to emigrate). After graduation Gorbachev returned to Stavropol where he worked in the Komsomol and party apparatus, later completing a correspondence course at Stavropol Agricultural Institute. In 1966 he became first secretary of the city party committee, in 1970 he was appointed to head the territorial party organisation, and the following year he joined the Central Committee as a full member. In 1978 Gorbachev replaced his mentor Fedor Kulakov in the Central Committee Secretariat, taking responsibility for agriculture. In 1979 he became a candidate, and then in 1980 a full member of the ruling Politburo.

It is not customary for a Soviet leader to discuss his personal affairs with the mass media, but Gorbachev did venture some information on this subject when he was interviewed by the Italian communist paper *L'Unità* in May 1987. His main weakness, Gorbachev believed, was that he had too many interests. He had enrolled in the law faculty at university, for instance, but had originally intended to study physics. He liked mathematics, but also history and literature. In later years he had turned more and more to the study of economics, while remaining interested in philosophy. This was not, to put it mildly, the intellectual background of his immediate predecessor. Interest in the general secretary's personal life was hardly satisfied by such revelations and there were further queries in the spring of 1989. Did Mikhail Sergeevich, for instance, like fishing? And why did *glasnost'* not apply to the person who had invented it? Gorbachev obliged with some further information in an interview in a Central Committee journal later the same year. He earned 1200 rubles a month, he explained, the same as other members of the Politburo, and neither he nor any members of his family owned a private holiday home of any kind. He had a considerable additional income from royalties and other sources (his book *Perestroika* alone had appeared in more than 100 countries), but he had donated any earnings of this kind to the party budget and to various charitable causes. Literature, theatre, music and cinema remained his hobbies, although he had less and less time to devote to them.

As well as his personal characteristics, there were also clues in Gorbachev's speeches before his assumption of the general secretaryship as to the direction of policy he was likely to pursue. Perhaps the clearest indication of this kind was a speech Gorbachev delivered to an all-union conference on ideology in December 1984. The speech contained positive references to self-management, which Lenin had 'never counterposed to Soviet state power'. It acknowledged the various interests of the different groups in Soviet society, and the need for a greater measure of social justice (which had become a coded form of attack upon the Brezhnev legacy). There was enormous scope, Gorbachev went on, for the further development of the Soviet political system, and of socialist democracy. This was partly a matter of developing all aspects of the work of the elected soviets, and of involving workers more fully in the affairs of their own workplace. It was also a matter of securing a greater degree of *glasnost'* or openness in party and state life. Gorbachev's electoral address of 20 February 1985, made at a time when Chernenko's serious illness was widely known, repeated many of these themes, combining almost populist references to Soviet power as a form of rule 'of the toilers and for the toilers' and to the need for the party 'again and again to check its political course against the rich experience of the people' with more abrasive remarks about the need for self-sufficiency in enterprise management and for greater labour discipline. These speeches, in effect an election manifesto to the Central Committee 'selectorate', made it clear that Gorbachev would continue Andropov's emphasis upon efficiency and discipline but also that they would be placed within a broader framework involving democratic reform and a reassertion of the moral values that were, for Gorbachev, implicit in socialism.

The direction of reform became still clearer at the April 1985 Central Committee plenum, the first that Gorbachev addressed as party leader. There had been significant achievements in all spheres of Soviet life, Gorbachev told the plenum. The USSR had a powerful, developed economy, a highly skilled workforce and an advanced scientific base. Everyone had the right to work, to social security, to cultural resources of all kinds, and to participation in management. But further changes were needed in order to achieve a 'qualitatively new state of society', including modernisation of the economy and the extension of socialist democracy and popular self-government. The key issue was the acceleration of economic growth. This was quite feasible if the 'human factor' was called more fully into play, and if the reserves that existed throughout the economy were properly utilised. This in turn required a greater degree of decentralisation of economic management, including cost accounting at enterprise level and a closer connection between the work that people did and the payment they received. The months and years that followed saw the gradual assembly of a leadership team to direct these changes and the further extension of what was already a challenging reform agenda.

Of all the policies that were promoted by this new and Gorbachevian leadership, *glasnost'* was perhaps the most distinctive and the one that had been pressed furthest by the early 1990s. *Glasnost'*, usually translated as openness or publicity, was not the same as freedom of the press or the right to information; nor was it original to Gorbachev. It did, however, reflect the new general secretary's belief that without a greater awareness of the real state of affairs and of the considerations that had led to particular decisions there would be no willingness on the part of the Soviet people to commit themselves to his programme of *perestroika*. 'The better people are informed', Gorbachev told the Central Committee meeting that elected him, 'the more consciously they act, the more actively they support the party, its plans and programmatic objectives'. Existing policies were in any case ineffectual, counterproductive and much resented. The newspaper *Sovetskaya Rossiya*, for instance, reported the case of Mr Polyakov of Kaluga, a well-read man who followed the central and local press and never missed the evening TV news. He knew a lot about what was happening in various African countries, Polyakov complained, but he had 'only a very rough idea what was happening in his own city'. Nor was this an isolated case. In October 1985, another reader complained to the same paper, there had been a major earthquake in Tajikistan in Soviet Central Asia, but no details were made known other than that 'lives had been lost'. At about the same time there had been an earthquake in Mexico and a volcanic eruption in Colombia. Both had been covered extensively with on-the-spot reports and full details of the casualties that had been suffered. Was Tajikistan really further from Moscow than Latin America?

Influenced by considerations such as these, the Gorbachev leadership made steady and sometimes dramatic progress in removing taboos from the discussion of public affairs and exposing both the Soviet past and the Soviet present to critical scrutiny. The Brezhnev era was one of the earliest targets. It had been a time, Gorbachev told the 27th Party Congress in 1986, when a 'curious psychology – how to change things without really changing anything' – had been dominant. A number of its leading representatives had been openly corrupt, and some (such as Brezhnev's son-in-law, Yuri Churbanov) were brought to trial and imprisoned. More generally, it had been a period of 'stagnation', of wasted opportunities, when party and government leaders had lagged behind the needs of the times. The Stalin question, however, was clearly the most critical one, as it had been for all Soviet reformers. Gorbachev, to begin with, was reluctant even to concede there was a question. Stalinism, he told the French press in 1986, was a 'notion made up by enemies of communism'; the 20th Party Congress in 1956 had condemned Stalin's 'cult of personality' and drawn the necessary conclusions. By early 1987, however, Gorbachev was insisting that there must be 'no forgotten names, no blank spots' in Soviet literature and history, and by November of that year, when he came to give his address on the 70th anniversary of the revolution, he was ready to condemn the 'wanton repressive measures' of the 1930s, 'real crimes' in which 'many thousands of people inside and outside the party' had suffered.

In the course of his speech Gorbachev announced that a Politburo commission had been set up to investigate the political repression of the Stalinist years, and this led to the rehabilition of many prominent figures from the party's past (and thousands of others) during 1988 and 1989. The most important figure to be restored to full respectability in this way was the former *Pravda* editor Nikolai Bukharin, whose sentence was posthumously quashed in February 1988 (later in the year his expulsions from the party and the Academy of Sciences were both reversed). Two other old Bolsheviks, Grigorii Zinoviev and Lev Kamenev, were rehabilitated in July 1988. Trotsky had not been sentenced by a Soviet court and there was therefore no judgment to be quashed; but his personal qualities began to receive some recognition in the Soviet press, and in 1989 some of his writings began to appear in mass-circulation as well as scholarly journals. An extended discussion took place about the numbers that Stalin had condemned to death: for some it was about a million by the end of the 1930s, but for others (such as the historian and commentator Roy Medvedev) it was at least 12 million, with a further 38 million repressed in other ways. Perhaps still more significant, a number of mass graves of victims of the Stalin period began to be uncovered, the most extensive of which were in the Kuropaty forest near Minsk. The victims, as many as 100,000 or more, had been shot between 1937 and 1941; this, and the other mass graves that began to be discovered in the late 1980s, was an indictment of Stalinism still more powerful than anything the historians and writers could muster.

Glasnost' led to further changes in the quality of Soviet public life, from literature and the arts to statistics and a wideranging discussion on the future of Soviet socialism. Public information began to improve, with the publication of statistics on crime, abortions, suicides and infant mortality. Subjects that had been taboo during the Brezhnev years, such as violent crime, drugs and prostitution, began to receive extensive treatment. Many events of the past, such as the devastating earthquake in Ashkhabad in 1948 and the nuclear accident in the Urals in 1957, were belatedly acknowledged. Figures for defence spending and foreign debt were revealed for the first time to the Congress of People's Deputies in 1989. The Congress itself was televised in full and followed avidly throughout the USSR; so too were Central Committee plenums, Supreme Soviet committee hearings and other public occasions. Still more remarkably, the Soviet media were opened up to foreign journalists and politicians, and even (in a few cases) to emigres and unapologetic opponents of Soviet socialism; and the first 'spacebridges' were instituted, linking together studio audiences in the USSR and many Western nations. Opinion polls suggested that *glasnost'*, for all its limitations, was the change in Soviet life that was most apparent to ordinary people and the one they most valued.

The 'democratisation' of Soviet political life, of which *glasnost'* was a part, was also intended to release the human energies that, for Gorbachev, had been choked off by the bureaucratic centralism of the recent past. The Soviet Union, he told the 19th Party Conference in the summer of 1988, had pioneered the idea of a workers' state and of workers' control, the right to work and equality of rights for women and all national groups. The political system established by the October revolution, however, had undergone 'serious deformations', leading to the development of a 'command-administrative system' which had extinguished the democratic potential of the elected soviets. The role of party and state officialdom had increased out of all proportion, and this 'bloated administrative apparatus' had begun to dictate its will in political and economic matters. Nearly a third of the adult population were regularly elected to the soviets and other bodies, but most of them had little influence over the conduct of state and public affairs. Social life as a whole had become unduly 'governmentalised', and ordinary working people had become 'alienated' from the system that was supposed to represent their interests. It was this 'ossified

system of government, with its command-and-pressure mechanism',
that was now the main obstacle to *perestroika*.

The Conference duly approved the notion of a 'radical reform'
of the political system, and this led to a series of constitutional and
other changes in 1988 and 1989 (see Chapters 4–6). An entirely
new electoral law, for instance, approved in December 1988, broke
new ground in providing for (though not specifically requiring) a
choice of candidate at elections to local and national-level authorities. A new state structure was established, incorporating a relatively
small working parliament and (from 1990) a new executive Presidency. A constitutional review committee, similar to a constitutional
court, was set up as part of a move to what Gorbachev called a
'socialist system of checks and balances'. The Communist Party
agreed to abandon its constitutionally guaranteed 'leading role' in
February 1990, and the party itself began to be 'democratised',
although in practice the changes were less dramatic than in other
parts of the political system. Leading officials, it was agreed, should
be elected by competitive ballot for a maximum of two consecutive
terms; members of the Central Committee began to be involved
much more directly in the work of the leadership; and much more
information became available about all aspects of the party's work,
from its finances to the operation of its decision-making bodies.

Together with these changes, for Gorbachev, there must be a
'radical reform' of the Soviet economy (for a full discussion see
Chapter 9). Levels of growth had been declining since at least the
1950s. In the late 1970s they reached the lowest levels in Soviet
peacetime history; growth, in the view of Soviet as well as Western
commentators, may in fact have ceased altogether during these
years, at least per head of population. Indeed, as Gorbachev
explained in early 1988, if the sale of alcoholic drink and of Soviet
oil on foreign markets was excluded, there had been no real growth
in the USSR for at least the previous fifteen years. Growth, at least
for many reforming economists, could not be an end in itself; what
was important was the satisfaction of real social needs. But it was
equally apparent that without some improvement in living standards
there would be no popular commitment to *perestroika*, and no
prospect that socialism would recover its appeal to other nations as
a means by which ordinary working people could live their lives in
dignity and prosperity. There was indeed a real danger, in the view
of economists like Nikolai Shmelev, that without radical reform the
USSR would enter the 21st century a 'backward, stagnating state
and an example to the rest of the world how not to conduct its
economic affairs'.

Radical reform, as Gorbachev explained to the 27th Party Congress and to an important Central Committee meeting in the summer of 1987, involved a set of related measures. One of the most important was a greater degree of decentralisation of economic decision-making, leaving the broad guidance of the economy in the hands of the State Planning Committee (Gosplan) but allowing factories and farms throughout the USSR much more freedom to determine their own priorities. They should be guided in making such decisions by a wide range of 'market' indicators, including the orders they received from other enterprises and the profits they made on their production. Retail and wholesale prices would have to reflect the costs of production much more closely so that enterprises could be guided by 'economic' rather than 'administrative' regulators and so that the massive subsidies that held down the cost of basic foodstuffs could be reduced. Under the Law on the State Enterprise, adopted in 1987, enterprises that persistently failed to pay their way under these conditions could be liquidated; some economists were willing to argue that a modest degree of unemployment was not simply a logical but even a desirable feature of changes of this kind. The state sector, more generally, should be gradually reduced in size and cooperative and even private economic activity should be expanded in its place. Gorbachev described these changes, which were gradually brought into effect during 1987 and 1988, as the most radical to have taken place in Soviet economic life since the adoption of the New Economic Policy (NEP) in the early 1920s.

Gorbachev, *Perestroika* and Soviet-type Systems

What, finally, did the 'Gorbachev revolution' mean for the way in which a communist political system has traditionally been conceptualised? The authors of this volume can offer no single response to such a question; but as we suggested at the outset, there would be a wide measure of agreement that the Gorbachev revolution had generated more questions than answers in this connection by the start of the 1990s. What, for instance, was the 'socialism' to which such a system was supposed to be committed as part of a transition to a fully communist society? Khrushchev had promised that the USSR would construct a society of this kind by 1980 in the Party Programme that was adopted under his leadership in 1961. His successors swiftly dropped that commitment and began to describe the USSR, from the early 1970s, as a 'developed socialist society', whose evolution into a fully communist society was a matter for an unspecified point in the fairly distant future. Brezhnev's successors in turn made it clear that the USSR was at the very beginning of the stage of developed socialism, whose proper development would require a 'whole historical epoch'. Gorbachev, for his part, has avoided the term 'developed socialism' and opted instead for 'developing socialism', in effect a postponement into the still more distant future of the attainment of a fully communist society.

It remained unclear, these generalities apart, how a 'developing socialist society' was to be conceived and how its further development was to be assured. It certainly excluded some of the utopian emphases of Khrushchev's Party Programme of 1961: Gorbachev's revised Programme of 1986 avoided any mention of dates or stages by which full communism was to be reached, and there was no longer any commitment to the increasing provision of public services to all who needed them without charge. It was not, evidently, a society that would be based upon state ownership and control – there would certainly be a substantial private and cooperative sector, and foreign as well as domestic ownership – and it was not a society in which it was assumed that all its members had a basic identity of interests. Gorbachev set out a vision of the 'qualitatively new state of society' that he hoped to achieve at the 19th Party Conference in 1988, but it was clearer in its denunciation of the 'deformed' socialism of the 1930s than in its depiction of the society that he hoped to construct in its place. Addressing a Central Committee meeting in July 1989, Gorbachev could offer only the 'broad outline' of the socialist society of the future. It would, he explained, be a 'society of free people . . . built on the principles of humanism, socialist democracy and social justice'; it would be a society in which the people had 'absolute power and all human rights'; and there would be a 'rich inner life and a high level of culture and morality'. Statements of such a kind, whatever their merits, could hardly hope to offer practical guidance to party members and the broader public in their daily life; nor did they necessarily carry conviction at a time of manifest economic difficulty, nationalist discontent and the open acknowledgement of all kinds of mistakes and shortcomings by those who exercised political authority.

An obscurity about objectives was compounded by some uncertainty on the part of the instrument that was supposed to realise those aims, the Communist Party of the Soviet Union. Traditionally, a centralised Marxist–Leninist party exercising a 'leading role' in the society had been taken as perhaps the single most important defining characteristic of a communist system. The role of a party of this kind, however, became more difficult to sustain in a society in which a wide range of political forces had taken advantage of the opportunities of 'socialist pluralism'. Perhaps the most serious challenge to the party's political leadership came from the process of electoral reform which allowed the return of deputies armed for the first time with a genuine popular mandate. The March 1989 elections, which were the first exercise of this kind, saw a series of senior party officials defeated at the ballot box in a manner that clearly called into question the party's claim to rule. How could the party, for instance, insist on its own ministerial candidates if 'the people's representatives' wished otherwise? How could it oppose the claims for resources that those representatives made of it? And how could it resist even a demand for outright independence if the voters returned a majority of nationalists at a subsequent election, particularly if local communists sided with nationalist opinion rather than with Moscow?

Gorbachev had hoped, in his speech on political reform to the Central Committee in January 1987, to combine control 'from below' with the continued maintenance of political leadership 'from above' by the Communist Party. His assumption appears to have been that the Soviet people were basically committed to collectivist values, and that they would respond enthusiastically to his call for a more open, pluralist socialism in which human rights would be respected and a diversity of interests could express themselves. His emphasis upon leadership change equally reflected the view that the Soviet system was fundamentally sound and that it had been 'subjective' causes, above all the failures of party officials at national and local level, that had led it into a pre-crisis or even crisis situation. The experience of his first five years was that the appointment of his own management team made relatively little difference (within two or three years he was being forced to sack the people he had himself appointed). The opportunities that were provided for 'socialist democracy' led to no obvious improvement in economic performance but rather to the open articulation of national and other differences (and indeed to substantial loss of life). The Communist Party itself, confronted by such challenges, began to experience what was frequently described as a 'crisis of confidence' and found itself increasingly divided and at odds with a resentful society. By the early 1990s it was this question of political authority, or more generally of the manageability of the processes of change he had encouraged, that was perhaps the most fundamental of all those the Soviet leader still confronted.

2

Rethinking Soviet Socialism

ALFRED B. EVANS, JR

The Soviet political regime traces its origins to the revolution of October 1917, under the leadership of Lenin, which brought the Bolshevik wing of Marxism to power in Russia. That regime bases its legitimacy on the claim that it directs Soviet society in accordance with the principles of Lenin and the Bolsheviks, who in turn considered themselves followers of the ideas of Marx and Engels. Thus to an unusual degree the Soviet regime is justified by and identified with a distinctive and comprehensive set of ideas – the ideology referred to as Marxism–Leninism. By presenting themselves as the interpreters of that world-view, Soviet leaders stress the notion of a direct continuity of intellectual heritage from the Marxist classics through Lenin and the October revolution to the present day. Since 1985, Mikhail Gorbachev has embarked upon the most sweeping revision of Soviet Marxism–Leninism since the 1920s. But paradoxically, the questioning of many previously established tenets of the ideology has intensified the need for the reaffirmation of faithfulness to its original sources. Gorbachev continues to assert that correct Marxist–Leninist theory must be the source of guidance for the policies of the Soviet state. Therefore, contemporary Soviet reformers are engaged in the search for a new model of socialism which can combine the most valuable principles of Lenin's thought with features adapted to contemporary conditions.

Stagnation and Reform

Gorbachev is preoccupied with the infusion of greater vitality and technological dynamism into the Soviet economy. Soon after coming to office as head of the party he sounded the alarm over the pace of technological innovation in his country, warning that the USSR's fate as a powerful and respected force in world affairs was at risk. Joseph Stalin had set the goal of overtaking the West in economic production, and Nikita Khrushchev had promised that the Soviet Union would surpass the most advanced capitalist countries in per capita output by the 1970s. However, by 1987 Gorbachev was bluntly admitting that the USSR was not catching up with the most developed economic systems, but was falling steadily farther behind. 'A country that was once quickly closing on the world's advanced nations began to lose one position after another', he told the Central Committee. 'Moreover, the gap in the efficiency of production, quality of products, scientific and technological development, the production of advanced technology and the use of advanced techniques began to widen, and not to our advantage'. Thus less than a year after Gorbachev took the helm, the 27th Congress of the CPSU adopted a Programme for the party which focused on the priority of the acceleration (*uskorenie*) of economic and technological development in the USSR.

Gorbachev sees the acceleration of Soviet economic development as impossible without radical political and social changes. He can view the last several decades from the vantage point of one familiar with several failed attempts at reform in the Soviet economy. He seems to believe that previous leaders who tried to make the Stalinist economic system work better – whether they attempted major organisational changes, as Khrushchev did, or whether they only tinkered with the details of the economic mechanism, like Brezhnev – failed to create mechanisms which would insure political support for economic change. Gorbachev is striving not just to build a broad popular base of support for the current economic reform, but more importantly, to restructure the Soviet system so as to institutionalise the dynamic of constant adaptation. He has emphasised that he considers successful political reform an indispensable prerequisite for economic reform in a system of the Soviet type. The principal mechanisms which Gorbachev hopes to build into the Soviet state and economy are not unfamiliar to Western and Asian readers; they are to be the Soviet socialist versions of democracy and the market.

The conviction on the part of reform-minded Soviet sources that no economy can long remain competitive by advanced world standards without incorporating substantial elements of democracy and the market is encouraged by their analysis of Soviet experience. Since 1917, that experience has been interpreted in relation to the 'stages of communist society' foreseen by Karl Marx in the *Critique of the Gotha Programme*, and described by Soviet sources as the historical phases of socialism and communism. Lenin argued that the Bolshevik Revolution had created a state of the working people which was engaged in the construction of socialism, and that communism would be the ultimate goal of Soviet society. Stalin claimed that Soviet society had entered the phase of socialism during the 1930s and subsequent Soviet leaders have agreed with that position. In 1959, Khrushchev asserted that the Soviet Union had moved into a period of 'full-scale construction of communism', and in 1961 the 22nd Congress of the Communist Party of the Soviet Union adopted a Programme for the CPSU setting forth plans for the transition to full communism by the beginning of the 1980s. The rapid and direct transition to communism was to be accompanied by the achievement of the world's highest standards of productivity and affluence.

The extravagant promises of the 1961 Party Programme were quietly abandoned after Khrushchev's downfall, however, and by 1971 Brezhnev introduced the thesis that the Soviet Union had entered the stage of 'developed socialism'. The concept of developed socialism was used both to demonstrate the great progress which Soviet society had made since the 1930s and to suggest that the realisation of full communism was not in prospect for the foreseeable future. Further development of the society within the stage of mature socialism was to realise the full potential of socialism by more thoroughly applying the principles of that phase, rather than initiating the replacement of features distinctive to socialism by traits which would be characteristic of communism. The theory of developed socialism, as elaborated at great length by Soviet scholars, provided a model of an authoritarian party-state regime functioning in a mature industrial society, and enjoying a base of stability derived from growing abundance and social consensus. This was the hope of the Brezhnev leadership: that the result of decades of steady economic growth would be the effacement of the unevenness of development which had plagued the society under the tsars and had been accentuated by Stalin's policies, and that with the integration of all segments of society into the industrialised socialist mainstream, all potentially destabilising conflicts of values would be eliminated. Brezhnev addressed a task which had been faced by every other Soviet leader since the early 1950s, the task of defining the nature of the current stage of development of Soviet society and identifying the main problems to be resolved within that stage.

Both the policies and the theory offered by Brezhnev have been repudiated by Gorbachev, however. Criticism of Brezhnev became increasingly open from 1986 on, with the 1970s and early 1980s being referred to as the 'period of stagnation' in the Soviet Union. At the 27th Party Congress in 1986 Gorbachev pointedly observed that during that period, 'the situation demanded changes, but in the central organs and also in the localities a unique psychology began to take hold: how to improve things without changing anything'. That observation implied an attack on the Brezhnev administration on two levels: on the level of practice, for lacking the boldness to deal with the mounting problems of the Soviet system; and on the level of theory, for cautiously endorsing the gradual improvement and perfection (*sovershenstvovanie*) of established institutions and practices. Gorbachev and his supporters complain that the concept of developed socialism furnished a theoretical façade of complacency and self-congratulation which concealed the growth of problems threatening to debilitate the Soviet system. Soviet sources now speak of their society as being one of 'developing' socialism, implicitly emphasising the amount of work which remains unfinished before the achievement of genuine maturity. Most Soviet scholars seem to regard mature socialism as a goal of contemporary Soviet society. The repudiation of the concept of developed socialism reflects a dramatic change in the Soviet leadership's interpretation of the current stage of their country's history. While Brezhnev believed that the Soviet system was entering a period of the consolidation of unprecedented stability, Gorbachev views the system as embarking on a transition which is fraught with the potential for disruption.

Stalinism and Overcentralisation

The criticism of the leadership's attitudes and policies of the 1970s and early 1980s has led to a search for the sources of stagnation in Soviet society. Gorbachev's supporters do not feel that the society was merely going through a temporary slump in those years; they see stagnation as having been the product of long-term trends rooted in the nature of the Soviet system, which threaten the health and even the survival of that system. It should not be supposed, however, that there is unamimity among Soviet politicians or Soviet scholars on the causes of the problems of the Brezhnev period. In the 1970s, Soviet publications gave evidence of disagreement on most policy issues, though public debates tended to be phrased in cautious and guarded tones. With the spread of greater openness of discussion under Gorbachev, a wide spectrum of opinions is now evident on most questions of social analysis and policy prescription. Even among those who generally support the kinds of reforms which Gorbachev has initiated there is often vocal disagreement. An effort will be made here to identify the positions of the dominant forces within the current Soviet leadership.

Gorbachev has traced the sources of stagnation back to the 1930s, or the years of the emergence of Stalinism. All Soviet reformers affirm that the essential features of the Soviet system were forged in that period, and have persisted down to the present time. All agree that the Stalinist system was distinguished by extreme centralisation, with heavy reliance on what Gorbachev calls 'administrative-command methods' of economic management and political leadership. In 1987, Gorbachev's book *Perestroika* implied that the primary explanation for the nature of Stalin's system was to be found in the 'objective conditions' of the late 1920s, such as economic underdevelopment and capitalist encirclement, but that some blame might be ascribed to subjective conditions or the errors in judgement that were coloured by Stalin's personality. By 1988 G. L. Smirnov, the head of the party's Institute of Marxism–Leninism, identified subjective factors as the 'main reasons' for negative phenomena in the Soviet system from the 1930s on, and Vadim Medvedev, a member of the Politburo who oversees ideology, insisted that the problems of Stalinism resulted not mainly from superficial 'tactical errors' but primarily from 'deformations of socialism' consisting in 'the deviation [*otstuplenie*]' from Lenin's conception of socialism.

The repudiation of Stalin's legacy has encouraged most Soviet reformers to reaffirm the heritage of Leninism, which they see as illuminating the true meaning of socialism and offering examples of pragmatic flexibility in policy-making. Gorbachev claims that his reforms are designed, not to borrow alien elements, but to realise more fully the principles of socialism in the USSR. He has reported that contemporary Soviet reformers are turning for guidance to Lenin's ideas at the time of the adoption of the New Ecomonic Policy and to Lenin's last writings, which expressed his disquiet at the damage caused by the bureaucratisation of Soviet political institutions. There even has been a revival of interest in the thought of Nikolai Bukharin, which is said by some to have offered a Bolshevik alternative to Stalinism, and was credited in *Pravda* in October 1988 with trying to protect 'Lenin's conception of socialism against Stalin's distortions and deviations from it'. The true essence of socialism as depicted by Lenin is said to be based on democratic and humanistic values, which were distorted by Stalin's rule.

There have been a few diverse attempts to discover the historical or social roots of Stalin's authoritarian version of socialism. A rare effort to attach some of the blame for Stalinism to Lenin's thinking was made in an article by Vasilii Selyunin in the literary journal *Novyi mir* in 1988, which attributed an inordinate fear of market relations and the restoration of capitalism to Lenin, though it also credited him with gradually realising the danger posed by the Soviet bureaucracy and fostering the development of limits on its power. Despite the softening of Selyunin's criticism, he implies that an authoritarian potential accompanied the Bolsheviks' aim of rapid social transformation directed from above. Another perspective is found in an article in the party's theoretical journal *Kommunist* by G. Arbatov and E. Batalov, which contends that the tendency for the state to dominate Soviet society 'stretched its roots . . . into the prerevolutionary Russian culture'. That thesis has been familiar enough in Western writings on Soviet history and politics for many years, but its appearance in a publication of the Soviet Communist Party is evidence of a sharp change in thinking. Of even greater significance in indicating theoretical change is the admission in *Kommunist* in November 1987 by Leonid Abalkin, one of Gorbachev's main economic advisers, that the tendency toward authoritarianism in the Soviet system may reflect a threat which is inherent in socialism's principles of public ownership and government management of the means of production. 'Historical experience testifies that the very system of socialised property and state leadership of the economy potentially contain in themselves the danger of extreme centralisation of management which will become a reality in the absence of corresponding counterbalances'. Abalkin concludes that the thorough enforcement of centralisation under Stalin, precluding necessary democratic counterbalances, led to the deformation of socialism in the USSR.

The highly centralised 'administrative-command' pattern of control established by Stalin is the chief target of criticism by Soviet reformers, who blame that system for the main problems of contemporary Soviet society. As Gorbachev complained at the Party Conference in June 1988, 'it is in that ossified system of power, in its command-pressure mechanism, that the fundamental problems of restructuring are grounded today'. Gorbachev has increasingly hinted that the system was ill-conceived to a major degree even when it was introduced, in his statement at a Central Committee plenum in June 1988 that the methods of leadership which were developed in the 1930s 'had a pernicious effect on various aspects of the development of our society'. At the same time, Gorbachev decried the straitjacket the state had imposed on popular initiative, and the disparity between 'democratic principles in words and authoritarianism in deeds'. Soviet reformers commonly charge the system originating under Stalin with a tendency toward the 'statification' (*etatizatsiya* or *ogosudarstvlenie*) of society, or the drive toward the absorption of all political, economic, and social activity into the administrative apparatus of the state. Like the general secretary, they openly describe the Soviet state as authoritarian, if not worse. By referring to the attempt to subordinate society to a 'total "all-embracing" "apparatus" state' and to 'the atmosphere of general fear' surrounding Stalin's 'state Leviathan with its hypertrophied punitive organs', Arbatov and Batalov in effect apply the concept of totalitarianism, previously scorned as a slander concocted by Western bourgeois ideologists, to the analysis of the heritage of Soviet politics.

Alienation and Dogmatism

The consequence of the adoption of authoritarian methods of control in Soviet society, according to Abalkin, is 'the alienation of the masses from property and the system of management'. Before 1985 Soviet sources insisted that alienation was confined to capitalism and other formations based on private property and exploitation but was absent from socialist societies, which were rendered immune to the problem by social ownership and control of the means of production. Under Gorbachev, the term 'alienation' has become widely used in Soviet scholars' criticisms of their society. Gorbachev and his supporters contend that true socialism as conceived by Marx and Lenin entailed self-government of political and economic institutions by the working people, but that the authoritarianism which became entrenched in the USSR by the 1930s stifled popular independence and initiative, depriving the workers and peasants of real control over the state and the economy. They argue that the loss of power over the means of production spawned apathy, passivity, and indifference among the working people.

As the working masses virtually lost control of economic institutions in the Soviet Union, according to reform-minded Soviet scholars, power gravitated to a strategically placed minority of the population, the bureaucracy. Abalkin notes that management bodies whose purpose is supposedly to defend the general interest actually 'acquire interests of their own' which 'can differ significantly from the interests of society'. In 1988 Anatolii Egorov, who at an earlier time was a prominent spokesman for older ways of thinking, admitted that in practice the interests of representatives and administrators sometimes got the upper hand over the interests of the people as a whole. Anatolii Butenko wrote in the philosophy journal *Voprosy filosofii* in 1987 of 'supercentralistic tendencies' in the

Soviet system as finding expression in 'bureaucratic centralism'. Most contemporary Soviet theorists recognise that the pattern of command from the top down has protected the concentration of power in the hands of a few, displacing the democratic elements in democratic centralism. That criticism of Soviet socialism for permitting the virtual dispossession of the labouring classes from control over the means of production and substituting the ascendancy of the bureaucracy carries strong undertones of previous themes in the writings of Eastern European revisionist Marxists and Soviet Marxist dissidents. Like those sources, who at an earlier time were stigmatised as servants of the class enemies of socialism and in many cases forcibly silenced by the Soviet regime, contemporary Soviet reformers focus their criticism on the institutional and ideological heritage of Stalinism.

Gorbachev has charged that from the 1930s on, the entrenched institutions of Soviet society were protected by a rigid ideological façade. He argued in February 1987 that since the features of the Soviet system under Stalin were 'equated with the essential characteristics of socialism, regarded as immutable and presented as dogmas leaving no room for objective scientific analysis', Soviet leaders' theoretical conception of socialism was protected from adaptation, and the actual dynamics of Soviet society were not subjected to penetrating scholarly research. Gorbachev has encouraged a reexamination of the theoretical tenets which were used by Stalin to justify the conclusion that Soviet socialism was exempt from the dialectical process of change which had been delineated in Marx's analysis of history. Stalin had asserted that the correspondence of productive relations to productive forces was guaranteed under socialism, so that a radical transformation of the superstructure would never be necessary. He also had emphasised that in Soviet society by the late 1930s, because of the abolition of private ownership of the means of production, class struggle had been replaced by the social, moral, and political unity of society as the main determinant of social change. Soviet theorists decided that the only conflicts in a socialist society were the superficial 'non-antagonistic contradictions' among groups whose interests were in fundamental harmony with one another, and that such conflicts could be resolved under the direction of the state. The guidance of change by the political superstructure ensured that social transformation would always be gradual, and revolutions from below unnecessary. In his last writings, Stalin sketched out a view of the future of Soviet society consisting of progress toward the complete absorption of productive property by the state, the elimination of remaining elements of market relations, and the subordination of all economic activity to administrative control. As Gorbachev has observed, all of those assumptions continued to exert a substantial influence on Soviet Marxist–Leninist analyses of Soviet society in the 1980s. However, all of them have been challenged by reformist thinkers in the USSR, most of whom were beginning to express their ideas cautiously during the Brezhnev period, and all of whom have more openly voiced their arguments in the more favourable climate provided by the Gorbachev leadership.

Gorbachev himself has led the way in repudiating the thesis of the correspondence of productive relations to productive forces in socialism. At the 27th Party Congress he observed that 'practice [had] shown the inaccuracy of notions, according to which in social- ist conditions *the correspondence of productive relations to the character of productive forces* is obtained, so to speak, automati- cally'. He has repeatedly complained that the system of manage- ment which took shape under Stalin gradually became more and more inappropriate as the Soviet economy reached higher levels of development, so that the administrative mechanisms inherited from the 1930s became a hindrance to further economic growth. In other words, outdated modes of planning and control are considered by Gorbachev to be the cause of economic stagnation in the USSR. That conclusion implies that nothing in the nature of socialism guarantees that productive relations will be adjusted to take account of changes in productive forces, and indeed suggests that without continuing adaptation in administrative structures growing contra- dictions between the base and superstructure are inevitable. In Gorbachev's view, the failure of political leaders to carry out timely and effective changes in economic management during the 1950s, 1960s and 1970s, by widening the lag in development between productive forces and productive relations, allowed those contradic- tions to grow so severe that by the 1980s they could be overcome only by an historical leap of 'revolutionary' restructuring. While Leonid Brezhnev expected that further economic growth and tech- nological development would provide a more stable base for estab- lished political and administrative institutions, Gorbachev argues that the political and managerial superstructure is now blocking further advances in technology and productivity. Reformist Soviet scholars add that unevenness of development is an inherent aspect of each stage of progress within socialism, since the advancement of the economy naturally tends to create inconsistencies between productive forces and the mechanisms used to control them. It follows that periodic renovations in the superstructure of socialist society are imperative, and that the more such changes are post- poned, the more radical and traumatic they must be.

The Market and Socialist Pluralism

Nowhere has the adaptability of the ideslogy been more evident in recent years than in the treatment of the relationship of market economics to socialism. Stalin predicted that the movement toward full communism would be marked by the steady reduction of the sphere of 'commodity-money relations', and even as late as the Brezhnev period the possibility of 'market socialism' was scorned by Soviet sources. Yet by 1987 Gorbachev was setting the theme for reformist scholars by promising that the 'advantages of planning will be increasingly combined with stimulating factors of the socialist market'. Leonid Abalkin soon pointed out that market relations had not been invented by capitalism, but had 'general-economic import' for various social systems. Alexander Yakovlev, a full Politburo member and close Gorbachev associate, faulted Soviet theorists for associating the properties of the market exclusively with capitalism and derided those who had made market socialism 'a bugaboo', calculated to frighten scholars 'with accusations of ideological unreliability'. Soviet leaders have traditionally described the market as a setting of dog-eat-dog competition in capitalist societies, and praised the alternative of the more comradely 'socialist emulation' among workers in their economy. However, P.G. Oldak contended in the economics journal *EKO* in 1987 that the repudiation of capitalist competition had been carried to exaggerated lengths, since while justifiably rejecting the motives and methods of that competition, Soviet sources had forgotten that it contained 'a sort of rational kernel'. The desire to introduce more vigorous competition in the Soviet economy has led Abalkin to conclude that the market has features pertinent to any system 'based on a developed division of labour and an commodity form of economic ties'. His statement virtually concedes that no highly developed economy can operate efficiently without large elements of market relations.

The effort to conceive of socialism with varied forms of ownership and a wider scope for market relations is encouraged by the recent emphasis on the necessity of stimulating the 'human factor' in production. Many contemporary Soviet scholars complain that the approach of Soviet leaders from Stalin on was to channel ever greater quantities of raw materials and machinery into the economy, while regarding labour resources as analogous to physical inputs, but neglecting the need for the motivation and qualitative improvement of human labour. They imply that the crude direction of labour with command methods and its stimulation with simple economic rewards and stereotyped propaganda campaigns has become less effective with the emergence of more educated and technically skilled workers in the post-Second World War years, the satisfaction of most basic material necessities for Soviet citizens, and the premium placed on a higher quality of work by new industrial technology. They also argue that a major problem in the motivation of workers in the contemporary Soviet economy is the growth of serious deviations from socialist principles of 'social justice'.

The emphasis on social justice has been used by Gorbachev and his supporters primarily to urge that the distribution of economic benefits be coordinated more closely with each worker's productive contribution. Soon after becoming general secretary Gorbachev complained that 'levelling tendencies' in wage policy had violated social justice by guaranteeing the same amount of pay for both diligent and sloppy workers. His commitment to greater wage differentiation was indicated by his statement in 1987 demanding that 'the actual wages of every worker be made closely dependent on his personal labour contribution to final results and not be limited by some sort of ceiling'. In addition, the current leadership has abandoned the thesis that 'public consumption funds' should be used to carry out a transition to distribution according to need. The 1961 Party Programme's predictions that payments from collective consumption funds would grow more rapidly than wage payments and that social funds would provide half of the real income of Soviet people within the near future are conspicuously absent from its 1986 successor. Gorbachev's report to the 27th Party Congress implied the need for a precise delineation of the functions of such funds, asserted that 'these are by no means philanthropic funds', and argued that 'they are also a means of encouraging skilled, conscientious labour'. Since 1985 a number of Soviet scholars have more openly advocated the restriction of the role of public consumption funds, with the expansion of services paid for directly by their users, and even the reduction of subsidies for housing and food. The last suggestion is particularly controversial. By allowing greater differentiation in wages and insuring that consumption would be determined more fully by money incomes, reformist economists and sociologists hope to reduce the impact of government subsidies, institutional perquisites, personal connections, and illegal activity on each citizen's standard of living, and more reliably link the enjoyment of material benefits with skills and achievements, as demonstrated in a more competitive society.

The recent emphasis on the differentiation of economic rewards reflects the growth of recognition in Soviet ideology of the variety of clevages and interests in Soviet society. In January 1987 Gorbachev accused Soviet ideologists of previously exaggerating the degree of uniformity in their socialist system: 'The social structure of society was depicted in an oversimplified fashion, as devoid of contradictions and the dynamism of the multifaceted interests of its various strata and groups'. Contemporary Soviet reformers see social homogeneity as a myth of Stalinist origins, used as a façade for bureaucratic domination of society. Their view that the growth in the complexity of the social system creates a greater variety of groups and interests has been endorsed by Gorbachev. Both the acceptance of the thesis of increasing complexity and the exposure of the superficiality of distinctions based on formal property relationships have encouraged a reduction of emphasis on the differences between the social classes of workers and collective farmers and a greater degree of attention to a multitude of other social divisions, such as those arising from departmental, occupational, regional, ethnic and generational differences. The implication is that non-class differences will not fade away with the further development of socialism, but on the contrary will continue to produce a variety of social interests which will demand attention from the Communist Party in order to prevent conflicts from building into crises. The current stage is seen, not as a period of the consolidation of uniformity through the reduction of the disparities between the more industrialised and less industrialised sectors of society, but as a stage in the intensification of the unevenness generated by the interaction of pre-industrial, basic industrial and advanced industrial segments within the same society.

Divisions among the nationalities of the USSR are also recognised to be a potential source of conflict and instability, as the traditional dogmas of Soviet ideology concerning nationality relations have been called into question during the last few years (see Chapter 8 for a fuller discussion). Gorbachev has criticised the earlier depiction of relations among Soviet nationalities as tranquil and harmonious, and has conceded that contradictions between nationalities will continue to arise. He has virtually abandoned the previous claim that a 'new historical community' signifying a higher stage of unity among Soviet nationalities had taken shape, while the 1986 Party Programme replaced the 1961 Programme's hints of the obsolescence of Soviet federalism with the promise of the 'further enhancement of the role' of the union republics of the USSR. Gorbachev, like many Soviet scholars, has declared that with the further development of socialism in the Soviet Union the self-consciousness of each nationality is growing. In an inversion of previous Soviet doctrine, contemporary Soviet ideologists conclude that higher levels of economic and social modernisation, rather than undermining differences among nationalities, heighten the psychological importance of such distinctions.

Soviet reformers of the Gorbachev period charge that previous Soviet leaders, by perpetuating the Stalinist myth of socialist social homogeneity and rationalising the domination of society by the state bureaucracy, suppressed the expression of social interests and stifled the initiative and enthusiasm of the Soviet people. Gorbachev has argued that the development of socialism stimulates the variety of interests in society, that the interaction of groups' demands is essential for progress, and that the policies of the Communist Party and state should take account of that diversity of interests. To a far greater degree than any other Soviet leader since Lenin, Gorbachev has accepted the conclusions that, first, the vitality and dynamism which Lenin expected to drive the advance of socialism must be impelled by enthusiastic mass participation in the construction of the new society; secondly, that the majority of the people will not display genuine enthusiasm unless their participation in political affairs and material production is motivated primarily by their own individual or group self-interest; and thirdly, that citizens and workers will not see chances for the satisfaction of their interests unless they are granted opportunities for independent political participation and economic activity. The adoption of 'socialist pluralism' as a positive slogan in Soviet ideology by 1988, presenting a deliberate and dramatic contrast with the previous repudiation of 'pluralism' as an alien and subversive concept, symbolised the acknowledgement, not only of the existence of a diversity of competing interests in Soviet society but also of the need to provide channels for the representation of those interests and the resolution of conflicts among them in the political system. So far, Soviet ideology has gone farther in recognising diverse interests than in devising stable mechanisms for representing and managing conflicts among them.

While the implications of *perestroika* for the Soviet political process are riddled with ambiguities, Gorbachev has made it clear that he would rather accept the risks accompanying the uncertainty of change than preserve the rigidity of political institutions, which has blocked popular political and economic initiative. Gorbachev's belief that political restructuring is a prerequisite for successful economic reform has led him to campaign tirelessly for the 'democratisation' of the Soviet political system, not only to build a broad and deep base of support for the current wave of economic reform but, more fundamentally, to institutionalise channels for popular pressure which will insure the continuing revitalisation of the system and guard against periods of stagnation in the future. Later chapters discuss the details of Gorbachev's attempts at reform in the electoral process, representative institutions, the government bureaucracy, and the Communist Party, showing the results of such changes and the problems they have encountered (see Chapters 4 and 5). At present, it may be noted that the theme of responsibility figures in the rationale for such reforms in two major ways. First, if demo-cratisation of the political process can ensure greater responsibility of political leaders to the people, the potential of bureaucratic resistance to present and future adaptation in the system will be drastically reduced. Secondly, if the workers in each economic enterprise realise their responsibility for the operation of the enter-prise, they will be more likely to appreciate the impact of its performance on their wellbeing. In other words, Gorbachev looks on democratisation as the antidote to the bureaucratic appropriation of control over political and economic institutions which has prod-uced a sense of alienation in the Soviet people, and has fostered the apathy, indifference and cynicism that have contributed to the stagnation of Soviet society.

'New Thinking' in International Relations

In addition to questioning the dogmas underlying Soviet political and economic institutions, Gorbachev has also reexamined some of the ideas guiding Soviet foreign policy. He has argued that leaders both in the West and the Soviet Union have long followed outdated conceptions, while contemporary conditions demand 'new political thinking'. The core of that new thinking was articulated in Gorbach-ev's report to the 27th Party Congress in early 1986, which outlined the main conflicts or 'contradictions' found in the contemporary world. Like previous Soviet leaders, Gorbachev gave due attention to the conflict between socialism and capitalism in the world arena, though he called for greater cooperation to moderate the conflict between those two social systems. He also followed Soviet tradition in discussing the internal contradictions of capitalism, though he expressed less hope than any previous Soviet leader concerning the prospects for destabilisation of capitalism through class struggle, rivalries among capitalist nations, or challenges to capitalism's influence in the Third World. The most original feature of his report was his description of 'yet another group of contradictions' never before accorded such attention on a theoretical level, arising from common problems on a global scale such as the pollution of the environment and the depletion of natural resources. These were problems faced by socialism as well as capitalism, with the greatest common problem – the danger of nuclear war – threatening the existence of all human civilization. Gorbachev implied that common problems were generated not so much by the predatory nature of capitalism as by the consequences of technological change, and concluded that technology was producing greater interdependence among nations, leading to the emergence of an 'integral world [*tselostnyi mir*]'.

The advocates of new political thinking in the Soviet Union have argued, in the face of some opposition in the highest circles, that because of the growing common problems of civilisation, the protection of common human values must take priority over the waging of class struggle. They stress the cooperative aspects of peaceful coexistence between capitalism and socialism, denying that peaceful coexistence is essentially a form of struggle, and suggesting that the relations between different social systems must go beyond mutual toleration. In June 1988 at the 19th Conference of the CPSU, Alexander Yakovlev contended that as socialism prepared for self-renewal, it should 'turn to the theory and practice of all world development, both socialist and non-socialist' for inspiration, and in October 1988 Vadim Medvedev, another member of the Politburo, was quoted by *Pravda* as rejecting the 'outdated' notion that socialism and capitalism could develop in parallel fashion, and saying that the paths of development of those systems 'inevitably intersect', since 'both systems inevitably interact within the framework of one and the same human civilization'. In Gorbachev's view, the appreciation of interdependence and common values should impel a search for 'mutual security', based on the realisation that relations between the USA and USSR are more secure when neither feels inferior to the other. In order to reduce Western fear of the Soviet military threat the Gorbachev leadership has introduced into Soviet military doctrine the ideas that 'reasonable sufficiency' should be the criterion of adequacy of the country's forces, and that force structure and strategy should be designed for the 'non-offensive defence' of the USSR rather than having the potential for swift and far-ranging counteroffensives against aggression.

Gorbachev's initiatives in foreign policy refute the charge that the rhetoric of 'new thinking' has not had an effect on concrete actions. However, the interpretation of Gorbachev's new ideas concerning international relations remains the subject of lively controversy among Western scholars. New political thinking in the USSR is influenced by genuine revisions in Soviet leaders' perceptions of world realities (encouraged by innovative analyses by some Soviet specialists on international relations), by the desire to find more effective means to attain the foreign policy objectives of the Soviet state, and by the hope to create a more favourable image for the USSR in the rest of the world. In other words, the new thinking is to be taken seriously as indicative of real changes in Soviet foreign policy, but is somewhat inflated by propagandistic pronouncements, and is ultimately and decisively shaped by the national interests of the Soviet Union. Gorbachev is striving to reduce the burden of military spending on the Soviet economy while simultaneously achieving greater success for Soviet diplomacy. For instance, he seeks sharp reductions in conventional military forces in Europe and the complete elimination of nuclear weapons from that region not only in order to free more resources for the Soviet civilian economy and stimulate the acceleration of its growth, but also to reduce the American military and diplomatic presence on the continent and encourage closer rapprochement between Western European countries and the USSR. In the long run, the main contribution of Gorbachev's new political thinking to Soviet ideology may be its challenge to the intellectual isolationism inherited from the Stalin period. Stalin's effort to ensure not only the economic but also the political and psychological autarchy of Soviet development is now identified as one of the principal causes of stagnation in the Soviet system. Gorbachev implies that the price of isolation is perpetual technological and economic inferiority. His attempts to overcome the seige mentality buttressing that isolation interact in an intriguing fashion with his insistence that Soviet society must continue to develop in accordance with its own, distinctive Leninist and socialist principles.

Conclusion

The effort to explain the stagnation of the Soviet system in the 1970s and 1980s and to devise a viable programme of change has led to the progressive radicalisation of Gorbachev's ideological position. Paradoxically, Gorbachev is a pragmatic reformer who has initiated sweeping revisions in ideological theory. His starting point for criticism of the overly centralised Soviet command system is that it does not work: it fails the tests of the rapid introduction of contemporary technology and the efficient use of economic resources. As Arbatov and Batalov put it, 'The all-embracing "total" state is not only difficult to manage and expensive, but simply ineffective and even counterproductive'. However, Gorbachev has found that the discovery of the causes of the practical ineffectiveness of that system entails an analysis of the theoretical premises as well as the historical consequences of the pattern of political and economic institutions that were established by Joseph Stalin in the 1930s. Gorbachev has not only concluded that the Stalinist system is unsuited for contemporary Soviet conditions, but has also questioned the validity of the values which were infused into the system at the time of its inception. Scholars who support Gorbachev's programme of restructuring accuse Stalinism of retarding the dynamism of socialist society by crushing popular initiative under the weight of an omnipotent bureaucracy. They contend that the Soviet system can be revitalised only by recognising the sources of conflict and alienation in the society and freeing human striving through the limited growth of democracy in the political sphere and the partial acceptance of market relations in the economy. Though the details of the system which would result from such reforms are still unclear, it is apparent that the general shape of the new society would consist of a unique synthesis of central planning and the market, and of single-party direction and political pluralism.

Though Gorbachev has initiated a search for a new model of socialism, he insists that the ideas on which that model are to be based are those expressed several decades ago in Lenin's conception of socialism. By invoking the authority of Lenin's works, Gorbachev is legitimating the acceptance of practices which had previously been regarded as anathema to Soviet socialism, including competitive elections, private entrepreneurship, and family farming. As he presses further in the course of reform Gorbachev may well encounter the implications of the contradictions which are integral to Lenin's theoretical contributions, such as the contradiction between conscious elite direction and enthusiastic mass participation, or the conflict between centralised economic planning and workers' self-government. In practice, after coming to power, Lenin tended to come down on the authritarian side of each of those polarities, and though his last works showed his regret over the consequences of some of the choices which he had made, the suggestions for institutional reforms offered in those writings would have proved superficial and ineffective. Thus Gorbachev is in the ambiguous position of presenting his reforms as a continuation of the Bolshevik revolution even though those reforms are directed against some of the defects of the society which originated in that revolution. The difficulty of reconciling the spontaneity of independent mass initiative with the 'guiding and directing role' of the communist party goes to the heart of the dilemmas faced by those who seek a new model of socialism.

The most fundamental theoretical contribution made by the scholars supporting *perestroika* is the realisation that the major problems in the Soviet system are generated from within. Some reformist scholars recognise that diversity and conflict are natural phenomena within a socialist society, and that the most important internal contradictions of socialism are caused not by the vestiges of previous phases of history or the nefarious influence of Western capitalism but are generated by the autonomous tendencies of the system, and are derived from the inherent principles of socialism. Contemporary Soviet reformers are confident that opening the Soviet system to greater economic and intellectual interaction with the non-socialist world will not corrupt the system, but will simulate its modernisation. Some Soviet scholars see a potential tendency toward authoritarianism as inherent in the nature of a centrally planned and administered economy under the guidance of a single political party, and argue that the restructuring of the Soviet system must create channels for the articulation and satisfaction of diverse interests as a means of countering the thrust of excessive centralisation and conformity. They implicitly acknowledge that the outcome of Gorbachev's reforms will depend on the achievement of radical change in the Soviet political culture, which has deep roots in the pre-revolutionary Russian past, but their analysis points to the conclusion that the failure to carry out such change would endanger the stability of the Soviet system and degrade its position in the modern world.

PART TWO

The Contemporary Political System

3

The Political Leadership

JOHN P. WILLERTON, JR

The Soviet political leadership – like the political process in which it operates – is now in the midst of profound change. Its composition has been radically altered in the past few years, with few high-level officials from the long-ruling Brezhnev regime maintaining power into the 1990s. Even a non-party member has been given an important portfolio in the USSR Council of Ministers, while increasing numbers of non-Communists fill influential positions in subnational governments. Meanwhile, elite norms of behaviour are being transformed, as politicians are encouraged to adopt more consensual, yet more outspoken leadership styles. The most basic system values, political structures, and policy priorities are now being reevaluated and, in many cases, transformed.

These changes, directed by a bold group of reformers and spurred on by strong socioeconomic pressures for significant policy change, have contributed to the reawakening of long dormant elements within Soviet society. They may well be changing the relationship between the elite and the masses, as politicians must cope with growing pressures from numerous societal elements. Even high-level party officials – once viewed as immune to mass interests and attitudes – have become vulnerable to such pressures. The July 1989 forced 'retirement' of Leningrad party boss and Politburo candidate member Yuri Solov'ev is dramatic evidence of this. Defeated as a candidate to the Congress of People's Deputies by an overwhelming majority of voters (and in an uncontested race), Solov'ev (and the Leningrad party leadership) received a vote of no confidence which led to his replacement. Other regional party leaders suffered similar fates, necessitating much rethinking about party norms and policies. The vulnerability of Solov'ev and other politicians qualifies our traditional understanding of power relations in the Soviet system. Today, the important political pressures operating on Soviet officials come not only from above.

The ongoing transformation of Soviet politics has been conducive to the emergence of a new policy programme with domestic and foreign policy initiatives revealing the contemporary leadership as more flexible and innovative. As this programme takes root and compels all society members – elite and mass – to reconsider basic values and expectations, pressures mount for the development of an elite cohort which is more able in training, ability, and attitude to address the challenges of a complex and heterogeneous society. The past half decade has already witnessed a major change in the composition of the governing elite. Yet contemporary developments, both in Moscow and in the varied Soviet periphery, increase the momentum for an even more profound transformation of the attitudes and behavioural proclivities of aspiring younger politicians.

There is a dynamism to the Soviet politics of the late 1980s and early 1990s that rivals that earlier period of experimentation and reform, the 1920s. Institutional arrangements long in place are being altered. There is a changing balance of power among major institutional actors, with long-favoured institutions (such as the CPSU Secretariat and the Central Committee apparatus) experiencing a diminution in power and authority. New – or newly enfranchised – actors (such as the Congress of People's Deputies and its Supreme Soviet) are addressing issues which until recently were under the exclusive purview of top party organs. The always precarious balance between national and regional interests and responsibilities is now in question: challenges from the Baltic, Caucasus, and other regions compel Moscow to reevaluate the relevance of restructuring to the administration of political and economic life in the Soviet periphery. The prospects of greater power sharing between the national leadership and lower-level officials were clearly enhanced by the wake of the reconstituted Supreme Soviet's August by 1989 approval of economic autonomy for the three Baltic republics.

All of these developments leave the Soviet society and polity dynamic and fluid. They contribute to an uncertainty and confusion which touches all levels of authority. Both politicians and the Soviet populace are unclear as to appropriate policy expectations, future directions, and opportunities for additional change. Politicians are necessarily anxious about their own responsibilities and conduct. Motivated primarily by their own career aspirations, they are cautious in acting on conflicting signals coming from Moscow. The prerequisities for career mobility for aspiring officials are not clear, and politicians must necessarily be wary. There are differences at the highest levels regarding the pace and direction of reform. There is also every likelihood that obstacles to the restructuring process – foreseen and unforeseen – will require further changes in policy and in the proscribed behaviour of officials.

Any observer of Soviet politics must also be cautious in characterising the evolving political leadership and its reform efforts. The presence of a strong and active general secretary and the emergence of a coalition of powerful politicians and interests committed to political and socioeconomic change have led to the rapid development of a wide-ranging reform programme. Yet powerful and deep-seated forces, within the political leadership and without, are hindering the restructuring campaign. Those forces are institutional and attitudinal. They include many high, middle-rank, and lower-level officials. While pressured by a reforming top leadership, the more orthodox and conservative party-state apparatus continues to favour the preservation of the status quo. As a result, any genuine transformation of the Soviet political regime and system is a long-term process: one requiring decades and, perhaps, more than one national leadership.

Continuities from the Past

Were one to describe the essential characteristics of the Soviet political system, one would note its centralised, hierarchical nature: its massive set of interconnected bureaucracies linking all institutions and interests into an entity ruled by a small and relatively homogeneous cohort of Slavic and Russian *apparatchiki*. The political system was moulded by Lenin's thinking and the CPSU's early experiences, with important rules such as the principle of democratic centralism directing it by the early 1920s. The set of party and state apparatuses, and the norms governing their operation, were more fully developed during the Stalin period. Each succeeding regime has attempted to leave its mark on the Soviet political process, with frequent reorganisational schemes of selected *apparats* or sectors characterising the Stalin, Khrushchev, and Brezhnev periods. While certain reforms constituted important efforts at redistributing power or political responsibilities (e.g. Khrushchev's *sovnarkhozy* or regional economic councils, an initiative designed to weaken the power of central ministries while strengthening the position of regional interests), most did little to alter the nature or operation of the Leninist–Stalinist system. Continuity, not change, characterised the Soviet system from the 1930s up to the 1970s.

There was also a great deal of continuity in the composition and behavioural norms of the political leadership. For most of Soviet history, the political process was dominated by a cohort of party functionaries whose careers were made during the tenure of Joseph Stalin. A generation of revolutionaries – generally highly educated, cosmopolitan, sophisticated, and fairly heterogenous in background and experiences – did govern in the early years of Soviet power, but they gave way by the 1930s to the Stalin generation of *apparatchiki*. These officials – committed to Stalin and his programme, of rural or small town origin, technically trained, little aware of the outside world, and much more homogeneous in background and experiences – would dominate the Soviet polity for nearly fifty years. They generally enjoyed rapid mobility, with their careers based on service in various institutional and regional settings. Their behavioural norms reflected the character of the 1930s and 1940s: a period of purges and war. They were conservative, little prone to risk-taking, deferential to superiors, and highly reluctant to assume responsibility or to initiate.

The term *nomenklatura* has come to symbolise this powerful and conservative elite group which for so long dominated Soviet political life. This term is derived from the system of lists of both official positions and politicians aspiring to those positions: lists controlled by party leaders and used at every level of authority in the recruitment and mobility of subordinate officials. The Stalin-generation *nomenklatura* proved to be stable and predictable in its composition and behavioural tendencies. The continuity in its ranks, in its members' behavioural tendencies, and in its commitment to the basic Stalinist system, norms, and issue agenda, contributed to a discernible political and societal stability which continued for several decades. It ultimately led, however, to a Brezhnev period of political lethargy and policy stagnation that would facilitate the dramatic developments of the latter 1980s.

The Brezhnev Legacy

Examined from a perspective of the early 1990s, the Brezhnev era (1964–82) is one of genuine contrasts. this is especially true in considering the mixed record of the Brezhnev national leadership. After the tumultuous Khrushchev years (1953–64), with de-Stalinisation, reform, and often erratic policy changes, the Brezhnev regime brought a regularising of the policy process and a stabilising of the political elite that were desired by most officials. Under Brezhnev, a broad-ranging coalition emerged which governed Soviet society for nearly two decades. That coalition encompassed all major elements within the political establishment. Its governing style favoured accommodation of institutional interests, continuity in personnel, and gradualism and caution in any policy change. Some (for instance Bunce and Echols, 1980) have described the Soviet system of the Brezhnev years as corporatist. Institutional interests were protected, while a welfare statist policy programme supported by all elite interests was seen as helping to bond the governing coalition to the broader society.

During the Brezhnev regime's first decade of rule, a number of important policy payoffs were reaped through a massive 'guns and butter' investment programme. Employing any of a number of measures – including agricultural growth rates, availability of housing and various consumer goods, military procurement figures, external trade and military agreements – the first half of the Brezhnev regime entailed major policy successes. Brezhnev's authority as primary policy initiator, and the general stability of the governing coalition, were greatly enhanced by these policy successes.

However, as has often been true of long-governing regimes, the continued application of the very programme and means by which initial gains were achieved ultimately led to important dilemmas which subsequently weakened both the regime and society. Political stagnation set in. The leadership aged and became ever more cautious and reluctant in addressing the society's problems. The officials and interests which comprised the governing coalition retained their standing for nearly twenty years. Illness and death accounted for most of the limited turnover in personnel. By the early 1980s, both society and the elite were awaiting a succession which would reactivate the Soviet political process.

The accommodationist and status quo orientation of the Brezhnev regime was conducive to the emergence of powerful and often corrupt patronage machines in many regional and institutional settings. Whole republics were run as the bailiwicks of influential party leaders and networks (for instance, the now well-publicised cases of Dinmukhamed Kunaev in Kazakhstan and Sharaf Rashidov in Uzbekistan). Provincial networks likewise governed with little interference from Moscow. In sum, the latter Brezhnev years entailed a political malaise in which continuity and stability were secured at the expense of policy inertia and corruption.

With Yuri Andropov's succession as general secretary in November 1982 there emerged a growing consensus within the national leadership to resolve these political dilemmas, as well as to address mounting social and economic problems. The early 1980s entailed a political leadership turnover which transcended the death of Brezhnev to include the passing of the Stalin generation of officials. All important interests and institutions were affected. A new cohort of officials assumed the reins of power. It included a wide range of politicians, more diverse in background experiences and in political orientations. First inspired by Yuri Andropov's short-lived reforming regime (1982–4), this cohort of politicians would institute a 'restructuring' programme which would far surpass the modest efforts of Andropov.

The Recurring Succession and Regime Formation Dilemma

An important dilemma not resolved in the Brezhnev regime's efforts at routinising the political system was the regularisation of the leadership succession and regime formation process. The succession and regime formation problem has dogged the Soviet system since its earliest days. This centralised and hierarchical system has needed a strong leader and political centre to operate effectively. Yet no leader, or regime, has developed a mechanism for the predictable and smooth transfer of power to another politician and governing team. There is no precedent, or formula, for retiring an aged or tired top leader. Only the physical infirmities, and ultimate death, of the top party leader have set the timetable for a succession. Konstantin Chernenko's leadership (1984–5) is illustrative. Chernenko was frail and nearly incapacitated during much of his tenure as general secretary, but he still retained power until his death in March 1985.

The processes by which a new regime emerges and a new governing coalition of politicians moves into place are subject to the vagaries of elite high politics. These processes have not been subject to Soviet law, as the experience of changing regimes in the 1980s demonstrated. Extensive manoeuvring by high-level officials characterised the emergence of all three national regimes. Each emerging regime was comprised of a rather different mix of institutional interests, with differing elite mobility practices undertaken. The policy lines pursued by these regimes also varied, even though all of these changes occurred during less than one decade.

Much Western scholarly work focuses on the succession and regime formation processes, and there are disagreements as to the informal rules and norms which underly them. Some contend that there is a 'honeymoon' period for a new leader and regime, with that honeymoon constituting the most opportune moment for significant policy change (Bunce, 1981). Others focus on what are seen as longer-term regime-building efforts of new leaders (Breslauer, 1980). Still others contend that it is only after a governing coalition has emerged, with the coalition spanning numerous interests and political networks, that new leaders are empowered to address the society's overarching problems (Willerton, 1987). There is widespread agreement, however, regarding the importance of leadership successions as critical transition periods when new regimes coalesce and the potential for significant policy change mounts.

The Gorbachev Succession and the Process of Regime Formation

The March 1985 succession which brought Mikhail Gorbachev to power occurred against the backdrop of simmering policy dilemmas which required the national leadership's attention. Most high-level officials were agreed on the need to address these problems, though their policy preferences varied enormously. The restructuring, openness, and democratisation campaigns which became central initiatives of the reformist Gorbachev national leadership emerged only after several years of regime consolidation. Even as the reform programme was taking shape, there was resistance in high places to its apparently more extreme nature. Gorbachev could use an authoritative setting such as the January 1987 Central Committee plenum to press for political reforms (including secret and multicandidate election of state and party officials), and yet see his proposals essentially tabled by the party leadership. Many Stalin-generation officials and other remnants of the old Brezhnev regime, to paraphrase Gorbachev, needed to be swept out of the way. A governing team committed to a reform programme was needed.

A review of past Soviet national regimes reveals that it takes a new leadership approximately five to seven years to consolidate its position, and therefore be in a position to advance a new comprehensive policy programme. The geriatric realities of the aged Soviet leadership enabled Gorbachev and other reformers to speed up this timetable, with a massive turnover of officials occurring at all levels between 1985 and 1989. Thus, of the twenty-five politicians who comprised the combined membership of the ruling party Politburo and Secretariat at the time of Brezhnev's death, only two (including Gorbachev himself) retained power in late 1989. By the end of 1989, four-fifths (twenty out of twenty-five members) of the Politburo and Secretariat had been recruited under Gorbachev, with all of those top officials having experienced career promotions during the 1985–89 period (for the leadership as it stood in January 1990, see Table 3.1).

This turnover of personnel was important because the broad contours of the reformist restructuring programme were already being outlined by 1987. However, the dilemmas of fashioning a coalition supportive of a new policy line have been constant. The extraordinary 19th Party Conference held in June 1988 failed to result in a consolidation of power by the reformers, and no personnel changes resulted. Only the September 1988 leadership shakeup, as the culmination of a hastily-called Central Committee plenum, and the unanticipated April 1989 purging of over one hundred Central Committee members, left the coalition of reformers in a relatively more secure position. Most of the one hundred and ten ousted 'deal souls' (officials retired from their formal positions but still holding Central Committee membership) were holdovers from prior, more conservative regimes. Their removal at least temporarily checked the prospects of a conservative Central Committee majority successfully challenging the reformist national regime.

Yet even in the wake of these important power-consolidating moves – and nearly six years after Gorbachev's succession – there are still important elements within the governing coalition which are sceptical about the full restructuring programme. At a contentious July 1989 Central Committee (CC) meeting, a number of top leaders openly pressured the general secretary and reformers to alter some of their major policy initiatives. Influential Politburo members such as prime minister Nikolai Ryzhkov and CC Secretary Yegor Ligachev argued for a reversal of important party organisational reforms and for serious limitations on *glasnost'*. Lower-level, but still influential, Central Committee members were themselves emboldened to articulate positions at variance from the official (reformist) policy line.

This diversity in the ranks of the national leadership reflects an essential reality of Soviet political life: governing administrations include many competing interests and actors. The guiding leader (general secretary) and his prominent proteges and allies are compelled to work with, or at least accommodate themselves to, many diverse elements which are important parts of the governing team. Among these are resistant and unsupportive elements, but elements well ensconced within the party-state bureaucracy. This dilemma is not a new one: all previous regimes have faced the same problem. Gorbachev and his supporters have come to terms with it more rapidly and, apparently, more effectively than a number of predecessors. Notwithstanding official resistance, as evinced at the July 1989 Central Committee meeting, they have been able to advance a radical reform programme which surpasses any set of reform measures attempted by a national regime in the past sixty years. However, that programme and its consequences heighten the concerns of numerous conservative elements within the governing

TABLE 3.1 *The Soviet leadership, January 1990*
(*years of birth in parentheses*)

Politburo

Full members (12):
Mikhail S. Gorbachev (1931), General Secretary of the CC CPSU
and Chairman of the USSR Supreme Soviet (President)
Vladimir A. Ivashko (1932) First Sectretary, Ukrainian Communist Party
Vladimir A. Kryuchkov (1924) Chairman, KGB
Yegor K. Ligachev (1920) CC Secretary
Yuri D. Maslyukov (1937) First Deputy Chairman USSR Council
of Ministers and Chairman, USSR Gosplan
Vadim A. Medvedev (1929) CC Secretary
Nikolai I. Ryzhkov (1929) Chairman, USSR Council of Ministers
Eduard A. Shevardnadze (1928) Foreign Minister
Nikolai N. Slyun'kov (1929) CC Secretary
Vitalii A. Vorotnikov (1926) President, Russian Republic
Alexander N. Yakovlev (1923) CC Secretary
Lev N. Zaikov (1923) CC Secretary

Candidate Members (7):

Alexandra P. Biryukova (1929) Deputy Chairman, USSR Council
of Ministers and Chairman, Bureau on Social Development of
the USSR Council of Ministers
Anatolii I. Luk'yanov (1930) First Deputy Chairman of
the USSR Supreme Soviet (Deputy President)
Yevgenii M. Primakov (1929) Chairman, Council of the Union,
USSR Supreme Soviet
Boris K. Pugo (1937) Chairman, Party Control Committee
Georgii P. Razumovsky (1936) CC Secretary
Alexander V. Vlasov (1932) Chairman, RSFSR Council of
Ministers
Dmitrii T. Yazov (1923) Defence Minister

Secretariat (13 members):

Mikhail S. Gorbachev (see above)
Oleg D. Baklanov (1932)
Ivan T. Frolov (1929); also editor of *Pravda*
Andrei N. Girenko (1936)
Yegor K. Ligachev (see above)
Yuri A. Manaenkov (1936)
Vadim A. Medvedev (see above)
Georgii P. Razumovsky (see above)
Nikolai N. Slyun'kov (see above)
Yegor S. Stroev (1937)
Gumer I. Usmanov (1932)
Alexander N. Yakovlev (see above)
Lev N. Zaikov (see above)

coalition, leaving the contemporary national leadership scene dynamic and unstable.

Primary Political Institutions of the Soviet System

Party Actors

Any contemporary judgements as to the relative standing of the political institutions responsible for the conduct of the Soviet policy process must necessarily be tentative. This is certainly true for top-level actors, for the period of *glasnost'* has not shed a sufficient amount of light on their operation. In examining these actors we are dealing with a set of moving objects, as institutional reforms, personnel turnover, and changes in political norms continue. New sets of responsibilities and new inter-relationships among the major institutional actors are not fully clear, but five years of Gorbachev-era reforms permit us to draw some conclusions.

In the 1980s the office of CPSU general secretary has once again proved to be all-powerful in the Soviet political system. Nikita Khrushchev's difficulties in shepherding projects through to their conclusion and his ultimate ouster in October 1964, together with Leonid Brezhnev's consensual decision-making style, had led some to wonder whether the top party leader was becoming but a first among equals (Hough and Fainsod, 1979). Gorbachev's rapid consolidation of power, his high profile and energetic manner, and his ability to initiate a wide-ranging set of policy changes have all reinforced the common understanding of the general secretary as the USSR's single most authoritative and influential guiding political force.

Traditionally, the party general secretary sets out the broad political agenda directing the CPSU and Soviet society. As the leading member of the party Politburo – the party's and country's top decision-making body – he guides the policy process. As the 'general' secretary within the party Secretariat, he has broad supervisory power over all other secretaries and all departments of the party apparatus. His access to information and his ability to comment on all policy matters make him a most formidable actor in the highly bureaucratised Soviet system. Of equal or perhaps even greater importance is his ability to affect personnel recruitment matters. General secretary Gorbachev has shown himself to be influential not only in the operation of top Party bodies but also in their composition. As noted earlier, he has overseen a transformation in the membership of the Politburo and Secretariat. Through powerful and well-placed proteges and allies (such as the Party Secretary overseeing cadres policy, Georgii Razumovsky) he has directly influenced the recruitment of other high-level politicians, be they Central Committee apparatus officials, regional party leaders, or members of the Soviet government.

The institutional powers of the general secretary are reinforced when that leader's style permits him to enhance his authority. Gorbachev's ability to take the initiative, to use the element of surprise to outflank opponents, to exploit the media and public appearances to further his political ends, and to forge short-term and long-term linkages with powerful politicians and interests should not be discounted. At the same time, in promoting a radical reform programme, he has drawn upon an impressive 'kitchen cabinet' of advisers. The Gorbachev braintrust includes specialists from diverse settings, including a former party Secretary (Anatolii Dobrynin), a former Armed Forces General Staff Chief (Sergei Akhromeev), long-serving advisers to several previous leaderships (Georgii Arbatov and Fedor Burlatsky), and reformist academics (Abel Aganbegyan and Tat'yana Zaslavskaya) less well connected to the Soviet political establishment. These advisers have enabled Gorbachev to remain on the cutting edge of establishment reform thinking, helping him to outmanoeuvre numerous rivals.

Historically, an important base of power for the general secretary has been the party Secretariat. As the primary administrative organ of the CPSU, the Secretariat supervised the execution of policy. Responsible for the day-to-day running of the party apparatus, it monitored subordinate party organs and, through them, government agencies. Since the Secretariat's subordinate departments researched information and helped in the drafting of resolutions for the policy-making party Politburo, its position in the political process was considerable. When dominated by a general secretary and his allies, the Secretariat and its subordinate apparatus are a primary resource upon which the top party leader can draw.

Under a reform-oriented Gorbachev, however, the Secretariat and party apparatus have proven to be sources of resistance. While the Secretariat includes members who broadly share Gorbachev's political vision (including Alexander Yakovlev, Vadim Medvedev and Razumovsky), its membership also includes leading opponents (such as Ligachev) and others who are apparently sceptical about important aspects of the reform programme (such as Lev Zaikov). Beneath these officials are thousands of party *apparatchiki*, working in Central Committee departments, who have been resistant to many initiatives of the governing leadership. As a result of this organisational resistance, both the Secretariat and the party (Central Committee) apparatus have become the objects of important organisational reforms and streamlining efforts. Under Gorbachev, the Secretariat has undergone a redistribution of responsibilities among Secretaries. The subordinate apparatus has experienced a consolidation of departments and the cutting back of administrative staffs. These changes have taken a number of forms, and they have assumed political significance.

At the November 1988 Central Committee plenum an important set of organisational reforms, agreed to earlier by the Politburo, were introduced which altered the distribution of power and responsibilities among top-level party organs. Six Central Committee commissions were created and given a wide range of responsibilities, including oversight of the party apparatus. While their roles are still not fully defined, these commissions appear to be subordinate only to the Politburo, assisting in the preparation of draft materials for that top decision-making organ (see also below, pp. 75 and 219–20). Positioned between the Politburo and the Central Committee apparatus, these commissions have apparently usurped the position of the Secretariat as the critical party monitoring actors. The emergence of these commissions – combined with the decision to consolidate the Central Committee apparatus into a smaller number of streamlined departments – has diminished the power of both the Secretariat and the central apparatus.

The six new commissions are all chaired by high-level party leaders. Three commissions – Party Development and Cadres Policy, Ideology, and International Policy – are headed by close Gorbachev proteges, Razumovsky, Medvedev, and Yakovlev respectively. All three politicians are important members of the governing coalition, and all are publicly committed to the reformist programme. A fourth commission, on socioeconomic policy, is chaired by an apparent ally of Gorbachev and his proteges, Nikolai Slyun'kov. Only two commissions – agriculture and legal policy – are headed by non-reformists, Ligachev and (until late 1989) Viktor Chebrikov. But the performance to date of the Commission on Legal Policy, under Chebrikov's guidance, has been more than compatible with the legal and political reforms being championed by Gorbachev. In effect, the emergence of these commissions, with their chairmen and members including many prominent reformers, has represented a structural initiative apparently designed to circumvent the organisational resistance of more conservative party *apparatchiki*.

What of the political power of the Central Committee apparatus in the period of restructuring? That apparatus, traditionally operating under the guidance of the Secretariat and Central Committee, previously served as the primary actor monitoring lower-level party organisations and officials and governmental and other bureaucracies. Just a few years ago, this apparatus was composed of twenty-four departments, with thousands of officials. The organisational reforms of 1988, combined with the streamlining efforts of the past few years, led to their consolidation into nine departments (plus a special organisation, the Main Political Administration of the Soviet Armed Forces). Once these departments played an influential role in the formulation of policy, if only in the provision of information and draft proposals to top party bodies. Today, their ability to influence policy and to supervise the activities of lower-level party organisations and especially governmental agencies is suspect. There is mounting evidence of a significant turnover in the composition of these departments, with high-level reformers (including commission chairmen) overseeing the recruitment of many new workers, often from influential, Moscow-based, think tanks. It has been estimated that over three-quarters of all workers in the influential International Department (primarily responsible for foreign policy matters) have been newly recruited during just the past three years.

Traditional party apparatus influences are being eased out of the Soviet policy process. The primary focus of these central party bodies increasingly involves internal party affairs and information gathering activities. One Central Committee department head was quoted in mid-1989 as predicting that the recently formed Supreme Soviet standing committees would replace Central Committee departments as the major originators of policy.

Under Gorbachev, the party Politburo continues to be the country's top policy-making body, though it apparently meets less frequently than in the past. The Politburo's membership includes all top party and governmental officials, with its superior organisational position only reinforced by the apparent downgrading of the Secretariat. It issues directives to party and state organisations, with many such contemporary directives constituting the foundation of the restructuring programme. The Politburo's wide range of potential interests makes it dependent upon subordinate party and state agencies. While members have areas of special responsibility, specialists often are brought into Politburo meetings for purposes of consultation.

Historically, the membership of the Politburo has spanned many institutional and regional interests. This continues to be true today, though the representation of non-Slavic and non-Russian interests has been minimal in the Gorbachev period: as of January 1990, only four of nineteen full and candidate Politburo members were non-Russians, and only two were non-Slav. In practice, among the diverse members of the Politburo, the preferential position has gone to those who are locally based in Moscow (who serve in either a national party or state apparatus). These politicians, and especially those who are simultaneously members of the Secretariat, constitute the top decision-makers within the Soviet system.

One must be cautious in describing the relative power balance among politicians and interests found within the combined membership of the Politburo and Secretariat. There appears to be a complex set of orientations among members, leaving a dynamic general secretary considerable room for manoeuvre, but not without limits. As already noted, Gorbachev has overseen a transformation of this membership, with numerous proteges and allies being promoted into this highest echelon of authority. A number of top politicians, including Anatolii Luk'yanov, Medvedev, Razumovsky, Shevardnadze and Yakovlev, have staked out public positions supportive of a more profound political and economic restructuring programme. Others, led by Ligachev, and including such powerful politicians as Ryzhkov, Zaikov and Vitalii Vorotnikov, have taken much more cautious stances. We thus find a checks and balances of sorts operating within the top Soviet leadership. Reforming initiatives appear as half-measures, as officials who supervise important sectors (such as Ligachev and Soviet agriculture) rely on their own preferences in interpreting and applying those initiatives.

The Gorbachev years have entailed an overhauling in the composition of the party's other deliberative and representative body, the Central Committee. We have also been witnessing a more subtle shift in the Central Committee's political role, as the reconstituted USSR Supreme Soviet assumes an ever wider set of responsibilities. Traditionally, the Central Committee was the top representative body within the CPSU, drawing its membership from a wide range of elements within the party. All top officials – party and state – were to be found within its ranks, with leading figures from other important institutions and sectors also included. This wide-ranging membership served an important legitimating function, suggesting important links between the top policy-making elite and various elements of the Soviet establishment and society.

The Central Committee has been the most authoritative forum where important issues were raised and important party decisions were ratified. Its two or more plenary sessions every year were critical settings where the party leadership set out policies. Various political elements had the opportunity to comment on such policies, as well as to raise other matters. However, the Central Committee's large size, with upwards of 400 full and candidate members, made it an unwieldy decision-making organ.

The April 1989 removal of 110 members served to make the

Central Committee a smaller and more cohesive body. Combined with the selective elevation of a limited number of new members, the Central Committee membership appeared increasingly to favour reformist interests. The representation within its ranks of party apparatus workers declined (their overall proportion of members dropping from approximately 45 per cent to under 34 per cent). In addition, certain types of politicians, who in past years would have been seated in the new Central Committee, were either passed over or only included as candidate members (for instance, regional party officials). In many cases these officials were conservative in orientation and at best dubious supporters of the national reform programme.

During 1989, the emergence of a revitalised and more influential Supreme Soviet clouded the assumed political primacy of the Central Committee. Important issues, once understood to be under the exclusive purview of the Central Committee and party hierarchy, were addressed in lively sessions of the popularly elected Congress of People's Deputies and Supreme Soviet (see Chapter 5). While the overwhelming majority of the 542 Supreme Soviet deputies are also CPSU members, only a fraction of those party deputies are Central Committee members. Indeed, among the top leaders, only Gorbachev (Supreme Soviet Chairman), his protege Luk'yanov (First Deputy Chairman) and Vorotnikov are Supreme Soviet members. As a result, numerous important policy matters (for instance, laws on agricultural leasing arrangements, taxation of cooperatives, limited economic autonomy for the Baltic republics, and even the resolution of workers' strikes) are now considered by a Supreme Soviet which is dominated by the general secretary and his allies, and not by the central party apparatus.

The contemporary Central Committee includes members with a wide range of orientations and differing levels of power and authority. Today, barring certain legal restrictions, the more influential members of the Central Committee are generally either deputies in the Supreme Soviet or members of the six Central Committee commissions. And it is not coincidental that within a still more conservative central party setting, a significant number of such Central Committee deputies or commission members are reform-minded politicians.

State Actors

Our traditional understanding of the Soviet party-state system has emphasised the policy-making and supervisory roles of party organs, and of policy-implementing role of state organs. While simplified and not fully accurate, this description does properly emphasise the decision-making prerogatives of top party actors. It does not, however, fully reveal the important role governmental organs assume in the overall policy process. There is an interlocking of party and state organs at all authority levels, with overlapping (and not entirely clear) domains of responsibility. In addition, there is an overlapping membership across party and state institutional actors, with leading governmental officials generally holding positions within top party bodies (such as membership in the Central Committee or, in a few select cases, membership in the Politburo).

The Council of Ministers, the most authoritative organ of the Soviet government, is a large body standing atop a massive set of state bureaucracies. Led by a chairman (prime minster), it is composed of over 70 governmental ministers, state committee chairmen, and top government officials. The Council of Ministers addresses a wide range of policy matters, including economic, education, legal, and social welfare concerns. Its primary focus has entailed the country's economic administration and, in particular, the development and approval of an economic plan. It has a varied membership, which primarily includes government officials with long-standing professional expertise in their domains of responsibility.

The unwieldy size of the Council of Ministers, combined with the considerable range of issues for which it is responsible, has enhanced the important guiding role of the Council's Presidium: a smaller working group of senior officials. Real executive authority rests with the Presidium, which directs the work of the dozens of ministries and state committees. Problems of 'departmentalism' – when officials in a particular institutional setting such as a ministry pursue their own interests or those of their organisation and not broader party-state interests – are addressed by this body. The party Secretariat, and its subordinate Central Committee departments, have traditionally monitored such problems, but the Presidium also assumes a supervisory role.

The Presidium is directed by the prime minister and includes approximately a dozen first and deputy chairmen. It meets regularly and sets the broad contours of economic and governmental policy. The Presidium works in concert with the top decision-making body, the party Politburo, acting on the latter's broad policy line and specific decisions. An important decision such as the 1989 Draft Programme on Republican Self-Management is developed by the Council and its Presidium, with the Politburo's approval, before it is submitted for ratification by the Supreme Soviet. Because leading members of the Presidium (such as prime minister Ryzhkov) are

also members of the Politburo, the relationship between the leading
party and governmental bodies is a direct one.

Similar to the recent experience of party organs, the Council
of Ministers and its subordinate institutions have also undergone
important changes during the 1980s. Its Chairman, Nikolai Ryzhkov, has become an increasingly respected and influential prime
minister. This has been due not only to his administrative skills,
but also to the leadership he demonstrated during the late 1988
Armenian earthquake disaster and to his role in resolving the
summer 1989 miners' strike. During his tenure, the Council of
Ministers' primary role as major administrator of the economy has
been reinforced. Ryzhkov has been a cautious supporter of the
reform programme, and that programme has heightened the government's role in carrying out policies in all areas. However, during
the past five years, there has been a significant cutting back of
government bureaucracies. Initially, many agencies were consolidated into larger administrative entities (for instance, the merging
of several agricultural ministries and state committees into Gosagroprom, the State Agroindustrial Committee). The Council of Ministers was subsequently streamlined through the abolition of bureaucracies such as Gosagroprom. The April 1984 Council of Ministers
numbered over 100 members, not including 15 republican representatives, while today's Council is reduced to approximately 70 members (excluding republic officials) and 57 ministries. Traditionally,
ministries had staffs of a thousand or more workers. Between 1985
and 1990, many were halved in size.

The composition of the Council of Ministers and its Presidium
has also been transformed. Only 10 per cent of the ministers are
from the pre-1985 period, while all Presidium members have been
appointed during the Gorbachev period. As in the past, most top
government officials are career professionals who were recruited
from within. However, many ministers are now from outside the
bureaucratic establishment. An increasing number favour system
and policy reform.

Ministers must be nominated by the prime minister and formally
approved by the Supreme Soviet. Unlike the past, the new Supreme
Soviet has exhibited real independence in its evaluation of potential
top government officials, and a number of nominees recommended
by Ryzhkov were rejected by the Supreme Soviet. Nikolai
Vorontsov, a non-Communist and supporter of more radical reform,
was selected to head the USSR State Committee for Environmental
Protection after previous nominees had been rejected. Some powerful ministers were subjected to intensive questioning, and then confirmed in split votes. Defence Minister and candidate member of

the Politburo Dmitrii Yazov is a case in point: he underwent several hours of gruelling questioning, with 77 deputies ultimately voting against his confirmation. In the period of restructuring the Council of Ministers may have gained enhanced responsibilities, but it has become more openly accountable, and to a wider range of political and societal interests.

Contemporary Developments and Future Dilemmas

Developments of the past few years – including the examination of leadership practices, the investigation of corruption, the introduction of secret and multi-candidate elections – point to a new ethic of political accountability. Decision-makers at all levels are increasingly answerable to a wide range of actors which includes not only superiors, but peers, subordinates, and the broader populace. Ongoing institutional reforms may represent a fundamental change of the policy process as power is shared among a wider range of actors and interests. Because we are still in a transition period, what we are witnessing could end up as little more than another reorganisation of existing bureaucracies. However, as this chapter has suggested, we are probably witnessing a more profound redistribution of power.

The new Congress of People's Deputies and Supreme Soviet stand as an alternative power base for Gorbachev and the reformers. Their deputies are popularly elected representatives with genuine legitimacy in the eyes of the populace. To date, these deputies have not been afraid to address contentious issues. If the Congress and Supreme Soviet's first sessions are any guide, these bodies may well come to possess the power necessary to effect policy change. Under a politically strong Gorbachev, they could become the most authoritative – if not the most powerful – political actors in the Soviet system.

One of the most critical questions before the Soviet polity is the future legitimacy of the CPSU leadership to govern the country. The results of initial popular elections do not bode well for that leadership if it must rely on popular support. Unopposed candidates from the CPSU leadership were defeated. Many top party leaders chose not to run, or became members of the Congress of People's Deputies only through intra-organisational selections. Challenges to the CPSU, and calls for a multiparty system, have been rebuffed by Gorbachev himself, who notes it is the CPSU which originated and continues to direct the restructuring and democratisation programme. However, the demands of more radical reformers, such as Boris Yel'tsin, could eventually compromise Gorbachev's stated position. One can only wonder if the July 1989 appearance of the 'Inter-regional Group' – composed of around 250 Congress deputies, and led by Yel'tsin and the prominent physicist and dissident Andrei Sakharov – is but the first step in the emergence of a rival national party. Similar challenges in subnational and especially non-Russian settings were likely to follow the Lithuanian parliament's decision, in December 1989, to abolish the communist party's constitutionally guaranteed leading role; indeed, the CPSU itself agreed to introduce a change of this kind at a Central Committee plenum in February 1990 (see pp. 85–6).

On 27 May 1989, a late Saturday afternoon session of the Congress of People's Deputies laboured over the selection of its First Deputy Chairman. Anatolii Luk'yanov, a candidate member of the Politburo and protege of Mikhail Gorbachev, had been nominated for the position by the Congress Chairman Gorbachev. Deputies' concerns over Luk'yanov's qualifications quickly emerged, requiring a postponement of the decision until the following Monday. It was only after intense questioning, and a weekend of uncertainty, that Luk'yanov's nomination was approved (and not unanimously). Whether or not Luk'yanov's eventual selection was a foregone conclusion, the confirmation process revealed that this top-level party official – and his powerful sponsor – must be responsive to subordinate political and societal interests. The confirmation process also revealed the dynamic character of a popularly-elected national legislative body. Luk'yanov's confirmation dilemmas anticipate the challenges which are likely to beset those desiring to channel deputies' activities. Indeed, the first sessions reveal the difficulties before Gorbachev and the top leadership in controlling fully the issues and agenda that will arise.

The 1990s will be a period of experimentation, as the national leadership continues to implement the restructuring programme. Further institutional and behavioural changes appear to be in prospect; in 1990, in a dramatic change of this kind, a newly created executive Presidency was introduced, elected by the Congress of People's Deputies and then latterly by the population as a whole, with powers that included the dismissal of the government, the dissolution of the Soviet parliament and the declaration of martial law. Assuming these changes continue and gain additional momentum, we may safely predict that the Soviet political leadership of the 21st century will look quite different from all its predecessors not only in its personnel but also in its structure and functions.

4

The Party

RONALD J. HILL

The Communist Party of the Soviet Union (CPSU) is, according to its own claim and by common consent, the central political institution in the Soviet political system. As the USSR Constitution of 1977 (Article 6) accurately expressed it, 'The leading and guiding force of Soviet society and the nucleus of its political system, of all state organs and public organs, is the Communist Party of the Soviet Union'. The same source outlines the party's principal functions: determining the general perspectives of the development of society and the course of the home and foreign policy of the USSR, directing 'the great constructive work of the Soviet people', and imparting 'a planned, systematic and theoretically substantiated character to their struggle for the victory of communism'.

What is today one of the most powerful political and social organisations anywhere in the world is the inheritor of a revolutionary tradition that goes back way into the 19th century. Its status as the ruling party, however, dates from the revolutionary seizure of power in October 1917. In the early 1920s, the dominance of the party (which changed its name to Communist Party of the Soviet Union in 1952) was made real, and it has never shown any inclination to forfeit that privileged position. Its relative strength as an institution has fluctuated according to the power of individual leaders, and its precise role has varied alongside that of other institutions, notably the Soviet state: but it has never so much as hinted that it performed any role other than that of directing the general course of Soviet development. Under Stalin, the country may have been ruled mainly through the powerful ministerial empires, and the dictator himself undoubtedly wielded massive personal power; hundreds of thousands of loyal party members were expelled and put to death in the purges of the 1930s: yet the party as an institution has maintained a continuity with its revolutionary origins, a fact that has always been a cause of inspiration, especially in times of leadership transition.

The Party in the 1980s

By the beginning of the 1980s, after some fifteen years under the indulgent leadership of Leonid Brezhnev, the CPSU could truly be said to have expanded its role into that of a major social and economic institution, as well as a ruling force. Since 1961 it has referred to itself as the party of the whole Soviet people, and has gone out to recruit 'the best' representatives of all social categories – workers, peasants, members of the intelligentsia, and a multiplicity of national and ethnic groups. By 1989 its membership embraced almost 10 per cent of the adult population, standing at 19,487,822 on 1 January and continuing to rise, although at a far slower rate than in previous times. Of these, 45.4 per cent were classified as workers, 11.4 per cent as collective farm peasants, and the remaining 43.2 per cent as white-collar employees, including the intelligentsia; these were drawn from a wide variety of specific occupations and professions. Increasingly, it has become an institution of the best-educated Soviet citizens, with higher education now common among members: some 34.3 per cent enjoyed that status in 1989, while 81.3 per cent had completed secondary education or beyond. It numbers representatives of 'over 100' nationalities. It has members, moreover, in virtually all workplaces.

As an institution, the party has developed a complex set of offices and committees, which intertwine with those of the state, economic management and the trade unions: taken together these offer a career structure that appeared increasingly attractive under the Brezhnev leadership's policy of trusting cadres (personnel). Party membership thus became the *sine qua non* for a successful career in administration, and many millions of Soviet citizens have grown dependent on the party in their working life; millions depend on it for their very livelihood. The party, as a massive organisation which functions through thousands of local offices, has become an important employer in its own right, offering jobs not only to politicians at all levels, but to auxiliary staff such as secretaries, typists and general office staff, janitors, chauffeurs and (increasingly) information processors – computer operators, office managers, and even social scientists (employed to conduct public opinion research and to rationalise administration).

By the same token, the CPSU in the 1980s played a significant role in the Soviet economy. It owns or uses (probably rent-free from the state) significant amounts of office space and other property, which has to be heated, lit, cleaned, maintained and repaired; it possesses fleets of vehicles, and is able to call on those of other organisations: these too use fuel and require maintenance; it runs publishing houses, hotels and vacation homes, plus canteens for its workers; and its normal functioning as a political organisation means that it uses large quantities of office furniture and equipment, and it consumes vast amounts of paper, ink, typewriter ribbons, floppy disks and other office stationery. Thus, the CPSU makes a significant contribution to the creation of work for the Soviet population: or, seen from a different perspective in an economy characterised by shortages, it consumes significant quantities of the products of the Soviet economy. In short, the CPSU as an institution not only charts the course of the Soviet economy, but is directly involved as an economic actor in its own right.

Moreover, it collects subscriptions from its members, on the basis of a percentage of their monthly earnings, and as earnings rise, so does the party's subscription income (the other basic source of income are the profits of its eleven publishing houses, and there are other subsidiary enterprises; also, new recruits pay an entrance fee). In fact, in recent years the party has disposed of funds to the tune of about one-tenth of the official defence budget (admittedly an artificial figure). In 1988, according to figures released in June 1989, membership subscriptions, at 1,349,900 million rubles, covered 82 per cent of expenditure, which goes mainly on the salaries of party officers and employees and the upkeep of various party facilities. Running the Central Committee apparatus alone devoured 52.3 million rubles, or 3 per cent of expenditures; some 76,800 party primary (branch) organisation secretaries and other full-time workers were also paid by the party. Quite apart from its political power, therefore, the CPSU also possesses a substantial amount of economic power.

It is, nevertheless, principally a *political* institution, and it is as such that it will be considered in the remainder of this chapter.

The Party's Political Role

The CPSU possesses three different identities, which it is important to bear in mind in attempting to understand its role in the Soviet system. It is, first, a *collection of nearly twenty million members*, who give it a complex social identity; they bear little in common except adherence to a particular set of values associated with the building of a communist society, to which they have declared their commitment (and it is far from certain that their understanding of those values is identical). The CPSU is also an *institution*: a hierarchy of roles, offices and organs that function as a unit to devise policy for implementing the prescriptions of the ideology (that is, for 'building communism'), and to lead and supervise the application of those policies. Thirdly, the party is a *hierarchy* of professional officers who at any one time speak in the name of the party: they determine the official *line* of the party as an institution, to which the party as a collection of members is formally committed. When we speak of 'the party' it is important to distinguish which identity we have in mind, for there are certain tensions among them, which the current policy of intra-party 'democratisation' is attempting to address.

Ideology and the Party

Traditionally, the CPSU has claimed the right and responsibility to rule the Soviet Union on the basis of its special relationship with the ideology of Marxism–Leninism. This body of doctrine is said to be 'scientific', and, mediated by the 'party line' (the official position on a given problem at a given time); this is said to permit the party as an institution to devise 'correct' policies. In view of this, 'ideology' is frequently seen as being something immutable, carved on tables of stone, and, indeed, it has sometimes been treated in such a dogmatic fashion.

Nevertheless, in practice neither the party line nor the ideology is unchanging: the line can be adapted to changing circumstances, and the ideology is modified as new phenomena demand fresh interpretation, sometimes with the use of new concepts: the notion of 'developed socialism', for example, was introduced in the Brezhnev era. Developments in the ideology are signalled in the speeches of politicians, principally the party leader, and especially in the party's basic documents, notably the Party Programme. The third of these, originally adopted in 1961, was revised in 1986, to be further revised at the 28th Party Congress in 1990. This constant reinterpretation and development of the ideology gives the party a degree of flexibility in its search for policies to solve some of society's problems. It has been suggested that ideology serves to rule out certain policy options, even if it does not prescribe specific policies. Even that may not be an accurate perception, however, and the most that can reliably be said is that the ideology appears to make it more difficult for the party to defend some policies than others.

The utility of such a body of doctrine for charting the way forward may be in doubt as the last decade of the century dawns. It may be that the ideology has lost much of its inspirational power, and is used principally as a means of verifying the credentials of party recruits, while supplying the political rhetoric with many of the concepts used to justify policy. *Perestroika* has raised anew the question of the nature of the ideology and the party's relationship with it, and a definitive formula remains elusive. (For further detailed elaboration of the nature and role of the ideology, see Chapter 2).

The Party and the State

One of the most complex issues in Soviet political life is the relationship between the party and the representative and administrative organs of the Soviet state. This is partly because the CPSU has traditionally presented confusing versions of the relationship. Soviet writers have quoted Lenin to the effect that not a single important decision is taken by a single state organ in the Soviet Union without guiding instructions from the party Central Committee – which strongly suggests that the state is subordinate to the party. Nevertheless, the soviets of people's deputies have been granted all manner of constitutional and legal rights to regulate affairs within their territory, including control over the state administrative arm. Spokesmen have insisted that the party rules not by giving orders to the state, but by the political method of persuasion: by placing its members in key positions and using them to convince non-members of the correctness of the party's policy. In practice, the party has exploited a variety of political conventions to ensure that its policy is given the force of law; subsequently, the party monitors the administration of the policy.

The general result is that the Soviet state has never enjoyed an independent existence. It has been politically beholden to the Communist Party, which has devised policy and selected, or at least approved, those who gave legal force to party policy, and it has carried out that policy under pain of party sanctions. The relationship is such that many Western observers have seen it as party dictatorship over the state, and in Soviet commentary the problem of *podmena* has been identified as something that prevents both the party and the state from performing their functions effectively.

Podmena, which means 'substitution' or 'supplantation', refers to the tendency of the party, its organs and officers to interfere with the legal and legitimate functioning of the state, essentially by giving direct orders in administrative affairs. It has been identified as a problem since the earliest post-revolutionary days, despite repeated exhortations to overcome it. Under Gorbachev there appear to be serious intentions to tackle the problem with more than exhortation, including separating the functions of the party and the state more clearly, and imbuing party and state officials with a clear sense of their role and duties in the process of government. But since this problem has a number of causes that are proving exceedingly stubborn – not least the powerful tradition that the party knows best – the successes to date have been limited.

Party Structures

Primary Organisations

One of the elements of party structure that has remained intact since the pre-revolutionary days is its base in the factories and other places of employment. The original 'cells' have been replaced by some 441,949 primary party organisations (PPOs) or branches (January 1989), formed in factories and offices, on farms and building sites, wherever at least three party members work (see Figure 4.1). It is in these organisations that party policies are ultimately implemented, through the allocation of specific 'party assignments' to individual communists. The PPO holds a monthly meeting to discuss various party concerns, including the allocation of assignments and the admission of new members. The organisation is headed by a secretary, and if large it may elect a bureau and be subdivided according to workshop or shift into party groups, each headed by a party group organiser (*partgruporg*). These local officers are formally elected at the autumn 'accounting and election' meeting, and this may be the start of a political career, depending on their success in running their organisation.

Conferences and committees

Every five years, the PPO elects a delegation (normally headed by the secretary) to the district or city party conference, which in turn elects the district or city party committee (*raikom* or *gorkom*) and delegates to the next higher conference, at the province (*oblast'*, *krai*) or republic level, and so on up the hierarchy to the all-Union party congress. This discusses broader policy matters and elects the Central Committee, which ultimately elects the Politburo and the

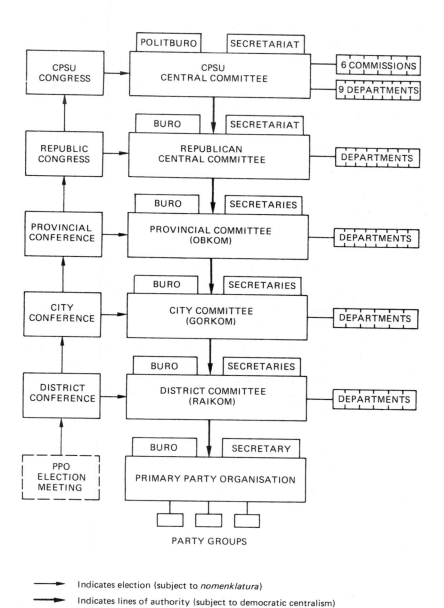

FIGURE 4.1 *The structure of the CPSU (simplified)*

general secretary, the highest party office. This system of indirect election means that rank-and-file members have no say over the selection of the party leadership, a process that in any case is subject to further constraints, principally the appointment system known as *nomenklatura* (see below). Moreover, the closer to the centre a particular party committee is, the higher will be the proportion of party officials from lower levels sitting on it. It appears, indeed, that places on party committees have been virtually 'reserved' for the occupants of specific posts in the party and state hierarchies. In this way, more than five million party members serve on party committees – over a quarter of the total membership.

The apparat

As a large and relatively complex organisation, the CPSU requires a substantial apparatus to handle its internal affairs. Each committee elects a bureau from among its voting members, headed by a first secretary and two or more secretaries. The first secretary is the most powerful politician in the locality (and from 1989 it is intended that he shall normally become the chairman of the local soviet). His deputy is usually in charge of recruitment, and it is significant that this post frequently goes to a Russian in the republican organisations. The work of the party organisation is administered through the *apparat* (apparatus) – hence the designation *apparatchik* for a worker in the party administration – which has a number of administrative departments. These stand in a supervisory position with regard to the state organs charged with directly administering the economy and society.

A key department, normally supervised by the second secretary, is the department for party organisational work (*otdel partiino-organizatsionnoi raboty*), which is responsible for staffing the administration through *nomenklatura*. In this political convention (which is not sanctioned by law) each party committee possesses lists of posts which it is responsible for filling, and lists of individuals deemed suitable for occupying them (some of whom already hold posts at that or a different level). The posts covered extend way beyond the party to embrace the state, economic management, the Komsomol (Young Communist League), trade unions, and practically all other positions of responsibility. The party committee has the final word of approval before the individual is appointed or even 'elected'.

In the autumn of 1988, a restructuring of the *apparat* began at the highest level. In place of twenty departments, some of them (for example, machine-building, chemical industry, or transport and communications) quite plainly duplicating the sectoral ministries of the state, nine new departments and half a dozen prestigious 'Central Committee Commissions' were created. These commissions (as noted above, p. 59) cover party construction and personnel policy (that is, appointments to leadership positions), ideology, social and economic policy, agriculture, international affairs, and legal policy. Each is headed by a Politburo member who is also a Central Committee Secretary, and they also have members drawn from the Central Committee. The function of the commissions is to review and devise broad policy in their areas of concern, for presentation to the Politburo and the Central Committee, and in doing so they have the power to confer widely with professional and political opinion. Their full role, as already noted, is not yet developed, and their work has begun somewhat irresolutely. The new departments (see above, pp. 59–60) are broader in their allocation of responsibilities than previously, and their role is intended to be more one of guidance than of detailed supervision. The party apparatus at lower levels is undergoing a similar restructuring, and its establishment of staff has been cut by more than a quarter as the CPSU seeks to equip itself to perform its leading role more effectively than in the past.

The *Apparatchiki*

The individuals who run the party's affairs – known as *apparatchiki* or cadres (*kadry* in Russian) – are an important group in Soviet society and the political system. The apparatchiki of the party are linked by *nomenklatura* with people in similar administrative offices in the state and other structures; there is much switching from one apparatus to another, especially at local levels. They are responsible to their superiors through patronage links, and *nomenklatura* allows them in turn to dispense patronage by arranging appointments for associates. Estimates of the party apparatus alone have varied from 100,000 to twice that figure, and under Gorbachev's rationalisation programme many are being re-deployed: he reported in the autumn of 1988 that the Central Committee apparatus alone had 1,940 officials, plus a further 1,275 technical or support staff. However, 679 persons were removed from the Central Committee payroll in 1988.

Similar changes are taking place at the local level, as the old are weeded out and replaced by a smaller contingent of more sophisticated officials. As an example, in Leningrad city and province, fifteen departments were abolished in 1989, resulting in the transfer of 110 persons to other jobs and the demotion of a further twenty-six. One hundred new recruits had been appointed during the previous year, and the total establishment of responsible party officials stood at 258 in the autumn of 1989, plus typists, secretaries, cleaners and other support staff. All the *apparatchiki* had higher education, including twenty-eight with research degrees, and almost half were trained engineers; approximately the same number were under forty years of age, indicating a measure of rejuvenation.

The party *apparatchiki* have traditionally formed a privileged elite, their position justified and protected by slogans such as Stalin's 'cadres decide everything' or Brezhnev's 'trust in cadres'. Brezhnev also took steps to improve the technical competence of administrators, and to support their work with better equipment and other facilities, a necessary corrective to Khrushchev's reliance on amateur administration in a society that was growing more, not less, complex. By 1987, the party press was reporting that 99.9 per cent of party committee secretaries from the district level upwards possessed at least incomplete higher education, as did 66.4 per cent of primary organisation secretaries. This was already a far cry from the Stalin years, when individuals were promoted from the ranks principally for their devotion to the cause (and to Stalin personally) and their willingness to use extreme measures to ensure the plans were fulfilled. In 1947, according to the same set of statistics, only 12.7 per cent of PPO secretaries and 41.3 per cent of committee secretaries had completed higher education.

The *apparatchiki* function largely in secret, taking administrative decisions of great moment, and having them applied by party members, including those working in the state and other organisations. This is how the problem of *podmena* arises. In addition, the party *apparatchiki* can enhance their own prestige by using their power to intervene to unblock bottlenecks in the economy: the power of the telephone call from the local party committee office has long been an important form of lubricant for the administrative wheels of Soviet society – part of the 'command-administrative system' that Gorbachev is dismantling.

In the very real sense, these important individuals set the tone of the whole system, and their understanding of how society is actually run, plus self-defensive networks among themselves, is proving an extremely effective hindrance to the reforms initiated by Gorbachev. The image of the faceless bureaucrat as typical of the *apparat* is proving depressingly accurate, as those whose privileged and comfortable lifestyle (including many perquisites) resist the reforms that will undermine their authority and mode of operation, and may threaten their jobs. This very resistance is an important reason for Gorbachev's assault on the apparatus and the *apparatchiki*, cutting a swathe through the swollen, complacent block that stands in the way of his new approach: and the *nomenklatura* appointees are one major group of employees not protected by job security legislation. Many have indeed been sacked, yet their successors often appear to fall quickly into the standard mode of operating, as Gorbachev has complained.

Party Discipline and Indiscipline

In all their activities, party organs and institutions are subject to the principle of *democratic centralism*, which means that ultimate authority lies at the centre, while lower party bodies are subject to firm guidance by their superiors. Party Rule 19, as amended in 1986, defines democratic centralism in terms of five elements:

1. the elective principle for all party organs from the bottom to the top
2. periodic accountability of party organs (i.e. committees) before their party organisations and before higher organs
3. strict party discipline and the subordination of the minority to the majority
4. the binding nature of decisions by higher bodies on lower bodies
5. collectivity in the work of all party organisations and leading organs, and individual responsibility on the part of each communist for the fulfilment of obligations and party assignments.

A more succinct definition goes back to Lenin's day: party members have the right to voice their opinions until a formal decision is taken; afterwards they must strive for its implementation, and they are not permitted to seek a reversal of the policy. In practice, however, party policy can be reversed, sometimes in response to an organised campaign in which party members and even officers participate.

In fact, in more senses than this, party discipline is not as effective as the strict centralist image would hold. It has become abundantly clear since Gorbachev came to office and introduced his policy of *glasnost'* (which entails giving publicity to many negative features of Soviet life) that in many parts of the country the party became a hotbed of corruption, which was exploited by local party secretaries acting as chieftains in their areas. From Uzbekistan under Sharaf Rashidov (who reportedly committed suicide in 1983) and his successors, to Kazahkstan under Dinmukhamed Kunaev (a Politburo colleague of Leonid Brezhnev), to Moldavia under Ivan Bodyul (sacked from his central government position soon after Brezhnev's death in 1982) to the capital city, Moscow, under Politburo member Viktor Grishin, the Communist Party seems to have turned into a benefit society for bestowing privileges on the elite of Soviet society at all levels. Not only did the top central and republican leaders live in luxury while living standards for the masses stagnated and declined, but the principle applied at lower levels too, as party members sought to use their connections in order to enhance their position. As a trainee diplomat said to me in the 1970s, 'Everyone wants to live well'.

Such an attitude flatly contradicts the principle, enunciated with great regularity by Brezhnev and other leaders of that period, that individuals are admitted to the party speaking Leninist words not for the sake of any privileges but out of a genuine devotion to the cause. Nevertheless, as the ailing Leonid Brezhnev lost his grip, so his subordinates around the country exploited the situation. His successor, Yuri Andropov, set about injecting discipline into the party, and at the 27th Congress, in February–March 1986, the leadership under Gorbachev put forward the slogan of 'pure and honest' (*chisty i chestny*) as representing the desired qualities of all communists. In the ensuing period corrupt party members have been removed, and in some cases put on trial, following a change in Party Rule 12 to allow this without prior expulsion from the party.

Indeed, given the contrast between such reality and its lofty self-proclaimed goals and its self-image, the CPSU by the time Gorbachev was consolidating his power was showing all the signs of an organisation in crisis. Many millions of Soviet citizens benefited from association with it, yet such a social position appeared to contradict some of the party's basic principles. It had quite manifestly not retained the confidence of the masses, and the more puritanical of its leaders were clearly concerned about its stability. Gorbachev at the close of the 1986 congress quoted Lenin on the phenomenon of 'revolutionary parties that have perished', and in the spring of 1988 a ministerial official suggested reducing the party's size as a means of restoring its position as a political vanguard. This concern reflects contradictions in the various images that the party attempts to present, which directly affect recruitment policy.

Membership Recruitment

As this discussion indicates, CPSU membership is not freely open to all. Although Party Rule 1 indicates that all Soviet citizens may join provided they 'acknowledge the Programme and Rules, actively participate in building communism, work in one of the party organisations, carry out the party's decisions and pay their membership dues', this wording is really a formula for the *retention* of membership. Obstacles are placed in the way of potential recruits, who have to be more or less coopted. There is a complex admissions procedure, after which the individual is subject to party discipline, and must accept assignments at the party's behest and seek the party's permission to make basic life decisions, such as changing employment. Even when travelling away for more than a few days, the party member becomes temporarily attached to an organisation at the destination. In principle, the party sees its members as troops to be deployed wherever the cause of building communism demands it. It places high demands on them, and the greatest sin is to be passive: 'losing contact with one's organisation' is a principal ground for expulsion from the party.

In view of this vision of its role, the party is selective about whom it admits. But other considerations also affect recruitment policy, in contradictory senses. The party has striven to be simultaneously the party of the working class and a ruling party, and a body that imposes discipline on key sectors of society, including, again, the managerial and 'thinking' sectors. Since 1961 the CPSU has also proclaimed itself the party of the whole Soviet people, which therefore needs to recruit representatives of all sectors of society, including a variety of occupational groups, women, and the many national minorities, and perhaps also to spread its membership to all geographical areas. But its self-image as a 'vanguard', comprising the foremost, the most politically conscious, members of society, means that it must retain stringent entry requirements and limit its size.

The need to adjust the party's membership in order to meet these various requirements was clearly recognised in the Brezhnev era, when positive attempts were made to recruit more women and more workers, and to attract members in the peripheral regions. At the same time the expulsion of passive members permitted the party authorities to adjust the membership. Steady adjustment, both to reflect changing social realities (the number of peasants appears to have peaked in 1986) and to incorporate priority groups, appears to have been the policy as the membership stabilised at around 10 per cent of the workforce.

By 1989, however, new trends appeared to be in evidence. In particular, the apparently inexorable expansion of the party's membership had apparently halted: after steady expansion of around 2 per cent a year in the 1970s, a natural decline may now be in prospect. There has been a fall in membership in at least the republics of Estonia and Armenia, and there are indications of similar developments elsewhere. Moreover, following the abolition of quotas that favoured certain groups, the number of blue-collar workers among new recruits has slipped, and even the number of women candidates for membership fell in 1988 (as did, surprisingly, the proportion of women holding official party positions). In addition, there is a crisis of confidence at the revelations of corruption of party officials under Brezhnev, so members are effectively resigning and significant numbers of candidate members are not presenting themselves for advancement to full membership. Even some leading figures – including a Supreme Soviet deputy – have left the party.

These trends appear to signify a change in public perceptions of the party. No longer is membership seen as a desirable enhancement to the individual's status which is expected to accompany and facilitate higher education and career advancement: to that extent, the slogan of 'pure and honest' may have had some impact. Moreover, the 'attestation' of party members, approved in 1988 for later implementation, echoes a similar measure – an exchange of party documents in 1972–4 – which had the effect of weeding out members deemed undesirable, thereby cutting off the benefits of membership. At the same time, the expressed intention of promoting non-members to positions of responsibility removes the necessity of party membership as a qualification for a high-flying career. But, more significantly, perhaps, the unwillingness of some groups to join the ranks of the ruling party will leave important groups 'unincorporated' and perhaps alienated. That cannot be good for the morale of the party, and it makes the task of governing the country even more difficult. In fact, the deliberate restructuring of the balance between the party and the state may be in part a response to the crisis of confidence.

The Party and Restructuring

A major thrust of Gorbachev's policy, particularly in the wake of the 19th Party Conference in the summer of 1988, has been political reform. Not only does this imply modification of the party's structures, outlined above, but it entails other changes too, affecting both internal party affairs and the party's relations with other institutions, notably the state. As a commentator observed in the spring of 1989, '*Perestroika* has demanded a reinterpretation of the party's role, which means also the principles of party leadership of state and public organisations in the spirit of loyalty to Lenin's behests'.

Intra-party Democratisation

A significant part of Gorbachev's policy of regaining respect for the CPSU comprises attempts to exorcise the nepotism, venality and corruption of the Brezhnev era, and to bring the practice of intra-party life into closer correspondence with the long-enunciated democratic principles, and the principles of 'communist morality' set out in the Rules. He has referred to the need for a new conception of democratic centralism, in which responsibilities will be decentralised, in order to relieve the centre of the excessive burden of trivial work, and democratic principles in relations between centre and localities will be given full-bodied application. Following a devastating attack on the way the party had been run, made at a Central Committee plenum in January 1987, he has led the way in promoting contested elections for party office, and also in restricting the holding of individual offices to two five-year terms. After January 1987, the principle of contested elections to committees and secretaryships quickly began to be applied at the local level. The 19th Party Conference, called to devise measures to democratise Soviet political life, endorsed this principle (without making it mandatory), and in August 1988 a new Central Committee Instruction was issued on the holding of party elections. As a result, in the 1988 party election campaign, almost a half the secretaries from the primary organisation level up to the province were reportedly elected in competition with at least one other candidate; at other levels, though, the principle of electoral choice is being tardily introduced.

A new regulation of 1988, limiting the holding of any single party office to two consecutive five-year terms, is reminiscent of a similar restriction adopted under Khrushchev in 1961. Even though there was an 'escape clause' that permitted exceptions for individuals of 'particular merit', the rule was repealed in 1966 as part of Brezhnev's moves to reassure the party's cadres. There was discussion at the 19th Conference of whether the new rule was intended to apply to the top leadership. Politburo member Yegor Ligachev replied that it was: 'we very calmly accept the proposal concerning two consecutive terms of election into leading organs; for many of us in the present composition of the Politburo and Secretariat may

God grant us enough strength for just five years'. The conference, in the event, agreed there should be no exceptions.

This raises an important issue which requires urgent resolution in Soviet political life: the question of honourable retirement from the stage. The purge is an all too familiar feature of Soviet political experience: sudden removals from office, usually into obscurity, at best under the cloak of a vaguely plausible pretext such as 'advanced years and deteriorating health' (the formula used to justify the removal of Nikita Khrushchev in October 1964), and more frequently under the empty phrase 'in connection with his transfer to other work'. As a party member commented in 1986, such a phrase gives the party members no indication whatsoever of the reasons for the removal – promotion or demotion. This is but one reason for the tendency to hang on to power until death or incapacity force it to be relinquished, which led to grave embarrassment and practically rudderless leadership under Brezhnev, Andropov and Chernenko in the first half of the 1980s. With few exceptions, the Soviet system has not allowed its political leaders to retire with dignity.

Gorbachev has made some moves that indicate a change in this respect. For example, at the 27th Congress, several prominent individuals who had left their senior office were re-elected to the Central Committee. These included Boris Ponomarev, long-serving Central Committee Secretary in charge of the International Department, and Nikolai Baibakov, who had retired after twenty years as head of Gosplan, the state planning committee. In September 1988, when Andrei Gromyko retired as president at the age of 79, Gorbachev made the remarkable suggestion that he might still play an active part in public life. Gorbachev similarly wished good health and an enjoyable retirement to 110 Central Committee members and candidate members and members of the Central Auditing Commission who tendered their joint resignation in April 1989. Whatever the machinations that induced them to act in this way, Gorbachev was signalling to the party and the world that retirement does not always mean disgrace. If the 'two terms' rule is to be effectively applied, these developments of the past few years must be seen as modest steps towards creating a new atmosphere for the withdrawal from party and public office of what will eventually be large numbers of officials and activists for whom 'retirement' in the past would always have been accompanied by suspicions of disgrace.

The Party in the Political System

In addition to changes in the party's internal life, Gorbachev is also evidently modifying its role *vis-à-vis* the state. The problem of *podmena* has already been mentioned, and with it come other problems such as 'petty tutelage' and 'parallelism': the tendency to scrutinise the state's functioning in minute detail, and to discuss the same issues and propose solutions in party committees prior to their formal adoption by the state. The party manifestly was finding it difficult to cope; but equally significant was the effect of debasement of the state institutions (particularly the 'representative' soviets of people's deputies) and the consequent cynicism that this generated among the Soviet public. Moreover, since everyone recognised the impotence of the soviets in the face of the party's authority, if policies failed it was the party, rather than the state, that was blamed for the failure. Politically, this was disastrous for the party.

Gorbachev's approach – foreshadowed by writers in the Brezhnev era – is to demarcate the spheres of responsibility of the two sets of institutions and their officials much more sharply, and to induce the party *as an institution* to avoid taking operative decisions and simply passing on instructions to the state for implementation. Instead, it should step back from the day-to-day management of Soviet society, and concentrate on broad strategy and political leadership. In other words, it should apply in reality the traditional 'explanation' of the relationship, which is that it is political, based on persuasion. In pursuing that end, contested elections to the soviets have now become the norm, and the state institutions have been reorganised so as to give elected representatives an opportunity for genuine debate and political argument (see Chapter 5). This has the effect of taking the power of control away from party *apparatchiki* and replacing the entirely predictable, party-controlled selection and functioning of the deputies with a degree of spontaneity that many see as incompatible with the Soviet form of socialism. As a result of this development, in the electoral experiment of June 1987, and again in the national election of March 1989, leading party figures failed to win sufficient votes to secure election.

Moreover, in positively enhancing the role of the elected soviets and encouraging the deputies to speak out about matters of public concern – for example, in the stormy ten-day opening session of the Congress of People's Deputies in late May–early June 1989, or the first sessions of the revamped Supreme Soviet – Gorbachev is effectively shifting the party from the centre of the public stage to some less prominent role. At the same time, while also supplying far more information about the party than ever before (particularly with the publication of the monthly *News of the Central Committee – Izvestiya TsK KPSS* – from January 1989), he appears to have been bypassing its organs to some extent, and eliminating the context of secrecy in which they have been privileged to operate. It has been reported that even the Politburo has not been meeting with the weekly regularity it enjoyed under Brezhnev, and the role of the central Secretariat has been reduced, with some of its functions transferred to the new commissions, and others to new structures of the newly constituted Supreme Soviet. With Gorbachev's election to the powerful new post of Chairman of the Supreme Soviet, he now has an important operational power base independent of the party structure.

This strategy carries considerable risks, since the system has traditionally functioned according to certain well-understood rules of the game. One of these is the notion that the party knows best, because of its understanding of the ideology, and that it therefore has the right to intervene to guide other institutions and correct mistakes. As Gorbachev has noted, 'it seems such a well-trodden path: exert party pressure and the plan is fulfilled!'. Once the pressure is removed, and the party accepts that mistakes will be made, chaos may ensue.

Such, at least, is the fear of many so-called conservatives within the party, who see, for example, editors' eagerness to publish information about 'negative' features of Soviet reality as licence to slander the form of 'socialism' developed under the party's benevolent guidance over the past half-century. This 'licence' also includes pointed questions about the party's own role in the system and its monopoly of political power. Although Gorbachev and other leaders repeatedly stated that a multi-party system not an appropriate development for the present, the question of the party's political monopoly came under repeated criticism in the press. The distinguished sociologist I.V. Bestuzhev-Lada, for instance, in an article in 1988, indicated a pluralistic party system as his preferred option for the development of the Soviet political system 'if we could create it'. Other authors, too, have raised provocative questions about the harm the party has wrought with its monopoly on power and information, arguing that this is incompatible with democracy, in the party and in society at large. In February 1990, at an historic plenum, the Central Committee agreed to renounce this prerogative, and also to concede greater independence to party organisations in the republics. Given these and other well-argued assessments by leading reformist thinkers within the party as well as outside it, Gorbachev has taken the view that the party has to earn the right to rule. Speaking at the opening of the 1989 Soviet election campaign, he pointed out that the party now had to present a programme in competition with those of other organisations. He added, 'Trust in the party's policies and support for them in society are increasing in the course of *perestroika*. Naturally enough, however, the credit of trust is not granted for ever. Each time, at every new stage of building socialism, the party has to justify it with its practical and theoretical activities. This is true of today as well'.

The Party and the Future

All of this raises serious questions about the long-term development of the Communist Party and its role in the Soviet system, which at the beginning of the 1990s is quite unclear. The whole political and economic system is in a state of transition from the modified Stalinism that had become entrenched to a system whose contours remain indistinct. There is a clear sense of groping towards a goal that is ill-defined, but that is referred to by the terms 'socialist pluralism', 'democracy' and similar, fairly vague epithets. Although the CPSU remains at the centre of the political system, and still retains the right to decide ultimately what is compatible with the goal of 'building communism' which it has set for society, its relationship with the society and with the institutions it has established for bringing about that goal is undergoing a profound change whose outcome is impossible to predict. A special plenum of the Central Committee in February 1990, as already noted, opened the way for the removal of Article 6 from the USSR Constitution, and party leaders indicated with a degree of equanimity their acceptance that the CPSU's political monopoly might sooner or later be broken. The party, it was asserted, would have to stand on its performance and programme alongside other parties. The 28th congress, brought forward to the summer of 1990, would introduce changes to the rules and further programme revisions to enshrine recent changes in practice and other changes in the traditional way the party has functioned, both internally and in the system at large. With members leaving the party in significant numbers, others withholding their subscriptions, and the party in Lithuania leading the way in declaring its independence of Moscow (leading to a split in the party in that republic), the chances that the party will retain its traditional identity for long into the new decade look decidedly slim.

There are still further indications of a somewhat uncertain future in the wide divergences of views expressed in the mass media by party members and others and in increasingly open and public forums in the Gorbachev era. Some of the divergences came to the surface at the 19th party conference, in the summer of 1988, and others in the provocative speeches by party members elected to the Congress of People's Deputies and the new USSR Supreme Soviet, both of which met for the first time in the spring of 1989. It is quite possible that these revitalised organs of power will come to displace the Communist Party at the centre of the Soviet political system. If that turns out to be the case, and if Gorbachev's proposals to bolster the role of the state president are fully implemented, the effect of his *perestroika* will have been to produce a configuration of power that is virtually without precedent: because up to the present a communist party playing a leading role has been not simply a feature of Soviet political life but its central and defining characteristic.

5

The Soviet State System

JEFFREY W. HAHN

The Background to Reform

The first two years of Mikhail Gorbachev's tenure as general secretary of the CPSU gave little indication of the dramatic changes
to come in the Soviet state system. In his speech to the 27th
Congress in February 1986 his remarks on the subject contained
few new initiatives, and these lacked specifics. Thus, he promised
'the development of socialist self-government for the people', but
noted that the party was to be the 'leading force and chief guaran-
tor' of that development. He announced that new proposals were
being developed to enhance the authority of local councils – called
soviets – in economic affairs and spoke of the need to 'strengthen
the prestige' of the deputies who were elected to these councils,
but offered no details. He hinted at 'necessary adjustments' in
Soviet electoral practice. Finally, he alluded to the problem of the
dominance of administrative personnel in political life and the need
to hold them more accountable before the people's elected representatives. But such proposals had been heard before. As far as
Soviet parliamentary institutions and practices were concerned, it
was a speech that Brezhnev or Chernenko could have made.

In the light of subsequent reforms, Gorbachev's comments on
state institutions at the 27th Congress seem limited and cautious;
in retrospect, they may one day be seen as tentative first steps in
the revival of democratic aspirations reaching back to the time of
the Russian Revolution of 1917 and before. In origin, the term
'soviets' (from the Russian word meaning 'advice' or 'council') was
used with reference to workers' councils which began to be elected
in Russian factories at the start of the century. Intended as a means

for workers to communicate economic grievances to management, the soviets took on a political character at the time of the 1905 Revolution. The most significant of these was the Soviet of Workers' Deputies in St Petersburg led by Leon Trotsky, then a Menshevik. In 1917, the emergence of the Petrograd Soviet of Workers' and Soldiers' deputies as a political force with *de facto* veto power over decisions by the Provisional Government contributed greatly to the downfall of that government and to the Bolshevik victory in the October revolution.

Lenin's attitude towards the soviets was essentially instrumental: they were the means for making a revolution. It was with this in mind that he declared in his 'April Theses' that Bolsheviks would not support the Provisional Government; he insisted instead on the slogan 'all power to the soviets'. The political problem for Lenin was that, at the time, the Petrograd Soviet was dominated by Mensheviks. It was only in September when the Bolsheviks gained majority control of the Executive Committee that Lenin explicitly identified the soviets as the 'new state apparatus', and used them to overthrow the Provisional Government. When he did declare power on 7 November 1917, he did so in the name of the All-Russian Congress of Soviets of Workers' and Soldiers' Deputies.

Lenin's designation of the soviets as institutions of state power may have been motivated by pragmatic considerations, but their role was justified on ideological grounds. In his conceptualisation of the state in socialist society Lenin drew on contradictory elements found in the writings of Karl Marx: Marx's analysis of the Paris Commune of 1871 with its emphasis on proletarian self-rule and direct democracy from below, and his view of the state as a 'dictatorship of the proletariat' necessary during the transition to the social ownership of the means of production. While the view of the state as a dictatorship of the proletariat is elaborated by Lenin in his *State and Revolution* (1917), in other writings Lenin clearly saw the soviets as the embodiment of the communal form of government described by Marx as the prototype of proletarian democracy. After all, the soviets were the political expression of the industrial working class. Moreover, in Lenin's conception those elected to the soviets would retain their status as workers while serving in government. In this way, the creation of a professional class of politicians as found in bourgeois parliamentary systems would be avoided. Executive and legislative powers would be fused with those making decisions simultaneously responsible for implementing them. In this conception, there is a strong emphasis on active political participation from below; most decisions would be made locally, not centrally, although all the soviets were organically linked by common class interests in a 'unified' system.

In understanding the current efforts to 'democratise' the Soviet state system, it is important to recognise the ideological ambiguity in Lenin's thinking on the state. Gorbachev himself has repeatedly justified his political reforms as a return to the 'spirit of Leninism'. But what does this mean? It is arguable that the state system which emerged in April 1918 (after Lenin's brief fling with pluralism in the Constituent Assembly ended in the abolition of that body on 19 January 1918) moved inexorably in the 'dictatorial' direction in response to the exigencies of survival during the civil war (1918–20). The centralisation of state institutions and their strict subordination to the will of the party, both of which took place during this time, created the conditions for Stalin's rise to power. In this view, the state system as it developed during the early years of 'war communism' and under Stalin and his successors was an aberration, and it was time to 'reconstruct' the state along the lines that Lenin originally intended. What Lenin really intended is, of course, an open question. What seems clear is that the legitimacy of present efforts at 'democratisation' rests on the conception of the soviets as representative institutions based on mass political participation with those elected accountable to the electorate.

Certainly, the state system Gorbachev inherited was the antithesis of the participatory self-government from below implicit in the original conception of the soviets. The problem is both structural and functional. The structure of the Soviet state is defined by the 1977 USSR Constitution. Until amended on 1 December 1988, it remained essentially unchanged from Stalin's Constitution of 1936. The state system was subdivided into a complicated network of administrative–territorial units arranged hierarchically. At the top, a national parliament was established known as the Supreme Soviet. It was made up of 1,500 directly elected deputies holding five-year terms from among whom was chosen a government, called the Council of Ministers, and a collegial head of state, named the Presidium. One level below the USSR Supreme Soviet, and reflecting the federal character of the state system, were the Supreme Soviets of the fifteen union republics and twenty autonomous republics. The organisation of executive agencies at this level replicated that of the national body.

Below the national and republican level, all soviets are called local soviets. There were 52,568 of them in 1987, subdivided administratively into 6 *krais* or territories, 123 *oblasts* or regions, 8 autonomous regions, 3,127 districts, 2,164 cities, 667 city districts (or boroughs), 3,864 settlements and 42,599 rural soviets. In 1987,

2,322,421 deputies were elected to these soviets ranging in size from about 32 deputies per rural soviet to 800 members of the Moscow city council. Terms of office at this level were two and a half years. Day-to-day affairs in the local district were run by executive committees (*ispolkomy*) whose dozen or so members were elected from among the deputies. Within this highly centralised structure all lower units were subordinated to the centre by the principle of 'democratic centralism'.

But the real problem with the soviets has less to do with their centralised structure than with how they came to function in practice. Constitutionally guaranteed the exclusive right to make laws and take decisions, the soviets at all levels had become legislative councils in name only by the time of Stalin's death. Nor had matters changed much by 1985 when Gorbachev took over despite resolutions and legislation advocated by Khrushchev, Brezhnev and even Chernenko aimed at reviving the soviets and strengthening the role of the deputy. Why did these efforts fail?

In theory, the executive organs of the soviets are elected by and accountable to the deputies; in reality, the executive branch came to dominate the legislative. The pattern for this was established under Stalin, but it continued under his successors. The executive body, frequently chaired by the corresponding party secretary, is chosen unanimously from a single slate of candidates. The determination of who is nominated falls within the *nomenklatura* or patronage of the party secretary. Sessions of the council as a whole were held only infrequently during the year, and then for short periods of time. At a typical city council meeting perhaps 200 deputies would meet for two to three hours four times per year. At these sessions deputies would unanimously approve legislation drafted by the executive body. The executive committee was also responsible for determining the agenda, the list of speakers, the amount of time each item would receive, and even the content of the speakers' remarks during carefully staged 'debates'.

As a result, the deputies' legislative role was largely reduced to a ritualistic confirmation of what had already been decided in advance by members of the bureaucracy and party apparatus. Candidates for deputy who might have challenged this system were simply not nominated; control of the single slate belonged, ultimately, to the local party secretary. Suffice it to say that from 1937–87 all decisions by the 1,500 members of the Supreme Soviet were made unanimously in two sessions a year, each lasting only a few days. Obviously one had to look for real political power elsewhere; it certainly didn't belong to the soviets.

It is against this background that Gorbachev's proposals to

'restructure' or 'reconstruct' the Soviet state must be seen. Broadly speaking, the most pressing overall goal of his reforms is the modernisation of the Soviet economy. But by 1987 it became increasingly clear that a major obstacle to economic reform was the resistance of those in the state bureaucracy from top to bottom whose personal interests were served by preserving the status quo, not by changing it. How to undermine this entrenched resistance? What Gorbachev needed was a way to replace those within the state bureaucracy and party apparatus who were opposed to his programme of *perestroika* with those who supported it. He may have found the key in the reintroduction of a degree of competition in elections to party, state, and economic institutions, an approach he outlined in his watershed speech to the Central Committee in January 1987.

With respect to the soviets, a cautious experiment with competition was carried out in connection with elections to the local soviets held in June 1987. Less than 5 per cent of the deputies elected were chosen from multimember districts in which there were more candidates than seats. What made this experiment interesting, aside from offering the voters a choice which they had not enjoyed since the early days of the revolution, was that in many of the multimember districts the candidates who lost, or were reduced to 'reserve' status, were those in executive positions, especially among those regarded as part of the old leadership. These results were not lost on Gorbachev. A year later, he proposed to the extraordinary 19th Conference of the CPSU, apparently with the support of the Politburo, that competitive elections become the norm, starting with elections to a new Congress of People's Deputies to be convened in the spring of 1989. In making this proposal, he explicitly praised the 1987 experimental elections for having 'increased the deputies' sense of responsibility'.

Competitive elections were only one element, though a critical one, in the comprehensive set of proposals on political reform introduced by Gorbachev at the 19th Conference which began on 28 June 1988. With respect to the institutions of the Soviet state, he proposed to increase the decision-making authority of the local soviets and their budgetary discretion; he called for a restructuring of executive–legislative relations within the soviets to ensure greater executive accountability; he outlined a major reorganisation of the parliamentary system at the national level; and he sought the creation of a Constitutional Review Committee as part of a broader effort to establish a more genuine rule of law. Perhaps most significantly, he insisted on ending the substitution (*podmena*) of the authority of the party for that of the state, calling for, in his words, 'the demarcation of the functions of party and state agencies'.

In scope, Gorbachev's proposals were breathtaking and engendered lively debate and open criticism at the Conference, itself a major change from past practice. In the end, Gorbachev's proposals, essentially unchanged, received CPSU approval in a series of resolutions adopted by the Central Committee in July 1988. Draft legislation on national elections and on amendments to the 1977 Constitution to implement the proposals was forthcoming in late October. After a month of 'public discussion' which resulted in comparatively minor, but important, revisions, the draft legislation was adopted as law by the old Supreme Soviet in December 1988. But, for the first time in at least fifty years, the vote, while overwhelmingly favourable, was not unanimous. In what follows, the major changes introduced into the Soviet state system will be examined in greater detail, starting with the new electoral process, then moving to changes in the national parliament, and ending with an assessment of the implications of these changes.

Elections

The purpose of elections in democratic societies is to provide citizens with a mechanism for changing elites. The fulfilment of this purpose presupposes an element of choice; elections lacking choice serve only to perpetuate elites in power. The inertia which had gripped the Soviet system when Chernenko died in 1985 in no small way reflected the effects of a lack of choice over a long period of time. The introduction of a competitive element in the elections to the USSR Congress of People's Deputies held on 26 March 1989 was almost certainly aimed at breaking this inertia by replacing, or at least threatening, those in positions of power who opposed Gorbachev's programme of reform. In light of this, two questions would seem to follow: (1) How much of a choice did the voters have? (2) Who won?

The elections to the USSR Congress of People's Deputies (hereafter, the Congress) were undertaken in three stages: preliminary nominations, or primaries, were held from 26 December 1988 to 24 January 1989; district pre-election meetings to determine the final list of candidates took place from 25 January to 23 February; and campaigns were conducted from 24 February to 25 March, with elections held on Sunday 26 March 1989. In two important respects, however, the outcomes in each stage were conditioned by decisions reflected in the Law on Elections adopted in December 1988. First,

in addition to the 1,500 seats in the Congress to be filled by election
in 750 territorial and 750 national-territorial districts, 750 additional
seats were allocated to public organisations specified in article 1 of
the Law on Elections, including 100 to be chosen by the CPSU.
Secondly, the elections were to be conducted in accordance with
the decisions of a thirty-five-member Central Election Commission
and 1,500 district election commissions comprised of eleven to seventeen members each. In all cases, appointments to these commissions ultimately depended on those already in power. The commissions were in place and functioning prior to the opening up of
nominations on 26 December.

The nomination process (26 December to 24 January) was quite
remarkable by previous Soviet standards. Candidates could be
nominated, as before, at places of work or from military units, but
now this right was extended to public organisations and to residents
at meetings attended by at least 500 of those living in the district.
The number of those nominated was 'unlimited', a choice of words
which allowed for single, as well as multiple, candidacies. At nomination meetings, anyone in attendance was free to propose (or
oppose) any nominee including themselves. Individuals were nominated if 50 per cent of those present voted for them. In a significant
departure from past practice those holding positions in government
were excluded from running, with the exception of the Chairman
of the Council of Ministers. This rule ultimately resulted in a sharp
reduction in the number of those in the administrative apparatus
simultaneously holding elective office.

The results of the nomination process, completed on 24 January,
offer a mixed picture with respect to the issue of public choice and
involvement. On the one hand, there is a good deal of evidence to
suggest that in many cases people took part in the selection of
candidates to an unprecedented degree. This was especially the case
in nominations for the 1,500 district seats where 6,132 candidates
were put forward and many more were discussed. The average of
better than four nominees per seat is misleading, however; in some
districts there were many more nominees than four, while in others
the absence of a requirement that more than one candidate be
nominated resulted in a single candidate running as before. Moreover, the existence of a numerical requirement (500) for nomination
from residences, but not from labour collectives, worked to the
advantage of those who ran the nomination meetings in the workplace. There, a decision to nominate by a show of hands rather
than by a secret ballot could be an inhibiting factor for voters whose
wellbeing depended on voting the 'right' way.

The element of choice is even more limited when it is remembered that 750 seats were reserved for public organisations with national constituencies. Here nominations were made at plenary sessions convened by their central bodies. Although it was possible for these meetings to produce a list with more nominees than the number of spaces allotted to them, many did not, including the CPSU whose plenary session approved 100 nominees for their 100 seats. Overall, the public organisations nominated only 880 candidates for the 750 seats reserved for them in the Congress.

During the next stage of the elections (25 January to 23 February), pre-election meetings were held in those districts where more than two candidates were nominated. The delegates to these meetings were chosen by those groups which had nominated the candidates, according to norms established by the district election commission which was also responsible for calling and running the meeting. At the meetings, the nominees presented their programmes, which, according to article 45 of the Law on Elections, could not be 'in contradiction to the USSR Constitution, or to Soviet laws'. Nominees receiving a majority vote – by open vote *or* secret ballot – from those present were then registered as candidates.

Pre-election meetings were held in 836 of the 1,500 districts. Nearly 400,000 delegates took part in their proceedings – an average of about 450 delegates per meeting. Out of the 4,875 nominees considered in these district meetings, 1,720 survived and were registered as candidates; 3,155 were rejected. The large drop-out rate must be attributed, at least in part, to two undemocratic features of the pre-election meetings. First, the fact that individuals could be nominated by an unlimited number of groups meant that those nominated in several different places could pack the meeting. For example, Konstantin Masik, the party first secretary in Kiev, was nominated by thirty different groups ensuring him a majority of delegates. Not surprisingly, he alone survived among five nominees. Secondly, the meetings were open to manipulation by the district election commission. There is a good deal of evidence in the Soviet press to indicate that, in some cases, these commissions interfered on behalf of one or another nominee, or pressured others to withdraw.

When the four-week campaign finally got underway on 24 February a total of 2,895 candidates were registered to run for 1,500 seats, a competitive situation unknown in Soviet history. However, in 383 of the 1,500 seats only one candidate was registered. In 953 districts there were two candidates, and in 149 there were three or more (in the Gagarin district of Moscow, twelve contenders vied for one seat). If one includes the 750 seats assigned to the public organisations it could be argued that the possibility for truly competitive campaigns existed for fewer than half of the 2,250 seats in the new Congress.

Where the opportunity for the voters to choose existed, however, the campaigns were vigorous and public interest appears to have been intense as large numbers of voters attended meetings at which the candidates debated their positions and answered questions from the voters. Campaign staffs were limited to ten persons and although the law was silent on campaign finance, except to guarantee equal access to the media, it was clear from the widely varying quality (and quantity) of the campaign literature that some candidates, or their supporters, had spent more than others despite a ruling by the Central Election Commission that fundraising was impermissible.

In past years, election day had been a dull affair. On paper, 99 per cent of the electorate turned out to vote for the single candidate in their district, but only because of an army of party 'agitators' who noted with displeasure those who refused to vote, or due simply to false reporting in the interest of closing the polls early. The election of 26 March 1989 was different. 89 per cent of the electorate turned out, but without prodding. When they received their ballots, in all but 399 cases offering a choice of candidates, they were required to vote privately in an area secured for that purpose. There they crossed off the names of those against whom they wished to vote, leaving one name or none to be deposited in the ballot box. On the whole, the elections appear to have been run honestly. The presence of foreign observers and journalists, as well as the participation of competing campaign staffs in the vote count, helped to ensure this.

One unexpected result of the elections was the large number of seats not decided on election day. To win, candidates needed to receive more than 50 per cent of the ballots cast. However, because of the negative voting procedure and because in 149 districts there were more than two candidates to split the vote, the possibility that none would receive the necessary majority was increased. In the 149 districts with three or more candidates, 76 runoff elections were held on 9 April between the top two vote-getters. In 199 of the 1,424 districts where one or two candidates were nominated, none received the necessary majority and new nominations as well as new elections had to be held. One conspicuous example was that of Yuri Solov'ev, head of the Leningrad regional party organisation and a candidate member of the Politburo, who was defeated in an uncontested election. The first round was held 14 May with final runoffs scheduled for 21 May, only four days before the Congress was convened. Even more surprising, perhaps, was that, in some cases, those nominated by the plenary sessions of the public organis-ations failed to receive the necessary 50 per cent from those mem-bers of their organisations who were able to vote. Although these candidates were presented as a list, those voting could cross off individual names. The most dramatic case was that involving the Academy of Sciences in which only eight of the twenty proposed were elected. Repeat elections yielded seats for a number of promi-nent critics, including Andrei Sakharov (who died the following December).

What about the results of the elections? Who won? Demograph-ically speaking, the freest elections in Soviet history yielded a Con-gress whose composition was less representative than the Supreme Soviet elected in 1984 under the old system. The percentage of women declined from 32 to 17 per cent; workers from 16 to 11 per cent; and collective farm workers from 16 to 11 per cent. Youth (representatives under 30) also lost. Among the 'winners', two groups stood out statistically: the percentage of party members increased from 71 to 87 per cent and so did the proportion of specialists, especially among the scientific and creative intelligentsia, whose share increased from 1.8 to over 12 per cent. These data are misleading, however. In previous elections, certain groups would receive a more or less fixed share of seats in accordance with an informal 'quota system' determined in advance by the CPSU. It is possible to do this when only one candidate is nominated for each seat; in genuinely competitive elections, it is extremely difficult.

Looked at qualitatively, the elections appeared to have resulted in a stunning victory for reformers both in and out of the party, and an embarrassing defeat for party regulars. Probably the most dramatic evidence of this was the election of Boris Yel'tsin to the Moscow national-territorial seat. Only a year earlier Yel'tsin had been ousted from his position as Moscow party secretary by those in the party who found his support for reform too radical. He was also dropped from the Politburo. Though a member of the party, he beat the organisation-backed party candidate by garnering 89 per cent of the vote. During the campaign, the Central Committee's attempt to discredit Yel'tsin by initiating a formal inquiry into his political views appears to have actually increased his popularity among Moscow voters. Other well-known critics elected included Andrei Sakharov, Nikolai Shmelev, Tat'yana Zaslavskaya, and Gavriil Popov. Equally indicative of the strength of the new oppo-sition was the success, especially in the Baltic republics, of the 'popular front' movements whose candidates campaigned for greater autonomy from central control. In Lithuania, the popular front movement (Sajudis) won thirty-two of forty-two possible seats out-right and were favoured to win eight more in runoffs.

On the other side, many party organisation candidates fared poorly. Out of approximately 160 regional and city party secretaries nominated, about forty lost. What makes this figure remarkable is that only twenty-five of the seats were contested. All of these were lost plus about another fifteen in which there was no opposition (in other words, their names were crossed out by more than 50 per cent of those voting). It seems clear that if the party organisation's candidates had not been protected by inclusion in the single candi-date lists drawn up by public organisations with guaranteed seats, their losses would have been even greater.

Still, the results of the 26 March elections to the Congress need to be put into perspective. The real organ of legislative power under the new system is not the Congress, but the Supreme Soviet elected by the Congress at its first session. And here, as will be shown in the next section, the reformers' euphoria turned to frustration, leaving the question of 'who won?' much less clear than it seemed at first.

The New State System: National Level

When the 2,249 newly elected deputies met for the first session of the Congress of People's Deputies on 26 May 1989 there was a great deal of uncertainty about what was going to happen. According to the amendments to the Constitution adopted in December 1988, some items of business were clear. The Congress was responsible for electing 542 of its members to a continuously functioning USSR Supreme Soviet; deputies were to choose a Chairman and First Vice-Chairman of the Supreme Soviet, and a Constitutional Review Committee; they had to confirm (or reject) the appointment of a Prime Minister, the Chairman of the People's Control Committee, the Chairman of the Supreme Court, the Prosecutor General and the USSR Chief Arbiter. In addition to these items, the proposed agenda included reports by the newly elected Chairman of the Supreme Soviet and the Chairman of the Council of Ministers on their foreign and domestic programme for the country. The Constitution, however, also granted the Congress the right to exam-ine and resolve any issue it wished, including amending the Consti-tution. Moreover, given the widely divergent points of view known to be held by many members of the Congress and the absence of clear procedures as to how contentious issues would be handled, no-one could predict the outcome of this first meeting.

It became clear within minutes after the Congress was called to order at 10 a.m. by V.P. Orlov, Chairman of the Central Election Commission and presiding officer, just how different this legislative body was going to be compared with the old Supreme Soviet. The first speaker to take the rostrum was a deputy from Latvia who promptly asked a moment of silence for those killed by police in anti-government demonstrations in Tbilisi, Georgia, on 9 April 1989, and then demanded the names of those responsible. Even the two main items of business, the approval of the Credentials Committee report and the election of the Supreme Soviet Chairman, proved contentious and provided deputies with opportunities to raise whatever issues were on their minds, no matter how tangential. It was late in the evening before Gorbachev was elected Chairman of the Supreme Soviet, but not until after one candidate had compared him to Napoleon and another insisted that he first resign as General Secretary of the CPSU. Although Gorbachev eventually won in an uncontested race, eighty-seven deputies (out of 2,210 voting) voted against him. Most remarkable, perhaps, was an unknown design engineer from Kola named A.M. Obolensky who proposed himself as a non-party candidate to run against Gorbachev; 795 deputies, more than a third of those voting, supported the idea of adding Obolensky's name to the ballot!

The election of deputies to the Supreme Soviet which took place very late on the second day of the Congress was also a struggle, but one which served to confirm the minority status of those considered anti-establishment reformers. The process by which the 542 members of the Supreme Soviet are selected proved cumbersome and somewhat complicated. The new Supreme Soviet, like the old one, is divided into two chambers, the Council of the Union and the Council of Nationalities (see Figure 5.1). Each chamber is comprised of 271 deputies who meet in continuous session to consider and adopt legislation. One fifth of these members are replaced annually at meetings of the Congress. Members of the Council of the Union are elected from among the 1,500 deputies representing territorial districts and public organisations. Like the USA House of Representatives, seats are apportioned by population. Members of the Council of Nationalities come from among the deputies elected from national-territorial districts and public organisations according to the following norms: eleven deputies from each of fifteen union republics; four deputies from each of twenty autonomous republics; two deputies from each of eight autonomous regions; one deputy from each of ten *okrugs* (areas). Deputies to the Congress decide who the 542 members of the Supreme Soviet will be by crossing off the names of those against whom they wish

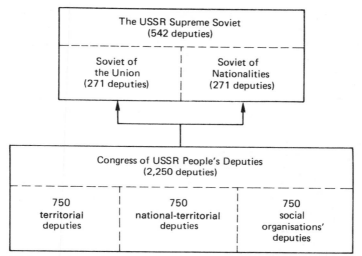

FIGURE 5.1   *The USSR Congress of People's Deputies and Supreme Soviet*

to vote. Those who receive less than 50 per cent of the votes cast are defeated. If necessary, repeat or runoff elections may be held.

At this first Congress, 600 deputies were nominated for the 542 seats. But how were these deputies nominated? With what results? Nominations to the Council of the Union took place in regional caucuses based on population. Thus, the Moscow regional caucus was allotted twenty-nine seats; they chose to nominate fifty-five candidates. This was probably a tactical mistake since it gave the more conservative majority a chance to reject those it did not like. In the Council of Nationalities nominations were by republican caucuses. The Russian Republic, like the other republics, had eleven seats. It chose to nominate twelve including Boris Yel'tsin who was the one defeated when 964 of the 1,500 cast votes against him. He was, however, appointed later as a result of a vacancy in the Russian delegation.

On the whole, the results proved disappointing for those advocating a faster pace of reform. A series of procedural votes prior to the election to the Supreme Soviet indicated that a decided majority – perhaps 70–80 per cent – of the deputies of the Congress were comparatively more conservative. The composition of the Supreme Soviet reflected this even though the social and professional profile of those elected had changed considerably from the one elected in 1984 (see Table 5.2). According to one of the deputies considered a progressive, Yuri Afanas'ev, the Director of the Institute of

Historical Archives, 'an aggressively obedient majority' had elected a Supreme Soviet so much like its predecessor in attitude that he labelled it a 'Brezhnevite–Stalinist' Supreme Soviet.

TABLE 5.1 *Social composition of the USSR Supreme Soviet (1984), Congress of People's Deputies (1989) and the USSR Supreme Soviet (1989)*

	Supreme Soviet 1984 (%)	Congress 1989(%)	Supreme Soviet 1989 (%)	N
Top political leadership	1.5	0.7	0.2	1
Top and middle-level managerial personnel*	40.0	39.8	32.8	178
Lower echelon managerial personnel**	6.6	25.3	35.3	191
Workers, collective farmers, non-professional office employees	45.9	22.1	18.3	99
Highly professional intellectuals	6.0	10.2	12.5	68
Priests	–	0.3	–	0
Pensioners	–	1.6	0.9	5
Total	100%	100%	100%	542

Source: *Moskovskie novosti*, no. 24 (1989).
Notes:
* Republican, regional and territorial-level party leaders, responsible employees of the CPSU Central Committee, leaders of the Supreme Soviets of the USSR and the union republics, government ministers, top military leaders, directors of research and educational institutions, etc.
** Chiefs of workshops, departments, work teams, laboratories, collective and state farms, etc.

Although the major functions of the Congress – the elections of the Supreme Soviet and its chairman – were accomplished in its first three days of work, the Congress remained in session longer than anticipated. When the final session ended on 9 June 1989, those in attendance and those watching the proceedings on television – it set a record for the number of viewers – knew they had observed events unique in Soviet history. Each day seemed to outdo the day before it. On one day, Yuri Vlasov, a former Olympic weight lifter, condemned the KGB as 'an underground empire' which was incompatible with a democratic society. On the next, KGB Chairman, Vladimir Kryuchkov, called for the creation of an intelligence oversight commission citing 'the experience of the

Americans'. On 8 June, a large number of the delegates from the
Baltic republics walked out to protest against the election of the
Constitutional Review Committee, only to return after Gorbachev
promised to meet with them and to respond to their concerns that
such a Committee would encroach on Baltic independence. The
day before, Valentin Rasputin, a writer sympathetic to Russian
nationalism, argued that Russia should secede from the USSR at
an organisational session of the Council of Nationalities. Andrei
Sakharov was booed and vilified as a traitor when he demanded a
criminal investigation into the actions of the Soviet Army in Afghanistan. In the meantime, Anatolii Luk'yanov was elected First
Vice-Chairman of the Supreme Soviet, albeit with 179 voting against
and 137 abstaining; Nikolai Ryzhkov was nominated to be Chairman of the Council of Ministers at the first session of the Supreme
Soviet held on 7 June 1989. Ryzhkov was chosen with nine opposed
and thirty-one abstaining.

As indicated above, the work of the Supreme Soviet actually got
underway while the Congress was still in session. The constitutional
changes introduced in December 1988 create a potentially more
powerful parliamentary body than the previous one. These powers
as specified in articles 113–117 include the right to confirm (or
reject) long- and short-range economic plans and to change the
state budget; to initiate and pass legislation on any issue related to
government which is not exclusively within the jurisdiction of the
Congress; to reverse edicts of the Presidium of the Supreme Soviet,
decrees of the Chairman of the Supreme Soviet, and resolutions
and decrees of the Council of Ministers; to ensure the uniformity
of the law for all areas of the USSR and to interpret the laws; and
to supervise national security issues, including mobilising troops and
declaring war. The differing jurisdiction of the two chambers is
spelled out in greater detail (article 116); both must approve the
legislation proposed by the other. Differences in proposed legislation are to be resolved in a joint committee or, failing that, by
the Congress of Peoples' Deputies.

One of the main reasons for the potentially greater impact of the
Supreme Soviet is that it will meet in two continuing sessions in
the spring and in the autumn, each lasting three to four months.
At least some of the deputies will be freed from other professional
work, although efforts to extend this to all deputies of the Supreme
Soviet were rejected. Among the truly 'full-time' deputies, the
chairmen of the standing committees appear likely to become focal
points of legislative activity. While the Council of Nationalities has
four additional commissions to deal with specific ethnic issues, there
are fourteen joint committees: Agriculture and Food, Construction

and Architecture, Defence, Ecology, Economic Reform, *Glasnost'* and Citizens' Rights, Health, International Affairs, Legislation and Legality, Science–Education–Culture, Local Government, Veterans' Affairs, Women, and Youth. In order to involve deputies elected to the Congress, but not to the Supreme Soviet, in the work of the new parliament, 50 per cent of the membership of the standing committees will be drawn from deputies not chosen for the Supreme Soviet. While they may participate, they do not have voting rights.

While it is still too early to draw conclusions about the work of the new Supreme Soviet, one encouraging sign of independence is that nominees for ministerial positions have not been routinely approved as before. At least two nominees were rejected by the Supreme Soviet, while six more failed to be forwarded for approval by the standing committees responsible for reviewing their credentials. Prime Minister Ryzhkov, whose nominees they were, was reported to have said afterwards that 'this is something we're going to have to get used to'. Given the lack of real executive accountability before the legislature which characterised the old Supreme Soviet, the assertiveness of the deputies regarding appointments takes on added significance. For the first time in memory, members of the executive and administrative branch may feel dependent on the deputies' goodwill if they are to retain their offices.

In the fulfilment of their responsibilities, the deputies will be assisted by the Presidium of the Supreme Soviet consisting of the chairman and First Vice-Chairman of the Supreme Soviet, fifteen vice-chairmen (comprised of the chairmen of the republican Supreme Soviets), the chairmen of both chambers and of their standing committees, and the Chairman of the Peoples' Control Committee. Although the constitutional amendments assign the Presidium ceremonial roles, such as awarding medals and receiving diplomatic missions, it will also perform a potentially important administrative function in organising the work of the deputies and coordinating the work of the standing committees. It also has the right to issue edicts and pass resolutions. Past practice saw much of Soviet legislation emanating from this source; subsequent unanimous ratification by the Supreme Soviet was merely a formality. Whether this will be repeated is not yet clear.

Also unclear at this point is how much of Gorbachev's authority derived from holding the position of Chairman of the Supreme Soviet, and then from March 1990 the newly created executive Presidency. In theory, his powers are substantial. As President, he has the right to define the political and legislative agenda of the Soviet state. He also heads the powerful Defence Council and conducts international negotiations, and nominates the Chairman of the Council of Ministers who heads the Soviet government. At the same time, he is elected by – and, in theory, accountable to – the Congress of Peoples' Deputies, and then from 1994 onwards will be directly elected by and accountable to the Soviet people as a whole. How this balance will develop, only time will tell. As one deputy put it: 'Gorbachev is the head of the party, the head of state and the leader of the opposition all at once'. What is clear now, however, is that any incumbent is constitutionally limited to two terms. Moreover, if the incumbent dies in office, he will be succeeded by the chairman of the USSR Supreme Soviet. These two changes create, for the first time, the conditions for an orderly succession of power in the USSR.

Summary and Conclusions

In summary, the changes in the Soviet state system discussed here – both those already implemented and those proposed – represent a significant departure from past practice. Taken together, the introduction of competitive elections for the Congress of Peoples' Deputies, the restructuring of the national parliamentary system, and the proposals to revitalise the local soviets all seem aimed in one direction: to transfer the power and authority to make decisions for Soviet society from the executive to the legislative institutions, and more generally from party to state. As suggested at the beginning of this chapter, such a shift may have been prompted by Gorbachev's shorter-term political needs to wrest power from the bureaucrats, where he perceives the greatest opposition to his economic reform programme, to elected representatives of the people whom he may believe are more sympathetic. But it is the potential long-term effects of these changes that may ultimately prove more significant, for they have restored the idea, if not yet the reality, that real power should belong to the soviets and to those who elect them. If this direction is not reversed, then the Soviet Union will have taken a major step towards 'democratisation'.

6

The Rule of Law and the Legal System

WILLIAM E. BUTLER

Law and the legal system are at the very heart of *perestroika* and *glasnost'* in two respects: as objects of reform themselves, and as vehicles of reform in all realms of political, socioeconomic, and cultural life. No reform of consequence fails to affect the legal system or rely upon law for its ultimate success and even implementation. A principal objective of *perestroika* has come to be the creation of a 'socialist rule-of-law state' (*pravovoe gosudarstvo*), and as that objective is pursued a momentous debate is occurring about the role of law in Soviet society. The outcome of the debate may decide whether *perestroika* and *glasnost'* succeed or fail and in any case will affect the structure, powers, and role of the legal profession, the courts, and law enforcement agencies.

Towards the Rule of Law

What are the Russians talking about when they advocate a 'rule-of-law state'? Partly it depends upon what sort of 'law' they have in view. The classics of Marxism–Leninism have been construed as predicting that law will play a minimal role after a socialist revolution occurs and in due course will die away under communism. Lenin indeed is widely quoted as saying 'law is policy', which was interpreted to mean that it had no eternal value as a restraint upon the state. But what kind of 'law' did he have in mind?

The Russian language has two principal terms for law: *pravo* and *zakon*. The former is basically the equivalent of *droit* (French), *recht* (German), *derecho* (Spanish), *diritto* (Italian), and the like. The second, *zakon*, refers to statutory law of the highest parliamentary type: enactments of the Congresses of People's Deputies and the Supreme Soviets. *Pravo* carried with it connotations of right and justice, consistency with moral principles, that prevail always and everywhere, that may not be transgressed by citizen or state – a species of natural law originating in the community, nature, divine will, or some other source. *Zakon* suggests man-made law, positive law, which may or may not be consistent with *pravo*.

No special knowledge of the Russian language is required to see that it matters enormously which rule of *law* one has in view. If *zakon* is meant, then the rule of law means whatever the majority as the highest parliamentary body should decree, irrespective of whether the substance conforms to deeply-rooted community rules or values; and even if the state is expected to behave in accordance with its own laws, there is no higher authority or standard to evaluate its degree of compliance. Referendums may be a partial antidote, but in practice they are an expensive, time-consuming, and clumsy institution.

Translating *pravovoe gosudarstvo* as the 'rule-of-law state' gives the benefit of the doubt to those who advocate the broader and more fundamental concept of law. Other translations widely used include: 'legal state'; 'law-governed state'; 'law-ruled state', 'law-based state'; and '*Rechtsstaat*'. These tend to accept the '*zakon*-minded' approach, but the key point for the Western student is to be aware of a vital subtle dimension to the dialogue about the nature of law in the Soviet Union which turns on these terminological distinctions difficult to draw sharply in the English language.

Towards the Improvement of Legislation

To say that the Soviet Union is seeking to introduce a rule-of-law state is not to suggest that even in the darkest days of Stalinist terror they lacked laws, or legislation. *Zakon* was plentiful, especially at the level of subordinate legislation issued by ministries, state committees, and local levels of government. No precise figures are available, but one is speaking of literally millions of enactments issued at all levels of the state apparatus, mostly unpublished and limited in circulation. 'Knowledge of the law' became physically impossible and the opportunities for arbitrary behaviour boundless. This was the most tangible symptom of what in the Gorbachev era has come to be called the 'administrative-command' system, and it operated both within the normal state apparatus and within those portions charged with exercising repressive functions on behalf of the leadership.

The antidote being developed under *perestroika* is diverse in its response. The bodies of states that are democratically elected – the Congresses of People's Deputies and their organs, the Supreme Soviets – are in permanent session and make laws more frequently; in doing so they displace the need for so much subordinate legislation and are able to hold local agencies of government more accountable. The courts are being enjoined to be more rigorous in their evaluation of state behaviour. In certain situations collegial decisions taken by officials can be appealed to a court. The USSR Constitutional Supervision Committee, although its role is rather limited, has powers to review the constitutionality of subordinate legislation. And a variety of other legal institutions are being reshaped or reinvigorated to become responsive to the challenges of *perestroika*. The economic reforms are intended to buttress the politico-legal measures, for by decentralising or eliminating state responsibility for enterprise management they reduce the need to rely on 'administrative-command' methods and use law rather to 'regulate' relations among parties enjoying equal legal status – which is much the same way that law is used in the West.

Crucial to the success of the legal strategy of *perestroika* are the legal profession and legal institutions in the Soviet Union.

The Legal Profession

The October 1917 revolution abolished Imperial Russian legal institutions and recast those deemed essential in a proletarian guise. But the principle that individuals should have a right to representation in court and should retain and pay a professional if they wished was continued. Soviet lawyers who specialise in representing the interests of individual clients, what we in the West would classify as a private practitioner, are called 'advocates'. They practise law, as a rule, as members of the *Advokatura* in each union republic or large city or region (Moscow, Leningrad, Kiev) and are usually grouped into law offices in urban and rural areas sited to serve population catchment areas. Their fees are based on a tariff fixed by the USSR Ministry of Justice. A few advocates, mostly of retirement age, have registered to offer their services as a form of 'individual labour activity' under the legislation of November 1986.

In the pre-*perestroika* era the advocate was often portrayed as an unavoidable anachronism whose private income paid directly to the law office by the client contrasted sharply with the socialisation of other walks of life. The anachronism was rationalised on the grounds that to require an individual client to employ a state-salaried advocate in a case where the investigation, judge, procurator and people's assessors were also civil servants or possibly so would be unjust with respect to the client. And in certain areas – alimony, dismissal from work, and others – the advocate was required to render services without a fee.

Under *perestroika* the advocate, together with other segments of the legal profession, is being called upon to perform an enhanced role. Rather than an anachronism, the advocate's economic independence is viewed as a positive factor to be emulated in other domains of Soviet society. Ceilings on monthly earnings 'voluntarily' accepted in the Brezhnev era by advocates have been eliminated, enabling the most gifted to offer their services as demand requires. Advocates are at liberty to negotiate 'contract prices' with foreign clients – that is, to agree whatever fee is appropriate. As foreign investment in the USSR increases, advocates will be in increasing demand to advise, and this represents a fundamental reorientation of their traditional areas of practice.

Reforms in Soviet criminal procedure give the advocate an earlier and more active role in defending client interests at the stage of preliminary investigation. Normally excluded in the past from this vital stage of any serious criminal case, the Soviet codes of criminal procedure as amended in 1989 allow, and sometimes even require, the presence of defence counsel.

The role and prestige of the profession is intended to be increased through a new body, the Union of Advocates of the USSR, founded in February 1989, and through advocates' membership in a larger social organisation, the Union of Jurists, created in June 1989. There are about 26,000 advocates in the Soviet Union and in excess of 300,000 'jurists' – the general term for persons holding a degree in law or employed or otherwise engaged in jobs that fall within the rubric of the legal profession.

The formation of both the Union of Advocates and the Union of Jurists contribute – and are intended to do so – to a sense of professional identity amongst those legally trained. In pre-revolutionary Russia the emergence of a law-trained elite during the 19th century contributed significantly to the limitation of tsarist absolutism and the emergence in 1905 of a constitutional monarchy. Destalinisation from 1953 has accentuated the restoration of socialist legality, and economic reforms since 1965 required a massive expansion of the legal profession, principally the *jurisconsults* (see below). Gorbachev is the first Soviet leader since Lenin to bring legal skills to that position. The rising *perestroika* generation is in part the product of the gradual rehabilitation of law as a positive and desirable force in Soviet society. That jurists should feel a sense of professional community, an awareness of values and principles which have enduring implications for the wellbeing of Soviet society, is a natural outgrowth of factors and forces gestating during the past nearly four decades and potentially a powerful element driving policies towards the rule-of-law state.

The jurisconsults, perhaps 150,000 or more in number, are the other type of legal practitioner who has clients in the Soviet Union. They serve as legal advisers to ministries, departments, local government, state enterprises or farms, collective farms, and the like. Unlike advocates, they are salaried employees and are not dependent upon fee income for their livelihood. Their numbers increased dramatically from 1970 as a direct of the 1965 economic reforms: a certain decentralisation in economic management and greater autonomy to state enterprises disciplined by contracts among the enterprises and larger numbers of legal advisers to assist enterprise managers. The jurisconsult was positioned to help the manager, but also to verify whether the manager acted in accordance with law. Accordingly, the jurisconsult may refuse to sign or 'visa' documents which in his view are contrary to law, and if management proceeds notwithstanding, the jurisconsult must report to the superior agency or share equal liability with management for the unlawful activities.

Perestroika in principle seems likely to alter the role and perhaps the status of the jurisconsult. As a 'check' on the legality of management decisions in the past, the jurisconsult needed to be protected against dismissal or other management reprisals should his views prove to be unpopular. In this respect the jurisconsult was viewed as extending planning and contractual discipline into enterprise operations on behalf of the superior agency, who was his 'protestor' in this situation. A jurisconsult cannot be dismissed, demoted, transferred, or regraded without the consent of the superior agency. To the extent that *perestroika* further loosens the bonds between ministries and enterprises, the jurisconsult increasingly is the enterprise's lawyer alone. His role may more and more approximate that of a company legal adviser in the West.

The Courts

Under the Soviet Constitution there exist two types of courts: the courts of the USSR (the USSR Supreme Court and the system of military tribunals) and union republic courts (all other courts in the

Soviet Union, which vary in importance depending upon the hierarchy of administrative-territorial subdivisions within each union republic). The lowest level of courts is the people's courts, which exist at district or city level. Probably they decide initially 95 per cent of all criminal and civil cases brought in the Soviet Union. But the Soviet court system is unusual in that *any* level of court, including the Supreme courts, can and sometimes sit as a 'court of first instance', that is, as a trial court. At all times a court of first instance must consist of at least three persons, a judge and two people's assessors, and under 1989 reforms can be enlarged in cases when capital punishment or ten year or more deprivation of freedom may be assigned.

The Judges

The judiciary has been a major object of legal reforms under *perestroika*. The judges have been accused of being too passive, of being subject to local external influences of various kinds, of being too easily disposed to accept the procurator's version of the law. Under the amendments to the USSR Constitution of December 1988 an attempt has been made to address these concerns. In order to give the judiciary greater independence, their terms of office have been extended from five to ten years. Except for the Supreme courts, which are elected by the respective all-union, union republic, or autonomous republic supreme court, all inferior courts are elected by the local soviets at the next immediate superior level. This new procedure does away with the popular election of judges at people's court level and likewise attempts to remove judicial selection away from the levels of government at which the judges will serve. Judges may be recalled by the agency which elected them.

Although Soviet constitutions have provided for decades that 'judges . . . shall be independent and subordinate only to law', the 1988 constitutional amendments sought to add substance to the phrase by stipulating that conditions must exist for the 'unhindered and efficient exercise of their rights and duties'. Further, 'any interference whatever' in the activities of judges is 'inadmissible' and punishable. The question arises often in practice: what is 'interference'? In a Law enacted in August 1989 'On the Status of Judges in the USSR', the Soviet legislator has attempted a more precise answer by prohibiting: (1) interference in the activities of judges when they are 'effectuating justice'; (2) pressure in any form whatever with a view to obstructing the 'comprehensive, full, and objective consideration' of a specific case or to obtaining an illegal judicial decision; prejudgement by the mass media when reporting the proceedings in a case or otherwise pressuring a court before its judgement has entered into legal force. Sanctions for violations are set out in special legisation adopted in November 1989.

The qualifications for judicial office have been increased under *perestroika*. All people's judges must have a higher legal education, be 25 years of age on election day, have at least two years' work experience in law, and have passed a qualifications examination. All of these except the age limit are new, although in recent Soviet practice most judges had a degree in law. Judges of Superior courts must have at least five years' work experience in law including two, as a rule, as a judge.

In a fascinating departure from earlier practice, where Soviet judges wore ordinary dress while sitting on the bench, the 1989 Law authorises USSR Supreme Court judges to wear a gown with the State Arms of the USSR. The union republics are at liberty to determine their own models of judicial dress. This is a formal reintroduction of the symbolism of judicial power – the first such since the October 1917 revolution.

People's Assessors

While *perestroika* is leading to further professionalisation of the judiciary, the lay element in dispensing justice is being preserved through the people's assessors. These are laymen who have reached 25 years of age and have been elected by meetings of citizens at their places of residence or work for a term of five years to serve on a people's court. Each assessor will give two weeks each year to the service with paid time off from his or her regular job. Thus, each people's court will have 50–75 people's assessors per judge, and in 1987 more than 850,000 Soviet citizens were elected to this position. The superior courts also have people's assessors available wherever the courts sit at first instance; in this event the assessors are elected by the respective local soviet at the same level.

The people's assessors have equal rights and an equal vote with the judge and in theory, and sometimes in practice, can outvote the judge. In most cases it is likely that the expertise and experience of the judge dominates the assessors. As a result, the Soviet Union allows the replacement of the people's assessor in selected situations with a jury containing more people's assessors or jurers.

Guiding Explanations

Soviet law does not recognise the doctrine of judicial precedent. Although some court decisions are published, to help guide the legal profession, they are not binding on other courts. However, the supreme courts of the USSR and union republics do issue 'guiding explanations' which interpret difficult or controversial legislative provisions in the light of judicial practice. These guiding explanations are binding upon all lower courts, are published and amended when necessary, and comprise an extremely important adjunct to the legislation.

The Procuracy

Very much a Russian institution with roots dating back to Peter the Great, the modern procuracy has long been the most prestigious component of the Soviet legal profession. There are more than 18,000 in the USSR. Highly unified and centralised, the Procuracy is sometimes called the 'fourth estate'. The Procurator General is appointed by the USSR Supreme Soviet and confirmed by the USSR Congress of People's Deputies for a term of five years; he in turn either appoints or confirms, depending on the tier of government involved, all inferior procurators.

The Procuracy performs four basic functions, all of which have been strengthened under *perestroika* but not altered in concept. Most important is the exercise of 'general supervision' by the Procuracy over the execution of laws by ministries, state committees, enterprises, local government on the executive and administrative sides, collective farms, social organisations, officials, citizens and others. 'Execution' for these purposes encompasses the enactments adopted by those entities and officials and their implementation. If the procurator considers that a ministry has issued a decree whose provisions violate superior legislation the procuracy will file a 'protest', giving reasons, and demand that the illegal decree be repeated or altered to remove the offending formulation. In some cases the act is suspended for ten days while the agency receiving the protest considers the matter. It is important to note that the Procuracy may not itself repeal or change the legislation it considers to be illegal; through the protest, the matter is drawn to the attention of the issuing agency, which must consider the protest within a particular time period, and either concur with the protest (and rectify the matter) or decline to do so. If the Procuracy disagrees with the rejection of the protest, the superior procurator will submit it to the next higher agency and seek satisfaction there. Theoretically, protests and rejections could reach the USSR Council of Ministers, whose decision would be final.

Where the Procuracy encounters behaviour by an agency or official which is in clear violation of the law, under 1987 amendments it may issue a written instruction to eliminate the violation. The instruction must cite the provision of law being violated and suggest corrective steps. The instruction may be appealed by the recipient within ten days to the superior procurator, whose decision is final; an appeal does not suspend the instruction in the meantime. The concept extends even to unlawful acts at a preparatory stage on the part of an official or a citizen; in this event a written warning is issued. Prosecution may follow if the warning is not heeded. If a violation has caused financial harm to the state the procuracy may initiate a civil suit for recovery of damages.

The other branches of supervision exercised by the procuracy concern the execution of laws by agencies of inquiry and preliminary investigation, the conformity of judicial decisions to law, and the administration of correctional labour institutions. In the case of court decisions, although the procuracy acts as prosecutor on behalf of the state, it is nonetheless required to ensure that the court has considered the case thoroughly and objectively and that all court decisions, in whatever form, are in conformity with law, well-founded, and executed in a timely way. This is merely one illustration of a plurality of roles which on the face of it would seem to involve the procuracy in conflicts of interest. These are avoided to some extent by depersonalising the conflict through the distribution of responsibilities: prosecutions are brought by the section concerned with such activities, whereas protests against judicial decisions are filed by the procuracy section specially charged with reviewing criminal or civil cases.

Although the procuracy is said to enjoy a high success rate when bringing protests, courts, state agencies and officials can and do reject protests if they do not agree with the reasons adduced to support the protest. In this event the procurator either must acquiesce or carry the protest to the next higher level. The essence of 'supervision' is to persuade agencies to rectify their own errors; except in certain aspects of inquiries and preliminary investigations, the procuracy has no power to change the state of affairs by itself. Aptly the procuracy has been called the 'eye of the state', but its vision is limited to the executive and judicial brances of government below the highest agencies of state power and administration. It also seems to be the case that the procuracy, amongst all the agencies involved in the administration of socialist legality, is the most responsive to Communist Party guidance in the sense of influencing the concentration of procuracy activities. In 1989, for example, the procuracy was directed to concentrate on organised crime in the Soviet Union and on smuggling.

Just as there exists a system of military tribunals to deal with crimes by military personnel, so to is there a military procuracy to supervise the execution of laws in the USSR Armed Forces.

Police and Investigative Agencies

Law enforcement functions are the responsibility of primarily two agencies. The Committee of State Security of the USSR (KGB) exercises both intelligence and police functions, the latter involving the investigation of the most serious crimes against the state. Under *perestroika* the KGB has assumed a more positive and public image. As a State Committee its chairman is appointed by the USSR Supreme Soviet, and the present chairman, Vladimir Kryuchkov, was given a thorough interrogation by deputies before being confirmed in July 1989. The basic legislation on the KGB, however, is not available.

The Ministry of Internal Affairs performs the ordinary day-to-day functions of keeping public order, crime prevention and traffic control. As a union-republic type of ministry, it has inferior units at all levels of local government. Also within the jurisdiction of the ministry are inspectorates for cases concerning minors, correctional-labour institutions and certain therapeutic-labour institutions, among others. At the lower operational levels internal affairs agencies conduct inquiries and preliminary investigations and are involved in passport, motor vehicle inspection and juvenile matters.

Glasnost' has brought public criticism of police corruption, especially in motor vehicle cases, and considerable concern with the enforcement of regulations on public demonstrations. Major debate, however, broke out over the preliminary investigation.

Soviet law, just as continental Europe, Japan, China, and numerous other countries in the world but unlike the Anglo-American tradition, relies upon separate professional services within the police and procuracy to investigate crimes. The gravity, place, and nature of the crime principally determine which agency is responsible for the investigation. Under the codes of criminal procedure the investigation must be comprehensive, thorough, and objective – that is, the investigator must assemble and evaluate *all* the evidence in a case and not merely that prejudicial to any specific individual who may be under investigation.

In Anglo-American eyes the Soviet model of preliminary investigation has had several objectionable features: (1) the weight of the investigator's findings are believed to influence the court unduly; (2) with few exceptions, individuals held in investigative detention have no right to defence counsel; and (3) the investigative model is prejudical to the principle of the presumption of innocence. *Glasnost'* and *perestroika* have addressed all three criticisms.

The danger is recognised, for instance, that the weight of the investigator's evaluation of the evidence in a case may predispose the court against a person on trial. The remedy is not an easy one: primarily instructing the investigator to perform his duties comprehensively and the court to conduct a trial rather than merely a review of the investigation. After decades of procrastination, the Soviet criminal procedure legislation now admits defence counsel to the preliminary investigation and at an early stage. Although it will take some time for advocates to master the forensic skills of investigative defence tactics, the intention is better to protect the rights of the person under investigation and to improve the quality of investigation by introducing an adversary element into the collection and evaluation of the evidence at that stage.

The admission of defence counsel to defend clients during the preliminary investigation is part of a larger effort to reinforce the presumption of innocence in Soviet law. The expression itself, consigned to perdition in 1958 by the utterance of a Supreme Soviet deputy who described the doctrine as a 'bourgeois worm-eaten dogma', has finally been introduced in criminal procedure legislation. How much it adds to the pre-existing balance of rights and responsibilities of the participants in an investigation and trial remains to be seen, but at a minimum the words themselves rhetorically strengthen the burden of persuasion which the investigator and prosecution must sustain for a case to go forward to trial and which the court must accept before finding an accused person guilty.

Criminal law reforms generally under *perestroika* have been subject to conflicting pressures. In a *cause célèbre* during the spring of 1989, the provisions of criminal legislation governing 'anti-Soviet agitation and propaganda' and the 'defamation of the Soviet state and social system' were liberalised significantly, but the same edict introduced new crimes more draconian in character relating to the 'insulting or discrediting' of a state or social organisation or of an official. So orchestrated was the legislative process that the Presidiums of the USSR and RSFSR supreme soviets acted on the same day (8 April 1989) and within a fortnight the USSR Supreme Court had issued a Guiding Explanation defining the scope of the edicts – and all before the full USSR Supreme Soviet had been given an opportunity to confirm – that is, to endorse – the edict.

The substance of the edicts occasioned vigorous public debate, almost entirely hostile. Confirmation of the edict, however, because of the March elections, fell on the agenda of the new USSR Congress of People's Deputies, which on 24 June 1989 repealed the most objectionable features and left it to the USSR Supreme Soviet to polish the final formulations. More or less as a matter of routine the Congress or the full Supreme Soviet now examines and amends enactments of the Presidium.

The 1990 Fundamental Principles of Criminal Legislation of the USSR and Union Republics reflect contrary concerns of *perestroika*. One is the desire to 'humanise' criminal legislation and 'decriminalise' many acts previously deemed to be crimes. In pursuit of those aims, capital punishment is confined exclusively to males between the ages of 18 and 65. For a smaller group of crimes the penalties have been reduced, and many petty offences have been transformed into administrative offences. Reforms of this order have been a welcome reaction against the harshness of the preceding period. However, at the same time the increased rate of reported crimes has generated severe pressure to respond by increasing punishments. The overall crime rate in 1989 showed a 33 per cent increase over the preceding year and a 40 per cent increase in grave crimes. Thefts of personal property were up by 66 per cent and the stealing of cars by a massive 84 per cent.

Perestroika can be expected to continue to press against the frontiers of the criminal law. As the socialist market economy develops and the private sector increases in importance, the criminal law is likely to give greater and perhaps even equal protection to personal and private property as compared with state and cooperative ownership. Offences such as speculation, acting as a commercial middleman and the like may be removed from the codes or be drastically revised. On the other hand, new protections will need to be introduced into the criminal law – company fraud, restrictive practices, stock manipulation, and the like – which are related to a mixed economy.

Other Law Enforcement Bodies

There is a vast range of other entities in the Soviet Union, both state and non-state, which 'administer' justice. Many are novel and have no precise equivalent in the Anglo-American legal system.

State Arbitrazh

Throughout virtually all of Soviet history economic contract disputes between state-owned enterprises have been excluded from the ordinary Soviet courts. A special system of tribunals whose origins date from 1922 has taken jurisdiction over such disputes. Presently called

State *Arbitrazh*, it is not to be confused with voluntary 'arbitration' widely used in international commercial disputes, including in the USSR. State *Arbitrazh* functions on the basis of a Law adopted in 1980, as amended in the *perestroika* period. It is not part of the Soviet judicial system, although it possesses many attributes of a court: it hears and settles disputes solely on the basis of law (and not economic policy). The parties have a right to legal representation, and its awards are binding and are executed in the same manner as court civil judgments.

On the other hand, the proceedings are not open to the public as a matter of right. They are highly informal, and arbitrators enjoy neither the stature nor the rights of a judge. Moreover, *Arbitrazh* considers a category of dispute inconceivable under Anglo-American law: a pre-contractual dispute, which arises when the parties are required by the plan to conclude an economic contract but cannot agree on those few terms left to the parties to negotiate. The *Arbitrazh* system handles more than a million cases a year, including more than 50,000 pre-contractual disputes and 10,000 cases initiated by State *Arbitrazh* itself.

Under *perestroika* the State Arbitrazh system has become more centralised and elevated in status. The Chief State Arbitrator of the USSR is, just as the USSR Procurator General and the Chairman of the USSR Supreme Court, confirmed in his post by the USSR Congress of People's Deputies. The long-term role of *Arbitrazh*, however, must be in doubt under *perestroika*. State *Arbitrazh* has been a creature of the planned economy, an instrument through which contract discipline pursuant to planning directives was enforced in a highly expeditious and expert way. As socialist market relations develop and economic planning becomes increasingly long-term and general, the case for maintaining the *Arbitrazh* system diminishes. Indeed, joint enterprises with Western and developing countries and Soviet cooperatives are not subject to *Arbitrazh* jurisdiction. If there is a case for *Arbitrazh* continuing to exist in a socialist market economy, it may be in the form of a special economic court rather than as an extension of the planning system.

Administrative Commissions

The Anglo-American legal system has traditionally distinguished between criminal and lawful behaviour, with nothing in between. Illegal behaviour is a criminal offence to be punished accordingly. Under Soviet law certain anti-social behaviour may not be criminal at all, or may be criminal only if previously punished administratively. It may nonetheless be punishable as an 'administrative offence' under the union republic codes on administrative responsibility adopted in 1982–8. The administrative sanctions can be quite serious, ranging from a warning up to administrative arrest for a term of as long as fifteen days. An enormous number of agencies have the right to impose administrative sanctions. Amongst them are the district and city people's courts or judges, state inspectorates, internal affairs agencies, and other officials or agencies specially empowered by law.

Although certain administrative cases are dealt with by judges sitting alone 'in administrative session', a large number, perhaps the majority, come before administrative commissions attached to local soviets. Special systems of administrative commissions deal with juveniles, alcoholics, and drug addicts.

People's Guards

Volunteer citizen groups which perform auxiliary policy and public order functions date back in the USSR to the early 1920s. Under Khrushchev the people's guards were instituted on a large scale as part of the devolution of state functions to non-state bodies. Although vigilante actions in the early days by some local groups brought the scheme into disrepute, the notion of auxiliary civic police has proved to be a durable one and the red-arm-banded citizens have become a familiar sight in the streets and at public events.

Comrades' Courts

Together with the people's guards, the Khrushchev era reshaped informal social courts as an elective agency (not a state judicial institution) intended to nurture citizens in the spirit of a communist attitude towards labour, socialist ownership, and compliance with the rules of socialist community life. In its Khrushchevian version the comrades' court did not 'punish' offenders; it applied 'measures of social pressure'. The terminology of the legislation stressed the persuasion and educational functions of comrades' courts rather than the coercive functions associated with ordinary courts. During the Brezhnev era the legislation on comrades' courts was amended in the direction of greater procedural formality and due process, but the voluntary lay element was retained intact.

The administrative commissions, people's guards and comrades' courts have not figured significantly in law reform proposals under *perestroika*. Whether this means they are peripheral or are performing satisfactorily on the whole is difficult to assess in the absence of empirical data on their respective caseloads and other activities. The fate of the people's guards and comrades' courts will be particularly interesting to follow, for the sense of social collectiveness and discipline needed to make them effective may come under pressure as *perestroika* inevitably accentuates factors of differentiation based on skill, attainment, and individuality.

Citizen Initiative

The ultimate restraint upon arbitrariness and illegality in the Soviet Union must be citizen complaint, or 'whistle-blowing'. Recourse to the courts or other official or non-state bodies would be unreasonable if the objects of recourse were given no opportunity to learn of their inefficiency or maladministration through direct notification by the victims. Purely in their capacity as citizens, individuals are expected to serve as guardians of legality through a complaints procedure based on a 1968 Edict on the Procedure for Considering Proposals, Applications, and Appeals of Citizens, as amended in 1980.

The procedures are straightforward: citizens may make proposals, applications, and appeals orally or in writing to all state or social agencies, to criticise shortcomings, and to complain against the actions of officials. The appeal is, first, directly to the immediate superior of the object of the appeal provided that the superior has direct jurisdiction over the matter in question, or if there is no superior, to a court or to the executive or administrative body of the agency. Regular office hours must be kept to receive complainants, and reasoned decisions must be issued usually within a specified time period. Since 1988 anonymous complaints are no longer considered.

Although extensively used, the system has been widely criticised as inadequate. Provision was made in the 1977 USSR Constitution (article 58, para. 2) for giving courts the power to review either the constitutionality or the legality of acts of officials and state agencies. But to be effective, that clause required a separate enabling statute stipulating which acts could be reviewed and by whom. Not until *perestroika*, ten years later, was the relevant legislation produced, and even then in a version which is ineffective. On 30 June 1987 the USSR Supreme Soviet adopted, after unprecedented stormy debate, a version of the enabling Law which required further alterations on 20 October 1987. In effect, even in amended form, the 1987 Law precluded from judicial review the decisions of officials taken collegially. Few actions have been brought as a result. On 2 November 1989 the 1987 legislation was replaced by a new Law allowing the unlawful actions of state agencies or officials to be appealed to a court with effect from 1 July 1990, irrespective of whether the decisions were taken collegially or individually.

While *glasnost'* and *perestroika* are making an undoubted impact upon the course of Soviet affairs, the 'rule of law state' may be the most enduring revolutionary innovation of the Gorbachev era. It postulates – for the first time in Soviet history – adherence to *universal* legal values, which presumably are to exist so long as the human community does. Law as an instrument of class struggle and temporary social change en route to a communist society where state and law are not required is being supplanted by law as an eternal value, an end worthy of protecting and preserving for its own sake.

In November 1989 the USSR Supreme Soviet formed a commission to draft a new Constitution for the USSR. How the rule of law is to be accorded constitutional expression will be among the salient issues for the 1990s.

7

Patterns of Participation

NICHOLAS LAMPERT

The ideal of public participation in political life, along with the concept of popular sovereignty, has gained a powerful hold on the modern political imagination. But 'participation' is an elastic yes-word, with different connotations in different political cultures. In liberal democratic regimes the meaning of participation has been given above all by electoral politics. Political power is legitimated by the preferences of individual voters, and political choice in turn implies a domain of civil society in which political parties and pressure groups can carry on an open political struggle. In the Soviet tradition 'participation' is understood differently. The Communist Party of the Soviet Union has claimed the right to a monopoly of political power, on the grounds that Soviet society, having rid itself of capitalism and class antagonism, is fundamentally harmonious. The party rules in the interests of the people as a whole; there is therefore no room for political competition and electoral choice, and no place for an autonomous domain of civil society.

However, the Soviet tradition attaches great importance to popular participation. First, an intense effort has been put into ensuring regular manifestations of support for the political order, in the form of huge turn-outs at elections, officially organised demonstrations and other political rituals. These have served as regular symbolic reminders of the social unity that the 'leading role of the party' is held to embody. Second, the party has succeeded in enlisting vast numbers of ordinary citizens in the business of ruling – not in the sense of sharing power or articulating group interests, but in the sense of sharing responsibility for the implementation of official policies and directives. This has meant fostering mass participation in the party and in elected state bodies, and in a variety of 'non-state' organisations such as the trade unions, people's control committees and volunteer police. Soviet citizens have also been encouraged to make use of a number of channels for individual petitioning and complaint, to make submissions to party and state agencies and the press.

The compulsion to maintain the appearance of political consensus has ruled out any honest study of political attitudes within the USSR, so that until very recently, at least, one could have only impressionistic ideas about how Soviet citizens viewed their involvement in the political system. One should not infer from this that public participation has been simply coerced. Indeed it has provided an important form of social 'cement' for the Soviet regime. However, the weaknesses of the traditional forms of participation are now very apparent and have come under strong attack during the Gorbachev period.

The regimented participation of the 'command-administrative system' now seems intolerable for a modernising government that wants a freer flow of information and wider opportunities for public debate about pressing economic and social problems. The Gorbachev regime has placed a strong emphasis on the democratisation of the political system, introducing a degree of electoral choice and a sitting parliament, and creating conditions in which 'informal' political movements could begin to develop outside the party-state apparatus. Although *perestroika* left the party in a dominant if no longer monopolistic position, the spectre of political choice has been raised. It is not therefore surprising to find that the development of new forms of participation is highly contested. The traditional forces within the political apparatus would like to keep *perestroika* within the bounds of a campaign from above in which the party leadership might enlist the support of the population for already-determined policies. Radical reformers, on the other hand, see the need to establish a different type of relationship between state and society, in which social diversity is openly recognised and social interests can find a political voice. Whether the Soviet system can move towards a more participatory system in this sense while coping with acute economic problems and national tensions remains the unanswered question.

Participation in the Soviet Union:
The Traditional Model

Soviet thinking about popular participation in politics was in its origins shaped by an ideal of direct democracy that Marx adopted in his enthusiastic reaction to the Paris Commune, and that was adopted in turn by Lenin (especially in his *State and Revolution*, completed in 1917). The representative organs of the state were to act not as parliamentary talking shops, but as a direct link between the executive and the citizens. They were to be administrative as well as legislative organs. And the tasks of administration could be simplified to such an extent that any literate and numerate person could carry them out. The gulf between the bureaucracy and the people, and therefore 'bureaucrats' as a professional stratum, would disappear.

The idea that professional administration could be abolished was quickly dropped by the Bolsheviks in the early years after the revolution. It was replaced by a concept of professional administration supplemented by citizen participation, a principle that has been retained to some degree up to the present. The emphasis on public participation in this sense was encouraged by the huge growth of the state in the post-revolutionary years. In the 1930s the mass collectivisation of agriculture and a crash programme of industrialisation brought a rapid increase in state regulation and thus in the size of the political and administrative apparatuses. They were now directly responsible for the planning and management of the vast bulk of economic activity as well for education, health and housing.

This development has posed fundamental problems of control for the Soviet political leadership. In a highly bureaucratised structure the pursuit of particular bureaucratic interests has tended to undermine centrally determined policies, leading to regular accusations of bureaucratic mismanagement and stagnation. In response the political leadership has resorted to corrective action from above, and citizen involvement from below has been encouraged by drawing people into a variety of agencies to assist in implementing central policies and, in principle, to help keep control over a ramified bureaucratic apparatus. At the same time mass membership in the party and other social organisations, together with orchestrated elections and other political rituals, have served to reaffirm in symbolic fashion the unity of state and people.

In such a setting participation becomes a matter of 'organised enthusiasm', mobilising the population in support of policies determined by the leadership. there is little room for *voluntary* political commitment. where there is no political choice, party membership and political activism tend to become social duties, and to leave the party becomes an act of political defiance. Behind this regimented participation is an extreme fear of social spontaneity, an unwillingness to countenance any political activity that is not closely managed by the ruling party.

In the post-Stalin period the official approach to citizen participation underwent a number of shifts. During the leadership of Khrushchev a strong emphasis was placed on recruiting citizens to assist in local government tasks (for example through 'non-staff' departments to which about 100,000 volunteers were attached by the end of the Khrushchev period), and a system of volunteer police and lay courts was revived. These changes were carried out under the banner of the 'withering away of the state', involving a transfer of government functions to voluntary organisations.

Under the Brezhnev leadership that banner was taken down and greater importance attached to professional administration as opposed to popular government. However, the structures of popular participation remained and the regime sought to strengthen its ties with society by enlisting growing numbers of citizens in voluntary tasks. In particular, as political decision-making drew on an increasing body of technical knowledge, some support was given to a technocratic type of participation. Specialists were coopted on to government bodies and given limited scope for public debate in the pages of the press and professional journals. Certain channels were thus established for the muted articulation of different views.

However, the mobilisational mode of participation remained basically in place. It was only with the advent of the Gorbachev leadership that the traditional pattern of relations between the citizen and the state began to come under scrutiny. In order to make better sense of the changes that have occurred in the second half of the 1980s, it will be helpful to outline the main forms of participation as they had become established in the Brezhnev period.

Elections and Deputies

The Communist Party of the Soviet Union has traditionally attached enormous importance to elections, although up until June 1987 no choice of party, policy or candidate was offered to the population. Official claims of 99 per cent and more turn-outs in elections to local and national soviets are almost certainly exaggerated. For example, many voters are known to have avoided the ritual by obtaining certificates of absence and then failing to vote in other constituencies. Nonetheless very high turn-outs have been secured by a well-developed system of canvassing under the supervision of a huge network of electoral commissions. Little effort was spared to pull out the voters and get them to do their social duty.

The amount of energy devoted to electoral success – i.e. an extremely high turn-out – requires explanation. Most commentators (for instance Zaslavsky and Brym, 1978) have stressed the legitimising function of orchestrated elections. One should be careful in interpreting this, since the average Soviet elector is evidently well aware of the 'fictitious' character of the electoral process. Nonetheless the mobilisation of a mass vote does lock the voter into the public pretence that the population chooses its rulers, and in that sense provides another 'demonstration' of social unity. Elections also involve large numbers of people in the nomination and canvassing process, enable the party to single out worthy people for future reward, and provide citizens with a relatively painless way of fulfilling social obligations.

The nomination process, closely managed by the party, has been used to guarantee that the currently defined correct proportion of workers, farmers, white-collar workers, men, women and others would be found in the local soviets. It has also been important in ensuring that a majority of non-party members, within a 'bloc of Communists and non-party people', would be elected. At the same time, by including important party and government officials as deputies, the regime could strengthen the status of its main servants.

The sheer weight of deputies within the system should also be noted. In the June 1987 elections the number of deputies to local soviets reached 2,321,766, a far greater density of representation than in Western democracies. The job of deputy was not an onerous one during the Brezhnev period. For example a sample survey covering two republics (Estonia and Armenia) at the end of the 1960s revealed that 81 per cent of deputies spent less than 10 hours per month on their duties. Those duties gave a little scope for representing aggrieved citizens – for example in connection with housing, residence or pension matters – but deputies' complaints about problems of access to the administration were endemic. Probably the most important channel of participation for deputies in the 1970s was the system of standing committees attached to soviets – a system which also drew in voluntary activists in an advisory capacity. In 1975 there were about 329,000 standing committees involving 1,776,309 deputies (80 per cent of the total) and 2,611,000 voluntary participants. Such paper claims tell one nothing about the meaning of participation for the activist, and it is clear that the typical deputy was largely impotent. Nonetheless the sheer scale of involvement is impressive, giving the participants a stake in the system and in that sense contributing to political stability.

Party Membership

Mass party membership has acted as a central mechanism of social integration (see also above, chapter 4). The party now numbers more than 19 million, almost 10 per cent of the adult population. Participation in the party has served a variety of social functions. First, it provides opportunities for advancement, since up till very recently party membership was a prerequisite for entry into almost any position of responsibility. Secondly, and for the same reason, membership has been a key mechanism of control over managers and administrators. Thirdly, it provides an important ideological and material link between the working class and the regime, with 45 per cent of members recorded as workers in 1987. Finally, it creates a pool of activists to manage the primary party organisations and, in some form or other, to supervise and contribute to all Soviet social organisations. Party members are the lynchpin of the whole system of officially-sponsored voluntary activity.

In emphasising the role of party membership as a mechanism of social advancement and a source of social control one should not give the impression of party members as a race apart, corrupted by privileges and standing over non-party members. Though it is usually a prerequisite for advancement, party membership in itself confers few advantages, and quite a few social obligations. At the same time, since the party is a mass organisation it is very heterogeneous in composition. In the event of major social and political conflict the party as a whole is therefore likely to be just as divided as the wider society.

The Controllers

The search for control over the apparatus has spawned a number of agencies whose declared task is to encourage citizens to provide 'criticism from below'. The People's Control Committees, established under their present name in 1965 (in their previous incarnation called Party-Government Control Committees), are supposed to investigate inefficiency and waste in a wide range of organisations and can appeal for intervention from higher level officials and law enforcement agencies. On paper the Committees have incorporated vast numbers of citizens. Their membership increased from 5 million to 10 million between 1965 and 1980, and 600,000 people were said to be participating in this work each year. In 1980 the People's Control employed 7,667 full-time officers; the rest were voluntary activists. The public profile of these committees has been rather high, since their activities have been regularly reported in *Pravda*. It is clear that their bark is worse than their bite, with a social reputation as havens for busybody pensioners rather than effective agencies of control. But even in that sense they have no doubt served a social purpose, providing an outlet for zealous citizens who take seriously the stated intention to uncover mismanagement and corruption.

Other forms of activity that allow the state to coopt volunteer participants into state institutions include the volunteer militia (*druzhiny*) and the comrades' courts. On paper there were 10 million members of the volunteer militia in 1980, providing support to the police in maintaining public order. Comrades' courts are lay courts held in workplaces and in residential areas to deal with domestic disputes, drunkenness, pilfering, hooliganism and a number of other petty offences. They are reported to have coopted 2.6 million people to their activities in 1980. Other voluntary bodies include residential committees (which play a mainly mobilisational role) and volunteer councils supplementing local council services. Mention should also be made of the trade unions, which in the early 1930s became in effect an extension of the state apparatus, and have retained that position up to the present. The most prominent function of Soviet trade unions has been to administer holiday and other welfare benefits. Trade union activists have thus become in the main a reserve of free labour for the welfare state.

Petitioning

In addition to the cooptation of volunteer labour into the agencies of administration and control, a number of channels have been established through which individuals can submit proposals and complaints to the authorities – in particular through the party and the press. The leadership under Brezhnev gave much attention to this procedure at the end of the 1970s, when a deteriorating economic situation and growing levels of corruption created considerable tension between officialdom and those citizens who were excluded from informal networks of privilege. For example, in 1978 the Central Committee of the party set up a letters department in order to deal with citizens' complaints that had come up against a brick wall lower down in the hierarchy.

Numerous press reports at the end of the 1970s and early 1980s showed that it was very difficult to make a complaint stick. Employees who took their 'controlling' responsibilities seriously and blew the whistle on corruption could expect rapid retribution, whatever bold words Moscow might be saying about the fight against abuses. Under Brezhnev local officials achieved an unprecedented degree of protection, and even if the centre made a declaration of support for an aggrieved citizen this hardly ever had serious repercussions for the official concerned. Nonetheless the petitioning mechanism seems to have served an important political purpose. The complainant had little chance of success, but the occasional success story could create the impression that Moscow was defending the ordinary citizen against the iniquitous behaviour of the local elite.

These different forms of popular participation have established many ties between the Soviet state and the population, drawing a significant section of citizens into the orbit of state-supervised agencies of administration and control. It can be argued that, taken together with certain other features of the system – in particular security of employment – they gave the Brezhnev regime a definite stability. What this meant in terms of popular attitudes is very hard to say in the absence of relevant research. A very carefully constructed survey of 2,793 Soviet emigres, carried out in the USA in 1983 by the Soviet Interview Project, did not suggest any acute sense of dissatisfaction with the Soviet way of life or with Soviet official values, even in a highly skewed sample of mainly Jewish, urban and well-educated people (see Millar, 1987). Only 43 per cent of the motives for emigration mentioned were political (as opposed to family, religious or economic motives); there was considerable support for state-controlled industry and a national health system (though strong support for private agriculture), and general satisfaction with jobs and housing (though not with consumer goods and services). Since the level of dissatisfaction in this sample could be assumed to be greater than among the wider population, it does not suggest that the high levels of formal participation concealed strong strands of popular sentiment hostile to the Soviet state and way of life.

However, it is also clear that under Brezhnev the Soviet regime was undergoing a loss of political authority as well as economic vitality. In the Stalin period the traditional model of guided participation had enabled the state to push through a process of rapid economic and social transformation. But it became increasingly ineffective in harnessing social energies. Mass membership of social and voluntary organisations allowed for the cooptation and reward of loyal citizens but 'criticism from below' had become a toothless affair as the *nomenklatura* gained an unprecedented degree of security under the Brezhnev leadership. The political and administrative elite was effectively beyond criticism. At the same time, guided participation, since it kept all social initiative in the hands of the leadership, encouraged a spreading apathy and cynicism about official values. This theme will be explored in the next section.

Challenging the Traditional Model

Perestroika is a response to crisis. From one vantage point the source of the crisis is economic: it lies in the failure of the command economy to meet its historical promises. Yet the economic crisis is at the same time a political and ideological crisis, which has placed democratisation at the centre of the banner of reform. The Brezhnev regime, though it maintained a kind of social peace and successfully squeezed out most dissident political activity, brought official values increasingly into disrepute. Political life became ritualised to a degree, with an enormous emphasis on outward political loyalty rather than inner belief. This did not, as we have suggested, create an 'anti-Soviet' public. But it did produce a systematic gulf between publicly declared values and private attitudes, a gulf that was increased by the glaring contrast between publicly stated collectivist values and the reality of growing corruption during the Brezhnev years.

The loss of political vitality was seen very clearly by many people in the 1970s as a threat to the future of the Soviet state. However, it was only in the dissident literature that the costs of Soviet authoritarianism were spelt out. A striking example was an open letter by Andrei Sakharov and others to the leadership in 1970, a letter which contained almost every item that was later to appear on the Gorbachev agenda (see Sakharov, 1974, pp. 116–34). The authors spoke of an 'urgent need to carry out a series of measures directed towards the further democratisation of our country's public life', stressing in particular the 'very close connection between the problem of technological and economic progress' and 'the problems of freedom of information, the open airing of views and the free clash of ideas'. Limitations on freedom of information made the leadership unaccountable and undermined all social initiative. The resulting loss of trust between politicians and the intelligentsia was particularly damaging. By contrast a course towards democratisation 'would inspire a wave of enthusiam comparable to that which prevailed in the 1920s'.

Such warnings were framed largely in terms of the dangers of a deteriorating relationship between the intelligentsia and the state, and the authors were careful not to question the principle of the leading role of the party. They were nonetheless ignored by the party leadership, although the leadership itself expressed concern about growing social apathy in the 1970s. The party did offer some limited support for public opinion studies (in particular research on the impact of the mass media), and issued a series of injunctions about the ideological state of the nation. However, the concept of public opinion that came to prevail was one that declared public opinion an instrument of social management. The aim was to bring popular attitudes into line with the wisdom of the political leadership, which could decide when public opinion was right and wrong. A competing conception, which had emerged in sociological writing in the late 1960s, saw public opinion as having a legitimate and independent status in relation to official ideology and as something to which public policy should respond. But this conception was squeezed out after an onslaught by the party on innovative social science in the early 1970s.

The Gorbachev era opened with strong attacks on the Brezhnev years, highlighting the loss of political vitality during the period of 'stagnation'. The sense of a crisis of political confidence was spelt out by Gorbachev in his book *Perestroika* (1987). The authorities had maintained a façade of economic success and had encouraged 'eulogising and servility' while ignoring the needs and opinions of the general public. But the pretence of a 'problem-free' reality backfired: 'a breach had formed between word and deed, which bred public passivity and disbelief in the slogans being proclaimed. It was only natural that this situation resulted in a credibility gap: everything that was proclaimed from the rostrums and printed in newspapers and textbooks was put in question' and 'all honest people saw with bitterness that people were losing interest in social affairs'.

The political reforms of the second half of the 1980s have begun to create the conditions for new forms of political participation. In 1985–6, when *glasnost'* was on everybody's lips, the main thrust of change was towards an improvement in the relationship between the political leadership and the intelligentsia through a radical loosening of restrictions on public discussion. From 1987 onwards, under the banner of democratisation, a more fundamental questioning of the inherited political system began. The introduction of multi-candidate elections and the establishment of a sitting parliament (the Supreme Soviet) have introduced a degree of political choice and accountability, while the strong emphasis on legal guarantees (the call for a 'law-based state') points to greater rights for individuals and groups that would make the moves towards democratisation more difficult to reverse (see Chapters 5 and 6). Meanwhile, in the most important development of all from the point of view of the culture of participation, there has been a rapid growth of 'informal' groups, standing outside the party-state apparatus, raising a variety of political, environmental and national issues. This development will be discussed in the next section.

To what extent these changes have affected public attitudes is hard to gauge. A survey of 200,000 readers of the weekly paper *Literaturnaya gazeta* in March 1989 gives an indication of the state of political involvement of a skewed (self-selected and relatively highly educated) sample. 1 per cent were either not interested in or did not understand politics; 10 per cent 'always participate in social and political life'; 7 per cent said that possibilities for participation had 'only just opened up'; 62 per cent felt that there was no chance of influencing political events; 33 per cent had 'defended their point of view' at party and trade union meetings; 28 per cent had signed collective appeals or protests; 22 per cent had written to newspapers; 9 per cent were involved in discussion clubs or societies; 4 per cent had attended demonstrations (excluding anniversaries); and 3 per cent had spoken at meetings or participated in the work of social associations.

These figures do not allow a comparison with an earlier period, but they do not suggest a state of political quiescence at the time of the survey. As soon as opportunities for unorchestrated participation and political choice emerged, they were taken up. The elections to the Congress of People's Deputies in March 1989 brought a huge vote for Yel'tsin against the official candidate, and the defeat of numerous local officials, including some who were standing unopposed (see Chapter 5). At the same time there are strong signs of dissatisfaction with the political reforms. For example in a poll reported by the Communist Youth newspaper *Komsomol'skaya pravda* in November 1988, 86 per cent of respondents were opposed to the indirect form of voting established for the Supreme Soviet, and 95 per cent thought that the president should be directly elected by the population, not by the Congress of People's Deputies. These figures point to a revolution of rising expectations started by the tentative experiments with a more competitive political process.

The urgency of the public discussion about a democratisation of the political system seems to reflect a serious crisis of political authority. The party still claims to unify society if not to exercise a 'leading role', but the form of authority based upon it is looking increasingly fragile. The role of the party is linked to its position as keeper of the sacrosanct (if changing) body of ideas called Marxism–Leninism. It is the special wisdom of the party, not its popular mandate, that provides the basis for the claim to a monopoly of power. 'Democratisation' brings a shift towards another language of legitimation. However, democracy is understood differently by different sections of Soviet opinion. The more conservative forces within political officialdom see it in terms of a mobilisation of support that would leave untouched the inherited political structure, and that would thus be carried out within the framework of the traditional forms of participation. The implementation of *perestroika* is a matter of rallying the troops around already-decided policies. For the radical reformers, on the other hand, *perestroika* promises a new relationship between state and society, new possibilities of political expression for a diversity of social interests. These differences will become clear when we look at official reactions to the informal movements.

The Development of Informal Groups

A radical reform of the Soviet political system is necessarily accompanied by changes in the patterns of participation, and that in turn is hard to envisage without an expansion in the scope of political activity for non-party groupings. A shift in this direction has occurred with the rapid development of 'informal' groups since Gorbachev's accession to the leadership, and especially since 1987. The term is used to refer to all manner of associations, ranging from sports and leisure clubs to Popular Fronts with far-reaching political platforms. It therefore conceals important differences. The label is nonetheless justified since these activities have all arisen out of initiatives by ordinary citizens, activities which are not supervised and controlled by the party-state apparatus in the way that has been customary for Soviet 'social' organisations in the past. The trade unions, for example, are defined as social organisations because they are not officially part of the state, yet in practice have acted as an extension of the party-state apparatus. The 'informals', although they have made a major political impact only in the Baltic republics, represent an important break with that tradition, bringing an element of social spontaneity of which the Soviet regime has in the past been mortally afraid. The extent of the change is reflected in the present serious worries about the consquences of the loss of the party's political monopoly.

In February 1988 it was estimated that there were 'more than 30,000' informal groups in the country, but this figure certainly increased thereafter. The great majority of members are young people, but in the case of the political groups youth can be taken to include anyone under 40. In late 1988 it was estimated that about 10 per cent of young people were active in an informal association, with another 5 per cent occasional members or supporters. Political groups, representing a variety of ideological currents (social-democratic, liberal, socialist, environmental, national) accounted for perhaps 10 per cent of all members.

The more politically-oriented clubs multiplied rapidly in 1987–8, taking advantage of a freer political climate to establish a position outside the party-state apparatus, raising a variety of national, ecological, social and human rights issues. The early political clubs – for example the Club for Social Initiatives, Citizen Dignity, *Perestroika*, Commune, Federation of Socialist Clubs, Democratic Union, Democracy and Humanism, Rescue, Council for the Ecology of Culture, Epicentre – were concentrated to begin with in the biggest cities (the clubs mentioned are Moscow or Leningrad-based), and drew their social support mainly from the intelligentsia. Thereafter there was an expansion of informal activity, especially in connection with growing environmental concerns. This drew in broader social strata and created a wider geographical presence. In 1988 and 1989 an increasing number of enterprises, ministries and local authorities were confronted with protests about high levels of environmental pollution. Mass activities (letter-writing campaigns, demonstrations and rallies), along with pressure from the scientific community and from environmental protection bodies, have helped to bring the environment to the front of the political agenda. In some cases popular action has brought a halt to production or speeded the introduction of anti-pollution measures.

All this is to be seen in the context of what are acknowledged to be alarming degrees of air and water pollution. According to Ministry of Health figures, the air in at least 104 Soviet cities is dangerous to breathe, and 50 per cent of the Soviet population is using water that does not come up to state standards. The consequences of a long period of unrestrained use of herbicides and chemical fertilisers, and a frequent absence of special waste sites, are now being felt. They have brought strong popular reactions in many Soviet cities, including Nizhnyi Tagil, Baku, Sumgait, Yerevan, Gorky, Yaroslavl and Kiev. In the town of Kirishi near Leningrad emissions from the Soviet Union's first bio-engineering plant are wreaking havoc with the health of the population. The incidence of bronchial asthma, for example, increased 35 times in the twelve years after the plant was built. Twelve thousand people out of a total population of 60,000 were said to have come out on to the streets in early 1988, and promises of improvement were made by the Minister for Bioindustry. In Ufa in 1988 the activities of the Social Council for Clean Air and Water were instrumental in getting a new chemical plant transferred beyond the boundaries of a city which already had three oil-refining plants and several chemical factories. This pattern of environmental activity is already a familiar part of the Soviet political scene.

The years 1988 and 1989 also saw dramatic developments in connection with nationalist activity, with the tide of Armenian protest action in support of a transfer of Nagorno-Karabakh to Armenia, and with the emergence of Popular Fronts in the Baltic republics of Estonia, Latvia and Lithuania. The development of the non-Russian Popular Fronts, discussed elsewhere in this volume, has brought a big challenge to the party's monopoly of power as well as to the management of national relations within the USSR (see Chapter 8).

Russian nationalism – partly in response to the demands of the minority nationalities – has also made a strong appearance within the political space opened up for informal groups. In its milder versions it is preoccupied with the preservation of Russian cultural and historical monuments and traditions. In the case of the *Pamyat'* association, national sentiment has taken the form of a virulent Russian chauvinism and anti-semitism. The emergence of extreme right political currents is thus part of the price to be paid for greater political openness – though there are different views about the potential of Russian nationalism as a political force.

Popular Fronts for Assistance to *Perestroika*, or organisations with similar names, have been set up in Moscow, Leningrad, Kiev, Lvov and a number of other cities. These have made less impact than the national groupings, but have been important in forming horizontal links and taking informal activity beyond the 'club' atmosphere of the early period. They played an important part in some cities in supporting alternative candidates during the 1989 elections for the Congress of People's Deputies.

All this open public activity, none of which was conceivable before Gorbachev, testifies to the erosion of the old political monopoly. It is not therefore surprising to find that the development of informal political groups is highly contested. There has been no shortage of hostile reactions, especially after the experience of the Armenia–Azerbaidzhan conflict over Nagorno-Karabakh and the explosive developments connected with the Baltic Popular Fronts. To the conservative-minded this activity appears dangerously anarchic. G.V. Kolbin, former head of the Kazakhstan party committee, while praising social initiatives on the environment and assistance from below with a variety of economic projects, warned in an interview in *Literaturnaya gazeta* in December 1988 that 'if one uses it [democracy] incorrectly one may go very far . . . When the party and soviet organs let slip from their hands control over the situation, then apolitical forces may get the upper hand'. In similar vein Alexander Vlasov, Chairman of the Council of Ministers of the RSFSR and candidate member of the Politburo, in a speech reported in *Pravda* in the same month, described centrifugal tendencies as possibly the 'greatest danger for our society':

Attempts to undermine the institutions of power, and moods of social nihilism must be countered by a policy of strengthening discipline and order in every way, of strengthening socialist statehood . . . We cannot permit a slide into anarchy and aimless holding of meetings.

These are the authentic voices of a conservative version of *perestroika*, with which the name of Ligachev has been closely associated. The fear is that if alternative political forces are allowed to operate, the party will lose its coherence and its authority may quickly evaporate. This came out clearly at a Central Committee plenum in April 1989, held soon after the elections to the new Congress of People's Deputies, at which numerous local party officials were defeated. There was a strong sense of unease about the election campaign itself, since local party organisations had been ill-prepared for it and simply did not know how to conduct it under the new conditions, thus often allowing non-party groups of one sort or another to exert an unwanted influence. *Perestroika*, said V.T. Saikin (chairman of the Moscow City Soviet), had started on the initiative of the party and 'this initiative must constantly remain in its hands'. 'Our party always had the right, and retains the right to be free from those who do not take its decisions and ideology, its world-view and politics into account.' Further:

For some reason a pluralism of views has been understood by some as the legal, open possibility of an indiscriminate denigration of socialist values, of all the achievements of socialism, of everything connected with the name of the communist party . . . in this direction a veritable mass attack on the heart and soul of the people is being carried out.

These conservative voices are not averse to popular participation in *perestroika*. Rather they want to ensure that it stays within the accustomed framework of political mobilisation. This frame of reference is likely to find a strong echo among wider sections of the Soviet population which are likely to equate 'freedom' with 'anarchy'. At a public meeting organised by some of the Moscow political clubs in May 1988, I overheard a bystander complain vociferously, before she had a chance to find out what the meeting was about, that such an event was 'not nice in our society', it was 'not normal'. In other words, it was acceptable for 'them' (in the West) to have such meetings, but here it was a sign of unwanted disorder and lack of respect for authority. This perception of things is undoubtedly very widespread, especially among the older generation. However, that is not to say that the equation of freedom and anarchy is an unchangeable national trait.

On the other side, the new non-party groups have been welcomed by the radical wing of the Soviet establishment as a fund of social enthusiam and ideas. That response has been well-articulated by Tat'yana Zaslavskaya, an influential reformist figure within the social science establishment. In an interview with the government paper *Izvestiya* at the end of 1988 she stressed that the 'striving for independent activity [and] direct participation in social life' was a vital element of *perestroika*. *Perestroika* would inevitably bring social conflict. If the conflict was to be successfully managed the political leadership would have to learn to enter into a genuine dialogue with independent social organisations, while maintaining public order in the face of the activities of 'chauvinistic, nationalistic and even fascist groups'. The same point was made more strongly by I. Vinogradov in an important collection of essays by radical reformers published in 1988 under the title *Inogo ne dano* (*There Is No Alternative*):

> We must inevitably come round to the idea of providing social organis-
> ations and unions – whether 'formal' or 'informal' – with *political* rights,
> fully and 'formally' entrenched in law and guaranteed by the possibility
> of recourse to the public and society through their own press and other
> media. Among [the rights given to social organisations would be] the
> right to form voting coalitions, to promote their own electoral
> programmes.

The conflicting pressures can be seen in arguments over the legal status of voluntary associations. The question is whether a new law, due to be published in 1990, will allow for 'self-registration' of associations, allowing access to printing and other facilities, or whether the local authorities are to decide if a club is worthy of registration and thus of entering the political arena. A decree on meetings and demonstrations, promulgated without public dis-cussion in July 1988, gives an idea of the likely shape of the new law. The decree details the right to demonstrate which was only vaguely stated in the constitution, but it also allows the local soviets to prohibit meetings whose purpose is deemed 'contrary to the USSR Constitution'. Such a formulation would allow for a variety of interpretations, depending on the current play of political forces.

Conclusions

The character of political participation is defined by the political culture of which it is part. In the Soviet Union it has been moulded by the efforts of the state to draw citizens into the process of administering state policies and controlling the apparatus from below. The Soviet Union has no doubt been able to boast higher numbers of 'participants' than Western liberal democracies. Furthermore the mobilisation and cooptation of a large section of the population has provided an important source of political stability for the Soviet system. However, the regimented style of participation has also been a source of great weakness, helping to create a widespread sense of political apathy and cynicism. The Gorbachev leadership has recognised that, in order to introduce some dynamism into the system, it is vital to create conditions for *voluntary* participation in the political process. This is especially important given the weakness of the popular constituency for economic reform, which so far has brought no tangible results for the great majority of the population. In this setting the role of non-party groups and organisations, standing outside the control of the established political apparatuses, becomes vital. The creation of a bigger political space for the non-party forces (including the 'informals'), if not for an official political opposition, is not a luxury. It is a necessary condition for the development of a strategy of reform and strengthening social support for it.

At the same time the expansion of such participation undermines the monopoly of political power on which the Soviet system has rested for seventy years, while the social tensions engendered by reform threaten to create serious political instability. In the short term this may benefit the more conservative political forces because the difficulties and disruption can be laid at the door of the radical reformers. However, the forces that have been unleashed will be very difficult to press back into the bottle. If the Soviet Union is to find a new economic as well as political vitality, it is essential for the system to find ways of accommodating greater social spontaneity and a less interventionist role for the party in economy and society. Alternative scenarios involving new forms of authoritarianism can also be imagined, especially in the event of a major economic crisis. The direction of political change, however, points towards the halting emergence of a new relationship between the Soviet state and its citizens in which changing patterns of participation will play a vital part.

8

The Nationalities

ZVI GITELMAN

Westerners often say 'Russia' when they mean the Soviet Union. Much to his embarrassment, Mikhail Gorbachev did the same while visiting Kiev, capital of the Ukraine, in June 1985, three months after becoming leader of the Communist Party of the Soviet Union. In the years following he has certainly become painfully aware that the country over which he presides is a multinational one and that many people are acutely conscious and proud of their nationality, to use the Soviet term, or ethnicity, a roughly equivalent term more often used in the West.

In 1926, when the first Soviet census was taken, there were 178 officially recognised nationalities. By 1979 their number had declined to 101, but when the results of the 1989 census are published in full they are likely to enumerate 128 nationalities. The number of nationalities at any given time is thus a function both of their own shifting demographics as well of government decisions about how to classify peoples. In 1989 there were 23 ethnic groups with populations over one million. Fifteen of them have Soviet republics named after them, and they are the majority of the population in all but one of those republics. As discussed in Chapter 5, the Union of Soviet Socialist Republics is a federal state. In addition to the fifteen republics it comprises 20 'autonomous republics', smaller units within four of the larger republics (16 of the 20 'autonomous republics' are in the largest republic, the Russian Soviet Federated Socialist Republic, RSFSR). Unlike the union republics, the autonomous republics do not have the legal right to secede from the USSR, but their official languages are those of the majority indigenous nationality. Smaller nationalities have autonomous national regions (*oblasti*). There are eight of these regions.

137

The smallest nationality unit is the national district (*okrug*), of which there are ten. The numbers of these units, including the republics, has fluctuated over the years, reflecting border changes and changes in Soviet nationality policy.

Russians constitute barely half of the Soviet population (50.8 per cent in 1989), and their proportion has been slowly declining. Some observers have concluded that once the Russians slip below 50 per cent, as they are likely to do before the end of the century, their unquestioned political, economic, and cultural dominance will be threatened. But there is no magic about being slightly more or slightly less than half the population. It should be remembered that in 1897, the year of the first comprehensive tsarist Russian census, and a period when Russians ruled over all other nationalities with no pretence at sharing power, they constituted only 44 per cent of the population. Nevertheless, some Russians are apprehensive about the prospect of their becoming a statistical minority in the country, though they will long remain the single largest nationality. In any case, together with the Belorussians and Ukrainians, the other two major Slavic nationalities, Russians constitute almost 70 per cent of the total population.

Between 1979 and 1989, while the Russian population was growing by 5.6 per cent, the Belorussians by 6, and the Ukrainians by only 4.2, four Central Asian nationalities were growing between 33 and 46 per cent. Another major Asian nationality, the Kazakhs, grew by a more modest 24 per cent, still four times the Russian rate. These differential growth rates mean that by the year 2000, 20 per cent or so of the Soviet population, already the fifth largest Muslim population in the world, will be of Muslim background. Later in this chapter we shall explore some of the political, economic, cultural and military implications of these ethnically differentiated growth rates.

The ethnic heterogeneity of the USSR naturally brings with it cultural diversity. There are significant numbers of people whose traditions, if not their current practices, are Russian Orthodox, Uniate, Protestant, Catholic, Muslim, Jewish, and Buddhist, among others. Georgians and Armenians have ancient and independent Christian churches. There are five alphabets in current use – Cyrillic, Latin, Hebrew, Georgian and Armenian – and there used to be more. About 130 languages are officially recognised by the state. They range across a wide variety of linguistic groups, and some are unique to the USSR. Some of the nationalities have been historic enemies, others historic allies, and still others have had little contact with each other. The life styles of Soviet peoples range from nomadic peoples of the far north-east of the country, related and

TABLE 8.1   *The major Soviet nationalities, 1989*

	Census population, 1989 (millions)	*% of total*	*Linguistic group*	*Traditional religion*
The Slavs				
Russians	145.1	50.8	East Slavic	Russian Orthodox
Ukrainians	44.1	15.5	East Slavic	Russian Orthodox*
Belorussians	10.0	3.5	East Slavic	Russian Orthodox
The Balts				
Latvians	1.5	0.5	Baltic	Protestant
Lithuanians	3.1	1.1	Baltic	Roman Catholic
Estonians	1.0	0.4	Finno-Ugrian	Protestant
The Caucasian Peoples				
Georgians	4.0	1.4	Karvelian	Georgian Orthodox
Armenians	4.6	1.6	Indo-European	Armenian Orthodox
Azerbaidzhanis	6.8	2.4	Turkic	Muslim (Shi'ite)
The Central Asians				
Uzbeks	16.7	5.8	Turkic	Muslim (Sunni)
Kazakhs	8.1	2.9	Turkic	Muslim (Sunni)
Tadzhiks	4.2	1.5	Iranian	Muslim (Sunni)
Turkmenis	2.7	1.0	Turkic	Muslim (Sunni)
Kirgiz	2.5	0.9	Turkic	Muslim (Sunni)
Others				
Moldavians	3.4	1.2	Romance	Romanian Orthodox

Source: Soviet census data and standard reference works.
Note:
* There is a substantial Roman Catholic (Uniate) minority in the Western Ukraine.

similar to North American Eskimos, to the Turkic peoples of Central Asia, to the Northern European types found in Estonia and Karelia, and many others.

Perhaps it is almost inevitable that in such a diverse country ethnic issues should play a major role in politics, as nationalities vie for recognition, resources, and representation. Until recently, Soviet politicians and scholars claimed that nationality conflicts had diminished to the point that the 'nationalities question' had been definitively solved, and the ethnic diversity of the country was yielding to a unity which would approach and eventually reach homogeneity. Like other dogmas long proclaimed as scientific truth, this one has been called into question both by policies of *glasnost'* and by dramatic events which seemed to contradict official beliefs. In fact, the nationality question is presently one of the most sensitive and troublesome. How it is handled will play a major role in determining the fate of the present reforms and the leadership proposing them. It would not be an exaggeration to say that the nationalities are testing the viability of the system as presently constituted. The system's future may depend to a considerable extent on whether or not most of the non-Russians will feel themselves accommodated in a reformed Soviet system.

The Ethnic Map of the USSR

There are several families and groups of nations and nationalities in the USSR. The three large Slavic nations inhabit the European, western part of the country, though members of all three have migrated eastwards and southwards over the centuries. The Russian Republic, by far the largest in the Union, stretches from Europe across Siberia and out to the Pacific Ocean, just across the water from Japan. Over 82 per cent of the 145 million Russians (1989 figure) live in the RSFSR. Ukraine is about one and a half times as large as neighbouring Poland, the largest country in Eastern Europe, and with its more than 50 million people is comparable to some of the largest countries of Western Europe. Ukraine is an important centre of both industry and agriculture. About 85 per cent of the 44 million Ukrainians live in the Ukrainian republic, the western part of which was annexed from Poland in 1939. Aside from Ukrainians, Russians and Jews constitute significant proportions of the urban population of Ukraine. Belorussia is considerably smaller than Ukraine, with a population of just over 10 million. Historically, Belorussian national consciousness and literature were not as developed as their Ukrainian counterparts. Western Belorus-

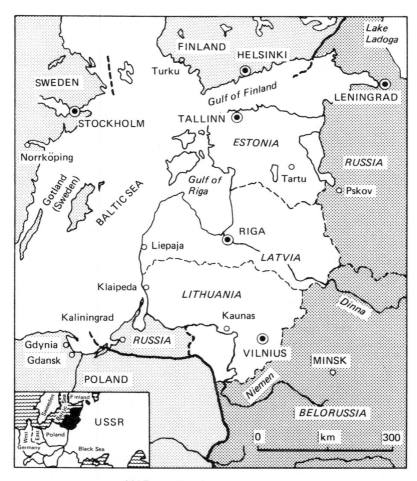

MAP 2 *The Baltic Republics*

sia, which used to have a mixed population of Russians, Poles, Belorussians, Jews and others, was also annexed from Poland in 1939.

The three Baltic republics, Latvia, Lithuania and Estonia, also were 'latecomers' to the Soviet Union, assigned to it in secret protocols of the Nazi–Soviet treaty of August 1939. Red Army troops moved into these countries and ensured that the 'elections' held shortly thereafter would show the great majority of the local populations asking to join the USSR. Exactly fifty years later, on

23 August 1989, two million people in the three republics joined hands in a human chain symbolising their protest at being forced to join the USSR, an act that would have been unthinkable twenty, ten, or even five years earlier. Estonia has less than two million inhabitants, ethnic Estonians constituting 65 per cent of the republic. The Estonian language is related to Finnish. This, together with Estonia's location and Protestant heritage, have made that republic more attuned to Western culture than perhaps any other. The Estonian legislature, in 1988 and 1989, adopted legislation which goes further than any other republic in asserting Estonian cultural, economic and even political autonomy. National feelings run so high here that many Russians are reluctant to speak Russian in Estonia, though Russian is the *lingua franca* of the entire country.

Latvia also has a Protestant heritage and a language that is unrelated to any other Soviet language except Lithuanian. About 54 per cent of the republic's population of some 2.6 million are ethnic Latvians. Here, too, a militant movement to wrest autonomy or even independence from the USSR has surfaced in the last few years.

Unlike the other two Baltic states, Lithuania has a Catholic background and was historically associated with Poland, though the two nations fought over possession of the present capital of Lithuania, Vilnius. The result was that the city was in Poland, where it was called Wilno, between the two world wars. A higher proportion of the population than in the other two Baltic states – about four-fifths – belongs to the indigenous nationality, and the rate of population growth is higher. Religion plays a greater role in Lithuania and buttresses national sentiment. Until the Holocaust, Lithuania was one of the most important Jewish cultural centres. Like the Latvians and Estonians, Lithuanians organised a national movement, called Sajudis, in 1988. It has led the fight to gain autonomy from Moscow and managed to elect three-quarters of the delegates from Lithuania to the new national Congress of People's Deputies which began to meet in May 1989. More controversially, its Communist Party voted for an independent status within the CPSU in December 1989.

The Caucasus mountains are inhabited by a great variety of nationalities with different religious and cultural traditions. The major nationalities, each of whom has a republic, are Armenians, Azerbaijanis and Georgians. The Armenian and Georgian languages are old and unique, as are their Christian churches. Azerbaijanis are Muslim and related to peoples in Iran and Turkey. The Armenian republic serves as a magnet for the large Armenian diaspora. Of all the republics, Armenia has the highest percentage of its population (90) made up of the titular nationality. It is ethnically the most homogeneous republic, although nearly two million Armenians live outside Armenia, where 2.8 million reside. Georgia has a larger population, over 5 million, and nearly 70 per cent of the population is Georgian. This republic has long had the reputation of being economically more independent and enterprising than the others. Armenians and Georgians, who have not always enjoyed the friendliest relations, have long been among the most educated nationalities and hence well represented in the national intelligentsia and in the economic and, at times, the political, elites. Nearly 6 million of the 7 million inhabitants of Azerbaijan are Azeris. In 1988–9 Armenians living in the Nagorno-Karabakh region of Azerbaijan protested against what they viewed as cultural deprivation and Azeri discrimination against them. Armenians in the home republic supported them, violence broke out, the two republic legislatures passed opposing resolutions about the proper jurisdiction under which Nagorno-Karabakh should fall, and a major ethnic, constitutional and political crisis ensued. The central leadership temporised by placing Nagorno-Karabakh under the direct jurisdiction of the federal government in Moscow, thus avoiding a decision as to which republic had the stronger claim to the region.

There are five republics in Central Asia: Uzbekistan, Turkmenistan, Kirgizia, Tajikstan, and Kazakhstan. The titular nationalities are all Muslim in background, and all the peoples but the Tajiks, who are of Persian stock, are Turkic. Some were nomads until forcibly settled by the Soviets, and nearly all were illiterate at the time of the revolution. Their alphabets and literacy were given to these peoples by the Soviets, partly out of a desire to socialise them politically through written media. Like the Caucasus, these areas had come under Russian rule before the revolution as a result of tsarist imperialism and wars that Russia had fought with her neighbours. All these peoples have high fertility rates: for example, in recent years, when fertility among Slavs was 13 per thousand, among Tajiks and Uzbeks it was 45 per thousand. Despite migration to their republics by Europeans, the proportion of indigenous nationalities in the population has grown because of this high birth rate. Only in Kazakhstan is the titular nationality less than half the population, 36 per cent in 1979, up from 30 per cent in 1959. The implications of the region's demography will be discussed later in this chapter.

There is a diversity of other territorial groups. The Moldavians, living in the southern part of the European USSR, are very closely related to the neighbouring Romanians, though, in order to justify their annexation of the area from Romania in 1940, the Soviets

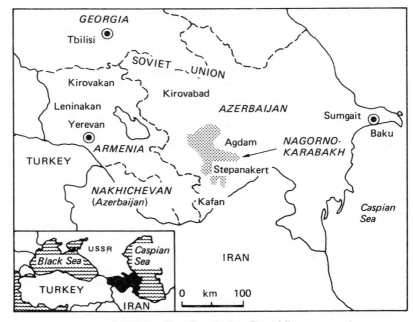

MAP 3   *The Caucasian Republics*

have insisted that the Moldavians are a distinct nationality. To widen the differences, the Soviets changed the Moldavian alphabet from Latin (Romanian and Moldavian are Romance languages) to Cyrillic (a decision that was reversed in 1989). The Buryats and Kalmyks are Mongolian by language and culture and Buddhist and Shamanist by religion. Yakuts and Chukchi are Siberian peoples, while the Turkic-speaking Tatars are Muslims by tradition.

Finally, non-territorial nationalities include Germans, Jews, and Poles, as well as smaller groups of Magyars (Hungarians), Greeks, Bulgars, Kurds and others. The two million Germans, some of whose ancestors came at the invitation of Catherine the Great to improve Russian agriculture, used to have an autonomous republic in the Volga River region but were deprived of it and forcibly exiled at the beginning of the Second World War when Joseph Stalin presumed they would collaborate with the Nazis. Germans were settled mostly in Kazakhstan and other parts of Central Asia, as well as in the Baltic. In the 1970s and 1980s over 100,000 Germans emigrated, almost all to the Federal Republic of Germany. Only in 1989 did articles begin to appear in the Soviet press which exonerated the Germans of the false accusations Stalin had made and which spoke sympathetically of their cultural and political demands. The 1.8 million Jews counted in the 1979 census are the most urbanised and educated nationality, but whereas they were once overrepresented in the government, party and military, for the last forty years they have been systematically excluded from the higher echelons of those hierarchies as well as from other positions where political loyalty or ideological considerations are important. Jews are the only nationality of any significant size who (until 1989) did not have a single school of their own. Since the late 1960s over 300,000 have emigrated, mainly to Israel and the United States. The Poles live mostly in Belorussia and Lithuania. Their linguistic assimilation is almost as complete as that of the Jews: only 14 per cent of the Jews and 29 per cent of the Poles listed their national language as their native one in the 1979 census.

Nationalities Policy: Ideology and History

Marx and Engels provided little guidance to their followers on how to deal with ethnic issues. The ideological forefathers of the Soviet state assumed that the fundamental cleavage in modern society was class, not ethnicity. They assumed that nations were an artificial construct of the capitalist epoch and that national sentiments were exploited by the bourgeoisie to pit one segment of the proletariat against another, thereby diverting workers from venting their spleen against the exploiting capitalists. It followed that in the classless society to be established after the socialist revolution nations would disappear as they no longer served any useful social and economic purpose. This theory did not prevent Marx and Engels from taking sides in the national disputes of their day or even exhibiting personal prejudices in regard to races and nationalities.

Lenin began thinking about nationalities issues from an orthodox Marxist point of view. He severely criticised the Jewish Labour Bund in the Russian Empire which had borrowed the concept of 'national-cultural autonomy' from Marxists in another multi-national empire, the Austro–Hungarian one. This provided for the right of nationalities to administer their own cultural institutions and make independent decisions in the cultural sphere even after the advent of socialism. Lenin rejected even more decisively the Bund's proposal that the Russian Social-Democratic Labour Party, from which the Bolsheviks emerged, allow the formation of national groupings within it which would deal with the cultural affairs of the respective nationalities. The Bolshevik leader felt that such concessions to the nationalities would divert attention from the overall objective, the overthrow of tsarism.

In the years before the revolution Lenin came to appreciate how sensitive and important the nationalities issue was in the tsarist empire, sometimes called the 'prisonhouse of nations'. He realised that ethnic issues were among the major grievances many people felt against the tsarist system, and was flexible enough to modify his earlier positions in order to make tactical use of these grievances. Thus, he conceded that geographically compact and distinct national groups might be granted territorial autonomy within a socialist structure. After the revolution he agreed to the establishment of a Commissariat of Nationalities, headed by Joseph Stalin, himself a Georgian, and even to the creation of nationality sections within the Bolshevik Party. Once the Bolsheviks reconciled themselves to at least the temporary existence of a state – ultimately, it was supposed to 'wither away' – they agreed to organise it along federal lines in order to meet the demands of the nationalities. In the course of the revolution and the civil war, several areas that had been wholly or partly in the Russian empire – Poland, Finland, the Baltic states – managed to break away from the Russian-dominated state. Others which attempted to do so – Ukraine, Georgia, Armenia, for example – were forcibly reincorporated into the USSR, successor state to the Russian empire.

In the 1920s the Soviet leadership declared that Russian chauvinism was the main problem in nationality relations and that the non-Russians, having been discriminated against for so long, should be assisted in developing their cultures. This would not contradict the ultimate Marxist–Leninist goal of the disappearance and amalgamation of nations, because if one thought 'dialectically' one would appreciate that oppressed nationalities needed to have their cultures flourish first in order to realise that this was not the main purpose of their existence. Once having maximised their cultural freedom, the nationalities could then move on to mutual assimilation. The concrete application of this paradoxical idea came in the policy of *korenizatsiya*, 'nativisation' or indigenisation. That meant that members of the non-Russian nationalities were encouraged to take government and party posts; schools in their languages were set up and vigorously promoted; courts, trade unions, and even party cells were encouraged to operate in the local languages; and the press, theatre, research institutes and other cultural organisations operating in the local languages were supported by the state. It was during this period of the 'flowering of the nationalities' that the peoples of Central Asia, many of whom were organised along tribal and clan lines, were given national status and written languages. This was the heyday of ethnic pluralism and cultural development.

When Stalin began his drive to modernise and industrialise the country as quickly as possible, he tried to shift all energies toward that goal. By the early 1930s the goal of promoting national cultures yielded to the overarching aim of rapid industrial development at any cost. What had been laudable efforts to develop national cultures just a few years before now became 'petit bourgeois nationalist deviations'. Cultural and political leaders of the nationalities were arrested and often killed. Cultural institutions were purged, closed down, or allowed to disappear by attrition. Parents became fearful of sending their children to national schools and many hesitated even to speak their native languages. Stalin declared that the cultures of the USSR were to be 'national in form, socialist in content'. That meant that ideological uniformity was to be imposed on all cultures, and only the linguistic and other forms of culture were to be preserved. Indeed, all of Soviet culture became subject to a deadly uniformity and conformity. At the same time, there were many who genuinely believed that the epoch of flourishing national cultures had passed and that it was time to move on to a more 'internationalist' mode. Marriages among peoples of different nationalities became more common. As people streamed from the countryside to the city, driven both by the horrors of collectivisation and the lure of modernity, they began to lose their traditional ways of life, native languages, distinctive dress, foods, and styles of life. Russian was the common language of the cities, housing and food became more uniform, and many began to abandon their former cultures.

Already in the 1930s, but certainly in the next decade, Stalin stressed the historical and contemporary qualities of the Russian people and made it clear that they were to be regarded as the 'elder brother' of all other peoples. During the war the Russian Orthodox church, severely persecuted in the two preceding decades, was revived. Historic Russian heroes were lauded, and the message was sent that the war was being fought to defend historic Russia as much as it was to safeguard the Soviet system. Simultaneously, several peoples, among them the Germans, Crimean Tatars, Chechen and Ingush, were deported *en masse* on the grounds that they had intended to collaborate with the German invaders or had actually done so. Collective punishment was meted out for what were often individual crimes.

In his victory toast in the Kremlin in 1945 Stalin singled out the *Russian* people for especial praise, and in the following years Russians were given credit for all kinds of inventions and achievements that properly belonged to people of other nations. This was part of a militant anti-Western and 'anti-cosmopolitan' campaign which sought to isolate the Soviet population from the world outside and which singled out the Jews, especially, as aliens and potential or actual traitors. The 'flowering of the nationalities' seemed long forgotten.

In his 'secret speech' to the 20th Party Congress in 1956, Nikita Khrushchev criticised Stalin for many crimes, including some – but not all – that had been perpetrated against the nationalities. Though Khrushchev curtailed some of Stalin's excesses in regard to the nationalities and opened up the elite to Ukrainians and some others he was not especially sympathetic to ethnic claims, having been Stalin's party secretary in Ukraine at the height of the purges. Khrushchev launched a vigorous campaign against religions, which indirectly impinged on several nationalities associated strongly with certain religions. In 1958 he initiated an educational reform which eliminated the required study of the native language in the non-Russian regions. His plan to divide the country into economic regions, known as *sovnarkhozy*, threatened to diminish the importance of the national republics.

Under Khrushchev's successor, Brezhnev, dissident nationality movements, among others, began to be more visible. Crimean Tatars demanded to return to their ancestral homeland in the USSR while Jews and Germans demanded to return to theirs outside it. Lithuanian Catholics pressed for religious and cultural concessions, as did Ukrainians. Brezhnev doggedly asserted, however, that the nationalities question had been solved definitively and that the protestors were deviants and criminals who should be punished accordingly – and many were. During the period of detente in the early 1970s, in order to improve relations with Germany and the United States, relatively large numbers of Germans and Jews, and later Armenians, were permitted to emigrate. However, many were denied permission to leave the country and were imprisoned or harrassed for their efforts to do so. In the 1970s also the concept of a 'Soviet people' was developed and widely promoted. According to one Soviet scholar, Academician P.N. Fedoseev, this was not a nation or an ethnic entity but 'a new historical form of social and international unity of people of different nations' which eliminated antagonistic relations between classes and nations and was based on 'the flowering and drawing together of nations'. It remained unclear whether this 'Soviet nation' was ultimately to replace the peoples of the Soviet Union, though this was presumably the intention.

The official doctrine explaining the present and future of the nationalities was for a long time and until recently encapsulated in the two terms, *sblizhenie* and *sliyanie*. The former means the 'drawing together', or rapprochement, of peoples, while the latter means their fusion into each other, or amalgamation. The two are presumed to exist in a sequential and causal relationship. That is, over time *sblizhenie* will lead to *sliyanie*, because as nations mingle with each other they will lose their specific characteristics and assimilate into one another. The prospect of fusion and loss of identity frightened those who cherished their particular cultures, but they were reassured that *sliyanie* was a rather distant prospect. Both components of the formula have come under empirical scrutiny and serious questioning in recent years, though no alternative formulation has yet emerged.

Regarding *sblizhenie*, Soviet commentators now admit that nationalism and ethnic prejudices and tensions exist in Soviet society. These evils were usually dismissed as 'survivals of the past' but, as one high official of an autonomous republic put it, the great majority of Soviet citizens today were born after the revolution, so how can the fiction of 'survivals' be maintained? It is suggested that nationalism exists because peoples' consciousness changes more slowly than the reality in which they live and because some peoples entered the USSR relatively recently and have not been fully resocialised. Moreover, religion survives and reinforces national exclusivity, and 'bourgeois elements' outside the country try to fan ethnic tensions. Furthermore, 'subjective' factors must be taken into account: insensitive bureaucrats insult people on an ethnic basis or attempt to hasten assimilation 'artificially'.

Soviet ethnographers discovered several years ago that national consciousness was not fading, as the theory had predicted, but was growing. Indeed, Gorbachev told the 19th Party Conference in 1988 that 'The development of our multinational state is, naturally [sic], accompanied by a growth in national consciousness. This is a positive phenomenon'. As for *sliyanie*, the 1986 Party Programme says that the 'complete unity of nations' will take place 'in the remote historical future'. In a speech to scientists and 'cultural figures' in January 1989, Gorbachev stated, 'Of course, we cannot permit even the smallest people to vanish or the language of the smallest people to be lost, nor can we permit nihilism with respect to the culture, traditions and history of both large and small peoples'. In theory, at least, this is a far cry from Lenin and Stalin's assimilationism. The judgement that national consciousness has not faded, and has even grown among some peoples, is borne out by recent events in the USSR and by several surveys of recent emigres from that country.

Soviet Nationality Policy

The Soviet Union has brought dramatically higher standards of living to many of the peoples of the Caucasus and Central Asia. Industry and modern agriculture were brought to these areas by the Soviet government, along with higher standards of health and education. Still, it has recently been revealed by the USSR Minister of Health that nearly half the hospitals in Turkmenistan have no running water. Infant mortality is shockingly high in parts of Soviet Central Asia, and the USSR as a whole ranks thirty-second in the world, behind Barbados and Mauritius, in this respect. For many nationalities there have been trade-offs between higher standards of living and improved economies, on one hand, and the loss of some or even much of their traditional cultures and religion, on the other. Jews are perhaps an extreme example of this trade-off: the revolution liberated them from the Pale of Settlement, allowing them to live where they chose, and opened educational and vocational opportunities to them that had been denied to them by the tsars. At the same time their religious institutions were almost completely destroyed, they were denied the opportunity to study Hebrew, and later they were discriminated against in education, employment and culture. Ukrainians are an example of a nationality whose very existence was denied by the tsars but who received republic status from the Soviets, though they were denied independence. Great economic progress has been made in Ukraine, and Ukrainian cultural institutions have flourished. However, there has been steady pressure for Russification within Ukraine, and few opportunities in their native culture for Ukrainians living elsewhere. Like most multinational countries, the USSR has tried to balance the perceived needs of centre and periphery, though ever since the 1930s the centre's interests have taken precedence.

How have the central authorities controlled this heterogeneous and potentially fractious population? This has been accomplished with a mix of normative and coercive incentives and through structural devices. First, the spread of Marxist–Leninist ideology throughout the country imbues the ideologically committed or conforming with the conviction that 'all-Union' interests and those of the party take definite precedence over the 'narrow, parochial' interests of this or that nationality. They are also taught to believe that nationalism is an evil and that 'internationalist' attitudes and actions are the only ones admissible under socialism. Nations are, in any case, transient. Thus, political elites of the nationalities are generally chosen for their 'internationalist' outlooks in addition to any other attributes they may possess.

Secondly, the Communist Party is organised as a hierarchical, disciplined organisation in which orders flow from the top down and must be obeyed. This is the device which effectively weakens Soviet federalism and makes inoperative and constitutional right of the republics to secede. The logic of this device is the following: since the nation is represented by its leading class, and since the leading class of all Soviet nations is the proletariat, and since, furthermore, the party is the only authentic representative of that class, ultimately it is the party which decides whether a particular nation will secede or not. Because the party is centralised and hierarchical, no republic-level party organisation can unilaterally recommend secession.

A third control mechanism is the cooptation of native elites. Promising people are recruited into the party and imbued with an 'internationalist' world view. Those who aspire to higher education must in almost all cases have an excellent command of Russian, the language of most higher educational institutions. The peoples of the USSR are given the impression that, at least on the republic and lower levels, they are being ruled by people of the indigenous ethnic groups. Of the 44 republic party first secretaries in 1954–1976, over 86 per cent were non-Russians. At present, the first secretaries of all republics are members of the titular nationality of that republic. As we shall see, the political mobility of non-Russians seems to stop at the republic level, but perhaps most of the non-Russians do not aspire to run the country as a whole and are more concerned with running the affairs of their respective regions. During the eighteen years of the Brezhnev period, now labelled in the Soviet media the 'era of stagnation', republic leaders, particularly in Central Asia, were given considerable lattitude in running republican affairs, apparently in return for their acquiescence to national policy as formulated by the Slavic leadership in Moscow. This resulted in the creation of fiefdoms in which the local leaders' power was enormous. That power was used, according to the Soviet press today, to discriminate against national minorities, mainly Russians, in the republics. It also resulted in enormous corruption and nepotism, with several of the republics looking like the personal possessions of local bosses.

On the other hand, traditionally the second party secretary in the republics is not of the indigenous nationality and has usually been despatched from the central apparatus in Moscow. He is assumed by many to be the 'eyes and ears' of the centre. About two-thirds of the second secretaries from the mid-1950s up to 1976 were Russians or other Slavs. While the second secretary probably does not run things in the republic, he may at least exercise some influence over his superior.

The centre can also exercise great economic leverage on the republics. Investment and trade decisions are, like most economic decisions in the country, highly centralised. It is Moscow which decides, though not always unilaterally, what is to be built where and how much is to be invested around the country. There is considerable debate about whether the centre has equalised the distribution of wealth through its policies, or whether they have tended to favour some regions, and hence peoples, over others. Gorbachev's reforms promise that the republics will have a greater say in economic decisions. Thus, Belorussia is promised that by 1991 republic authorities will control the disposition of half the goods and services produced in their republic, whereas at present they control less than 10 per cent. The Baltic republics have been promised even greater control over their economies, the trade-off apparently being that, as the most economically successful republics, they will be showcases for Gorbachev's reforms.

A sixth instrument of central control is coercion as exercised by the militia (police), KGB and armed forces. The KGB played a major role in the repression of nationality dissent in the 1970s and early 1980s. The police are used to break up ethnic and other demonstrations. In especially serious instances the armed forces are called in. When large-scale violence broke out between Armenians and Azerbaijanis or between Uzbeks and Meskhetis in 1988–9 several thousand troops of the regular army were brought in. On quite a few occasions the threat of army intervention has been used to head off nationality demonstrations.

Finally, there are policies whose obvious aim is to hasten *sblizhenie*, or more concretely, to nudge the nationalities in the direction of Russianisation. The Russian language is clearly the favoured one. Though official doctrine speaks of the 'mutual enrichment of languages', in practice the other languages have taken much of their scientific, technological and political vocabulary from Russian, while the latter has borrowed little from them. As pointed out, the educational system is heavily slanted toward Russian. The armed forces operate exclusively in Russian and they are supposed to have a role in the teaching of Russian to those of other nationalities. As a greater and greater proportion of recruits comes from Central Asia, and since large numbers of rural Central Asians have only a rudimentary command of Russian, the army's role in teaching Russian will increase.

Perhaps the dominance of Russian is the only practical arrangement in such a multilingual country, but non-Russians complain that the media and publications are disproportionately weighted toward Russian. Publication data seem to bear them out. About 41 per cent of the Soviet people consider their native language to be one other than Russaian, but in 1983 only 23 per cent of the titles and 16 per cent of the total runs of books and brochures were in non-Russian languages. Still, among most nationalities there has been little erosion of native-language loyalty. That is, the proportions of people declaring the language of their people to be their 'mother tongue' (*rodnoi yazyk*) have changed very little over the decades, though this is not the case for the non-territorial nationalities. Over 90 per cent of most nationalities consider the language of their people to be their native or mother tongues. At the same time, there has been an impressive growth in the Russian-language facility of all peoples, though a leading Soviet ethnographer has recently complained that in some republics the older generation is more conversant with Russian than the younger. There is some debate over the extent to which bilingualism has been achieved, or is even desirable, but on the whole Soviet citizens of all nationalities are able to communicate with each other through Russian.

Russian's influence has been exercised even in what might be called alphabet policy. When written languages were invented for the Central Asians, the first script used was Arabic. For fear of the spread of pan-Arabism and other reasons this was changed to a Latin script, but by 1940 all of these languages had gone over to a Cyrillic script, the script of the Russian language. As mentioned above, even Moldavian was switched, after the incorporation of that republic, to Cyrillic.

Russianisation is also promoted by migration of Slavs to non-Slavic areas. Not only the Russians, but Ukrainians and Belorussians also, tend not to learn the local languages and use Russian as the common language of Europeans as well as with indigenous nationalities. Caucasians are quite mobile, but Central Asians tend to stick to their own republics, even eschewing movement from the countryside to the city. Thus, they can afford to remain basically monolingual, since the countryside has few Slavs. Baltic peoples have complained about the migration of Slavs to their republics as a result of industrialisation. Factories bring Slavic workers and managers, thereby diluting both the ethnic and linguistic character of the countries. For this reason one of the current demands of the national fronts in the Baltic is to give the republican governments the right to limit migration into the republics. Moreover, they are demanding that the indigenous languages be learned by all non-native speakers and that all official business be transacted in the indigenous languages.

Compared to many other multinational countries, irrespective of political system, the Soviet Union has been quite tranquil until recently. Certainly, when one thinks of Yugoslavia, Lebanon, Iraq, Nigeria, or even Canada and Belgium, the Soviet record in granting opportunities to nationalities and maintained peace among them looks quite good. It might fairly be asked, however, whether this was due more to actual and implied coercion or repression rather than to genuine harmony and cooperation. Now that the reins have been loosened Soviet nationality policy is being severely tested, and the results are not as encouraging as the leadership would like.

Current Issues and Developments

In line with his effort to make people work more efficiently and thereby improve the economy, Gorbachev has attacked the 'affirmative action' practices of his predecessors whereby indigenous peoples in the republics, especially in Asia and the Caucasus, were favoured for jobs, promotions, political appointments and places in higher educational institutions. The current position adopted in most Soviet commentary is that while 'affirmative action' might have been justified when some of the nationalities were culturally and economically behind the others, at present this is no longer the case and therefore a system of proportional representation of nationalities is unnecessary and harmful. Merit, not ethnicity, should be the criterion for employment, promotion, and education. The abuses of 'affirmative action' must be reversed.

Gorbachev's first attempt to implement these principles aroused violent opposition. In December 1986 he removed from office the First Secretary of the Kazakhstan Communist Party, Dinmuhammed Kunaev. Kunaev was old, notoriously corrupt, and a close ally of Leonid Brezhnev. It was not his removal but his replacement who aroused controversy. Instead of appointing a Kazakh to the post, the party named a Russian, Gennadi Kolbin. Mass demonstrations broke out in Alma Ata, the Kazakh capital, and there were casualties and arrests. In a break with the tradition of not reporting such embarrassing occurrences, the events received national media exposure. Gorbachev stuck to his guns and the media soon launched a general campaign against 'affirmative action' and corruption.

Pushing the campaign along, Gorbachev replaced all five first secretaries in the Asian republics, and later was to do the same in the other republics. A massive purge was set off in Uzbekistan.

Thousands of officials lost their jobs on charges of corruption and incompetence. Leonid Brezhnev's son-in-law, a Russian, was implicated in Asian corruption, tried and convicted in December 1988. Thus, the anti-corruption campaign was linked explicitly to the Brezhnev regime whose practices were now repudiated.

A different kind of challenge was presented by the Baltic states. In the course of 1988, organisations calling themselves 'popular fronts' were formed, which became the spokesmen for Estonian, Latvian and Lithuanian national interests. They demanded the right to regulate migration, to issue their own currency and establish representation abroad. They also demanded that the indigenous languages be made state languages and that all residents of the respective republics be required to learn them. The pre-war national anthems and flags of the republics, previously banned, were restored to public use. In Lithuania two cathedrals seized by the state in the 1940s were returned to the church. The Estonian legislature passed a law giving itself the right to veto legislation emanating from Moscow. Moscow rejected this law but chose not to make it a *cause célèbre*. To date, Gorbachev has expressed his disagreement with several of the Baltic positions and has rejected some of their demands, but in a non-confrontational way. Clearly, he wishes to avoid a crisis but at the same time he has signalled that there are limits beyond which the federal leadership will not be pushed.

In Belorussian and Moldavia more narrowly cultural demands have been heard. Though Belorussians were long considered the most Russianised nationality, the Belorussian intelligentsia began to press for schools in the Belorussian language, especially in the cities, and other measures to strengthen their language and culture. Moldavians protested in less benign ways, organising several mass demonstrations in the capital republic, Kishinev. They won from the party the concession that in time their language would be transferred back to Latin script. Moldavians echoed the Baltic nationalities in their demand that Moldavian be made the state language, there were also calls, following the overthrow of Nicolae Ceauşescu, for a closer association with neighbouring Romania.

In February 1988 the ancient historical dispute between Christian Armenians and Muslim Azerbaijanis, who had territorial claims on each other, flared into violence in the Nagorno-Karabakh enclave of Azerbaijan. The claims of the local, overwhelmingly Armenian population that they were being discriminated against and denied cultural facilities were supported in the Armenian republic. At least 36 people were killed in Armenian–Azerbaijani clashes. In the autumn there were further clashes and casualties. By the end of the year at least 91 people had been reported killed. Out of approximately 165,000 Azerbaijanis living in neighbouring Armenia, about 136,000 were reported to have fled the republic; 170,000 Armenians out of the nearly half a million in Azerbaijan had also fled. Thus, about 300,000 internal refugees were created by these clashes. There was more violence in the area later in the year. In April 1989, in another dispute, Abkhazians living in an autonomous republic within Georgia demanded a republic of their own and Georgians, in turn, demanded independence of the USSR in a series of mass demonstrations and hunger strikes. Troops called in to restore order killed twenty Georgians and the events became a subject of heated discussion in the Congress of People's Deputies. Later in the year fourteen people were killed in Abkhazian–Georgian clashes, and about 100 were killed in attacks by Uzbeks on Meskhetis, a Turkic minority who had been exiled by Stalin from Georgia to Central Asia. All told, by the end of 1989 there had been nearly 300 deaths in ethnic clashes.

There are several longer term issues that involve the nationalities. We have already alluded to the impact that economic decentralisation might have on republics and nationalities. If the Yugoslav experience is any indication, there are likely to be republics which will benefit from being cut loose from the centre's apron strings, and those whose economic position will worsen when the centre no longer subsidises the local economies to the same extent. The degree of centralisation and federal subsidisation, or federal transfer of assets from one republic to another, would be a major political issue in a reformed, decentralised Soviet Union.

A second issue which has already emerged and is likely to sharpen in the future is the linkage between ecological and national concerns. As publics grow more concered with environmental deterioration and dangers, they begin to feel that decision-makers in Moscow are locating industries or mines or making use of natural resources in the non-Russian areas without regard to their ecological consequences, partly out of indifference to the environmental impact outside the Russian lands. Baltic, Caucasian and Central Asian peoples are saying, in effect, 'it is *our* land that *you* are ruining'. There have been protests in the Baltic against mining operations which leave the countryside scarred; in Central Asia against the excessive pumping of the Aral Sea for irrigation, excessive spraying of pesticides, and successive plantings of cotton with no crop rotation or letting the land lie fallow; and demands in Ukraine and in the Caucasus that, following the Chernobyl nuclear plant disaster, no further nuclear stations be built. A plan to irrigate the parched lands of Central Asia by diverting Siberian rivers was shelved, in part because Russians protested against the violation of the Siberian landscape, which plays an important part in Russian nationalist mythology.

Demographic trends have put at least two important issues on the agenda. Present and future population growth is concentrated in Central Asia, whereas industry is concentrated in the European republics. There is considerable migration within the country, mostly of the rural-to-urban kind, but relatively little among the Asians. They are reluctant to leave their own republics and even to move from the countryside to the cities within those republics. So the Soviets cannot count on recruiting significant labour reserves to work in the European industries, though attempts in this direction are being made. Of course, if they were successful, another issue would arise: would the state be prepared to depart from its traditional policy and allow schools and other cultural institutions for Asians (and other non-indigenous peoples) outside their republics? This would be an expensive and complicated undertaking.

The logical alternative to moving Asians to Europe is to move industry to Asia. But the lack of water, usually thought of as a barrier to agriculture, is also a hindrance to the development of industry. The terrible depletion of Asian water sources and the cancellation of the Siberian river diversion seem to indicate that industrial development in Asia will be insufficient to absorb the large numbers of Asians seeking to enter the work force in the coming decades. Moreover, Soviet social scientists point out that many young Asians do not aspire to employment in industry.

The expansion of the Asian population also has implications for the military. An increasing proportion of draftees will be of Asian origin. Since they generally have lower educational levels than Europeans, and since their Russian is often rudimentary, they cannot be assigned to the more technologically advanced forces (rocketry, the air force and the navy). Already, they form a disproportionate number of those assigned to labour battalions, often not trained for combat and used as cheap labour on both military and civilian construction projects. The leadership of the armed forces has made it very clear that it does not want to see those forces stratified by nationality: Slavs overrepresented among the officers and non-commissioned officers, and Asians disproportionately in the lower ranks. Gorbachev has pledged to cut the forces by half a million men, but this will not solve the problem. The military is now discussing going over to an all-volunteer force or to forces that are composed of a higher proportion of professional, long-term soldiers. These options, if adopted, may go some way to avoiding the ethnic differentiation of their ranks.

Having spent his entire career in his native Stavropol' province, in the south of the RSFSR, and in Moscow, Gorbachev has no direct experience in nationalities issues. In his first year or so in office he paid little attention to them. But *glasnost'* allowed people to express national sentiments and grievances and to criticise the clichés that had marked Soviet rhetoric about ethnic issues. *Perestroika* showed them the possibilities of institutional and policy change. The two together led to the explosion of national sentiment and demands that we have described. On one hand, Gorbachev has acknowledged that there is a much higher national consciousness among the Soviet peoples than his predecessors were willing to admit and that not all was well in relations among nationalities. He has tolerated actions and rhetoric in the Baltic that none of his predecessors would have countenanced. On the other hand, his personnel policies indicate a stronger inclination to promote Russian and Slavic dominance than that shown by any of his four predecessors. Over three-quarters of the members of the government have been replaced since 1985; yet only two of them are not Slavs, one a minister of Greek origin who presides over a minor food ministry, and the other Foreign Minister Shevardnadze, whose office has no domestic responsibilities. It is as if Gorbachev is telling the non-Slavs that while they may continue to wield some power in their republics, they will not have any share in running the country as a whole. In the party, as well, there has been a massive turnover in personnel, but traditional patterns have been followed. Non-Slavs are assigned to their own areas, but Slavs are assigned all over the country. On the whole Gorbachev is still searching for a new formula to guide nationalities policy and a new programme to implement it.

PART THREE

The Making of Public Policy

9

Economic Management and Reform

PETER RUTLAND

If there is any single issue likely to determine the success or failure of Gorbachev's reform programme, it is not going to be opposition from entrenched bureaucrats (they can be fired); it will not be the inherently authoritarian nature of Russian political culture (cultures change); nor will it be ethnic unrest (this can be suppressed). It is the economic 'base' of central planning which will determine the outcome of attempts to change the political 'superstructure'. Unluckily for Gorbachev, the economic system created by Stalin has shown itself incredibly resistant to attempts at reform, and has brought the USSR to the brink of economic disaster.

Economic Performance

During the first five year plan (1928–32) the USSR established a pattern of 'extensive' growth – i.e. growth generated by pumping capital and labour out of the agricultural and consumer goods sectors (group B) and pouring it into heavy industry (group A), which was seen as the key to economic accumulation. Only a small proportion of Soviet expansion was due to 'intensive' growth (the more efficient use of existing resources).

This approach turned the USSR into the world's second largest economy, but Soviet consumers saw little of the fruits of this growth. Real living standards halved during the 1930s, and only regained the 1928 level by the late 1950s. By 1960 it was clear to the Soviet leadership that the scope for further extensive growth was exhausted. Capital accumulation was at maximum levels, and the labour reserves of the country were fully mobilised. Indeed, the controversial 1950s programme of closing villages and encouraging migration to the towns contributed to the USSR's reliance on food imports, which began after the disastrous harvest of 1963. Popular pressure for improved food and housing was mounting: the Novocherkassk riots of 1962 seem to have been a turning point for the leadership. Attention turned to reforms designed to shift the Soviet economy on to a path of intensive growth.

Through the 1960s and 1970s, however, things continued pretty much as before. The annual growth rate slowly declined, from a respectable 6.5 per cent in 1961–5 to about 2 per cent in 1976–85 – with the bulk of this modest growth still coming from extensive sources (see Table 9.1). At least in this period consumers saw their living standards start to improve. A steady 3–4 per cent annual rise meant a rough doubling of living standards between 1960 and 1980.

TABLE 9.1 *Soviet economic growth, 1951–85 (official data, average annual rate of growth)*

1951–5	1956–60	1961–5	1966–70	1971–5	1976–80	1981–5
11.4	9.1	6.5	7.8	5.7	4.3	3.6

Source: *Narodnoe khozyaistvo SSSR*, various years (it should be noted that these and other official figures differ from Western estimates and are likely to be inflated to varying degrees).

It turned out that the USSR was living on borrowed time. Resources were poured into maintaining the current output of heavy and defence industry while investment in the social and economic infrastructure was neglected. Soviet industry was producing four and a half times as many tractors as the USA, but without the housing, schools and hospitals needed to retain the skilled technicians in the village to keep the tractors working effectively. Meanwhile the shortage of storage capacity and poor roads meant that 20–30 per cent of the harvest was lost between field and market. One farm in five lacked a paved road to town, for despite its huge size the USSR had roughly the same mileage of roads as India or Japan. Even in heavy industry, the most obvious beneficiary of the Soviet growth pattern, it turned out that the capital stock was critically out-dated, with the average machine tool being seventeen years old as opposed to eight years in the USA.

The crunch came in the late 1970s with crises in agriculture, transport and energy. The overloaded, underfunded rail network reached breaking point, disrupting the transport of food and industrial supplies. The exhaustion of easily accessible coal and oil deposits led Brezhnev to launch hugely expensive projects in oil and gas (the Tyumen fields in West Siberia), coal and hydro-electric and atomic power. At the same time Brezhnev and his allies in the big-spending ministries and regional parties were pressing ahead with costly prestige projects such as the Baikal–Amur railway and the 1982 'Food Programme'. Even in 1987 the land reclamation ministry still controlled projects worth 30 billion. The economy stalled. Real economic growth began to stagnate (some of Gorbachev's advisers suggest that there was zero overall growth in 1980–5), and rationing of consumer items began in outlying regions from 1978 onwards.

By the time Gorbachev arrived it was clear that the sorry state of the economy threatened the status of the USSR as a superpower. According to official figures the USSR's share of total world output slid from 15 to 13 per cent between 1960 and 1980 (while Japan, for example, rose from 3 to 10 per cent). As measured by crude quantitative indicators, in 1986 the USSR occupied first place in the world producers' league table only in oil, steel, iron ore, potatoes and sugar (hardly the sinews of a 21st century super-power). In production of radios they ran in sixth place (just behind the USA and Singapore); of passenger cars, in sixth place (behind Italy and France). Given the revelations which have been appearing in the Soviet press about poor product quality, false reporting and the unreliability of Soviet statistics, the real situation is likely to be much worse than these raw figures suggest.

The flood of information under *glasnost'* has also provided a clearer picture of the plight of the Soviet consumer. Purchasing power comparisons by Soviet economists show the average Soviet citizen's living standard to be roughly 25 per cent of that prevailing in the developed capitalist economies. One has to go to Turkey to find a comparison favourable to the USSR. This low level of personal consumption is not compensated for by social welfare benefits provided by the state. Health care spending has languished at around 4 per cent of GNP (compared to 8–10 per cent in the West). In consequence, according to health minister Yevgeny Chazov, the USSR occupies 50th place in the world in infant mortality, just behind Barbados. Despite Brezhnev's egalitarian rhetoric, it turns out that income distribution is seriously skewed, with 40 per cent of the population living on less than 100 rubles a month (£100/$160 at the official exchange rate).

Basic items such as meat, butter, sugar, coffee, soap and toothpaste are in short supply, and are rationed in many areas. In early 1989 one newspaper found periodic shortages for 188 out of 211 types of foodstuffs. It was officially reported that availability of 270 out of 880 types of consumer goods deteriorated during 1987. The deficit of consumer durables during the 1970s meant that consumers accumulated 280 billion rubles in savings accounts, up from 47 billion in 1970 (with probably 90 billion more in mattresses). This sum is equivalent to seven month's retail spending, and is clearly a major cause of the current goods famine.

Yet another bombshell hit the Soviet public in October 1988, when the finance minister revealed that the government was running a 36 billion ruble budget deficit on a 500 billion ruble budget. The deficit is equal to 7.3 per cent of Soviet GNP – compared to the US federal deficit of less than 3 per cent of GNP. The leading economics adviser Leonid Abalkin subsequently suggested that the deficit was in reality 100 billion rubles (20 per cent of GNP).

Western observers had long suspected that there was repressed inflation within the Soviet economy, showing up in shortages, disguised price rises (c. 35 per cent since 1970) and the dilution of product quality. Soviet figures consistently showed wages rising faster than output (as firms bid for scarce workers). In 1988, in the wake of a liberalisation of wages policy, average pay shot up by 7 per cent while output rose only 1.5 per cent. It seems clear that the state has been printing money to bridge the gap. This shows up above all in the 73 billion rubles expended on food subsidies (up from 2 billion in 1965). Subsidies to housing and to loss-making enterprises are additional drains. After 1985 these structural imbalances were compounded by a series of exogenous shocks. The exchequer lost 40 billion rubles due to falling world oil prices and 36 billion rubles because of the anti-alcohol campaign. Cleaning up after Chernobyl and the Armenian earthquake will cost another 20 billion rubles. The Rand Corporation estimates that subsidies to Soviet client states doubled at the turn of the decade, costing 37 billion rubles (5 per cent of GNP) in 1980–8.

What has gone wrong with the Soviet economy? It seems clear that it is not in the middle of a cyclical crisis which will clear up on its own accord after a few years. Rather, the economy is suffering from a long-run, secular decline in productivity, which is in turn a product of deep-seated contradictions within the central planning mechanism. These forces have brought the economy to the point of zero growth. It remains to be seen whether the trends will bottom out, or will continue and cause contraction in the Soviet economy (as happened in Poland and Yugoslavia in the 1980s). Gorbachev does not seem inclined to wait and see what happens. He wants 'radical reforms' which will set the Soviet economy on a new path of growth and prosperity. In the remainder of this chapter we will analyse the structural causes of Soviet economic stagnation, and then assess the adequacy of the measures proposed by Gorbachev to overcome it.

The System of Central Planning

The Origins of the System

Appearances can be deceptive. Looking at the USSR, with most of the trappings of a modern, urban, industrial society, it is easy to imagine that their economy somehow or other works in roughly the same way as the developed capitalist economies. While there are some points of overlap, it is easy to overlook the fact that the centrally planned economy (CPE) is a highly distinctive form of economic organisation. The Soviet economy is not a world in which profit or sales-maximising managers seek to sell to autonomous consumers. Most Soviet economists are not familiar with the sort of rudimentary supply and demand curves to be found in an introductory economics textbook.

It is tempting to regard the Soviet CPE as merely a scaled up example of a Western corporation or government bureaucracy. Economists in particular are prone to analyse the CPE using tools developed for studying the behaviour of Western bureaucrats – for example, through the application of 'principal agent' models, which look at how leaders select incentive systems so as to get subordinates to behave in ways which maximise the leaders' goals.

These approaches yield interesting insights, but tend to overlook the unique characteristics of the CPE. It is important to see the CPE not simply as a gargantuan bureaucracy, but as a particular system of property rights. With the abandonment of the New Economic Policy in 1928 the USSR tried to establish a state monopoly of the means of production. Private ownership of productive assets (stores, workshops, farms, tools, factories) was to the maximum feasible extent abolished. All such assets became the property of the state, managed by centrally-appointed directors. No capitalist economy has ever approached the level of state monopoly over legitimate economic activity found in the USSR (c. 90 per cent).

There were of necessity some exceptions to state monopolisation of productive assets. Labour itself remained the property of the individual rather than the property of the state, although up to 20 per cent of the labour force were in camps or in exile and thus in effect state property. Also, laws requiring all adults to work, and exercising close control over labour mobility (in force 1940–56, but weakly applied) restricted individuals' property rights over their own bodies.

The biggest exception to the state monopoly of production came in agriculture. Stalin lacked the managerial cadres to run all farms as state enterprises. Thus most peasants were grouped into collective farms (*kolkhozy*). These were nominally cooperatives, but in fact had no autonomy and were tied to state grain requisition quotas. Before the 1950s peasants rarely received any income from the *kolkhoz*, sustaining themselves from the small private plots that they were allowed to retain.

It is not clear why Stalin hit upon such extreme centralisation as the vehicle for managing the Soviet economy. The core concepts of the CPE were present in Lenin's scattered writings on economics. But Lenin's NEP of 1921 recognised the need for the state and private sectors to coexist (at least in the short run). The CPE model seems to have derived from Marx's vision of a unified economy which would run itself, free from the anarchy of the capitalist market. Stalin added to this vision a pragmatic concern with constructing an economic system which would buttress the CPSU's monopoly of political power, and which would enable him to impose his development goals on the economy. He wanted to break the peasant's control over resource allocation decisions (refusing to sell grain to the towns if consumer goods were over-priced, for example) and move labour and materials into the expansion of heavy industry. In this at least Stalin succeeded – by 1940 it is estimated that the defence sector accounted for 40 per cent of Soviet economic activity.

We have dwelt at some length on the origins of the CPE because the pattern of institutional relationships established in 1928–30 has remained largely intact to the present day. In order to find out how to dismantle the CPE, it seems necessary to go back to its roots, to understand *why* it was established in the first place. This at least is what many Soviet economists themselves have been doing. Some of the sharpest debates in the Soviet economic literature (in 1968, and again since 1984) have revolved around the correct interpretation of NEP. Was it merely a breathing space, or was it a model for a non-Stalinist growth path? The latter interpretation, associated with the figure of the purged 'Right Oppositionist' Nikolai Bukharin, seems currently to be in the ascendant. (In 1988 Bukharin was officially rehabilitated.)

How Central Planning Works in Practice

What then was the institutional structure installed during the period of the first five year plan? At the centre stands the State Planning Committee, Gosplan, which draws up a grid chart matching the flow of available inputs (labour, capital, raw materials) with the set of desired outputs. They do this for about 2,000 items (out of the 30 million plus product types in the economy). Beneath Gosplan are some 60 economic ministries, supervising 120,000 economic units (in industry, construction, commerce and agriculture).

Gosplan breaks down the output figures for each ministry, which in turn allocate output targets to individual enterprises in the form of an annual plan. Plans change so frequently that the five year plan itself is little more than a forecasting exercise. Gosplan also allocates the inputs which ministries need to meet their output targets. The State Committee on Supplies (*Gossnab*) handles the distribution of raw materials and industrial goods. The State Committee on Labour and Social Questions supervises labour allocation and renumeration, the State Committee on Prices sets all prices (except for example those in the free peasant food markets), and the Ministry of Finance and State Bank monitor monetary flows.

The 20 State Committees have the same status as ministries but generally execute 'staff' rather than 'line' functions – supervising a given activity across all enterprises in the economy rather than running their own enterprises. In practice the line between ministries and state committees is blurred. A further distinction whose practical significance is unclear is the separation of ministries into the categories 'all union' (headquartered in Moscow) and 'union republican' (based also in the 15 union republics of the USSR).

This system of central planning is highly complicated and difficult to manage. Indeed, it is probably more complex, and more bureau-

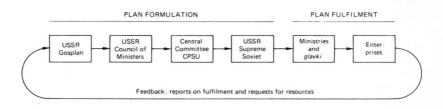

FIGURE 9.1 *The Soviet planning process (simplified)*

cratically ossified, than the outside observer can possibly imagine. Over time, however, the CPE has evolved certain operational rules of the game which enable it to function in a fairly stable fashion. Unfortunately by global standards it remains highly inefficient at converting economic inputs into usable outputs.

One thing which makes the planners' lives bearable is that they do not try to calculate the 'material balances' from first principles every year. Rather, they simply take the previous year's results as indicative of what the economy and individual plants can achieve, and tinker with incremental changes (adding new projects or mandating small productivity improvements). Soviet emigre economist Igor Birman has pointed to 'planning from the achieved level' as the key to the functioning of the CPE.

The national leadership seek to steer this incrementally planned economy by maintaining a network of political agencies which parallel the economic bureaucracies. Foremost among these is of course the Communist Party, whose 20 million members are grouped in Primary Party Organisations located directly in the place of production. They are charged with supervising the work of the economic managers (*pravo kontrolya*), while the officials in the party apparatus at district and regional level devote a lot of time to monitoring economic performance in their bailiwick. In theory party officials should not get involved with economic management on a daily basis (the sin of *podmena*): in practice they often use their political muscle to locate scarce supplies, persuade factory directors to send workers to help with the harvest, and so forth.

Apart from the CPSU, there is a host of other bodies called upon to eliminate waste, promote technical change and ensure plan fulfilment. They range from the press, through voluntary groups such as the 'Society of Rationalisers and Inventors', to mass organisations such as the Komsomol and Committees of People's Control.

It is difficult to assess whether these political interventions actually improve the functioning of the planned economy, or merely generate a cloud of political rhetoric behind which managers continue to work as before. The clearest pattern to political activities within the CPE is the way they impose a framework of priorities over the working of the economic system.

The party enjoys a monopoly of political authority, and uses this power to lay down priorities on an annual and even weekly basis. Priorities come in various shapes and sizes. The whole military industrial complex, for example, is considered a permanent priority sector, with Gossnab clearing their special (red-bordered) supply chits ahead of those of other factories. Any sector of the economy may come under the priority spotlight for a while – for example, grain silo construction in 1978, or railway wagon repair in 1982. During such a period party and Komsomol organs are mobilised to help the bottleneck sector. Unfortunately, there are so many 'priorities' in force at any given time that the centre loses the ability to make much of an impact. (For example, only 68 per cent of the priority construction projects selected for completion in 1988 were actually finished by year's end.)

Let us return to the question of how routine planning works. In drawing up the annual plans we find Gosplan and the ministries relying on crude quantitative indicators. The huge quantity of information flowing up and down the pyramid of planning institutions has to be simplified and made manageable. The planners rely on simple, physical measures of output (thousands of cars, tons of coal, square metres of housing) which crystallise in the 'gross output' target of *val*, given to enterprises in their annual plan. It is on the basis of *val* that Gosplan tries to balance the resource flows between the various sectors, so they are acutely sensitive to the fact that interruptions in *val* deliveries can disrupt the entire system. Over the years managers have learned that the *val* targets must be met first, even if it comes at the expense of other goals sent down from their ministry (improving labour productivity, widening the product mix, improving quality, introducing new technology, etc.).

An important behavioural feature of the Soviet planning system is the 'ratchet effect'. Planners monitor directors so closely that any productivity gains which enterprises make in year T will earn them handsome bonuses that year, but the targets for $T+1$ will be increased. This means managers have few incentives for long-run improvements in productivity. Planning takes the form of an iterative game, in which planners try to coax out of managers information as to the production reserves hidden away in their factories.

Relying on such a crude aggregate performance measure as *val* in part explains the insensitivity of the CPE to product quality. Niceties of design, reliability and consumer appeal are subordinate to the demands of volume production. Crude quantitative targets may not have done too much damage in the Soviet economy of the 1930s, when a few simple products dominated production (coal, oil, steel, hydro-electric projects), but they are grossly inappropriate for current circumstances. According to Soviet estimates only 15 per cent of their manufactured goods reach current world quality standards, leaving aside questions of reliability (e.g. one in three Soviet colour televisions break down during the guarantee period).

The other factor contributing to the quality problems of Soviet industry is the fact that the economy operates under conditions of permanent shortage. The biggest headache facing Soviet managers on a daily basis is the unreliability of supplies. Plans are so 'taut' that even the smallest interruption in deliveries of inputs can push a factory below 100 per cent plan fulfilment, leading to the loss of bonuses and a knock-on effect on other factories relying on their output. The fact that planning takes place on a calendar basis (annual, quarterly and sometimes monthly targets) means that the CPE works according to a bizarre rhythm. Factories 'relax' at the start of the cycle, while waiting for supplies to arrive. By the end of the month or year work speeds up to fever pitch, as overtime and safety rules are thrown to the winds and no effort is spared to 'beat out' the plan on time. This phenomenon, known as 'storming', is obviously not conducive to efficiency or high quality workmanship.

Managers resort to various strategies to try to overcome supply difficulties. They request more supplies than they need, and hoard the remainder. They use all sorts of 'horizontal' contacts to try to persuade other plants to release materials to them outside of strict Gossnab guidelines, from cooperative regional party officials through to an army of semi-legal roving expeditors (the *tolkachi*). It is not easy to explain why the CPE suffers from a chronic deficit of supplies – but there is no doubt that a persistent shortage of many types of industrial and consumer goods remains one of its most distinctive features. The most sophisticated analysis of this phenomenon comes from Hungarian economist Janos Kornai (1980). Three factors stand out.

First, there is the general orientation of the system towards the producer at the expense of the consumer (either individual or corporate). Consumers have been starved of resources (and are therefore glad of whatever they can get); they lack the option of shopping around because of the central allocation of supply contracts; and they are deprived of the means of effective legal redress to force suppliers to adhere to agreed quality standards and delivery times.

Secondly, it seems clear that the system suffers from chronic over-investment. The planners don't seem able to say no to ministries or local officials lobbying for pet projects. There are not enough construction materials to finish all the projects started, and there are not enough workers to staff the plants when they are finished. Perhaps only a mechanism such as unemployment can stop this chronic over-heating, which distorts the whole functioning of the economy.

The third factor contributing to the shortage phenomenon is the passive role played by money and prices in the whole system. Planning takes place in physical terms: monetary flows are calculated after the plan has been constructed. Prices bear scant relation to production costs and are not therefore relied upon as plan indicators. Retail prices cover only about a third of the cost of producing food, for example. Industrial goods are also under-priced. Managers worry far more about meeting their *val* targets than about whether their enterprise will turn in a paper profit at the end of the year. They know that their ministry will always transfer notional funds to cover their losses. (Hence some 15 per cent of farms and factories run at a loss.) Firms in a CPE thus face what Kornai calls a 'soft budget constraint': monetary calculations do not enter into their decision-making. This obviously feeds into the investment hunger we referred to above: capital is a gift from above, and managers do not have to worry about the rate of return on assets they manage to accumulate.

A further characteristic of the CPE worthy of note is its tendency to rely upon excessively large enterprises (easier to plan from the centre), which frequently enjoy a quasi-monopolistic position. This shows up not in high prices (their prices are of course centrally fixed), but in the cavalier treatment of customers when it comes to product range and quality. These oversized firms also develop strong autarchic tendencies, seeking to internalise uncertainty by bringing the production of spare parts, tools, etc. inside the firm. Unfortunately these auxiliary workshops are usually much less efficient than purpose-built plants. Many factories and mines even run their own farms in order to provide reliable supplies of meat and dairy produce for their workers. Roughly half of all housing in the USSR is built and allocated by industrial enterprises – an important incentive to dangle before the employees.

Autarchic tendencies have in part been encouraged by the central planners. After decades of under-investment in the consumer sector, Gosplan hit upon the idea of encouraging Group B plants to produce consumer durables on the side as a cheap, quick solution to the deficit of consumer goods. As a result, roughly half of all consumer goods production takes place in plants whose main output is something else entirely (coal, steel, or whatever). The trouble is that these auxiliary workshops are not equipped for mass, quality production, nor are they sensitive to consumer tastes.

Another characteristic of the CPE related to the 'ratchet effect' is its tendency to inhibit technological progress. While the USSR has enjoyed some spectacular successes (such as Sputnik and the Tokamak, a nuclear fusion device), it continues to lag 6–10 years behind the USA in leading edge electronic and computer technology. This is despite the fact that the leadership is firmly committed to science as a factor of production and has devoted considerable resources to the creation of a network of research and development (R & D) institutions (such that the USSR has one in four of the world's scientists).

Managers are discouraged by the fact that proposed innovations have to be pushed through the bureaucratic labyrinth, gaining approval from the main supervisory ministry and other interested bodies. The process takes years, the chances of success are small and the likely rewards paltry. In theory the State Committee on Science and Technology and the Academy of Sciences should be directing technical progress, but this top-down management is not conducive to successful innovation. The system can generate inventions, but it finds it hard to get rank-and-file factories to introduce these innovations into serial production.

The CPE also scores poorly as regards territorial coordination. The planning organs are arranged in a vertical pyramid: horizontal cooperation between different agencies located in a given territory is weak. Factories tend to dominate the urban districts where they are located in a way reminiscent of the US 'company town'. Bartering of materials, black market dealing and the exchange of political favours can only partly compensate for the absence of that great engine of horizontal exchange, a money-based market economy. Gosplan has tried and failed to come up with territorial planning agencies powerful enough to restrain firms answerable only to the central ministries. Local governmental organs – the soviets – lack the political connections and financial resources to take on the powerful national ministries. Even regional party secretaries may find themselves unable to exercise any influence over decisions emanating out of Moscow ministries.

Thus the CPE system suits some economic sectors better than others. The extractive and heavy manufacturing industries have not fared too badly, but agriculture, construction, and consumer goods and services have all encountered severe problems. This situation is not accidental, since in the 1930s raw materials and heavy industry were the priority sectors. Stalin, having dismantled the peasant and urban private economies, was not interested in developing planning mechanisms to cope with conditions prevailing in the agricultural and consumer sectors – geographical dispersion, variability of production circumstances and 'subjective' factors such as consumer tastes and the peasant/farmer's relationship to the land.

Construction is something of a special case. It has been a priority sector from the outset, but has proved difficult to handle for central planners (each project is a one-off). Planners have tried to standardise construction, for instance through reliance on industrialised apartment building techniques. However, the situation in the sector remains fairly chaotic. The State Committee for Construction struggles to coordinate the work of no less than eight separate construction ministries, and about half of all construction is in fact carried out by factories and farms on an *ad hoc* basis, either in-house or by hiring rogue building teams. The long-jam of unfinished construction projects tying up capital in the late 1970s contributed considerably to the onset of the current crisis.

Agriculture remains the Achilles heel of the Soviet economy. According to Soviet figures, while Soviet industrial labour productivity is about 65 per cent of US levels, agricultural productivity languishes at the 10–25 per cent level. Some 19 per cent of the labour force still work the land, and almost one third of capital investments have been poured into the 'agro-industrial complex', yet still the USSR has to import about 10 per cent of the food needed to provide its population with a barely acceptable diet.

It is now openly conceded that the system of huge state and collective farms, each with hundreds of workers, has broken the peasant's love of the land and 'sense of ownership'. The system of centrally-fixed procurement targets and strict controls over production techniques (which was borrowed from industrial planning) has proved fatally unsuited to farming. The system of administrative organs which carry out these central instructions is confused and decentralised, creating a morass of conflicting responsibilities which leaves local party officials with immense power over farms. Attempts in the late Brezhnev years to set up new territorial farm management agencies (RAPOs), and the fusion of five agricultural ministries into a single body, Gosagroprom, in November 1985, do not seem to have produced order out of the chaos (Gosagroprom, in fact was abolished in 1989). According to reform economist Nikolai Shmelev, RAPOs continue to function as 'instruments of forced labour'.

Previous Attempts at Reform

Beginning with the pioneering article by Yevgeny Liberman in 1962, Soviet economists have long argued that the 'administrative-command methods' which prevail in the CPE fatally constrain managerial initiative. Various ideas emerged during the Brezhnev years as to how to tackle this problem, some of which became the subject of experiments and attempted reforms.

The reform introduced by prime minister Kosygin in 1965 tried to lessen detailed ministerial supervision over industrial enterprises by phasing out *val* as the primary target indicator, relying instead on more financially-based and customer oriented performance measures such as profits, sales and product quality rating. Brezhnev was lukewarm in his support of the reform, and the measure was killed at the implementation stage by ministry bureaucrats hostile to the changes. The next major reform came in 1973, with the grouping of enterprises into broader industrial associations (resembling capitalist firms). The idea behind inserting an additional layer into the organisational pyramid was to reduce direct ministerial interference in factory life, and to get directors to focus on financial performance indicators, in place of the traditional obsession with keeping the production line flowing. In practice, the associations reform merely served to complicate the administrative structure of Soviet industry without breaking the planners' addiction to *val.*

Undaunted, the Brezhnev planners tried again in 1979, with the 'normative net output' (NNO) reform. The idea here was to plan on the basis of value added rather than gross flows of inputs and outputs, calculating coefficients ('normatives') to show average inputs for a given output and rewarding firms that improved their performance. In theory this could have overcome many of the problems the Soviet planning system was facing (above all, lack of concern for efficiency in the use of inputs). In practice, ministry officials seemed unable to operationalise NNO, and the reform sank beneath the surface of an economy reeling from bottlenecks and shortages.

The Gorbachev Reform Programme

Thus economic reform did not appear on the national agenda for the first time in 1985. On the contrary, the structural failings of the CPE had been analysed fairly openly in the Soviet specialist and popular press since the early 1960s. What has changed with the arrival of Gorbachev has not been the emergence of a new diagnosis of the USSR's economic ills, nor a new set of prescriptions about how to cure them. Rather, Gorbachev's leadership style has convinced people that this time around the measures will actually be implemented. Khrushchev's reform style was wilful and eccentric. Brezhnev's reforms compromised over sensitive issues in order to preserve political stability, and were abandoned at the first signs of bureaucratic resistance. Gorbachev was somehow able to convince people that he meant business, that he could take tough decisions and overcome vested interests.

The question of economic reform is often posed in purely political terms – does Gorbachev have the political will to reform? Is he powerful enough? Will he be able to overcome the conservative opposition to reform? and so forth. Important though these questions are, it is unfortunately only possible to answer them *post factum*. We will begin by looking at a slightly different set of issues: does Gorbachev have a clear understanding of the structural flaws of the Soviet economy, and are his reform ideas sufficient to cope with the daunting economic problems? Writing as of mid-1989, the answer to these questions would have to be no.

When Gorbachev took office in March 1985, it seems clear that he did not think that a radical overhaul of the system of central planning was required. His initial strategy was to redouble efforts behind the 'acceleration' (*uskorenie*) of economic growth. This approach seemed to stem partly from a naive faith in the productive potential of high technology, and partly from a belief in the utility of Andropov-type discipline campaigns (which had slackened off during the Chernenko interregnum).

Principal among the discipline measures of 1985 were a crackdown on corrupt officials and a huge anti-alcohol campaign. The former had Stalinist overtones (blaming the laggers and the bureaucrats for the malfunctioning of the economic system), but Gorbachev preserved a liberal image with rhetorical invocations of the importance of 'the human factor'. The alcohol drive was a typical Brezhnevite campaign. It relied on massive publicity and police measures (2.7 million moonshiners arrested); involved great haste and disruption (vineyards torn up, shops closed); and created a vast new bureaucracy (the 'Sobriety Society', with 6,500 full-time officials). Both the discipline and alcohol campaigns succeeded in their own terms (embezzlers were rounded up in droves, and alcohol sales fell by 40 per cent), but the expected boost in economic efficiency failed to materialise.

Thus Gorbachev's initial approach to reform was fairly traditional, with campaigns launched and monitored from the centre. A similar pattern was also visible in economic policy, with attention concentrated on shifting investment into the machine tool sector, using resources diverted from huge, costly irrigation projects. An important measure was the introduction of a new system of centralised quality control, *Gospriemka*.

Teams of outside inspectors were placed in factories and told to rigorously apply state quality control standards. (The idea was borrowed from the quality control system used in defence industries.) Previously, internally-recruited factory inspectors were in no position to go against their directors and fellow workers. Gospriemka rejected 8–10 per cent of output, leading to pay cuts and occasional wildcat stoppages. Workers rightly complained that quality problems were often not their fault, but the result of defective materials or managerial errors. Was Gospriemka a success? Presumably it has forced managers and workers to pay more attention to product quality. However, Gospriemka has more critics than supporters amongst Soviet economists. It is a top-down, administrative answer to a problem whose long-run solution must lie in managers being dependent upon customers, *not* on inspectors appointed from Moscow.

From mid-1986 on one can see Gorbachev starting to recognise that some sort of radical restructuring (*perestroika*) of the economic mechanism was necessary (while maintaining the pressure for economic acceleration). The main thrust of the reform programme which has emerged in an *ad hoc* fashion lies in three directions: decentralising decision-making; promoting new forms of ownership; and increasing the reliance on international economic integration. Rather than abandon the CPE model entirely, the idea is to make it work more effectively by casting aside outdated ideological dogmas and introducing greater flexibility in the design of institutions. Market-type forces are to be allowed a place within the CPE, although official language shuns the concept of 'market socialism', preferring to talk of 'commodity-money relations' or even the 'socialist market'.

Decentralising Decision-making

The centrepiece of Gorbachev's plans for a reformed planning system is the new Law on the State Enterprise, introduced in June 1987. This was a complex and contradictory measure. More than two years and a dozen supplementary decrees later, it is still not clear how the new planning regime is working out. The avowed goal of the new system is to increase enterprise autonomy and diminish ministerial interference. The main elements can be summarised as follows:

1. Planners are to rely on indirect 'normatives' designed to function as guidelines and quite different from the detailed operational instructions of the old system. Gosplan will concentrate on strategic forecasting (issuing non-mandatory 'control figures'). Rather than focussing attention on the annual plan, plan normatives will be set in advance for a five year period (and should not be frequently altered). Planners will steer economic activity through setting rules for enterprises regarding budget repayments, wage allocation, taxation, contract penalties, credit and price setting. Some prices will continue to be centrally set, but others will be open to alteration by producers (either within specified limits, or freely according to

supply and demand). Investment is to be generated from ploughed back profits and repayable credits. (The banking system is to be totally revitalised.) Only projects involving brand-new products are to be financed by central allocation of capital.

2. The new system will need fewer bureaucrats, so the staff of the central ministries was cut by roughly one third in 1988. At the national level power is being concentrated in a strategic planning team close to Gorbachev. Economic policy is to be formulated in six bureaux under the Council of Ministers (Agriculture, Engineering, Construction, Foreign Trade, Energy and Resources, and Consumer Welfare). The sectoral departments through which Central Committee officials monitored ministries have been abolished. There is talk of abolishing the equivalent departments in regional and district party organisations and getting the local parties out of economic management, but this has not yet happened.

3. Enterprises are expected to produce according to customer contracts, and not in response to direct production orders from their ministry. They will draw up their own production plans in cooperation with their customers. The *val* indicator has been abolished – but replaced by a new system of 'state orders' (*goszakazy*). These were supposed to be reserved for priority commodities, but have spread rapidly to cover 85 per cent of industrial output. The intention is to reduce the proportion of *goszakazy* to 30 per cent over the next few years.

4. Enterprises are to be granted real financial independence. There are several variants in use ('full cost accounting', 'self-financing', 'self-payment'), the general idea being that firms should be given fixed rules regarding repayments to the ministry budget and then be left free to plough back profits into new equipment, social projects or bonuses. These new arrangements now formally cover about 60 per cent of enterprises. There are also plans (most advanced in the Baltic republics) to promote regional self-financing, and more modestly to increase the financial autonomy of local soviets.

5. Central allocation of supplies is to be replaced by a system of 'wholesale trade', with firms free to purchase inputs from other firms or territorial supply agencies. However, a new system of centrally-imposed 'limits' controlling the allocation of scarce resources was also introduced. As of 1988 less than 5 per cent of inputs were being allocated through the wholesale network.

The transition to the new system is not going smoothly. GNP growth was only 0.5 per cent in 1987 and 1.5 per cent in 1988 (official Soviet data, which refer to produced national income, are given in Table 9.2). One survey of industrial directors early in 1988 reported that 80 per cent saw no diminution in the tautness of plan orders being sent down by their ministries. ('It's the same fist banging on the table all over again', as one director put it.) Some economists are saying that the Law on the State Enterprise was dead on arrival. The problems have been twofold.

TABLE 9.2 *Soviet economic growth, 1981–9 (official data, average annual rates of growth)*

1981–5	1986–90(plan)	1986	1987	1988	1989
3.2	4.2	2.3	1.6	4.4	2.4

Source: *Narodnoe khozyaistvo SSSR v 1988 g.* (Moscow: Finansy i statistika, 1989), p. 7; *Pravda*, 28 January 1990, p. 1.

First, the new system suffered from some serious design flaws. Several crucial issues were fudged or ignored – most notably bankruptcy, unemployment and price reform. There is no clear mechanism for winding up loss-making operations (and it is estimated that one in three farms and one in seven factories run at a loss). Thus ministries have little alternative but to subsidise bankrupt plants with funds taken from their more successful counterparts, robbing Peter to pay Paul. Similarly, any successful reform would involve shaking out large numbers of excess workers – some Soviet writers talk of as many as 20 million. This again is such a political hot potato that no systematic measures have been introduced to facilitate such lay-offs, or to help these workers adjust (retraining, public works projects, etc.). Finally, there is an urgent need for price reform of both industrial and consumer goods. Such a reform would mean substantial increases for virtually all commodities (food prices would have to rise by 200–300 per cent to eliminate subsidies). Thus price reform has been repeatedly pushed back over the future horizon. Initially there was talk of reforming prices in two years, now even the optimists think a reform would be unwise before the mid-1990s.

Second, there is the problem that the reform was introduced at the worst possible time. As we described above, after ten years of stagnation the USSR was hit by a series of additional economic shocks – falling oil prices, Chernobyl, the Armenian earthquake, the anti-alcohol campaign. This meant that the Soviet leadership could not afford to let the introduction of economic reform disrupt current production: they had no free resources to play with, no room for manoeuvre. As a result they opted for acceleration and restructuring, making firms meet their pre-existing targets for the twelfth five year plan (1986–90). This was why the ministries were allowed to enforce strict *goszakazy*. However, it meant that the enterprise reform, the cornerstone of *perestroika*, went off at half-cock. It may never manage to recover.

Promoting New Forms of Ownership

In 1987 new laws on cooperatives and 'individual labour activity' were introduced, designed to provide opportunities for hard work and initiative, and to help to satisfy the pent-up demand for consumer goods and services. Private and cooperative cafes, boutiques, taxis and repair shops have sprung up, employing 787,000 (out of a workforce of 130 million) by December 1988. They are unevenly distributed, being most numerous in the Baltic republics, Moscow and Leningrad.

Does this represent the creeping restoration of capitalism – or at least a return to the mixed economy of the NEP? Almost certainly not. While the cooperatives have made the lot of the Soviet consumer a little easier, they remain hedged in by restrictions. There are strict licensing requirements – thus for example only cooperatives, not individuals, are allowed to run restaurants. A second wave of legislation in the summer of 1988 liberalised the rules. This began with the Supreme Soviet's 'tax revolt' of May 1988, when with the first independent decision in its history it rejected a proposed 90 per cent tax on cooperatives. Subsequently, however, more restrictions have been introduced (for example, on printing and medical cooperatives).

There is considerable opposition to the new entrepreneurs, both from state managers who do not appreciate the competition, and from the public who attribute huge incomes not to hard work but to exploitation of shortages and the laundering of illegal income. It seems clear that the reform was indeed motivated by a desire to bring part of the burgeoning black economy into the official sector, where it could be monitored and taxed. It is true that some entrepreneurs earn very high incomes, but prices in the new firms are state controlled and most tales of profiteering are apocryphal. It has been interesting to see how the trade unions, searching for a new role in the post-*perestroika* economy, have leapt on this bandwagon, denouncing high prices and setting up teams to monitor the distribution of food and consumer goods.

On balance, then, we would conclude that the new forms are unlikely to grow to more than 5 per cent of the economy, which is roughly the share they have maintained in Poland, Hungary and East Germany since the 1950s.

Housing may be a promising avenue for new ownership forms. Less than 10 per cent of apartments are cooperatives in the USSR as compared with 35 per cent or more in East Europe. Housing cooperatives could quickly tap off the excess savings in the economy. However, the new youth house-building cooperatives report severe problems in getting hold of scarce building materials. This reflects the central problem facing all these initiatives: they remain islands in the sea of central planning, and can be dragged down by the failings of the state sector.

Leasing farmland offers the chance of dramatic improvements in agricultural productivity. The lease team, typically a family, is granted use of a plot of land for a given period (50 years according to August 1988 rules, for life under March 1989 proposals). They can sell at free prices whatever they choose to grow after having made agreed payments in kind to the leasing farm. Such experiments date back forty years, and have a track record of success (for example, 500 per cent increases in productivity in some cases). These schemes were halted in the late 1960s because they posed a threat to entrenched local party elites in the countryside. Gorbachev too has found it hard to convince regional officials to press ahead with leasing. About 40 per cent of farms claim to have some lease teams, but many of these exist only on paper. Also, there are many ways in which farm managers can make life difficult for leaseholders (by denying them access to equipment, transport and fertiliser.). Most peasants seem wary of making a commitment to private farming, since they fear that the political wind may blow in the opposite direction a few years hence. Gorbachev has tried to keep up the pressure for leasing with visits to successful farms in November 1988 and a special Central Committee plenum on agriculture in March 1989. However, the Soviet political agenda has become crowded with other more pressing issues, and rural conservatives seem to be winning out in the trench warfare over agricultural reform.

Apart from leasing, the new system of decentralised planning does not yet seem to have changed agricultural management. Farms remained locked into detailed procurement quotas and centrally fixed prices (although they are not allowed to sell up to 30 per cent of the procurement quota in the free market).

Leasing of units within factories took off rapidly in Hungary in the early 1980s, but only a handful of cases have been reported in the Soviet press. One interesting example is a car-parts cooperative in Naro-fominsk. They turned a loss-making workshop into a successful firm whose 950 workers earned twice as much as workers in the parent plant. However, the local party committee intervened and persuaded the Central Committee to curtail the cooperative's operations, on the grounds that the cooperative paid only 4 per cent of turnover into the state budget while the parent plant paid 40 per cent. Once more we see the paradox of reform in a CPE. Unless *all* the rules are changed at once, reformers may be penalised – but how can one expect everything to be changed simultaneously?

Increased International Integration

The problems of managing economic reform seem so daunting that several Soviet economists (most notably Shmelev) are of the opinion that the task can be tackled only with outside assistance. International factors can help the reform process along in various ways.

First, a transfusion of Western imports (from consumer goods to machine tools) could help the Soviet economy through the dislocations of *perestroika*, and provide incentives for managers and workers to embrace the new methods.

Second, it is suggested that only by using world market prices is it possible to introduce a quasi-market decentralisation of the Soviet economy. The monopolistic structure of Soviet industry makes it difficult for planners (working in a price vacuum) to come up with fair and realistic prices. A thorough price reform would be extremely disruptive, with some firms reaping short-run monopolistic profits while others face cash shortages. Making the ruble partially convertible and taking world prices as a benchmark should help shorten the adjustment period.

Third, expanding cooperation with Western businesses should encourage Soviet firms to attain the efficiency levels prevailing in global industry. Since mid-1987 new regulations on joint ventures have led to 164 projects involving Western partners. A complete overhaul of the foreign trade system began in January 1988, breaking the former monopoly of the Ministry of Foreign Trade and allowing many Soviet firms to trade directly with Western partners. By early 1989 roughly one third of all foreign trade was being conducted directly by enterprises.

These developments, encouraging though they are, face severe limitations. No one should imagine that internationalisation is somehow the magic wand which will rescue the Soviet economy. The Soviet economy is essentially autarchic: only 10 per cent of GNP is traded, and two thirds of this is with the socialist bloc. An abrupt change in this situation is unlikely, as Soviet export capacities are limited. The USSR has run a trade deficit in three of the past four years, and has accumulated debts of $40 billion. It is doing all it can with its core exports (oil, gold and weapons account for 70 per cent), but Soviet manufactures are generally not competitive in the West because of their low quality. Consumer goods imports had been cut back in 1987, but as an emergency measure for 1989 37 billion rubles (equivalent to 10 per cent of retail turnover) has been allocated for the purchase of such items as soap, razors, cassettes and ladies' boots.

The shortage of hard currency is one of the problems of joint ventures, since they must rely on re-exports to generate their own hard currency earnings. Joint ventures also experience difficulties with poor transport access, slack work discipline, unreliable supplies and bureaucratic obstacles, all of which make it harder to do business in the USSR than in Mexico or Thailand (where labour costs are lower too). Even Soviet firms are reporting that the restrictions stemming from the slow pace of domestic reform are preventing them from taking advantage of the liberalisation of foreign trade.

Increasing indebtedness to the West is a high risk strategy, since if the Soviet economy fails to respond positively to the stimulus a repayment crisis and drastic austerity measures to cut imports may be the result. The Polish and Romanian cases are vivid examples, close to home, of the perils of increased exposure to the world market. Increased integration with the socialist bloc economies carries fewer of these problems, and may turn out to be one of the few bright spots in the *perestroika* programme.

The other way in which international developments can help is in military affairs. Successes in arms control should enable Gorbachev to cut Soviet defence spending, now officially described as 70 billion rubles (15 per cent of GNP). This would ease the pressure on the budget, although it is not clear how smoothly resources could be transferred to the consumer sector. The CIA estimates that the elimination of INF, the withdrawal from Afghanistan and the 500,000 troop cuts announced in December 1988 will provide less than half of the 15 per cent savings which Gorbachev proclaimed as his target in May 1989. One wonders how much further Gorbachev can push these cuts without alienating the military and suffering the same fate as Khrushchev.

Conclusion: The Perils of *Perestroika*

As *perestroika* unfolded, it took on a life of its own which extended beyond the primarily economic categories we used to describe it in the preceding section. Gorbachev, frustrated with the slow pace of change, came to see the problem in political rather than economic terms. (He is, after all, a politician rather than an economist).

Two issues stand out in his presentation of the situation. First, there was from the beginning an understanding that certain social groups stood to lose from *perestroika*, and there was a consensus that their living standards should be protected. Thus Gorbachev and his economic advisers repeatedly stated that in the event of any future price reform workers and pensioners would be fully compensated and would not suffer a drop in living standards. Even 'liberals' such as Tat'yana Zaslavskaya stop short of calling for an austerity programme. (This despite the fact that Zaslavskaya had previously argued that an 'equality of misery' was not worth having, and that in the Soviet economy rewards bore no relation to effort.) It was worries over consumer unrest that pushed Gorbachev into trying to pursue both acceleration and *perestroika*.

This stance leaves the reformers with little room for manoeuvre. How can they promote the restructuring of industry when unemployment and bankruptcy are taboo subjects? How can the budget deficit be corrected if cuts in food and consumer goods subsidies (amounting to 100 billion rubles, or 18 per cent of the budget) are merely to be replaced by equal subsidies to wages and social spending?

Secondly, we have Gorbachev's characterisation of the state bureaucracy as riddled with 'anti-*perestroika*' elements and one of the key obstacles to reform. This fits into a general pattern. Gorbachev has tried to polarise the political spectrum into the 'friends' and 'foes' of *perestroika*, and anybody who gets in his way (for example, Boris Yel'tsin, or the Armenian nationalists) are condemned as opponents of *perestroika*, or at least the tools of these forces.

Gorbachev has been more vociferous in attacking the ministries, and more energetic in reorganising them and cutting their staff, than he has with regard to, say, regional party officials. There is an element of unfairness in the attacks on the ministries; a whiff of blaming the messenger who brings the bad news. It was after all the national political leadership which created the system, not the ministries, and it is the political leadership which continues to place contradictory demands on the ministries, insisting that they meet a host of goals while limiting the arsenal of instruments at their disposal.

In any event, Gorbachev's two political goals turned out to be set on a collision course. In 1986 *glasnost'* emerged as the device which Gorbachev hoped would reveal the inadequacies of the old administrative system and stimulate the desired reforms. Gorbachev seemed unhappy with the pace of change, however, and in January 1987 he turned to 'democratisation' as the means to overcome the bureaucratic forces who were seen as stifling economic reform. Accountability to the masses through competitive elections was the chosen path, applying not only in elections to the soviets but also in the selection of industrial managers. The Law on the State Enterprise also accorded an expanded role in the management of the enterprise to elective 'Work Collective Councils' (WCC).

It is not a good idea to try to democratise a political system while simultaneously trying to mount an economic reform programme (in the middle of an economic crisis). *Glasnost'* increased the opportunities for people to express their discontent with the economic situation. Investigative journalists filled the papers with articles showing people just how badly off they really were. They even turned up problems such as infant mortality which the public had not been aware of before. (Aggregate statistics had not been published since 1976.) Gorbachev's own 'meet the people' tours, in particular his visit to Krasnoyarsk in September 1988, brought him face to face with some very dissatisfied consumers.

Democratisation has had a similar impact. The dramatic March 1989 elections (see above, Chapter 5) threw up demagogic figures such as Boris Yel'tsin. In as much as one can find a unifying theme in the platforms of the successful 'anti-establishment' candidates, it is discontent. They are unhappy about meat rationing, poor housing, pollution, corrupt officials, and so on. They are even unhappy about phenomena such as the cooperative movement, which might have been thought to be part of the solution rather than part of the problem. One searches in vain through the election literature for any hint as to what sort of policies they think should be followed.

In elections of managers, candidates have often promised the workers that they would increase social benefits, particularly housing (by far the most sensitive shopfloor issue). Even though the new works councils have not yet really taken off, there are already some examples of councils mobilising in opposition to redundancy plans.

Thus by pursuing *glasnost'* and democratisation Gorbachev has sown a field of dragon's teeth for his *perestroika* programme. His political manoeuvrings were perhaps necessary for the consolidation of his own personal power, but they sharply reduced the leadership's room for manoeuvre in economic policy. Political liberalisation has made it much less easy to take tough decisions which hurt regional interests or certain groups in the population. It makes it unlikely that Gorbachev will be able to mount an austerity programme, which is probably what is needed to get the Soviet economy (reformed or unreformed) back on the road. Entering a new decade, the auguries for the Soviet economy could scarcely be described as hopeful.

10

Social Policies and New Social Issues

MARY BUCKLEY

At the 27th Party Congress in 1986 Gorbachev announced that during the years 1986–2000, the CPSU would 'raise the people's well-being to a qualitatively new level'. Due to *perestroika*, a 'decisive turning point' had been reached, which meant faster and more effective problem solving and a re-examination of social policy. Hereafter policy makers would take the 'growing significance' of the social sphere into account.

Perestroika certainly requires policy makers to rethink the goals of social policy. Although they remain loyal, in theory, to many past ideological commitments of welfare provision, they are now being encouraged to tailor social policies to economic changes. In addition, *glasnost'* has affected the extent of debate about social issues. 'Old' issues, such as housing shortages and queues for kindergarten places, which were examined in some depth in the 1970s, are receiving more widespread and critical exposure. 'New' issues which were taboo under Stalin, Khrushchev and Brezhnev, such as how to combat murder, drug addiction, prostitution, and the self-immolation of Muslim women, are now being aired, often in heated exchanges. Democratisation invites citizens to listen to experts express competing views in round table discussions and welcomes their reactions.

The objects of this chapter are: first, to highlight the factors which shape the making of social policy; second, to examine the meaning of 'social justice' under socialism; third, to introduce the current priorities of the CPSU in the selected areas of policy; and fourth, to explore how some of the 'new' social issues are being treated.

The Making of Social Policies

The formulation and implementation of social policy is affected by historical context, ideology, economic needs and pressures, political actors and social attitudes. But what is ideologically desirable, such as full employment and widespread kindergarten provision, may be historically difficult due to economic constraints. Immediately after the revolution, for example, meagre resources in a politically fragile state could not meet many basic needs. Communists had taken power in a predominantly agricultural country characterised by widespread illiteracy and rudimentary medical care. Pressing social issues included how to provide enough food to prevent starvation, how to teach citizens to read and write, and how to combat small-pox, cholera, typhoid and syphilis. Progress in many areas, such as the setting up of kindergartens and the provision of restaurants, was inevitably slow. The early Soviet state was unable to offer its workers and peasants generous pensions, spacious housing or excel-lent medical care. The tasks for social policy were enormous and dependent upon successful economic growth.

Economic resources limit the supply of goods and services that can be distributed. But political choices about the nature of pro-duction influence the pace at which resources will be channelled into consumer goods and social services. For example, Stalin's pri-orities of electrification and the production of steel and coal meant the subordination of light industry to heavy industry. The main goal after 1928 was to build a socialist economy through central planning and thereby to guarantee long-term welfare provision. Heavy indus-try was the 'means' to the communist 'end'. In the meantime, there were serious constraints on welfare policies. One result was that by the early 1950s, living standards were worse than they had been in the mid-1920s.

Leaders change, however, and so may their priorities. Khrush-chev stepped up housing construction, expanded the welfare state, and attempted to boost food production by cultivating more land; Brezhnev presided over the building of high-rise flats, wage increases, larger maternity benefits and general improvements in the standard of living. The concerns of a given leadership, as well as historical context and economic resources, affect the content of social policies.

Competing pressures on policy-makers from different institutions also influence policy formulation and implementation. For example, economists working in the trade unions may press for more part-time labour for women, while industrial managers resist in the name of plan fulfilment. In the fight against drug abuse, law enforcement institutions may press for an end to the poppy crop, while associations which process plants for medicinal purposes object. Institutions with competing interests may clash over how to tackle different issues. The implementation of social policy can also vary across regions, influenced by different social attitudes. Although since 1917 the state has been committed to an expanding system of childcare, Tajikistan and Uzbekistan have opened kindergartens with much less enthusiasm than many non-Muslim republics because their customs encourage women to stay at home and rear large families.

Resources for social policy are more plentiful in the 1980s and 1990s. As an advanced industrial superpower, the USSR enjoys the 'material-technical base' that it lacked in the 1920s and 1930s. Yet leaders and citizens are sensitive to the gap in living standards between themselves and capitalist systems and eager to close it. Increases in the quantity and quality of consumer goods are official goals of *perestroika*. As well as supporting higher living standards as ends in themselves, Gorbachev believes that the 'human factor' in economic production should not be neglected because an efficient economy needs a committed and contented workforce. Social policies should therefore pay more attention to workers' wellbeing than hitherto – for both ideological and economic reasons.

Social Justice and Gorbachev's Reforms

According to official ideology, 'the full and free development of every individual forms the ruling principle' of socialist society. The overthrow of capitalist property relations made this 'free development' possible; and the ownership of property by the socialist state in the name of the working class ensured 'socially just, public aims' through the 'planned development of the economy'. Ideologists contend that scientific planning has 'a socially purposeful orientation' because it is linked to the principle of 'from each according to their abilities, to each according to their work'. Under communism, this principle will become 'from each according to their abilities, to each according to their needs'. Socialist society is thus one of high morality since it gives 'a new content to the problems of humanism'.

The promotion of social justice is officially described as a process which establishes the political, social and economic equality of social groups. 'Deliberate policies' aim to 'promote the levelling of social conditions' irrespective of family status or level of pay. The right to work, rising real incomes, and extensive welfare rights, including the constitutional right to housing, are cited as evidence of the system's 'democratic nature' (see for instance Mchedlov, 1987). In keeping with this, at the 27th Party Congress Gorbachev declared that Soviet social policy 'clearly demonstrates the humanistic nature of socialist construction, its qualitative difference from capitalism.'

Since the 27th Party Congress and consistent with condemnations of Brezhnev's 'years of stagnation', it has become fashionable for social scientists and ideologists to argue that in 'the last ten years' the tendency to destroy social justice intensified due to 'formalism' and 'a braking of socialist democracy'. Leaders concerned with their own job security and party privileges caused disaffection, demoralisation and cynicism among the people. Social malaise resulted, and, in turn, provoked irresponsible behaviour. Some citizens coped with empty lives through alcohol; others, alienated in their public lives, failed to take initiative at work and became passive cogs in an inert system which they hesitated to criticise openly; still others who worked illegally on black markets, profited from immoral 'unearned incomes'.

Because social justice was being undermined under Brezhnev, a 'restructuring' of society and of social attitudes became vital. According to supporters of *perestroika*, social policies must struggle against bribery, corruption, unearned income and alcoholism; encourage a 'new psychology', 'initiative' and 'social responsibility' among citizens so that they will learn to solve problems independently and actively; continue past commitments to the provision of basic social needs, such as housing, education and healthcare – and to an increase in their quality; and promote more open discussion of social problems.

But social justice, according to Gorbachev's book *Perestroika* (1987), should not be confused with 'equalising', which was 'one of the prime deformities in the past few decades', resulting in 'the development of attitudes of dependence, consumerism and a narrow-minded philosophy of the type: "It is none of our business, let the bosses have the headache"'. Gorbachev argues that 'socialism has nothing to do with equalising' and 'only work determines a citizen's real place in society'. Social justice refers to the granting of benefits and privileges 'on the basis of the quantity and quality of socially useful work.'

The 27th Party Congress, as well as Central Committee meetings in 1985 and 1987, called for the adoption of the principle of 'socialist social justice' as one of the most important tasks of *perestroika*. In full agreement, the social scientist Tat'yana Zaslavskaya argues that socialist social justice must be connected to the practical question of how the 'human factor' can 'influence production effectively'. She believes that because different groups make different contributions to socioeconomic development, there should be a 'differentiated approach to social policy' which ensures a 'differentiated growth of the wellbeing of population groups'. Those who contribute most to the economy should receive a higher standard of living. Socialist social justice also entails the social control and economic regulation of the status of those who put narrow professional, departmental or local interests above those of society (Zaslavskaya, 1988, pp. 116–17).

Welfare Provision

Successive Soviet leaders have been committed to a welfare state, arguing that it services and benefits enable citizens to develop their abilities in similar fashion. This section looks at current social problems and social policies in the selected areas of employment, housing and healthcare.

Employment

The Soviet state was forged in the name of proletarian revolution to end the exploitation of the working class and poor peasantry. In 1917 a 'dictatorship of the proletariat' championed the liberation of workers who, according to the 1977 Constitution, became the 'leading force' in promoting the 'socio-political and ideological unity of Soviet society'. The consolidated alliance of the working class, collective farm peasantry and people's intelligentsia resulted in a replacement of the dictatorship of the proletariat by 'a state of the whole people'.

According to the 1977 Constitution, 'citizens of the USSR have the right to work' and 'the right to maintenance in old age, in sickness, and in the event of complete or partial disability'. These rights have been central principles of ideology since the revolution. Labour, consistent with Marxist theory, was seen by the Bolsheviks as the only source of value. Under socialism everyone was expected to work, since to do otherwise would be parasitic on others. As Lenin put it, 'Those who do not work, neither shall they eat'. In return, the state protected the infirm and the elderly.

Soviet ideology has consistently portrayed unemployment as an integral part of capitalism, alien to socialism. The new socialist state, however, was unable to guarantee jobs for all and unemployment was a problem throughout the 1920s. Unemployment and sickness benefits were formally available, but limited resources made payment difficult. It was not until Stalin's policy of industrialisation that the demand for labour significantly increased and unemployment fell.

Many fear that if *perestroika* is successful, its efficiency and streamlining will mean a return to the unemployment of the 1920s. In fact, rationalisation of the labour force has already begun. When *khozraschet* or cost-accounting was introduced in 1988, 400,000 workers were dismissed in three months. A temporary unemployment benefit was introduced, guaranteeing average monthly wages for not more than two months, or for three months in the event of a factory closure. Thus the right to work is no longer an automatic right because the logic of *khozraschet* makes surplus labour expendable. Employment is relative to the needs of the economy, as defined by economic policy. The encouragement of higher wage differentials in order to reward initiative and skill reinforces the need to shed workers so that higher wage bills can be met. These developments are designed to step up intensive economic growth and to produce more social wealth.

The growth of social wealth under socialism, according to official thinking, comes from the earned income of unexploited labour. But 'unearned income', such as profiteering on the black market, runs counter to socialist morality and saps energy from *perestroika*. Yet work which in the Soviet past would have been condemned as unsocialist, such as running private restaurants, is now legal. Entrepreneurial labour activity in the new cooperative sector has been encouraged since 1987 and is expected to provide better goods and services, thereby improving the standard of living. But the prices charged by cooperatives are often prohibitive and have already provoked resentment among citizens who cannot afford them. Expensive restaurants, for example, are out of reach for low paid nurses and unskilled cleaners. Economic cooperatives may be consistent with Gorbachev's aim to improve lifestyles, and with Zaslavskaya's advocacy of differential services, but the poor feel aggrieved.

With *glasnost'*, proverty has been acknowledged and hardships from low wages have become issues. In June 1988, the newspaper *Sotsialisticheskaya industriya* estimated that the average standard of living cost 125 rubles a month per person, but over half of the population spent less and one fifth were spending near the official poverty line of 70 rubles a month, especially pensioners, young couples with children and single mothers. Two million people had second jobs, according to *Izvestiya* in October 1988, in order to subsist. In December 1988 *Pravda* reported that although the average wage of workers and office employees had risen in 1988 from 203 to 217 rubles a month, almost three million people still earned under 80 rubles a month. Wage differentials date back to the early 1920s; they increased under Stalin and have persisted ever since, with some modifications. The urban–rural gap, for instance, has narrowed since Stalin, but remains: in 1988 the average wage of collective farmers increased from 170 to 178 rubles a month. By contrast, the gender gap has not been significantly reduced, and as in pre-revolutionary days, women, on average, earn two thirds of male wages, similar to the situation in the USA and UK today.

Many argue that the official poverty line of 70 rubles a month understates the problem and that hardship hits those earning more. Policy suggestions made in the trade union paper *Trud* in June 1988 included increased child support for the poor, guaranteed minimum family incomes of 70 rubles a month per person and higher pensions. Others see individual initiative, such as setting up a cooperative, as a better solution than help from the state. In January 1989, *Soviet News* reported that the lowest wages of those who were self-employed or working in a cooperative was 2 to 2.5 times higher than the average monthly wage.

Emboldened by democratisation, some workers are turning wages, output norms, bonuses, working conditions, economic decision-making, housing conditions, and pollution into political issues. In March 1989, *Izvestiya* reported that miners were staying underground in protest against excessive output norms, low pay and unpaid bonuses. Their 'just' demands were subsequently met. By July 1989, over 100,000 miners in Siberia and 250,000 in the Ukraine had struck for similar reasons. While there was occasional labour unrest in the late 1970s and early 1980s, it lacked the widespread publicity and enormous ripple effect that *glasnost'* triggers. In a context of fragile democratisation in an authoritarian system, strike action in 1989 vividly illustrated the necessity of taking the 'human factor' seriously since workers' discontent could threaten economic production, *perestroika* and political stability.

An extension of the right to work has always been the right to a pension. Pensions were first introduced after the Civil War, even though resources to provide them were scarce. Pensions did not increase significantly until after Stalin's death when Brezhnev, in particular, paid special attention to daily needs. One problem for Gorbachev is that the population is ageing, so pensions are a growing strain on budgets. Over the past 50 years the proportion of elderly people has doubled. Whereas in 1939, citizens over 60 accounted for 6.7 per cent of the population, by 1987 they made up 13.5 per cent, projected to increase to 17.5 per cent by 2002. Moreover, current discussions of the Draft USSR Law on Working People's Pensions, due to come into effect in 1991, recognise that the present mimimum old-age pension of 40 rubles a month is too low. Consistent with the principle of socialist social justice, some argue that a citizen's pension should be linked to qualifications and the number of years worked.

The relevance of socialist social justice for jobs, wages, bonuses and pensions, is that they be allocated according to merit. Training and performance are seen as necessary criteria for the distribution of rewards. Critics, however, worry that traditional socialist values are being compromised and that certain social groups, such as women with large families and low levels of training, will be disadvantaged. But supporters of the 'new thinking' view income disparities as necessary economic incentives. They also believe that the principle of socialist social justice should be extended to housing allocation.

Housing

According to the 1986 Party Programme, the housing problem is one 'of special significance' in need of 'an accelerated solution' so that by the year 2000 'each Soviet family will have separate housing – a flat or a house'. In comparison with the West, the housing situation is grave. Stalin's emphasis on heavy industry meant that investment in housing fell; then during what is called the Great Patriotic War (1941–45) about one quarter of Soviet housing was destroyed. Khrushchev and Brezhnev set out to rectify these shortages with the result that between 1956 and 1985 about 66 million flats were built, amounting to three quarters of all housing built under Soviet power.

Despite a commitment to massive housing construction, competing pressures on a declining economy have resulted in a reduction in the share of capital investment allocated to housing, falling from 23.2 per cent in the Sixth Five-Year Plan (1956–60) to 18.3 per cent in the Seventh (1961–5), 13.6 per cent in the Tenth (1976–80) and 12 per cent in the Twelfth (1986–90). Doubts have been raised about whether the CPSU can meet its optimistic housing target for the year 2000.

The main problem for policy-makers is that housing supply does not meet demand. Newlyweds, for instance, often begin married life by living with one set of parents and it is common for the lounge to be transformed into a bedroom at night. Overcrowding is particularly acute in the old communal flats, shared by several families. Each family has just one room in which to live and the kitchen and bathroom is shared with other families. A quarter of urban dwellers still live this way.

Overcrowding means little privacy and contributes to emotional stress, alcoholism and divorce. Journalistic accounts about the implications of cramped conditions for quality of life and work performance are now common. For example, in January 1989 *Izvestiya* reported the case of a thirty-year-old pilot who lived in one room of 9.6 square metres with his wife and two children. The young baby cried a great deal, which made rest in non-working hours difficult. Overstressed nerves meant that it was hard to maintain 'flight safety and a high level of service'. The article noted that most pilots in the North live in this way.

The quality of housing varies across republics. In September 1988 *Izvestiya* reported that in Tallinn there were 11.8 square metres of living space per person. This is 1 square metre more than in Moscow, Riga and Leningrad and 2 square metres more than in Kiev, Vilnius and Tbilisi. Rock bottom space is found at 6.8 square metres per person in Ashkhabad and 7.5 square metres in Dushanbe and Yerevan. The official minimum standard is 9 square metres per person. Although this is often not met, housing space has increased from 4.7 square metres per person in 1950 to an average of 8.6 square metres.

Since the late 1950s, an average of 2 to 2.2 million flats have been built each year, but waiting lists remain long. Even in Tallinn, 16 per cent of all families are on housing waiting lists. Figures range from 12 per cent in Moscow to 32 per cent in Kishinev. Aided by *glasnost'*, national and local newspapers address the problem in increasing detail. In November 1988, the newspaper *Bakinskii rabochii* reported that 133,000 families in Azerbaidzhan were on waiting lists. Of these, 20,000 had been waiting for over 10 years, including invalids and war veterans, living in ill-equipped buildings and hostels.

Waiting lists are not eased by corruption. In October 1987, *Pravda* exposed management personnel for illegally allocating housing 'in exchange for various services'. Apparently, 'Frunze City Soviet Executive Committee circumvented the existing waiting lists to satisfy requests from the business managers of Kirgizia's Communist Party Central Committee and Council of Ministers'. Seventy-eight flats were illegally set aside for them. *Pravda* commented that flats are frequently kept vacant just in case a special request is made by party officials.

Shoddily built flats which were thrown up in the 1950s and 1960s aggravate matters because resources have to be channelled into their renovation. The quality of building work has implications for the longevity of housing stock as well as for living standards. In 1986 projects began in six cities to renovate 20-year-old five storey blocks of flats. According to *Izvestiya* in October 1986, this work was essential because residents were 'plagued by poor sound and heat insulation' and 'constant leaks and freezes'.

Even harsher conditions are found in shantytowns in Kolyma, in the North East, where 'unplanned structures' are built from crates. The case of a man who ran wild with a gun in the city of Susuman drew attention to these conditions. In August 1988, *Izvestiya* commented: 'Arkady Buchuk grew up not only in a troubled family but also in Kolyma's worst slum'. Susuman had 600 'unplanned structures' with several thousand inhabitants. The town of Magadan had a further 8,000. Before *glasnost'*, slums and homelessness were depicted by ideologists as problems of the capitalist West, unknown in the USSR. Now both are recognised as Soviet social problems too.

Population growth and migration from rural areas into cities exacerbate housing problems. Over the last fifteen years, the Soviet population has increased by more than 38 million and rural areas have simultaneously lost about 10 million inhabitants. In this period, 232 new towns have been created. State housing predominates, although groups of citizens can form housing cooperatives, and perhaps with help from their trade union, pay for a block of flats to be built. Residents of state flats pay extremely low rents and bills by Western standards, about 4–5 per cent of an average family income, while owners of cooperative flats pay back much larger amounts over twenty-five years, similar to mortgage repayments. Factories also assume some responsibility for housing workers in hostels, but conditions are criticised as inadequate.

The quality of housing is repeatedly linked to medical, demographic, and employment problems, such as sickness, life expectancy, birth rates and work performance. Experts writing in *Izvestiya* in September 1988 claimed that the probability of a child falling ill 'decreases with each extra square metre'. They also argued that couples with an average of 9 square metres per person 'will have a second child 50 per cent more often than those who have 7 square metres per person'. Demographers who are keen for birth rates to increase, particularly in republics where one-child families are the norm in urban areas, view housing policy as a contributory factory to population structure. The profile of different age-cohorts, in turn, affects the changing size of the workforce and the proportion of different nationalities in the overall population. The extent of overcrowding endured by workers influences physical and mental health and hence job performance. Thus, housing policy is indirectly relevant to employment policy, nationality policy and healthcare.

Healthcare

'Strengthening the health of the Soviet people' and 'increasing life expectancy' are the main goals for healthcare enshrined in the current Party Programme. The CPSU aims to meet them by providing town and country 'with all forms of highly qualified medical services' of increasing quality.

After the revolution, the Soviet state pledged support for free medical care for its workers. The number of doctors per 10,000 population increased from 1 in 1917 to 4 in 1928, 7.9 in 1940, 20 in 1960, 27.4 in 1970, 37.5 in 1980 and 43.6 in 1987. The number of hospital beds per 10,000 people climbed from 40 in 1940 to 131 in 1987. Average life expectancy increased by 26 years between 1926 and 1972, but dropped again in 1985 to 69 (73 for women and 64 for men).

When ill, citizens visit polyclinics in the workplace or near their home. Medical care is free, but prescriptions are not and many drugs are hard to obtain. Paid private visits to doctors are common for faster and better care. Small payments to hospital personnel also make a patient's stay more comfortable. The second economy is neatly embedded in the running of many hospitals.

Consistent with *perestroika*, hospitals are encouraged to run efficiently and from January 1989 were supposed to adopt *khozraschet*. Detailed reports on how this is proceeding have not yet been forthcoming, but reports on the problems of healthcare are numerous. *Glasnost'* has triggered criticisms of insanitary conditions, poorly qualified doctors and a lack of equipment. The recent publication of infant mortality rates and abortion statistics has raised alarm. Particularly high death rates of children up to one year of age in Turkmenia, Tajikistan, Uzbekistan, Azerbaidzhan and Kirgizia have prompted discussions about reasons behind them. The highest infant mortality rates are found in Turkmenia, where unlike in other republics, differences between urban and rural rates are negligible. In 1986 in Turkmenian towns there were 56.6 deaths per 1,000 births up to the age of one, and 59.3 in the countryside. Particularly worrying is the fact that Turkmenia's rates are worsening, as Table 10.1 shows, and even in republics where improvements are apparent, like the RSFSR, they are often slight. Urban rates in the RSFSR fell from 22.5 deaths per 1,000 births in 1975 to 18.8 in 1986; and rural rates decreased from 26.2 to

20.4. But official statistics may be deceptive. In April 1987, *Nedelya* admitted that case histories were often falsified; thus infant mortality rates were previously higher than stated: 'Frequently, when an infant has died or has experienced a severe birth trauma, the mechanism for "correcting" mistakes promptly swings into action: the case history of the birth is rewritten (or, to be more precise, faked) to conceal the mistake or other incorrect actions.'

TABLE 10.1   *Infant mortality rates in the RSFSR and Turkmenia (number of children dying up to one year of age, per 1,000 births)*

	1975	1980	1981	1982	1983	1984	1985	1986
RSFSR								
Total population	23.7	22.1	21.5	20.4	20.1	20.9	20.7	19.3
urban:	22.5	21.2	20.3	19.5	19.2	19.9	19.8	18.8
rural:	26.2	24.0	24.3	22.4	22.4	23.4	22.8	20.4
Turkmenia								
Total population	56.5	53.6	55.9	52.5	53.2	51.2	52.4	58.2
urban:	54.4	57.4	55.7	54.7	55.3	49.1	49.0	56.5
rural:	58.0	51.0	56.1	50.9	51.8	52.6	54.7	59.3

Source: Goskomstat, *Naselenie SSSR 1987: Statisticheskii sbornik* (Moscow, Finansy i statistika, 1988) pp. 345–6.

Since 1987 there has been official recognition that infant mortality rates are worse in the USSR than in advanced capitalist countries. Comparative figures in Table 10.2 show that although Soviet rates are, on average, worse than Japan, Canada, the USA, UK, France, the FRG and Italy, they do not fall as low as lesser developed nations such as India, Vietnam, Angola, Burma and Mexico. Nevertheless, Soviet commentators find these figures embarrassing for an advanced industrial superpower and are keen to reduce them. The reasons for such high rates include poor conditions in maternity homes and inadequate pre-natal care. In August 1987, *Pravda* reported that in Turkmenia over 60 per cent of maternity clinics, maternity wards and children's hospitals lacked hot water. There was no running water in 127 hospitals and two-thirds of these lacked pipes for sewerage. In the summer epidemics were common, such as viral hepatitis, jaundice and intestinal infections.

Many pregnant women are also unhealthy. In February 1987, *Izvestiya* pointed out that anaemia among Muslim women, not eased by frequent births, contributed to infant mortality. In August 1987, *Pravda* noted that women agricultural workers were exposed to high levels of nitrates in fertilisers. A growing sensitivity to

TABLE 10.2 *Infant mortality rates in selected countries*

Year or years	Country	Deaths per 1,000 births
1980–5	Angola	148.5
1986	Australia	9.8
1980–5	Burma	70.0
1986	Canada	7.9
1986	France	7.9
1984	India	104.9
1985	Japan	5.5
1980–5	Mexico	53.0
1985	UK (England and Wales)	9.4
	(Scotland)	9.3
1986	USA	10.4
1986	USSR	25.1
1980–5	Vietnam	75.8

Source: *Statistical Yearbook 1985/86* (New York, United Nations, 1988) pp. 71–5.

ecological issues has made the link between the 'abuse' of inorganic fertilisers and infant mortality easier to draw. Pre-natal care is not improved by overworked gynaecologists. There is general agreement that a reduction in infant mortality rates requires higher standards of hygiene in hospitals, more medical equipment, available oxygen and hot water, improved pre-natal care and better working conditions for pregnant women.

Recently published abortion statistics have also prompted articles on why they are so high. In 1985, there were 100.3 legal abortions for every 1,000 women between the ages of 15 and 49. This compares with 28 legal abortions per 1,000 women in the USA and 12.4 in England and Wales. The Soviet average is exceeded in the RFSFR, reaching 123.6 abortions per 1,000 women. Apparently, only 15–18 per cent of women in this republic have never had an abortion. Lower figures in Uzbekistan, Azerbaidzhan, Tajikstan and Turkmenia of 46.9, 30.8, 39.5, and 40.9 abortions per 1,000 women respectively, are due to the high value placed on large families by Muslim cultures.

Abortion has long been the main means of contraception in the USSR. It was first legalised in 1920 as a necessary evil, banned in 1936, and made legal again in 1955. Many Soviet women endure six or more abortions in a lifetime. Writing in *Pravda International* in 1989, Professor Kulakov lamented, 'The Soviet Union holds a sad record: the highest number of abortions in the world. Every year, 23,000 teenage girls (under 17 years of age) have an abortion. Every year, for each 5.6 million births, there are 6.8 million abortions.' In the USA there are 425 abortions for every 1,000 live births.

According to women's reports, the abortion system is harsh. Patients experience disrespect from medical workers, queues for treatment and filthy bed linen. The operation is performed without anaesthetic and little sympathy is given for the pain and ill-health that results. The topic of abortion was clouded in silence until 1987, even though it was legal. Apart from a chilling description of the procedure in samizdat by Vera Golubeva (1980), little was written about it.

Glasnost' has drawn attention to a further problem. Although abortions are legal, some women seek illegal abortions because they do not wish those working in official channels to be aware that they need one. Others do so because pregnancy has gone beyond the legal limits for abortion. In order to try to reduce the number of 'late' backstreet abortions, the USSR Ministry of Health in 1989 extended the legal termination date to 28 weeks. This contrasts with the situation in the UK and USA. British conservative MPs have been pressing for reductions in the time limit for legal abortions and US Supreme Court judges in 1989 issued a ruling that made it easier for states to restrict their availability.

The main reason for high abortion rates is a dearth of contraceptives. Published abortion statistics, coupled with fears about the spread of AIDS, have led to criticism of the lack of protective condoms. According to a 1988 edition of the medical paper *Meditsinskaya gazeta*, just 220 million condoms are produced every year – clearly not enough in a population of over 280 million which lacks choice about contraceptive methods. Professor Kulakov describes the supply as 'laughable. Each male citizen in our country can count on four condoms per year!' Letters to the press complain that shops do not stock them and regret that a black market in condoms has developed, on which prices have apparently rocketed one hundredfold.

Articles in the Soviet press in the late 1980s generally concur that improvements in the health of Soviet citizens call for upgraded hospital facilities, better trained and less overworked doctors, higher quality medical equipment, regular supplies of drugs, easy access to contraception and fewer abortions. The link between good health and a less polluted environment is increasingly made.

New Social Issues

Social policies go beyond jobs, shelter and healthcare to address 'social problems' whose existence has only recently been acknowledged. These include taboo subjects of the past, such as crime, drug addiction and suicide. Other 'new' issues, such as prostitution and abortion, were discussed in the 1920s, but thereafter cloaked in disapproval and silence. Due to *glasnost'*, new social problems were given more media coverage between 1987 and 1990 than they had enjoyed in the entire half-century from 1930 to 1980.

Because these problems are 'new', policies on them are young, not fully worked out, and subject to debate. This section illustrates how the press presents new issues, traces how they have been tackled and outlines different policy recommendations.

Crime

Until recently, citizens were unaware of the extent of Soviet crime because statistics were not released. In stark contrast, by April 1989 journalists were allowed to report that 'In the first quarter of the year, 509,000 crimes had been registered in the country, which is 31 per cent up on the same period last year. The crime rate among minors rose by nearly 25 per cent'.

In April 1988, the Central Committee passed a resolution 'On the Status of the Struggle Against Crime in the Country and Additional Measures to Prevent Lawbreaking'. Party committees were criticised for their lack of vigilence and urged to step up 'law and order'. The soviets, trade unions and Komsomol were encouraged to fight crime by liaising with the comrades' courts. Gorbachev returned to the issue of crime at the Central Committee plenum of April 1989 when he called for 'an uncompromising struggle against criminal elements' and castigated party and government bodies for their 'slackening attention'.

In their coverage of crime, journalists have highlighted murder and kidnapping. In January 1988, *Pravda* regretted that the number of premeditated murders in the Ukraine, Kazakhstan, Latvia, Armenia, Tajikistan, Kirgizia and in some provinces of the RSFSR was increasing. Reporters revealed that in Central Asia and in the Caucasus, the kidnapping of young children is on the rise and one third of those kidnapped are killed. In exchange for their victims kidnappers demand money, authorisations for flats, and places in institutes for unqualified students.

According to *Nedelya* in January 1988, criminal codes do not adequately deal with kidnapping. No clause covers it in the Georgian Code, even though Georgia suffers the highest incidence of kidnapping. The Russian Criminal Code calls for 'deprivation of freedom' for up to seven years if the act is committed 'for mercenary purposes or from other base motives', and a one-year sentence in the absence of motives. Yet many commentators consider Russian law too lax and criticise redrafted criminal codes for leaving the law 'virtually unchanged'.

Press coverage of thefts by criminal gangs of state and private property has also increased, particularly in *Pravda*, as has the reporting of bribery, abuse of office and fights between gangs of youths. The prevalence of crime is usually linked to 'the years of stagnation' which gave rise to parasites, black marketeers, drunkards, home brewers and drug abusers.

Drugs

While marijuana, speed and acid were easily available in the 1960s and 1970s on student campuses in North America and Britain, they were unknown in Soviet universities. When discussions about the pleasures and dangers of drugs were commonplace in the West, they were unheard of in Brezhnev's Soviet Union. As heroin addiction spread through Western states, the Soviet Union prided itself on not having this blight. Drug addiction was characteristic of capitalism's moral decay.

By the 1980s that moral decay was part of Soviet society too, but initially hushed up. Once the growing strength of *glasnost'* forced it into the open, it became, according to two writers in *Izvestiya* in November 1987, 'an evil that experts acknowledge is growing around the world'. Three months later in *Izvestiya* the same writers (Illesh and Shestinsky) quoted the Head of Criminal Investigations, V. Pankin, to the effect that at the beginning of 1988, 131,000 people were on record for having tried drugs at least once. Of these, 50,000 were put on the medical register as drug addicts. These figures, however, probably underestimate the scale of drug abuse.

According to Illesh and Shestinsky, the authorities draw a distinction between 'classical drug abuse' and 'vulgar drug abuse'. The former refers to plant substances, such as marijuana; the latter includes 'new, homemade narcotic substances . . . produced by processing preparations of various kinds . . . similar to those that are produced industrially for medical purposes'. The distinction is similar to Western categories of 'soft' and 'hard' drugs. Whereas in 1984 'vulgar drug abuse' accounted for 2 per cent of all drugs used, in 1986 the figure climbed to 12–16 per cent, and in 1987 exceeded

30 per cent. Hard drugs are particularly popular in the Baltic republics, central Russia and the cities of Moscow and Leningrad. Alarmed at the pace of change, officials quoted in *Izvestiya* in November 1987 commented: 'It's hard to say what drug addicts will be using a year or two from now'.

Medical treatment and punishment are the two main responses to heroin addiction. In 1987, 77 per cent of registered addicts underwent medical treatment, allegedly voluntarily. Of these, 15,000 broke their habit, 21,600 suffered administrative disciplinary action and 4,000 failed to complete their treatment and so were sent to 'treatment and labour centres'. The trouble-shooting magazine *Ogonek* criticised, in February 1988, the quality of care available to addicts, questioned the success rate of treatment, and pointed out that track was often lost of discharged addicts.

The punishment of addicts was harsh in 1986 and 1987 when 30,000 drug users faced criminal proceedings and some were imprisoned for first time possession of small amounts. Reports by Illesh and Shestinsky suggest that law enforcement is now more lenient. Addicts who do not involve others in their addiction are viewed as ill, rather than as criminals, and small scale possession no longer results in imprisonment. But they also point out that addicts are regularly convicted for related criminal acts, such as forged prescriptions and domestic theft. In 1987 there were 35 recorded cases of addicts attempting to acquire drugs from chemists with forged prescriptions. Chemists were also broken into, with the result that 96 per cent of them now have burglar alarms. An estimated 35 per cent of illegal drugs in cities 'leak' from hospitals and in the first ten months of 1987, 73 medical employees faced related charges. By the end of 1987, 35 drug dealers had also been arrested because police campaigns were being stepped up. As in the West, burglary, robbery and murder are crimes performed by hardened addicts since they may have to spend 170–200 rubles a day to satisfy their habit.

Institutions other than hospitals, chemists, the police and courts have been drawn into the battle against drugs. For example, the Ministry of the Medical and Microbiological Industry and the Agro-Industrial Complex (before it was disbanded) agreed that the planting of poppies should cease. The decision, however, was taken reluctantly since oil-bearing poppies supply the needs of the All-Union Association for the Production, Procurement and Processing of Medical Plants, the Ministry of Grain products, the Ministry of Trade and the Agro-Industrial Complex. Pressure for the proposal to end planting came from the Department of Combatting the Embezzlement of Socialist Property and Speculation since it was spending a great deal of money on guarding the poppy harvest with police and dogs. According to *Izvestiya* of 6 October 1987, 'Chases, night ambushes, and the apprehension of addicts, often armed with knives and sawn-off guns' were common.

The destruction of crops, however, is proving difficult. Experts admit that they do not know how to destroy areas growing marijuana plants with herbicides without destroying other crops as well. Apparently, advice is being sought from the United States – how to deal with some new issues thus requires drawing on the experience of other countries. The international fight against drug trafficking also draws the Soviet Union to cooperate with other states.

Prostitution

Like drugs, prostitution was rarely mentioned in the press until 1986. The official line was that under Soviet socialism prostitution did not exist. Instead, prostitution was characteristic of capitalist systems where the right to work was not guaranteed and where unemployed women were 'forced' into prostitution in order to eat. Then, beginning in 1986, and escalating in 1987, newspaper articles on prostitution admitted its existence, deplored its extent, and provided descriptions of the lives of prostitutes and their pimps.

Sensational stories were printed in papers like *Literaturnaya gazeta*, *Komsomol'skaya pravda* and *Sovetskaya Rossiya* with explicit moral messages. Under-age schoolgirls who performed sexual favours in cars and then blackmailed their clients were examples of the depravity of youth. Young women who 'worked' hotels in tourist spots in Sochi, soliciting foreigners, were an insult to society. Madames who lured young women to work in brothels, taking advantage of their lack of residence permits and their poverty, were corrupt. Pimps who demanded 70 rubles a day 'protection' money, and who beat up prostitutes if they did not get it, were violent parasites. These early articles focused on moral degradation, deception, crime, violence and venereal disease.

By late 1987 more systematic analyses of why women turn to prostitution were being published in the sociological journal *Sotsiologicheskie issledovaniya*. Study of prostitutes in Georgia found that women saw discrepancies between the lives they dreamed of and everyday reality. Images of elegant and successful women in the media underlined the mediocrity of their lives. Unable to afford boots at 120 rubles a pair, women found prostitution a useful source of supplementary income. On average, young women earned fifty rubles for their services. Older streetwalkers earned just five or ten.

Recommendations for combatting prostitution vary. One argument voiced in *Komsomol'skaya pravda* in October 1986 held that 'this immoral business' could best be tackled by 'pooling the efforts of the police and the Komsomol'. Together they could rid society 'of this dirt'. A similar position put forward in *Sovetskaya Kirgizia* in May 1987 called for a 'war' against prostitution, arguing that non-resistance 'is the same as giving it one's blessing'. Another view expressed in *Trud* in July 1987 argued that prostitution should be made a criminal offence with sterner punishments than the administrative measures already taken. Prostitutes can be issued with a warning and a fine up to 100 rubles in the first instance and up to 200 rubles if the offence is repeated within the year. Critics question if this is an adequate deterrent: 'Can you really stop these increasingly brazen women with a 100 ruble fine?'. In fact, prostitutes are generally picked up by the militia for reasons other than prostitution; loitering in hotels, for instance, results in arrest for violation of hotel regulations. A more enlightened approach taken by *Sovetskaya Rossiya* in March 1987 pointed out that legislation alone could not deter prostitution. Young girls, especially those who leave their jobs and families, needed to be educated away from it.

Accurate statistics on prostitution are unavailable. Selected articles, however, draw attention to its extent in particular cities. According to *Sovetskaya Rossiya*, the files of one Moscow police chief covering the last fifteen years provide a record of 3,500 prostitutes, aged from 14 to 70. Academics call for further research into prostitution to discover more precisely its extent, sources and problems. They believe that sensible policy recommendations should be based upon more complete data. One problem which makes deterrence pressing is the spread of AIDS. Although by January 1989 there were only 102 known AIDS carriers in the USSR, modest in contrast with Western statistics, there is anxiety that far more cases exist and that prostitution is a major means of transmission.

Conclusion

As an integral part of *perestroika*, the rethinking of social policies has stimulated deeper reflection about social problems. *Glasnost'* has resulted in new issues being defined and in old issues being revisited and reassessed. More than ever before, journalists, academics and policy-makers express frank opinions; and citizens participate in debates and protests with increasing boldness as they worry less about upsetting officials or treading on party lines.

Democratisation broadens the scope for both policy debate and political protest. Although public opinion as a policy input is much weaker than in liberal democracies, it is a force with which policy makers have to reckon as political mechanisms change and as political culture is transformed. The enhanced accountability of the Supreme Soviet to the electorate through multi-candidate choice makes people's deputies with stronger legislative powers more sensitive to views held by voters and by demonstrators. Citizens, however, may have expectations that deputies cannot meet. Questions may be raised in the Supreme Soviet, particularly in its standing commissions, about job losses, low pay, poor housing, pollution and the lack of medical equipment, but scrutiny and debate do not guarantee results. Moreover, extensive discussion in the Soviet media about the goals of economic efficiency, higher quality consumer goods and an improved standard of living may raise citizens' expectations of what the state can deliver, despite the USSR's poor historical record and despite a deeply engrained cynicism among the population.

Poor economic performance, budget deficits and inflation mean that the state cannot necessarily provide what its citizens and leaders want, nor at the pace which they would like. Just as an overload of demands in the 1970s on West European states led to a questioning of the viability of social democracy and to heightened awareness of the weaknesses of Keynesian economics, so too the difficulties encountered in reforming the Soviet economy may provoke a crisis of distribution. Steady expenditure on housing and social services depends upon successful economic growth, or else contributes to budget deficits. According to the Soviet Minister of Finance quoted in *Pravda* in October 1988, although 24.8 billion rubles from the budget were allocated for healthcare in 1989 (a 15 per cent increase), 73.9 billion for social security, mostly for pensions (a 4.8 per cent increase) and 36 billion for housing, there was a projected deficit of 36.3 billion rubles.

The smoother implementation of social policies requires an end to superfluous red-tape, rigid centralisation, and to the reluctance of local officials to taking initiative. *Glasnost'* has gone some way to identifying the stifling effects of bureaucratic inertia, but those who implement social policies must break out of excessively rule-bound behaviour for the style of policy implementation to change. Some might see this as a vain hope since bureaucrats world-wide generally resist innovative changes in favour of the perpetuation of past patterns and structures. Corruption is deeply rooted in these patterns. For justice to be promoted in housing allocations and in other services, privileges for top officials, and for those well-connected to them through reciprocal favours, must cease. This is an immense hurdle to overcome given that 'violations of socialist legality' are embedded in the everyday practices of social networks and institutions.

A controversial aspect of *perestroika* for social policies is the application of 'socialist social justice'. According to this recently redefined concept, citizens should not expect to benefit equally from the state since rewards are linked to contribution; unequal efforts merit unequal benefits. Critics worry that this betrays revolutionary principles because it justifies wage differentials, pensions graded according to past work record and a growing gap between rich and poor; the humanistic potential of socialism is undermined by a system which reinforces inequalities, rather than reduces them.

The counter-argument holds that economic crisis makes efficiency imperative. Wage differentials are essential to reform, and morally just since contributions to economic restructuring should be encouraged, and laziness punished. A more appropriate target for ideological attack would be corrupt privileges and unearned incomes. Black-marketeers, however, pose a special problem for Gorbachev. The poor results of economic reform had, by the end of the 1980s, stimulated the very economic racketeering of the second economy that Gorbachev wanted to curb and rechannel. If economic fortunes do not improve, then 'unearned income' and the street corruption that goes with it could escalate. If unemployment rises, the temptation to seek 'unearned income' may outweigh the desire to set up a cooperative for uncertain rewards.

Social problems in the 1990s are likely to be complex, inextricably linked to the success of economic reform, and also to each other. If disillusioned citizens living in overcrowded housing find themselves out of work, they may turn to alcohol or drugs for comfort and to petty crime and 'unearned incomes' for financial gain. If energies are directed into illegal activities, the chances of the official economy working out its own problems are reduced. In order to tackle the social problems of drug abuse, crime, prostitution, suicide and the spread of AIDS, policy-makers need more funds and facilities. In order to begin to provide a very basic network of old people's homes – an area long neglected – budgetary allocations for care of the elderly must drastically increase. But one prerequisite of a successful economy is a reliable and committed workforce. The circular problem here is that without the confidence that economic reform *will* succeed, such a workforce will not exist in all sectors. Political reforms may generate some confidence in *perestroika*, but positive economic results must occur for many workers to shed their scepticism. Already some have resorted to industrial action and exert a new pressure 'from below'. Yet whilst everyday products such as soap and washing powder, generally available under Brezhnev and suddenly in 1989 not even attainable by Muscovites, remain scarce, the belief in economic reform will not blossom, and social problems may grow. Moreover, frustrations at low wages, scarce products, expensive goods and poor housing in a context of democratisation are likely to lead to more protests, demonstrations and strikes. These, in turn, give fuel to conservatives and critics of *perestroika* who view its results as politically disruptive, as well as unsocialist in economic terms.

So long as the state commitment to housing, healthcare, maternity grants, unemployment benefit and other social services persists, the charge that Gorbachevism is Thatcherism or Reaganomics in a different guise will not stick. A thorough rollback of the state so favoured by the New Right in the West will not occur in the USSR, so long as its leaders remain loyal to the concept of a welfare state. In fact, social policies demand an expansion of the state because attention to the 'human factor' calls for more dynamic, diversified and costly social policies. Nevertheless, the problem for adequate social policies in the 1990s remains their dependence upon economic growth.

11

The Politics of Foreign and Security Policy

ALEX PRAVDA

Issues of national security and external relations play an important role in the politics of all states. Their role, however, is in a sense more restricted than that of other major sets of issues. Policy on external relations is formulated and decisions taken by a narrower group of officials and politicians than is the case in most domestic questions. Foreign and security policy is normally the province of a small elite dealing with their counterparts in other states. Serious concern with foreign policy is confined to relatively few groups since it directly affects only selected areas of domestic policy related to external communications, the military, and international trade and commerce. Under certain circumstances, international conflicts being the most extreme, external policy may figure very prominently on the domestic agenda; but for the most part its domestic political presence is diffuse and indirect. The weight and especially the range of that presence has grown rapidly over the last forty years in OECD states as international economic developments, in particular, have impinged increasingly on domestic conditions. Ever-expanding international contacts, exchange and economic interdepence has fostered a growing politicisation of external policy. As international links, especially economic ones, have come to affect a wider range of interests, so a larger number of domestic groups and constituencies have sought to influence external policy.

Some growth in the domestic presence of international policy issues has become evidence even in the Soviet Union where foreign and security policy has traditionally penetrated domestic politics more narrowly, if arguably more intensely, than is generally the case in capitalist states. Traditionally the domestic political 'reach' of security and foreign policy issues in the Soviet Union has been restricted both in terms of the direct domestic affects of external policy and of the groups able to influence its development. The USSR has remained relatively cut off from intercourse with the international political and especially the international economic system. International contacts have certainly increased by comparison with the years of Stalin's autarkic strategy but remain minimal when compared with those of the non-communist states. As a result the spectrum of domestic issues affected by external policy and the range of domestic constituencies with strong vested interests in foreign policy remains relatively confined by world standards. Similarly the number of actors involved in influencing the content of external policy has traditionally been more restricted than in other states. Soviet policy making in general has long been highly centralised and secretive; this is all the more so in the case of defence and foreign policy, sectors universally associated with closed decision-making.

In recent decades and particularly in the course of the last five years – the *perestroika* period – the traditional place of foreign and security policy in Soviet politics has been showing signs of change, of a tendency to move in the direction of Western patterns. First, the nature and mix of traditional anxieties and values has altered. While sensitivity to ideological issues and especially to security concerns remains higher than in most states, external policies are coming to have a somewhat less intense and more 'normal' presence on the political scene. Second, the political 'reach' of security and foreign policy in Soviet domestic politics has started to widen. The expansion of international links, especially the recent efforts to expand economic interaction with the capitalist world, is multiplying the number of institutions and constituencies with an interest in external relations. Moves under *perestroika* towards higher levels of exchange with the capitalist world parallel steps to decentralise control over their conduct. Finally there are currently signs of some broadening of participation in the formulation of security and foreign policy as part of an overall effort to bring a greater variety of ideas to bear on policy making in general. The combination of wider interest and growing opportunities of involvement in external policy, when added to the rapid changes this policy sector has experienced, has produced a growing politicisation of security and foreign policy.

This chapter attempts to set these current developments, associated with *perestroika*, within the context of the overall connections linking security and foreign policy with Soviet politics under the more 'traditional' conditions of the Brezhnev years. To do this and bring out the significant changes now emerging we first outline the ways in which external policy is embedded in Soviet priorities, then consider the institutions and processes involved in security and foreign policy-making, and finally examine the way in which issues of external policy figure in domestic political concerns and debates.

Why and How Security and Foreign Policy Matter

In Soviet politics defence and foreign policy are made peculiarly critical by the sheer scale of security concerns and the salience of the ideological dimension of foreign policy. Security anxieties have traditionally loomed large in Russia and the Soviet Union. Historical memories of invasions, distant and long lasting (such as the Mongol) or more recent and brief (such as the French and German), have long fed a preoccupation with defence against threats from both East and West. Geopolitical facts make the task of defending the country a daunting one, as the USSR has the world's longest frontier (37,000 miles) bordering on no fewer than fourteen states. What is more, security has dimensions within and beyond Soviet national borders. The fact that the USSR is the last great land empire makes national security far more complex and sensitive a domestic political issue than in most other states. Tensions between the various nationalities and particularly between the centre and the union republics (by definition located in border areas) have traditionally increased Moscow's concern to maintain very high levels of military vigilance against external 'threats'. On occasion concern to prevent such perceived threats from destabilising vulnerable border republics has contributed to the use of force beyond areas of established Soviet dominance – the invasion of Afghanistan provides the most graphic recent example. More often concern about the stability of the 'inner empire' of republics has played a part in prompting direct or indirect Soviet action in the 'outer empire' of Eastern Europe. The existence of what was long an external empire of dependent states extended both the logistical and the political range of Soviet security policy. It has involved a major commitment of forces (almost half a million Soviet troops are stationed in the region) and the maintenance of the Warsaw Pact to integrate those and other Soviet contingents with East European forces and exercise control over them.

Additional extension of security concerns came with the acquisition in the 1960s and 1970s of a global military presence and capability, particularly in the Third World. The fact that Soviet superpower status has depended so heavily – some would argue exclusively – on military capability perhaps lends security policy even greater political importance than in the case of the US, whose world status rests more evenly on political and economic as well as military resources. The relative economic weakness of the Soviet Union, coupled with its extensive military commitments, has also given security policy exceptionally great weight in domestic priorities. Soviet military expenditure, according to the most widely accepted Western estimates, amounts to around 15–17 per cent of GNP, about double the figure for the US (and greater still if one includes military use of scarce material and human capacities). The wide range of security commitments we have sketched thus impose an immense burden on the economy and have traditionally occupied a commensurately central place in policy priorities.

Many of those security commitments reflect the ideological elements of Soviet external concerns and relations. The ideological dimension has affected the way in which security and foreign policy impinges on domestic politics in two ways: by complicating security tasks and by providing an additional visible link between external and internal policy developments.

Marxist–Leninist ideology has tended to compound and strengthen divisions between the USSR and the outside world which stem in large part from national interests and capabilities. For most of the last seventy years or so the international image of the Soviet Union has been coloured by its professed commitment to take advantage of the weaknesses of capitalism and help promote the spread of world socialism. This is not the place to assess the extent to which ideology has in fact played an active policy role, an issue perennially debated in the extensive literature on Soviet foreign policy. Suffice to say that the promotion of revolution as a high priority lasted for only a few years after 1917 and then in attenuated form; secular pragmatic national interests very quickly came to exercise a dominant and determining influence. Yet however pragmatic and indeed cautious Soviet leaders have proved in pursuing foreign policy objectives, their continued profession of a global ideologically-based mission challenging the status quo has helped to increase the perceived 'Soviet threat'. The ideological aspect of this threat has in turn contributed to an ideological rationale in the build up of military forces against the USSR, to contain communism, and has thus increased Soviet security problems.

As well as magnifying and complicating the security challenges facing Soviet policy-makers, the ideological dimension has long thickened links between Soviet foreign policy and major aspects of domestic politics; it has given external policy a more prominent domestic profile. To be sure, there is a link of this kind in all states, since all governments by definition seek not merely to secure frontiers but also to defend and promote national interests and values. An ideology/value link is embodied in the self-image of states, or more precisely of their diplomatic-strategic elite, which invariably includes an image of their place in the international order. Efforts to promote that image are often closely connected with the corresponding advancement of values at home. The Falklands War illustrates the tight connection at that time in British politics between the projection of values at home and abroad. While in many states the linkage is explicit and strong in exceptional circumstances, in the Soviet case it has had a more pervasive influence because of the peculiar role played by ideology in sustaining regime legitimacy.

The fact that the communist party has a monopoly on Marxist-Leninist ideology and thereby on what is claimed to be the key to scientific policy has traditionally figured as an element of its claim to legitimacy. Needless to say, sheer duration of time in power and economic performance have in practice constituted more important factors determining popular legitimacy. On the external front military performance has also played an important part. International performance in a broader sense has figured too as a self-set yardstick set by the leadership of the success, dynamism and even historical legitimacy of the Soviet system. The fact that the ideology points up the significance of the global 'correlation of forces' and competition between socialism and capitalism has meant that successes or setbacks in the progress of socialism throughout the world can rebound on the image and even the legitimacy of the domestic regime. It is of course difficult to disentangle ideological and material elements here, but doctrine reinforces a tendency of Soviet publics and especially elites to gauge domestic health partly in terms of such global competition. Concern with poor performance in this contest and the Soviet Union's rapid slippage in the international league table was a major element in forming the Gorbachev leadership's early judgement that the country was in a 'pre-crisis' situation.

As well as helping to point up international comparisons of Soviet performance, ideology in a broad sense provides a link between strategies of external policy and domestic development. The ideological connection here goes far further back than Marxism-Leninism; it involves notions of the proper orientation of Russian as well as Soviet development. The Soviet period has echoed many of the discussions under the tsars between those advocating Russian-centred paths of development and those favouring borrowing from and often copying West European experience. The difference is that the Soviet debate has been couched in new doctrinal terms. Under Lenin a pro-European strategy rested on a 'new' gradualist path to socialism and peaceful coexistence with capitalism. Stalin stressed the importance of class politics both within the USSR and in the international arena. Stripped of such ideological garb, these differing external and internal strategies can be described in terms of 'open' and 'closed' development.

It is important to understand the interaction of open and closed strategies in order to grasp the overall connection between Soviet foreign and security policies on the one hand and politics on the other. The terms themselves are fairly straightforward. In the domestic context closed strategies are associated with the monopoly and concentration of economic and political power and a mobilising, top-down style. Open strategies, by contrast, seek to decentralise, diversify and even pluralise economic and political power and increase accountability and participation. On the external front, closed strategies involve tendencies towards isolationism and autarky; open strategies strive to reduce barriers to cultural, economic and political interaction with the outside, particularly Western, world. In practice, of course, Soviet strategies have rarely been purely open or closed; yet one can discern dominant tendencies and patterns of external and internal strategies. The patterns have varied considerably over time, as has the strength of the linkage between domestic and international strategies. It goes almost without saying that domestic considerations have overwhelmingly taken priority over international ones.

The Lenin period saw strategy shift from early closure on both fronts to later openness in external policy and a mix of open economic and closed political moves at home. The significance of Lenin's opening strategy in the early 1920s was qualified by the tactical nature of NEP. Under Stalin development generally tended towards closure with obvious and important exceptions in the international arena in the mid- to late 1930s and in both domestic and external policies during the war. The post-war years saw a reversion to closed policies on both fronts, what may be termed 'congruent closure'.

Under Khrushchev, particularly in the early years, policies tended towards congruent openness with de-Stalinisation at home accompanied by efforts to mend fences with Yugoslavia and build 'peaceful coexistence' with the West. The later Khrushchev years saw less consistency within and between policies. At home continued attempts to open economically developed alongside political closure. Abroad Khrushchev tried to pursue open strategies by methods which fostered tension rather than cooperation with the

West. Overall, however, the Khrushchev period should be seen in terms of an inconsistent striving towards greater openness at home and abroad.

Divergence between closure on the domestic front and opening internationally marked the first decade of the Brezhnev era. Up to the mid-1970s reversal of internal decentralising reforms at home was accompanied by the active pursuit of detente with the West, notably the US. Inconsistent though these strategies seemed, their relationship, to use Alexander Dallin's term, was a reciprocal one. The material benefits of increased political and economic interaction with the developed capitalist states were seen by the leadership as almost a substitute for domestic economic reform. This required a compartmentalisation of external policy, with greater diplomatic and economic opening up being pursued alongside constraints on political contacts and in the later years what appeared as expansionist activity in the Third World and an offensive military posture in Europe. The contradictions between these elements eventually helped undermine the effectiveness of both the internal and external strategies. The strains between the open and closed directions produced incoherence and towards the end of Brezhnev's life the closure and immobilism that is now dubbed stagnation (*zastoi*).

Gorbachev assessed the legacy of *zastoi* in terms of systemic crisis (officially called 'pre-crisis') and launched under the label *perestroika* a strategy of economic and political modernisation. Critically important for purposes of our analysis is the fact that Gorbachev conceived and pursued this strategy as modernisation by way of opening up in both the domestic and international arenas. To a greater extent than any previous Soviet modernising leader Gorbachev has sought radically to restructure the economic and political system in a Western orientation by exposing the USSR to greater international influence and involvement. The degree and pace of openness has varied between policy areas. It took less time and effort, for instance, to make headway in security and foreign policy than in domestic affairs. Progress in the international dimension helped advances at home. Defusing East–West tension has contributed to creating a more favourable climate for domestic democratisation, the progress of which has aided Soviet international credibility. Under *perestroika* there is not merely congruence but also to some extent symbiosis between open strategies at home and abroad.

The fact that the strategies are mutually reinforcing does not mean that they possess equal priority or driving force. Domestic interests have come first throughout Soviet development. Even in the very brief early period of international revolutionary fervour

Soviet security took precedence over spreading socialism abroad, a priority exemplified by the Treaty of Brest Litovsk (1918) which ceded vast tracts of territory to the Germans. Stalin's doctrine of 'socialism in one country' set a seal on the dominance of domestic concerns. Khrushchev, however, on occasion seemed to place the promotion of international influence almost on a par with considerations of domestic security. While for the most part he sought to cut the cloth of defence capabilities to domestic rather than foreign policy needs, his attempt to pursue simultaneously ambitious domestic and foreign objectives helped to bring about his political demise. Brezhnev moved rather more cautiously and on the whole placed maintenance of the domestic political status quo first. The fact that his international policy helped only temporarily towards this end and may in fact have hindered its achievement was a product more of miscalculation than design.

What is certain is that Gorbachev has placed the needs of domestic respite and economic modernisation higher in shaping his international strategy than any post-war Soviet leader. The most obvious evidence is the string of Soviet moves on arms control including unilateral cuts and the acceptance of Western proposals on verification and asymmetrical force reductions. Equally important have been the moves to take a more flexible and accommodating line on political and human rights issues, to take ideology out of the conduct of international relations. To some extent, of course, such moves have served foreign policy as well as domestic goals. Yet under *perestroika* the rationale for improving relations with the West derives largely from domestic needs for respite and modernisation through interaction. Security and foreign policy shifts have served, *inter alia*, to reduce the burden of defence on the Soviet economy.

Arms control moves and budget cuts are symptomatic of a less obvious yet more significant policy shift which reflects the priority of domestic needs and the symbiotic relationship between internal and external strategies of open modernisation: an effort to reduce military priorities in security policy in particular and the Soviet system in general. 'New Thinking' has sought to de-militarise security by placing far greater stress on economic and political aspects of security. Mutual security and interdependence have become the new watchwords. Notions of 'reasonable sufficiency' and non-offensive defence have replaced traditional insistence on quantitative parity with all potential adversaries and counter-offensive strategy. On the domestic front de-militarisation has involved unprecedented criticism of the performance of the armed forces and a drive to convert and harness more military resources capacity to civilian use.

The de-ideologisation of Soviet international relations has formed the other major pillar of 'new thinking' and *perestroika* in foreign policy. 'New thinking' has explicitly elevated universal human interests above those of class and excluded ideology from the conduct of Soviet relations with other states. If, as we have noted, the role of ideology in Soviet foreign policy has long been in doubt, *perestroika* seems to have clearly resolved the matter in favour of pragmatic *raison d'état*. A similar, if far less sweeping reduction in the role of ideology is evident in domestic policy, particularly in the economic sphere. Here decentralisation and the introduction of market elements has facilitated the pursuit of greater interaction with the capitalist economies.

What effects have these policy shifts had on the overall connection between external policy and domestic politics? They have clearly weakened the traditional security and ideological links. The downgrading of the military element of security and the emphasis on mutual security and interdependence have diluted the intensity of policy concern with external threat. At the same time the questioning of traditional principles has involved more political controversy and salience for security issues.

De-ideologisation has also altered the nature without diminishing the overall strength of the link between Soviet politics and external policy. While the explicit secularisation of foreign policy has further reduced the doctrinal nature of the link, it has if anything thrust international relations more prominently into the domestic political arena. As with shifts on the military front, the attempt to downgrade ideology has generated political controversy and debate.

A higher profile for foreign policy over the longer term stems, however, from two dimensions of its secularisation. First, the stress on greater interaction, especially economic, with the outside world has brought foreign policy closer to a wider spectrum of domestic interests. Secondly, by disposing of the doctrinal fig-leaves, such as advancing the cause of world socialism, that traditionally covered ineffective foreign policy, and assessing it in secular cost-benefit terms, Gorbachev has exposed foreign policy performance to broader and more critical evaluation: more critical because the de-ideologisation of domestic policy-making has opened up greater scope both for a wider range of officials, specialists and elected representatives to exercise influence.

Policy Institutions and Processes

Perestroika has had a twofold effect on the structure and making of foreign and security policy. First, the general overhaul of party and government institutions and personnel policy associated with *perestroika* has started to rationalise traditional structures and appointment systems. Secondly, the shifts towards a more pragmatic and flexible external policy have generated calls for more imaginative and effective problem-solving approaches.

To set current developments into context, let us briefly examine the bodies and processes involved in the established system of foreign and security policy-making. The revolutionary origins of the Soviet state have left their imprint on the structure of institutions concerned with foreign policy. For a few months after the revolution of 1917 the Bolsheviks, and notably Trotsky who was briefly in charge of foreign policy, believed that they could dispense with the traditional paraphernalia of 'bourgeois' diplomacy, including a foreign ministry. As in other areas, so particularly in relations with the outside world, Soviet leaders faced with the tasks of consolidating power found they had to use traditional as well as new instruments. Chicherin laid the foundations of a traditional foreign ministry and professional diplomatic corps in the 1920s. This was engaged in formulating and mainly running 'normal' (what were called 'technical diplomatic') state-to-state relations. At the same time Moscow used the Comintern (the Communist International), its post-war successor Cominform and subsequently the CPSU International Department, to build links with other communist parties and help them advance the cause of socialism in a way that suited Soviet national interests.

This dual foreign policy was conducted by two parallel machines, the diplomatic, headed by the Ministry of Foreign Affairs and the ideological, run by the CPSU international apparatus. In theory the two have operated in tandem and with closely coordinating policies. In practice party/government dualism, as in other policy areas, has brought overlap and even inconsistency. The International Department of the CPSU Central Committee, while notionally limited to relations with communist and other 'progressive' parties, has typically exercised the major influence over the formulation of the CPSU's overall foreign strategy. In certain areas the influence of what amounts to the party's foreign ministry has been all-important, notably in relation to ruling communist parties and many Third World states. Relations with the communist world were handled after 1957 by the Central Committee Department of liaison with communist and workers' parties of socialist countries. This department, together with the International Department (into which it was reintegrated in late 1988), has shaped policy towards China as well as Eastern Europe, critical elements of overall Soviet foreign policy. The other key external policy area where both departments have predominated is the Third World, not just in countries, like Vietnam or Ethiopia, with established communist or socialist-oriented regimes, but in states such as Angola or Nicaragua. Even in non-communist and stable regions such as Western Europe the International Department has had considerable influence on Soviet strategy. The Department's long-time first deputy head, Vadim Zagladin, had a key say in overall policy towards the region, especially West Germany, a role continued and perhaps enhanced by Valentin Falin, the present head of the Department.

The tendency of these Central Committee departments to try and extend their policy 'reach' has long been a source of rivalry between them and the Ministry of Foreign Affairs. To be sure both government and party bodies have usually worked within the same strategic framework, yet each has had a different perspective on priorities. The International Department has often been particularly concerned with dimensions of policy relating to public opinion and 'progressive' movements. The Foreign Ministry has tended to look at options from more traditional state and diplomatic vantage points. For most of the post-war period the International Department under Boris Ponomarev managed to exercise – often *via* Mikhail Suslov, the Central Committee secretary in overall charge of international affairs and ideology and a key member of the leadership – the greater influence on the formulation of general foreign policy strategy. The Ministry, headed for almost thirty years (1959–85) by Andrei Gromyko, typically played more of an executive role, influencing strategy not so much through formulation as by means of interpretation and implementation.

Since the mid-1970s, however, the policy influence and authority of the Foreign Ministry have increased. Gromyko's appointment to the Politburo in 1973 gave the Ministry direct access to that key decision-making body. The deaths of Suslov and Brezhnev in 1982 further enhanced Gromyko's influence and he probably exercised effective control over Soviet foreign policy from the late 1970s to his replacement by Eduard Shevardnadze in July 1985. While the new minister does not seek to control foreign policy in the same way, his key position in the Politburo, where he counts as one of Gorbachev's closest allies, has given the Foreign Ministry a very strong political position.

As well as bringing the Ministry political access and clout, Shevardnadze has submitted it to a thorough-going internal *perestroika*.

Initiated in late 1985 and accelerated through 1986, this has involved rationalisation of Ministry organisation and working practice plus an overhaul of personnel and appointments policy. Such reforms were long overdue since the Ministry, in common with other Soviet bodies, had been allowed to tick over with outdated structures and inefficient practices over the previous twenty years. Shevardnadze oversaw a rationalisation of departments which corrected anomalies such as the grouping of Britain with its former colonies Australia and New Zealand (the UK is now grouped in the Second European Department with the Scandinavian countries). More importantly, this rationalisation exercise established new sectoral departments, notably ones for economic affairs and arms control. A more energetic pursuit by the Ministry and the diplomatic service of profitable economic contacts is one of Shevardnadze's favourite themes. This involves the new economic affairs department in coordinating policy information and ideas with the equally new government commission for external economic relations. It remains unclear whether effective policy cooperation takes place. Nor is the picture much clearer where the Ministry arms control department is concerned. Notionally it should cooperate closely with an equivalent section within the International Department, though there are apparently no specific institutional mechanisms for doing so. Whatever the case, the arms control department, headed by Viktor Karpov, an official with considerable experience in the field, gives the Ministry some input into the formulation of policy in an area where it has long been confined to conducting negotiations.

Alongside these reorganisations Shevardnadze launched a series of broadsides against the Ministry's established system of work practices and appointments. In tones even sharper than those applied by leaders to other ministry targets (and certainly more critical than any published speeches by reforming heads of Western foreign ministries), he railed in May 1987 against its 'stale atmosphere of protection, nepotism, money-grubbing and narrow-mindedness'. The extensive personnel upheaval which the Ministry experienced in 1986–87 replaced eight of the nine deputy ministers, most department heads and key ambassadors. Although Shevardnadze complained in 1988 that changes were still inadequate and not producing the new generation 'diplomatic technology' he wanted, the higher echelons of Soviet diplomacy have recently exhibited an increasing array of talent which has much impressed their Western counterparts.

Similar changes, if somewhat less draconian and publicised, have affected the International Department under *perestroika*. In June 1986 Ponomarev, department head for over thirty years, was replaced by Anatolii Dobrynin, the doyen of Soviet diplomacy who had served as ambassador in Washington for more than two decades. He brought with him other professional diplomats to fill key International Department posts previously held by men from ideology, propaganda and international communist organisation backgrounds. The 'diplomatisation' of the top positions in the Department reflected the wider thrust to de-ideologise Soviet foreign policy. Replacements lower down went in the same direction, with several high flyers recruited from the Foreign Ministry as well as the media. Dobrynin seemingly proved disappointing as a generator of new ideas and was replaced in September 1988 by Falin, a German specialist with a mixed propaganda and diplomatic background. Under his leadership the Department has continued to deal with a wide range of diplomatic issues and contacts outside its traditional brief of party-to-party relations.

This widening of the scope of International Department operations under *perestroika* has meant an expanding overlap with the work of the Foreign Ministry. Whatever tensions now exist stem not so much as in the past from a divergence between dominant ideologising and *raison d'état* perspectives. They more simply reflect the rivalry of institutions with overlapping policy coverage competing for influence over the direction and content of Soviet foreign policy. In theory such overlap and competition should be reduced by the International Department concentrating on formulating the broad strategic lines of external policy, still with particular emphasis on the socialist world, leaving operational tactics and policy towards non-socialist states to the Foreign Ministry. In practice both bodies concern themselves with strategy and the International Department has taken an active part in shaping and even conducting relations with certain non-socialist countries.

The Ministry may have gained in influence, by comparison with the Brezhnev period, over relations with various regions in the Third World. While its overall position is not as powerful as it was in the late Gromyko period, the Ministry has considerable political weight and access by virtue of being represented in the leadership of Shevardnadze. The International Department has less direct access *via* Alexander Yakovlev, chairman of the Central Committee Commission on International Policy, who is a key member of the Gorbachev team and in overall charge of party external policy. The Commission, a third of whose members are regional or republican party secretaries, also includes heads of the KGB, the armed forces General Staff and one of the first deputy foreign ministers. It thus has the potential to function as an inter-agency body for the coordination of foreign policy proposals. Indeed for two to three years before its establishment reports from Moscow suggested that the Gorbachev leadership was thinking of creating a functional equivalent of the US National Security Council. But the present Commission meets too infrequently and deals with too selective an agenda to meet this need; and Soviet foreign policy continues to be run on overlapping and parallel tracks.

Clearer structures and procedures have traditionally existed in the area of security policy. Here the military have long exercised firm control over the formulation of policy alternatives. The Ministry of Defence, wholly staffed by the military, has traditionally gathered and processed the technical information relating to security policy. Some processing of military data and much analysis on weapons systems and strategy is done by the General Staff of the armed forces. Data on the economic aspects of defence are the province of the Military Industrial Commission, which oversees and coordinates the production of the various defence ministries. These bodies have always jealously guarded their monopoly of military information to which even the KGB has had limited access. The areas of weapons development and military doctrine and strategy as well as arms control have traditionally exemplified the general tendency in the Soviet system to compartmentalisation. In arms control negotiations with the Americans in the 1970s military members of the Soviet team were reluctant to share what they considered sensitive data on Soviet capabilities with their diplomatic colleagues, even though the US side already possessed equivalent information. While perhaps an extreme example, it illustrates the widespread determination to keep institutional holds over technical and often therefore strategic policy formulation.

Under Gorbachev determined efforts have been made to break down such 'departmentalism' and compartmentalisation of information in security policy and indeed over the whole area of foreign policy. In the key sphere of arms control steps have been taken to undermine the military's monopoly by encouraging the establishment of special units at both the Foreign Ministry and the International Department. Their arms control units have provided civilian specialists with better access to information and decision-makers. Civilian arms controllers were able even in the 1970s to produce alternative analyses to those offered by the military, yet they made relatively little impression on policy. Under *perestroika* their ideas, culled mainly from Western strategic thinking, have made an incomparably greater impact on Soviet arms control policy; they have effectively shaped the security component of 'new thinking'.

This is partly because their recommendations have coincided with the de-militarisation thrust of Gorbachev's overall priorities. But they have also played a role in shaping that thrust. Top decision-makers are more than ever before in Soviet development inclined to assess issues and judge alternatives in pragmatic and often economic cost-benefit terms. They are thus more favourably disposed to careful and well-reasoned pragmatic policy advocacy and want to be able to choose from a full range of reasoned options. Gorbachev has on several occasions sought out and accepted civilian rather than military proposals on arms control and disarmament moves. These may well have found favour for instrumental as well as substantive policy reasons, but this does not alter the fact that civilians have recently come to exercise a remarkable influence not just on arms control but also on military doctrine. Not surprisingly this has occasioned considerable resentment among the professional military.

A similar if less spectacular broadening of specialist policy influence is evident in foreign policy. It has been less spectacular because specialists have in the past contributed important to foreign policy thinking. Yet under *perestroika* many more members of the various academic think-tanks have been able to gain access to policy-makers, and several have themselves risen to positions within the Foreign Ministry and International Department. A few have risen to the highest levels becoming, like Georgii Shakhnazarov, aides to the general secretary, or like Yevgeny Primakov, members of the Politburo.

The Politburo exercises effective decision-making power over all aspects of security and foreign policy. As an enormously overloaded cabinet-like executive body (see Chapter 3), the Politburo has sub-groups that specialise in particular policy areas. On security matters major decisions are normally taken by the Defence Council, formally a government body which seems to have traditionally operated functionally as a Politburo committee. The Council includes the party general secretary, the foreign minister, the Chief of the General Staff and other top military and defence industry officials. Under Brezhnev it was used sporadically, decisions being taken by a 'kitchen cabinet' of the general secretary's closest supporters. Under Gorbachev it seems to be playing a central role and apparently coming less under the influence of its military members.

The Defence Council has no foreign policy equivalent. External policy issues are regularly discussed at Politburo meetings though, not surprisingly, the foreign minister, the minister of defence, the head of the KGB and the Central Committee secretary in charge of ideology, all of whom are typically either full or candidate members, tend to dominate. The general secretary plays a key role in all foreign policy decisions and is frequently identified with particular initiatives. In expending a great deal of energy and staking much personal authority on foreign policy ventures, Soviet general secretaries resemble heads of government the world over. Unlike their Western equivalents Soviet leaders typically acquire real power in foreign policy several years into their incumbency when they have established pre-eminence within the Politburo. Gorbachev managed to get a firm grip on foreign policy within his first year and has since personally played a critical role in all the many initiatives Moscow has launched. His tenure of the office of president as well as that of general secretary gives him an added advantage in conducting foreign affairs. While *perestroika* has generally broadened the making of security and foreign policy and invigorated decision-making, it has if anything strengthened top executive steering.

Political Concerns and Debates

Security and foreign policy issues have impinged on political debates in different ways at various levels. They have occasionally figured very prominently in public political concerns; they have been a focus of debate and controversy for strategic groups with vested interests in the area; and they have provided one of the staple items for political dispute within the political leadership. The fact that under *perestroika* radical domestic changes have predictably attracted the greatest attention and controversy has led to a relative decline in the political salience of external policy issues. However, the radical nature of foreign and security policy change has produced an absolute rise, by comparison with previous periods, in the political profile at all three levels noted.

The opening up of contacts with capitalist states under conditions of *glasnost'* and democratisation has fostered a wider politicisation of foreign policy issues. Public interest in foreign affairs has traditionally been high yet unsatisfied, as the Soviet media typically provided nothing but the official line on international developments and Soviet policy. Though *glasnost'* came later to international than domestic issues, the media since 1988 have aired controversial historical questions (for example, Stalin's conduct of the war, the Katyn massacre and the Molotov–Ribbentrop pact of 1939) and more recent episodes, notably the deployment of SS20 missiles in Europe and the decision to intervene militarily in Afghanistan. Media discussion of such previously taboo issues has undoubtedly heightened critical public interest in the international field. Gorbachev's moves to correct past foreign policy mistakes, particularly in Afghanistan, have undoubtedly increased his popular standing. Equally, popular feelings, the groundswell of dissatisfaction with the Afghan war, probably figured importantly in his decision to withdraw Soviet troops.

Soviet public opinion may well come to play a growing role (from an admittedly extremely low base) on other policy issues that straddle the domestic and international arenas. For instance, active public support for reductions in the military budget beyond the 14 per cent announced in early 1989 may strengthen the leadership's hand in pressing on with deeper cuts. The policy weight of public opinion is likely to be enhanced by a more significant element making for the politicisation of foreign policy issues: the new role of the Supreme Soviet. Even in the first sessions in the summer of 1989 deputies showed themselves capable of probing sensitive security and foreign policy issues and scrutinising performance. They refused to sanction the reappointment of a key foreign trade minister and approved the defence minister, Yazov, only after a very rough ride. As the new Supreme Soviet gains further in self-confidence and its standing commissions on defence and international affairs become effective monitors of external policies, so parliament may increasingly air the debates that have traditionally been conducted behind closed doors among strategic groups.

The strategic groups that have the closest bearing and influence on external policy clearly include leading officials from the Ministry of Foreign Affairs, the ministries involved in international economic links, the Central Committee International Department, the KGB, the Ministry of Defence, the Military–Industrial Commission and the General Staff. Using their role in the formulation of policy alternatives and their access to top decision-making bodies, these groups have been central to the high politics of security and foreign policy. Notwithstanding the dominant authority of the party leadership, groups have been able to participate in a limited form of bureaucratic politics which has involved 'pulling and hauling' on major security and foreign policy issues. Democratic centralism and the powerful position of the Politburo in a hyper-centralised political structure has, however, made support within the top leadership indispensable to any group wishing to make a major impact on key decisions. As the Politburo has tended to reflect a range of policy views such support has typically been forthcoming, especially for those institutional groups such as the military and KGB who since 1973 have had almost *ex officio* representation in that body. Representation has often been as much a form of political control over the institution as as an instrument of influence. Nonetheless, through their involvement in leadership political struggles these groups have often injected security and foreign policy issues into broader agendas of contention.

Only on rare occasions (such as the treaty of Brest-Litovsk in 1918) have external policy questions provided the main cause and focus for leadership contention. More often contentious foreign policy issues have added fuel to existing wider domestic policy conflicts, as between Trotsky and Stalin in the 1920s or between Khrushchev and Malenkov thirty years later. The military and the KGB formed a critical part of the coalition that ousted Khrushchev in 1964 but his foreign policy failures assumed only a subordinate part in the indictment against him. This is not to say that leadership struggles and alignments have little effect on foreign and security policy. On the contrary, shifts in external policy are often made possible only by changing configurations in power within leadership and strategic group circles. These go a long way towards explaining the vicissitudes of policy under Khrushchev, who had to contend with pressures from the military and conservative colleagues. Military support and influence under Brezhnev was one of the reasons for the generous allocation of resources to defence and the elevated status of the armed forces for most of the 1970s.

At the same time, the power of the general secretary is usually sufficient to push through some personally favoured foreign policy initiatives; Brezhnev, for instance, became closely identified with detente in the early 1970s. Similarly Gorbachev has staked much of his personal authority on disarmament and a strategy of cooperative rather than competitive coexistence with the West. The extent to which he has been able to make moves to achieve these strategic goals seems to have been affected by his authority within the Politburo. In the autumn of 1986 and 1988, for instance, improvements in his position in the leadership preceded particularly vigorous pursuit of radical arms control initiatives.

Under *perestroika* differences on foreign and security policy within the leadership and indeed among strategic groups have emerged around three policy issues: the downgrading of class principles in international politics, the demilitarisation of security, and more open economic interaction with the capitalist world. Focussing on recent disputed issues is not meant to imply that foreign and security policy departures have met with particularly powerful opposition. In fact 'conservatives' have been largely preoccupied with fighting rearguard actions on domestic issues. The following brief review is meant merely to illustrate the way in which security and foreign policy has recently been contested and further politicised.

Considerable political debate has revolved around the lynchpin of 'new thinking', the elevation of human values above those of class in international politics and Soviet external policy. Particularly contested by conservatives such as Yegor Ligachev is the new line that takes class struggle out of peaceful coexistence and by implication downgrades the goal of promoting world socialism. This shift was the subject of a heated exchange of speeches between Ligachev on the one hand and Yakovlev and Shevardnadze on the other in the summer of 1988. Significantly, both sides linked the new position on international policy with the thrust of domestic economic and political reform. Conservatives in particular 'politicise' Gorbachev's innovations in foreign policy by identifying them with excessively permissive attitudes to anti-socialist ideas and developments at home.

A somewhat less polarised but equally significant debate has surrounded the attempt by Gorbachev to demilitarise security and cut military forces and resources. Here it is not simply a matter of political conservatives versus reformers but of those somewhat more cautious about the dangers of lowering the Soviet Union's guard allying with groups in the military to cast doubt on the degree and pace rather than the direction of change. Military opinion divides over the key issues along generational, sectoral and attitudinal lines. Some agree that the traditional principle of absolute security was based on military 'over-insurance'. Others feel uneasy about the idea of 'reasonable sufficiency' central to new security policy; even Gorbachev appointees such as Defence Minister Yazov prefer the term 'reliable' sufficiency. The military seem to have accepted the principle of a more defensive doctrine yet feel strongly, in contrast to Gorbachev's civilian advisers, that the armed forces must retain counter-offensive capabilities.

Such differences overlap with ones over arms control. While Gorbachev's general disarmament strategy has encountered little direct opposition, its speed and unfavourable asymmetries have aroused concern particularly in military circles. The fact that Gorbachev pushed through a unilateral cut of 500,000 men in December 1988 rather than following the military proposal for reciprocal reductions contributed to the resignation of the Chief of the General Staff, Marshal Akhromeyev. Military criticism, however, has on most issues been partial. Younger and more technically minded members of the military support the thrust of Gorbachev's security policies as they appreciate the importance of freeing resources for the technological modernisation that holds the key to sustaining a competitive edge in new types of conventional weaponry. The majority of the military establishment, however, view with apprehension the deep cuts in force levels and budgets, especially as these have been accompanied by a mounting chorus of deprecation of the utility of military force and the performance of the Soviet armed forces. There is little if any prospect of the military offering open political opposition to the new security politics, as the tradition and structures of political control over the armed forces are too strong. Yet the deeper the cuts – set to lop up to a half from the defence budget by the mid-1990s – and the more extensive the campaign to convert defence industry to civilian production, the more will security issues become enmeshed in domestic politics.

Closer economic interaction with the capitalist world is the third policy issue that has acted as a focus for debate and politicisation of foreign policy change under *perestroika*. Previous efforts to move in a similar direction attracted heated debate: sharp differences emerged in the early 1920s over the dangers of exploitation and dependency involved in the New Economic Policy. The 1970s saw considerable concern expressed over moves to accept Western credits, anxieties which continue to colour current debates. Moves under the pressure of popular discontent with persistent shortages to take on larger credits are likely to generate more criticism of the general strategy of opening up economically to the world economic system. Critics of joint ventures (which in late 1989 totalled over 1,000) and mooted special economic zones are also likely to raise traditional spectres of the dangers of capitalist exploitation.

If the new foreign economic policy continues to allow greater penetration of the Soviet Union by foreign commercial interests, so these issues will not only become the target of sharper controversy but the numbers of groups involved in those debates will multiply. The development of joint ventures and the decentralisation of foreign trade is likely to mean a dramatic extension of the range of groups with a vested interest in Soviet economic relations in particular and foreign policy in general. In 1989 5,000 ministries, local authorities, enterprises and cooperatives were involved in direct foreign trade activity. The decision to introduce part-payment in hard currency for farmers whose production makes possible savings on food imports means a further potential growth of the number of groups with stakes in foreign policy developments.

This multiplication of constituencies with international policy concerns will alter the environment for Soviet foreign policy makers. For the first time since NEP they will have to deal with a wide array of pressures from outside the traditional inner circle of institutional groups. And they will have to do so in the context of a changing political system which affords far better opportunities for group lobbying of a Western type. Powerful potential lobbyists include associations of foreign traders, economic regions (and special zones if and when more materialise) and, most importantly, republics. Union republics have been encouraged to pursue their own economic strategies and develop autonomous external economic relations. As far as future republican roles in foreign policy are concerned, Baltic developments suggest that we may see the increasing pursuit of distinctive foreign economic policies which will in turn inevitably affect the republics' general relations with key commercial partners.

All this, when added to the domestic social and political repercussions of direct foreign trade links and joint ventures, promises to make the running of Soviet foreign policy a far more complex political exercise than in the past. Opening up the USSR to global economic influence is likely to expand the role of what is often called 'low politics' in the foreign policy process. In this sense *perestroika* is changing the web of connections between domestic politics and external policy into something more akin to that found in Western states. A broader, more variegated and complex web does not of course necessarily mean a shift of Soviet foreign policy in any particular direction. Nonetheless it makes likely a more openly political foreign policy process and debate involving larger numbers of constituencies bringing to bear a wider range of domestic political considerations and interests. More 'open' contacts between the USSR and the West are therefore likely to bring closer links between Soviet domestic politics and security and foreign policy.

PART FOUR

The Future of the Soviet System

12

Perfecting the Political System of Socialism*

YEVGENY AMBARTSUMOV

As *perestroika* develops it is becoming increasingly clear that its success, as well as the success of its most essential component, comprehensive economic reform, depends totally on the state of the political system and the political life of society. The progress of *perestroika* itself, the changes in the order of priorities from technical and economic problems to political ones and the growing concern about social problems, reveals that it is impossible to solve any of these problems without radical change in the political sphere. The problems and difficulties that have been encountered under *perestroika* have made us aware of the essence and importance of democratisation, which alone is the means by which the full potential of genuine socialism can be realised and the human factor in its development utilised.

Economics and Politics Under Socialism

Radical economic reform and democratisation cannot be seen as two separate aspects of *perestroika*. They are so closely connected that one cannot be accomplished independently of the other.

A full democratisation of political life is not feasible so long as the economy is run according to administrative and bureaucratic methods and workers are unable to see a connection between their

* An earlier version of this chapter appeared in the book *Inogo ne dano* edited by Yuri Afanasyev published by Progress Publishers, Moscow, 1988. It has been adapted and abridged by Stephen White.

labour and the satisfaction of consumer demand. If none of these aspects changes then workers simply have no need of democracy either at state level or within the framework of factory self-management. Equally it will be impossible to switch over from administrative to economic methods of management without making society more democratic. This will be possible only when the individual has developed democratic characteristics and become aware of his interests and the need for solid political and legal guarantees and state protection. N.G. Chernyshevsky, the outstanding Russian revolutionary democrat, pointed out that a man could not be schooled to work independently in the field and then to remain submissive in front of the manager. Democratisation is therefore stipulated by the very nature of modern economic demands.

The results of democratisation are already being felt and are obvious to everyone. Above all, the social climate in the country has changed dramatically. Society has become vibrant, free and democratic – in short, just as it should be in a socialist society. The party leadership and population's active participation in *glasnost'* has played the central role in achieving this. Party work has become richer in content and more effective at all levels. There have been revitalising personnel changes affecting state organs and public organisations. However, no less obvious are the problems and lack of change in everyday life, the continuing and even worsening shortages. Obstacles to *perestroika* are growing as party personnel changes and good intentions translate into backpeddling rather than real progress. Inertia has proven difficult to overcome, as it is concealed within the enormous bureaucratic apparatus, which having acquired independent strength is trying to replace public power and the party leadership with a rigid and inflexible administrative and bureaucratic system of management. Inertia is also concealed in the system's monocentrism, limiting and suppressing local initiative in the absence of real and effective democratic control, in formalism, ostentatiousness and overorganisation of social life. Despite all efforts, the structure and method of organisation and work of our political system have in principle remained unchanged.

One cannot say that there have been no attempts whatsoever to change and improve our political system. Lenin had worked out such a plan towards the end of his life, and although some of his suggestions were realised following his death, the bureaucratic character of management and the political system under Stalin became more entrenched. Attempts to alter this situation were limited and suppressed. It is true that during extreme conditions such as industrialisation and the Great Patriotic War the command-administrative character of political organisation, turning all institutions into 'transmission belts', yielded results regardless of the cost to the political system. However, as the economy grew quantitatively and became more complex and as public consciousness, culture and workers' interests developed the system became less effective and society less governable.

Following the 20th Party Congress, Khrushchev attempted to reform the political system. Bureaucratic forces made good use of the chaotic, inorganic and inconsequential character of the reform measures he introduced and managed to oust him.

Some sensible decisions were made to adjust and improve the performance of some elements of the political system under Khrushchev and after him. From the mid-1950s several party-state decisions were adopted, the purpose of which was drastically to improve the work of the soviets, to realise their primary functions as the foundations of state power. However, they failed to achieve a result mainly because they were not fully carried through and were not sufficiently radical due to the traditional administrative nature of the decisions.

Attempts at economic reform in the 1950s and later have lacked firm foundations because they were not backed up by reform of the political system. The absence of such reform was the major reason for the crisis, or pre-crisis, situation in which a number of socialist countries, not excepting the USSR, have found themselves. It has not been accidental that all these socialist countries and their ruling communist parties have come to the conclusion that the combining of economic and political reform is imperative and must be implemented immediately. Moreover, the more thoroughly economic reform is implemented, the more demand there is for political reform.

It is now perfectly clear that the monocentric, administrative and bureaucratic system of power and management inherited from the past only hinders the necessary innovations, above all economic reform. It has to be added that the apparently bold decisions of the June 1987 CPSU Central Committee plenary meeting have been emasculated, that ministries and other upper echelons continue to govern mainly as they have always done, and that lower echelons continue to follow the trend. It is the obviously outdated political mechanism which feeds bureaucratism and other social deformations. It reproduces the old division between the governing and the governed, resulting in the passivity and low initiative of a large proportion of the population which is unsuitable for the modern requirements of socialism and social progress. The old system is obviously drifting away from the ideas and values of socialism, discrediting the ideology of the reform and *perestroika*, in the long run playing into the hands of the enemies of socialism and democracy. In short, the system has become both ineffective and harmful.

The conclusion is therefore that a genuinely revolutionary reform of the political system, of all its methods of functioning, has become essential. Experience has shown that reforms should neither be partial – in this case they will be futile and discredit themselves – nor should they be half-hearted, as this would lead to them being bogged down and reversed and possibly to counter-reform. The major directions of such a political reform are highlighted in the speeches of Gorbachev, who has gone further than ever before in working on concrete solutions to these problems. The basis of such a reform, for instance, was suggested in his speech delivered at the CPSU Central Committee plenary meeting in February 1988.

A delay in renewing the political system leads to growing tension in society, the emergence of a crisis of trust in the party on the part of the population, a growth of pessimism and apathy, the dissemination of a lack of faith in the politics of *perestroika*, the watering down of the socialist system of values and, most seriously, a disillusionment in the vitality and effectiveness of socialism as a social order. At the same time, urgent and decisive political reform, having channelled the social energy of the people into the political sphere, can produce a 'compensatory effect' for the shortages and faults in economic life. Having raised the political consciousness of the masses, it would support their activity in other spheres. If successful, it would set an example to be followed by other socialist countries and would facilitate a strengthening of their friendship with the Soviet Union.

It could be questioned whether political reform is in itself dangerous. Would it not be an attack on the most sacred aspect of Soviet life – the leading role of the party? It could be answered that it is precisely the lack of initiative, the refusal to introduce reform that undermines this role, as well as socialism as a whole. But most significant is that a well thought out and consistent reform programme can only raise the role and prestige of the party in the eyes of the people.

At the same time, we should not close our eyes to the complexity, even the uniqueness, of the suggested reforms. Unlike economic reform, political reform of such character and magnitude has never been undertaken in the Soviet Union, nor in the other socialist countries. Neither Lenin, Marx nor Engels left any instructions as to the concrete forms of the political mechanism of the socialist order. Moreover, the founders of Marxism, assuming that a socialist revolution would be carried through more or less simultaneously in all civilised countries, thought that both the state and state policy would begin to die out immediately and eventually disappear. Our revolution embarked upon another state direction with all its consequences. Lenin, towards the end of his life, gave much thought to reducing these consequences and preventing the negative phenomena we encounter today. Because of his illness and the then Soviet Russia's backwardness, Lenin was unable to develop his thoughts and apply them to present-day conditions. However, in their original form, Lenin's thoughts retain their meaning, which were ignored by Stalin and developed into an irreconcilable conflict with the latter's command-administrative, totalitarian view of socialism.

Perestroika and the Russian Tradition

The difficulty of reform of the political system also lies in the particularities of our traditions. Looking at the pre-revolutionary period, the experience of bourgeois democracy, inherent in Western Europe, was lacking. Such features prevailed as an absolutism of state power, a large and inert bureaucracy, an absence of judicial consciousness and respect of individuality, an absence of rights for some social groups and their acceptance of authoritarian methods of government. The revolution attempted to put an end to these traditions, but its isolation resulted in a prolonged atmosphere of 'siege' and limited democratic rights. Then there was the Stalinist period when there was an acknowledged neglect of democracy, from which a recovery is still not complete. So we are therefore discussing the plans for the first normal, genuinely adequate socialist political system in history.

The political system under Stalin was notable for its mimicry of democracy. This was acquired and reiterated in an expanded form in the ideology of the traditional bureaucracy. Should we take their quasi-democratic reasoning and evaluations seriously, then there is no need for political reform as the people have power and society is organised in an optimal manner. This distortion of the situation, this adaptability to changes and an ability to emasculate reforms clearly seem to be the major obstacle. The anti-*perestroika* stance was bluntly expressed in the article, 'I can't forgo principles', signed by Nina Andreeva and published in the paper *Sovetskaya Rossiya* on 23 March 1988. Under the pretext of defending the 'purity of principles' the author – or rather authors – stand for the preservation of an administrative and bureaucratic system which originated under Stalin, and in the exclusion of power of the masses awakened by *perestroika*.

If the urgency of political reform is obvious, then the question of pace needs particular consideration. Here, there is not only the danger of half-heartedness and indeterminateness, but also of haste. Our recent history has demonstrated the cost of maximalistic tempos and superficial rearrangements. It is therefore important that the order of priorities of the different stages of political reform be considered and determined, similar to the way it has been done as far as economic reform is concerned. Stagnation, sluggishness and bureaucracy within the political system which has formed in some socialist countries can be eliminated only when the centre's monopoly on political initiative, which stands in direct opposition to an insufficiently developed initiative of ordinary workers, is overcome.

We have irrationally become accustomed to departmental monopoly, having forgotten that it is competition that brings progress. Very often people who are genuinely interested in solving some of these problems suggest the setting up of special departments. We have continued with these methods, even in science where progress is based upon the free conflict of ideas and where the setting up of monopolistic centres is considered to be progressive. In a letter to a central newspaper in 1988 it was suggested that in order to improve Aeroflot's service it should be divided into two parallel organisations. This is not such a bad idea. However, even a good idea should not be carried to the point of absurdity.

Monopoly and monocentrism are incompatible with economic reform, which envisages independence and self-initiative at enterprise level. The reform demands a more accurate definition of democratic centralism, other than the one to which we have become accustomed. At the dawn of Soviet power Lenin pointed out that centralism, 'understood in a truly democratic sense, presupposes the possibility, created for the first time in history, of a full and unhampered development not only of specific local features, but also of local inventiveness, local initiative, of diverse ways, methods and means of progress to the common goal'. Marxism, in fact, attaches fundamental importance to local self-government. Engels suggested that the German Social Democratic Party's programme should read as follows: 'Full self-government in the provinces, regions and communes through state officials elected on the basis of universal suffrage. The abolition of all local and provincial powers appointed by the state'. Lenin especially quotes Engels in *The State and Revolution* (1917), pointing out that local self-government does away with bureaucracy, and he insists that local self-government and true democratic centralism are perfectly compatible. He adds with regret, 'insufficient attention has been and is being paid in our party propaganda and agitation to this fact, as, indeed, to the whole question to the federal and centralised republic and local self-government'. Because of civil war in Soviet Russia, the circumstances of the 1930s and the subsequent period, self-government has not developed as it was supposed to do.

However, a new understanding of democratic centralism in fraternal countries, which has pointed economic reform in the direction of giving more independence to enterprises, is manifested in the growing decentralisation of management and the granting of more authority to local organs of power. In Hungary, for example, local soviets now have control over their budget, taxation and land leasing, and can take out loans for local needs. According to our estimates, 35 per cent of all enterprises in the German Democratic Republic, a country which has particularly centralistic tendencies, are governed locally, whilst in the USSR only 5 per cent are. In principle, it is logically consistent to let local bodies deal with all problems that can be dealt with locally.

Economic reform, together with the political reform, create the preconditions for the development of diversity under socialism, which is its basic quality. Central command over individual enterprises would then not be possible so long as they were independent (in principle, direct economic links between enterprises leave no room for bureaucracy – its primary objective being to hinder and emasculate reform).

Under conditions of self-financing socialism, the political sphere would no longer be able to continue its unifying role in society, to which we have become accustomed. A democratic unity of diversities would replace an authoritarian monotony. Both the economic and the political spheres must become arenas in which social conflict is expressed and resolved. At the same time, the political sphere will become a source of information on these conflicts, their dynamics and inter-relations, for which not even the most qualified and contemporary sociological research can substitute. Accumulated experience, particularly under present conditions, proves that a democratic unity of diversity is stronger than an authoritarian unity of monotony. A democratic society is more able to negotiate a crisis, whilst an authoritarian one is destroyed by it. Internal adhesive forces function in a democratic society, whilst an authoritarian one functions according to external and crude coercive force.

Informal Organisations and Civil Society

Centralisation in the USSR is of an hierarchical and multi-stage nature. Not only are the intermediate levels of authority parasitic, in the course of passing down directives the information is distorted, deforming the interests represented (as with Chinese whispers). The system of hierarchical subordination should give more scope for the equality of self-initiated and independent associations, which were thought by Marx to be the primary cells of socialist society. The same idea is contained in Lenin's views on socialism as being a 'system of civilised cooperators'. Vertical links between management and labour must be complemented by horizontal ones, which are poorly developed in the USSR. Economic links will not be confined to the economy, but will overflow into other sectors. A tendency towards a socialist civil society will emerge.

The time has come to draw the necessary conclusions from the high evaluation given by Marx and Engels to civil society. As they put it in *The German Ideology* (1845–6), 'this civil society is the true source and theatre of all history . . . Civil society embraces the whole material intercourse of individuals within a definite stage of the development of productive forces. It embraces the whole commercial and industrial life of a given stage and, thereby, transcends the state and the nation'. It is civil society that provides stability to the state structure during governmental transitions by providing reinforcement of horizontal linkages. Civil society thus strengthens political power. At the present developmental stage of socialism, when practically the whole population lacks experience of an alternative system, socialist civil society would be a natural and revitalising alternative.

It cannot be said that no civil society whatsoever has formed in the USSR. However, having found itself in a position of forced opposition to the state, it is characterised by deformed, pathological links which permeate social relations within it. These links should be brought to the surface and society should be given the opportunity to eradicate them by using its own means and not having to rely on state repression.

Contrary to the Marxist–Leninist prophecy that the state would disappear, it has acquired enormous strength under socialism. This was necessary and inevitable when the new regime, fighting against both internal and external enemies under conditions of isolation, had to be strengthened. However, when the threat of a restoration of capitalism had been removed, the cost of an increased dependence on the state began to outweigh the benefits. Excessive, all-embracing intervention by the state stifles the self-initiative of society, associations, public organisations and of individuals, becoming a source of alienation and political passivity, and leading to anti-social behaviour, creating ideal grounds for the multiplication and diffusion of a parasitic bureaucracy. The contradiction between an inherent socialist tendency toward full self-government – i.e. a transfer of control to the citizens – and the growth in size and activity of the state apparatus has become the major issue in Soviet socio-political life.

To speak of a disappearance of the state today would be utopian. Equally disorientating would be the assertion that the state has ceased to exist. When Lenin talked about the socialist state as being a 'semi-state' he meant nothing more than its class character, which was a means of expressing the will and interests of a previously exploited majority. However, in stepping up his critique of the bureaucracy in the 1920s and in attaching a conceptual meaning to the development of a cooperative network Lenin was in actual fact pursuing a course of decreased dependence of society on the state, which would free it from the state's tutelage. Such an evolution is even more important at a moment when the creative energy and constructive ability of the population is accumulating.

At present the impression can be obtained that it is the right wing of Western democracy, the so-called neo-conservatives from Reagan to Thatcher and their successors, who are calling for the weakening of the state and a narrowing of its functions. Although this is the case, it must also not be forgotten that it was left wing democratic ideologists who were the first to talk of a narrowing of the state's functions in the West, particularly in the USA. Emerson wrote that 'The best government is the one that governs the least. The less government the better'. On the other hand, such reactionary forces as Russian tsarism and German militarism, Metternich and Bismarck, upheld the absolute power of the state. Marx and Engels sharply criticised Lassalle and Dühring's theory of state socialism, which has had a certain relevance to Soviet political development.

Today the opportunity to bring to fruition the Marxist vision of a reversal process in which the state's power is absorbed by society has emerged. Socialism in a state form has exhausted its potential and must now acquire new forms, which correspond more to its fundamentals, that of the individual realising his potential.

The hierarchical structure of the political system of socialism has hitherto placed the individual on the lowest level of the system, the smallest cog in the machine. The rights of the individual, currently, are certainly declared. But this is insufficient: the individual should be placed at the centre of the system, playing the role of the motive force. Human factors acquire primary importance in times of the information revolution, which by their inexhaustibility compensate for a growing deficit of more expensive resources. Due to its inherent nature, the socio-political system of socialism must become anthropo-centric, with a concentration on individuality. Furthermore, this notion corresponds to the future society which Engels considered was clearly defined by the founders of Marxism in the *Communist Manifesto*, 'the free development of each is the condition for the free development of all', and not otherwise.

Now, when for the first time in history we have the chance to achieve a practical organisation of social life which according to Marx would be worthy of and adequate for human nature, socialist society cannot but take into account and reflect in its political system the natural desire of the Soviet people to self-realisation and a broadening of their rights. Despite the extensive enumeration of rights and freedoms declared in the Soviet Constitution and the shifts that have taken place under *perestroika*, some fraternal countries have gone further than the USSR in the realisation and institutionalisation of civil rights. An example of this is the new post of public defence councillor or ombudsman elected by the Polish Sejm which was introduced in 1987.

The individual in socialist society strives to be a citizen in the highest meaning of the word, which is natural in this revolutionary period. However, this term appears to have been belittled in recent years and has taken on a more vulgar connotation. It is now time to return to the original meaning of the word.

A question of attitude toward spontaneity of social movements arises here. A negative evaluation of spontaneity still predominates in the USSR because it is viewed as a sign of immaturity. However, the soviets – the political foundation of society in the USSR – were born as a result of a spontaneous mass movement. Lenin spoke of 'the spontaneous formation of Soviets of Workers' Deputies' in 1905 and 1917. And was it not spontaneously that an active and critical approach towards Brezhnev's regime of corruption and stagnation grew among the masses? In the final analysis, has not this approach, this stance on the part of the people, led to *perestroika*? Under conditions of over-regimentation it could not have been otherwise.

'Spontaneity' should not be a word to be feared. It does not necessarily mean destruction or disorganisation. On the contrary, it is a rich and valuable aspect of life, the raw materials for an organisational framework so to speak. If organisations and structures attempt to protect themselves from the spontaneous flow of life by an 'iron fence' of restrictions and limits, they demonstrate their inability to respond to a spontaneous manifestation of activity and to govern them. They themselves become the victims of spontaneity and sooner or later find themselves fully intertwined. The value of such informal movements is that unplanned and undecreed self-initiative helps to form a democratic type of personality. This is one of the embryos of a society of socialist diversity and pluralism.

Regrettably, not all fully realise the importance of informal movements. At times some organisations, trade unions, the Komsomol and party committees treat them with prejudice. They see in them dangerous rivals and troublemakers that must be eliminated at all cost. This is a fundamentally incorrect and outdated approach. It is necessary to get accustomed to the fact that lively and varied self-realisation, in other spheres as well as the economy, is not a hindrance but a most important source and stimulus of development and a guarantee against stagnation. For this reason it is extremely important to remove all bureaucratic obstacles to these informal movements. The common principle here, as in other spheres of self-initiative, can only be that everything is allowed that is not forbidden by law.

It can be argued that the correct approach would be to grant a comprehensive right of self-organisation to all associations whose aims and activities do not contravene the law. This would enable at least two tasks to be solved. First, the negative tendencies in an informal movement would be removed internally under the pressure of public opinion. Secondly, the legalisation of a movement would help remove the 'halo' of secrecy and prohibitedness which exists around some of them, and which stimulates greater interest in them. This does not correspond with the essence and public significance of their activity. There is enough political experience in the USSR to understand that bans (modernism in painting, some trends in modern music, etc.) are less effective than legalisation from the point of view of securing public stability. In the long run, sound judgement will sift all that is alien, transient and unwise and select what is most valuable. The people have only to be trusted more.

This process of decreasing society's dependence on the state cannot but be accompanied by the creation of parallel centres of information and decision-making, which will lead to the emergence of independent public groups working together with the state organs. In some countries, socialist countries included, trade unions have an independent position on incomes, prices and wages (which in the USSR they have not). This is because they maintain their own statistics and calculations. In other countries informal and independent groups take the initiative in research on significant public issues, such as the environment. A comprehensive study of alternative and ecologically clean sources of energy could be within their scope in the USSR. Generally speaking, the introduction of competitiveness will not only help to assess all aspects of the problem in question and to increase involvement in the administrative process, but also to discover optimal decisions.

State, Party and *Perestroika*

In this connection, the practice of having multi-candidate elections and the promotion of alternative proposals, concerning above all local issues but within the framework of a unified electoral programme, seems to be of particular importance in the majority of socialist countries. The multi-mandate system used experimentally in the 1987 local election unfortunately represented only a modest improvement. In Poland, where such a system was tested but later rejected, prominent lawyers and specialists in state affairs have underlined the advantages of a single-mandate system with many candidates. In this case, the choice for the voter is clearer and simpler.

Taking everything into consideration, the use of a contested, electoral framework (in Yugoslavia, Hungary and now in the USSR) has turned out to be a good form of self-regulation and self-correction of development in different spheres and locations. As Kadar commented at the 13th Congress of the Hungarian Socialist Workers' Party in 1985, 'Let us make it quite clear that we are not creating anarchy at enterprise level. On the contrary, the manager will be dependent on the collective and there is nothing bad about him having to have a bit of worry sometimes when workers assess the running of the enterprise. However, work will be directed by the management'. Furthermore, the Hungarian Party Central Committee has explained the innovations in the electoral mechanism by the fact that 'Our people are politically mature and can be depended upon'.

Because people have different social interests, because there are many social groups participating in government and because each suggested policy has an alternative, it follows that conflict is not only possible but inevitable and that it is expedient to institutionalise it. Hitherto, the assumption of moral and political unity of the people has been used, which when there is an external danger does indeed exist. However, the growing diversity of socialist society and the complexity of its socio-professional structure, which refutes the hasty declaration of social homogeneity, should not lead to reluctance in admitting the existence of internal contradictions and conflicts. To deny this would mean 'hiding it away in the cellar', making it acquire destructive and anti-social forms. The problem is in the positive application of these contradictions and conflicts for the betterment of society and in their institutionalisation, so that conflict is taken into account within the system and some form of agreement negotiated.

Legality is an indispensable component of a genuine socialist democracy. Its development is a two-way process. On the one hand, it is necessary to implant legal consciousness, culture and a feeling of civil dignity in the masses, which has so far not been achieved due to the blatant neglect of the law by many organs of power not under legal jurisdiction. Legality must be taken seriously and by all without exception. On the other hand, Soviet law must be law in the full sense, not (as has often been the case) merely declaratory. There is a saying among lawyers that there are 'dead and semi-dead' laws. As I.I. Taranov put it at the summer 1987 session of the Supreme Soviet, 'Laws should be more demanding, concrete and clear'. To this N.I. Malkov, another deputy in the Supreme Soviet, added, 'The fact that our laws are quite often open to broad and inaccurate interpretation creates unnecessary complications'. The possibility of a direct application of the Constitution must be discussed before the appropriate laws are passed.

A constitutional court, as in Yugoslavia, Hungary and Poland, was demanded a long time ago in the USSR. It would have determined the conformity of laws, government and party-state decisions to the Constitution and would have annulled those that did not. At present, this function belongs to the Presidium of the USSR Supreme Soviet, which due to its character and composition is unable to perform this function and thus transfers it to the apparatus. Moreover, until the 1920s the Supreme Court of the USSR had the power to supervise the conformity of laws to the constitution at republican level, which had the same power over the decisions of executive organs. The USSR Supreme Court had been using its powers extensively until they were annulled and formally transferred to the Office of Public Prosecutor. However, under present conditions, the Supreme Court is overloaded with work as the highest court of appeal and it would have been improper to take on the functions of an entirely different character.

A constitutional court could be appointed for one or two terms of office by the Supreme Soviet, as the highest organ of power, to which the court could be accountable. Its members could enjoy immunity and irremovability until their term of office expired. Taking into account the experiences of fraternal countries, it could comprise such authoritative specialists as lawyers and policy experts and probably some most respected deputies of the Supreme Soviet.

Political reform, equally, cannot be imagined without a fundamental reconsideration of a number of outdated tenets of Soviet political theory or without a basic change in the Soviet view of democracy. The essence of democratisation can be expressed in a few words – the transition from formal to real democracy. However, the theoretical and practical tasks behind these words are immense in their revolutionary depth.

Modern representative democracy was born in the West and is one achievement for which humanity is indebted to the bourgeoisie. In its revolutionary adolescence, there were no class restrictions in those principles (a division of power, universal suffrage, freedom of speech, of the press and of political organisation, etc.) with which the bourgeoisie opposed the feudal political system. These principles were of a progressive character and had a generally civilising impetus. When the restrictiveness of bourgeois democracy is spoken about, it must be realised that it is not the democratic norms and principles at work in bourgeois society that are restrictive, but their actual content. Bourgeois democracy is historically restricted due to its inconsistency. Equality of political rights is not extended to the point of equality as far as the means of production are concerned, and this is why it is inevitably a political instrument in the hands of the ruling class.

Regrettably, for many decades the attitude to bourgeois democracy in Soviet political theory was unduly negative and indiscriminate. It turned out that, together with the class restrictiveness of bourgeois democracy, its generally civilising achievements were discounted and socialist democracy seemed to be something that had emerged outside of the traditions of world political thought, having no continuity with them. This process of negation is no more deeply rooted or stable than the logic of 'proletarian culture'.

Democratisation cannot but spread out into the way of life of the ruling party itself. This is the key condition for a better socio-political climate, ensuring the growth of society's trust in the party. It facilitates the absorption and development of democratic skills and approaches in communist-headed state and public organisations, the overcoming of bureaucratic elements and disregard of the needs and requirements of the people, which in turn stimulates democratic activity within society.

The perfecting of socialist democracy, whether it acquires a genuine or formal character, is above all dependent on the atmosphere within the party, the degree and effectiveness of the development of internal party democracy. In all spheres, it is the party and its members, with their way of life, that is destined to put the ideals of socialism into practice. This is both their duty and responsibility, as the behaviour of the nation's leaders sets the standards to be followed by society. The corruption and social egoism of responsible party workers must not be allowed to spread by rumour, but must be made public officially so that rigid legal, political and moral sanctions can be applied. The fact that leading party members and workers within the apparatus have material privileges has however to be accepted, at least to the extent that their material wellbeing should be dependent upon the performance of their subordinate organisations.

The costs of the party's monopoly of power and of having a one-party system must be taken into account. In 1921 A.A. Sol'ts, one of the leaders of the Party Central Control Commission, wrote, 'A prolonged stay in office during the epoch of the dictatorship of the proletariat has had a demoralising effect on a considerable part of old party workers. This is the origin of bureaucracy, of a highly arrogant approach to ordinary party members and the non-party masses and a horrendous misuse of their privileged position in access to goods. A communist, hierarchical caste has developed and come into being' (*Pravda*, 12 November 1921).

Lenin criticised the practice of the apparatus dictating its will to the party. His principle was that the apparatus should serve policy, not the other way round. Stalin placed the apparatus under his absolute control by ensuring social privilege and exclusivity on the one hand, and by terror and intimidation on the other. With Stalin's death and the ending of terror, the apparatus has become more successful in achieving independence and the subordination of society to its own interests. Khrushchev's reforms disintegrated when they stumbled against the power and inflexibility of the apparatus, and in the era of stagnation under Brezhnev it had its best period. Even now, long overdue social reform is 'bogged down' in the bureaucratic apparatus. Many letters to the press before the All-Union Party Conference of 1988 described how the apparatus had succeeded in their attempts to push the party rank and file aside and to prevent them forming a delegate bloc at the conference.

The ruling parties in such countries as Hungary, Yugoslavia, Vietnam and China are more definite in their recognition of the use of discussion and conflicts of opinion within the party, including real and meaningful exchanges of opinions between members on fundamental issues of policy. Whilst the current Party Rules of the CPSU treat discussion within the party as something extraordinary and an essentially negative phenomenon, it must become a norm of internal party life. At the 3rd Party Congress in 1905 Lenin pointed out the importance of the freedom of discussion and unity of action and proposed appropriate amendments to the Party Rules.

The CPSU Rules stipulate the member's right to 'express and defend one's opinion before a decision is adopted'. And what if the decision is incorrect? It seems that the condition stated here is contradictory to the party member's right 'to open discussion on party policy and activity at meetings, conferences, congresses, party committee meetings and in the party press'. (Why only the party press? And what about the government newspaper *Izvestiya* or in books published by Progress Publishers?

The Hungarian Socialist Workers' (now Socialist) Party, the Polish United Workers' Party, the Yugoslav League of Communists and some Bulgarian social scientists consider that if conflict and contradictions are manifest in society, then they must be reflected within the party. In these countries the minority's right to criticise the views and positions of the majority, even after the decision has been adopted, is guaranteed. At the same time the leaderships of these parties have warned against the danger of turning the party into a place of 'permanent discussion'.

The Hungarian Socialist Workers' Party and its leadership have long adhered to the interesting thesis that under the conditions of a one-party regime, the party must be its own 'opposition'. The party press in that country has also discussed the expediency of the creation of 'some form of counter-balance which would prevent the party adopting the wrong decisions and reduce the possibility of the emergence of formal and bureaucratic features in party work'.

So far as the Soviet party is concerned, a resolution unanimously adopted by the Central Committee in December 1923 stated: 'Only constant and animated ideological life can preserve the party such as it was before and after the revolution, with a constant critical study of its past, conviction of its mistakes and a collective discussion of important issues . . . It is essential that the leading party organs take account of the voice of the broad party masses without considering criticism as a manifestation of factionalism and in doing so, they should not push conscientious and disciplined party members into isolation and factionalism'.

It is now obviously time to return to the meaning and spirit of Lenin's approach to these questions, in which it was understood that without an animated internal party life it would not be possible in the party to resolve the serious tasks that faced it.

The problem of a differentiation of functions between the party and the state is and will remain a most difficult and topical one. As is known, Lenin in the 1920s was infuriated by the fact that without the Politburo it was not possible to resolve the most basic of problems, such as buying a batch of tinned food from abroad. While preparing for the 11th Party Congress in 1922 he demanded 'a more precise division of functions between the party (and the Central Committee) and the soviets . . . so that the general management of all state organs should be within the scope of the party and not, as is the case all too often at present, irregular and often minor intervention'. The Congress adopted an appropriate resolution: 'Under no conditions should party organisations interfere with the day to day current activity of economic organs and they should refrain from administrative decisions as far as the work of the soviets in general is concerned'. But these good intentions were never realised. Neither the Soviet party or any ruling party in other socialist countries has ever managed to refrain from interference in everyday situations, which is quite understandable.

The Polish concept of the party as not only being the leading social force but also an arbitrator in the relations between different social groups and organisations, between the state and the people, seems to be fruitful. However, in practice the Polish United Workers' Party is far from having restored its authority and the state enjoys much greater prestige. The leading role obviously cannot automatically be given to the party, it must live up to it daily by working effectively for the wellbeing of the people and the society. The other side of the question is a wider promotion of non-party members to leading positions in different spheres of social life, a practice that is followed in Poland, China and Hungary (but not so far in the USSR).

To summarise, in the course of *perestroika* the reform of the political system of socialism is becoming not only a theoretical and methodological problem but a practical one too, and a means of uniting and activating all healthy social forces.

Translated by Pavel Slavgorodsky and Graham Timmins

13

The Social Basis of
Perestroika

DAVID MANDEL

A troubling contradiction lies at the heart of *perestroika*. Officially, democratisation is the very essence of the *perestroika* that must proceed hand-in-hand with its other central component, economic reform. But in practice there is very little that is democratic about the manner in which the economic reform has been decided or is being carried out. Only one variant of reform is seriously discussed, the 'socialist market', presented to the Soviet people as the sole alternative to the discredited 'command-administrative system'. Details of the reform, some more important, others less so, become the object of public discussion, but there is no public debate about the kind of society people want. Yet any structural reform of the economy will necessarily have a profound impact on the nature of the society and on the socio-economic situation of all classes, groups and individuals in it.

This conflict between word and deed is an important clue to understanding the social nature of *perestroika*. In this chapter, we will follow Lenin's advice to 'seek behind any moral, religious, political or social phrases, declarations and promises the *interests* of one class or another'. What follows does not pretend to be a full portrait of Soviet society as it relates to *perestroika*. Limitations of space as well as knowledge of Soviet society, with its great social, ethnic and regional diversity, rule this out. Our aim is more modest: to analyse *basic* tendencies in the interests and attitudes of the three major social classes and strata of Soviet society – the bureaucracy, the working class and the intelligentsia, with particular emphasis upon the Russian heartland. While such an analysis omits such important elements as the national question (see Chapter 8), the commercial and service sectors and the peasantry, it is an important, if rough, tool for making sense of events.

The great majority of Soviet citizens are dissatisfied with the state of the economy and agree on the need for basic reform. The principal exceptions are among members of the various administrative apparatuses, the currently much-maligned bureaucrats, though even here not all oppose reform. But Soviet officials and publicists go much further when they present the market reform as a socially neutral operation in which all groups are objectively interested, except those bureaucrats who will become superfluous or refuse to adapt. This hardly accords with the less public or veiled admissions by these same publicists that successful promulgation of the reform requires a 'firm hand', even a 'Cavaignac' (the general who crushed the 1848 Parisian workers' uprising). Nor does it accord with complaints by social scientists that the Soviet people do not understand the difference between 'responsible democracy' and a 'democracy of wishes', implying that if they were allowed to decide collectively they would pursue wishes that conflicted with a 'responsible' reform programme.

Of course, if there really were no alternative to the market reform one could justifiably argue that it was socially neutral, even though it would cause short-term pain to some and perhaps long-term deterioration of their relative socio-economic situation. If this were the only way to progress, then these costs would be unfortunate but necessary. But is the 'socialist market', as conceived by the Soviet leaders, the only alternative to the discredited 'command system'? This admittedly complex issue – there is no experience anywhere with a 'third way' – has effectively been excluded from public debate. Logically, however, it must be part of any honest analysis of the social basis of *perestroika*.

'Revolution From Above'

Our thesis is that *perestroika* is an attempt by the more farsighted elements of the ruling bureaucracy to rationalise their system through the use of the market, necessarily accompanied by political liberalisation. Official rhetoric aside, the leadership sees in this transformation of the mode of domination a means of retaining the essential part of their power and privilege while avoiding a democratic revolution. There is no doubt that, compared with what preceded it, *perestroika* has many progressive aspects. But like the 1861 emancipation of the serfs and similar 'revolutions from above', it is in its conception a fundamentally anti-popular response to the crisis of the existing order. Of course the final outcome of the reform process may be quite different from this intention. But this will depend on the evolving correlation of political forces that the reformers have willy-nilly unleashed.

At the end of 1987, a visiting Central Committee secretary told a gathering in the southern town of Shakhty that if the party had not announced *perestroika* in time, the people would have taken to the streets. It is difficult to judge the immediacy of this threat. But there is no doubt that by 1985 the depth of popular discontent with stagnant living standards and with the corruption that infected all levels of government had finally convinced a majority of the political leadership that the system Brezhnev had left them was no longer capable of maintaining either the internal stability of their regime or its great power status (the first consideration being by far the weightier).

Although the reform project has involved much improvisation and continues to evolve under the impact of various economic and political influences, its logic is reasonably clear. The aim of the economic reform is to replace the centralised 'command economy', which, ideally, treats the Soviet economy as one huge enterprise, with one in which relations among enterprises are no longer based on administrative order from above, but on freely entered contracts. Vertical coordination by the huge party-state bureaucracy is to give way to horizontal economic coordination through the market. Overall planning and regulation will be achieved by means of indirect, economic levers, such as interest rates and taxation, which will set the parameters within which autonomous, competing enterprises make decisions.

This reform means the abandonment of the traditional socialist vision (reality was always rather different) of an increasingly egalitarian society with firm socio-economic guarantees for all its members. This vision is now said to be outmoded and to conflict with the demands of economic efficiency. If Soviet society is to progress economically, it must condemn 'levelling' tendencies and materially encourage enterprises and individuals that produce goods and services that society values. And the market is the only proven way for society effectively to express these judgements.

Soviet leaders assure the population that under the reform social policy will guarantee a basic minimum to all and protect those who cannot compete: the infirm, the elderly, those who lose their jobs to restructuring, and others. Nevertheless, as the current onslaught on the welfare state in the West shows, this does not resolve the fundamental contradiction between market rationality and social guarantees. Another unresolved contradiction is that between the market and enterprise self-management, officially an integral part of the reform. A coherent market reform requires functioning capital and labour markets: the market must be able to penalise inefficient enterprises through reduced profits and employee incomes and, ultimately, by forcing layoffs and bankruptcies. But Yugoslavia's lengthy experience with self-management shows that when workers hold power in the enterprise, they use it to secure their jobs and incomes. And today, as Yugoslavia's leaders attempt to strengthen the market, self-management is increasingly under attack.

The declared political objective of *perestroika* is 'democratisation'. But if democracy is a state in which citizens collectively decide the important issues affecting their lives, one must conclude this is not the real intention. Not only was the economic reform decided 'on high' and only then handed down to the public for discussion and amendment, but this has been the case for virtually all crucial economic and political questions. For example the basic contours of the 13th Five-Year Plan (1991–5) were established, as always, in secret, mid-way in the current plan. At some point they will be submitted to the public – and this is real progress compared with what went before – but the basic alternatives have already been excluded. The same occurred with the less-than-democratic rules governing the 1989 elections to the Congress of People's Deputies (see Chapter 5), which assured Gorbachev a docile majority but with enough critical voices to make for lively debate. Soviet citizens were delighted by the openness of the discussion, but all the items on the Congress's agenda, itself presented to the delegates as a *fait accompli*, passed as recommended.

Even the far-reaching liberalisation of the press has by no means meant free access to publishing or an end to state control of what appears. Gorbachev has criticised those who would 'detach the press from the party. In questions of principle there can be no concessions. There is the political line and the basic orientations that must define the direction of the press. In the rest . . . [there must be] full creative freedom, the right to pose questions and defend one's positions'. Demonstrations require prior permission of local authorities – offenders are open to stiff fines and up to two weeks in jail. As for the KGB, the ultimate pillar of bureaucratic power, it has retreated to the shadows, but remains quite intact and outside democratic control. Article 70 of the penal code – 'anti-Soviet propaganda' and 'slander of Soviet institutions' – used in the past to justify political repression, has been revised, but the changes made in April 1989 still declare illegal the 'defamation and discrediting of state organs and social institutions'. Also illegal are calls 'to change the social and political regime' of the Soviet Union. One might ask if this is an admission that *perestroika* itself does not really intend to do this?

Critics of 'Western-style' – that is, capitalist – democracy point out that while competitive elections and (more-or-less) freedom of speech and association afford a measure of popular control over government, they in themselves do not make a democracy. When there are systematic barriers that prevent certain ideas and interests from entering the 'political market place' and forces outside the formal political system that circumscribe parliament's power to carry out the popular mandate, competitive elections may, in fact, serve as an ideological substitute for popular sovereignty, a subtle and flexible means of domination.

The basic issue in the Soviet Union is undoubtedly the party's 'leading role', enshrined in article 6 of the Soviet Constitution. One of the political demands voiced by some coalminers in their July 1989 strike was repeal of this article, which in practice has meant the domination of society by the party-state bureaucracy. There are really two interrelated questions: will the party's 20-odd million members continue to be dominated by a self-appointing apparatus; and will the party cease to reserve for itself the exclusive right to set the country's political agenda and allow other parties with qualitatively different programmes freely to compete with it for power? Since his arrival, Gorbachev has conducted a large-scale purge of the party apparatus, and the rather open debate at 19th Party Conference in mid-1988, despite the undemocratic nature of the elections, was evidence of some liberalisation of the internal party regime. But five years into *perestroika* party officials are still appointed or 'confirmed' from above; and despite competitive elections in some lower party committees, there were few signs of a democratic revival of the party as a mass political movement.

Soviet leaders are, in fact, at pains to justify the party's continued 'leading role', even if, in 1990, they agreed to relinquish the constitutional guarantee that underpinned it. Noting that most of the people elected to the Congress of People's Deputies were party members, Gorbachev told the April 1989 plenum of the Central Committee that 'with their choice, the Soviet people confirmed that they see in the party the only real and dependable political force capable of securing the renewal of society and its consolidation'. But how real was that choice? He failed to mention the embarrassing defeat of many prominent party leaders, including the first party secretaries of Leningrad and Kiev, who ran in that part of the elections open to universal suffrage. The majority of prominent functionaries entered the Congress as delegates of the various 'social organisations', including the party, which were guaranteed one third of the seats (see Chapter 5). Gorbachev has been very clear: if the party, that is its apparatus, must henceforth forgo day-to-day detailed intervention in economic management, its political role under *perestroika* will only grow.

One need not belabour this point. There is some merit to the argument that the bureaucracy is not a ruling class in the historical sense. (It controls but does not own the means of production and, incapable of legitimising its domination, it has had to mask its real existence. Trotsky called it a 'cancerous excrescence on the body of the proletariat'). But it would be naive to believe that after sixty years of usurpation, during which it did not hesitate to use the harshest methods to maintain its rule, the bureaucracy's leaders, all of whom have risen through the ranks, have decided that it is time to restore power to society. To the degree that something resembling this occurred in Czechoslovakia in 1968 or in Hungary in 1956, it was against the background of a profound internal crisis within the bureaucracy and a powerful popular mobilisation. There are signs that these processes are maturing today in the Soviet Union, but they have not been prominent elements of *perestroika's* first five years.

The political and economic aspects of *perestroika* are intimately related. 'Democratisation' is intended to win support for the economic reform among a population that, in its mass, is mistrustful, all the more so as the economic situation has deteriorated since *perestroika* was proclaimed. Similarly, enterprise self-management – so far, scarcely more real than political democracy – is designed to win workers' acceptance of the far-reaching changes in relations within the enterprise required by the economic reform. It is also a precondition for workers assuming responsibility for the enterprise's profitability, which is to determine the size of their incomes. But 'democratisation' is also a means of harnessing popular hostility to the bureaucracy to help overcome the latter's resistance to the economic reform. Finally, open debate and criticism have now been recognised as necessary elements of efficient economic decision-making.

The Bureaucracy

The thesis that *perestroika* is the bureaucratic response to the system's crisis seems paradoxical in the face of its strongly 'anti-bureaucratic' thrust. Bureaucrats are enemy no. 1 in the Soviet media, the villains who are holding back the market reform and opposing 'democratisation'. But this paradox merely reflects the contradictory nature of the bureaucracy itself – a ruling stratum whose interests are in conflict with the very logic of the socio-economic system it administers.

The Soviet bureaucracy did not make the socialist revolution. It was a product of it, and its rise to power was an unintended consequence of the backwardness of Russian society and of the revolution's isolation. But the extreme deformation that the revolution underwent in the 1920s and 1930s under the bureaucracy's leadership did not lead to the restoration of capitalism. It led rather to the establishment of the 'command economy' and to the totalitarian attempt to control and guide all aspects of social life. The problem with such a regime is that, once established, it tends to be an inherently conservative and wasteful manager and itself to divide along functional, regional and mafia-type 'clan' lines, as each group pursues its narrow interests at the expense of national goals. Moreover, a regime whose basis lies in the usurpation of power and illegitimate appropriation of material privileges finds it very difficult to keep corruption and abuse of office within 'acceptable' limits, as functionaries constantly seek to draw additional benefits from the spheres entrusted to them.

The unfettered pursuit of their individual interests by the members of the bureaucracy thus leads inexorably to the undermining of bureaucratic power. The survival of this system calls for a strong leader to protect the bureaucracy from itself. Stalin kept the bureaucracy – and society – in line through a terror apparatus that he personally controlled. Khrushchev used non-terroristic measures to maintain the bureaucracy in a stage of insecurity, while he tried to build an independent political base through a mixture of populist politics and improvement of popular living standards. This strategy failed, and the bureaucracy replaced him with their own man, Brezhnev, who was content to let matters drift. His regime led to the profound systemic crisis of the end of the 1970s.

Soviet sources claim that there are today 18 million bureaucrats (though only 5.25 million themselves command subordinates) in an active population of 131 million. The majority of these functionaries do not view sympathetically Gorbachev's efforts to 'save them from themselves'. There are many reasons for this opposition. On the most general level is the justified fear that structural reforms are a risky undertaking whose consequences can never be predicted. Gorbachev's political liberalisation quickly revealed the depth and extent of popular hostility toward the 'bureaucratic parasites'. Nor is it clear that the reform will yield positive economic results.

Anyone so inclined would have little difficulty portraying in a negative light the reform experience of other Soviet-type societies. After an initial period of rapid growth, most of these economies have been hit by high inflation, foreign indebtedness and a renewed tendency toward stagnation. In Czechoslovakia (1968) and China (1989) reforms placed bureaucratic power in mortal danger. The Yugoslav federation is being torn apart by severe national tensions and growing labour strife.

The 'command economy' was the bureaucracy's response to the crisis of the mixed economy of the late 1920s. Administering the planned economy has since been the principal *raison d'être* of the huge party and ministerial apparatuses. These now face the prospect of losing much of this economic power. Whole administrations, hundreds of thousands of positions, are to be abolished. The available jobs in industry and services offer neither status, conditions nor remuneration comparable to those being lost. According to journalistic accounts, there is a feeling of betrayal in these administrations. It is 'heart attack season'.

Even for those whose positions are not being cut, *perestroika* has opened up a period of heightened insecurity. Gorbachev's early purges were undoubtedly welcomed by middle-aged and younger members of the bureaucracy, who found their careers blocked by Brezhnev's gerontocracy. (His regime's hallmark was 'respect for cadres'.) But functionaries would not be functionaries if they did not yearn for job security. *Perestroika* is directed against this fundamental interest. It aims to make job tenure depend upon strict, regular evaluations of job performance. What is even more distressing is that these evaluations are no longer to be made only by administrative superiors but also by elected popular delegates and employees. The dismissal in July 1989 of Yuri Solov'ev, first secretary of the Leningrad regional party committee, after his crushing defeat in the elections to the Congress of People's Deputies is a case in point. Sociological studies have shown uniform hostility among managers to democratisation of enterprise administration, and interviews with deposed ministers make clear that attitudes are shared at higher levels. Even the most competent administrators feel that public scrutiny and control only complicate an already difficult job.

'Democratisation' also poses a threat to the economic situation of members of the apparatus. In the Soviet context the bureaucrats' non-salary income and benefits are seen by the population as abuses of office. This system of privilege – special access to housing, to scarce and/or high quality goods and services at low prices (as well as income from bribes) – is not limited to the upper stratum of the *nomenklatura* but permeates all levels. Although there has been a campaign against the more blatant forms of corruption, bureaucratic privilege remains largely intact. Angry letters and exposes continue to appear from time to time in the press, and *glasnost'* has only intensified public hostility towards these privileges. Some Soviet analysts argue that bureaucrats should welcome the market reform since it will restore their dignity, replacing the hidden system of distribution, made necessary by generalised scarcity and 'levelling ideology', with legitimate, monetary incomes comparable to those earned by executives in capitalist countries. (Top US executives earn 93 times the average factory wage.) But it is an open question whether such a transition is politically possible in face of the strong egalitarian attitudes among workers, who typically feel that it is their labour supporting the army of bureaucratic 'hangers-on'.

Administrators in the repressive agencies of the state – the police, KGB and the army – share many of the same basic attitudes and interests as their colleagues in the party and economic apparatuses. These organisations, particularly the KGB, have been only slightly less spared by *glasnost'* from public criticism. Large-scale cutbacks are envisaged in the armed forces – half a million for the present, many of these officers. By July 1989, more generals have been cut than are on active duty in the US and West German armies combined. (The police force and internal security forces will probably grow because of the alarm over the increase in crime and social unrest.) But as police organisations, the KGB and militia cannot be very happy about the liberalisation and growing public activism in society, especially since the rules are no longer clear and tend to change suddenly with the political weather, adding a special element of insecurity to their situation. The armed forces have also been deeply affected by Gorbachev's new military doctrine of 'reasonable sufficiency', which has given rise to lively debate about what is 'enough'. The new thinking in foreign policy de-emphasises military might in favour of political actions. These have principally taken the form of unilateral Soviet moves, including cuts in the military budget and partial civilian reconversion of military industry, that many in the military feel weaken Soviet defence or can be seen as a sign of weakness by a potential aggressor. There is also discontent over the declining prestige of the uniform among youth, increasingly open to pacifist ideas and influenced by criticism of the armed forces in the media.

Genuine, active support in the bureaucracy for *perestroika* is thin. There are, of course, very competent, energetic and enlightened elements in all branches of the bureaucracy that understand the necessity of far-reaching reform and welcome the challenge. But nowhere are they a majority. Not even managers at the enterprise level, who are to be freed from bureaucratic tutelage, are always enthusiastic about the reforms. Those who have been successful in the past owe much of this success to relations they developed with superiors in the state and party bureaucracies. The market reform, if it is consistent, will make these irrelevant and demand very different talents. Then it is necessary to learn how to deal with the workers, who are losing their deference and fear of management. Even if genuine self-management never materialises, the economic reforms and political liberalisation have already produced a much less malleable work force.

As a social stratum, the bureaucracy is organised hierarchically and so cannot openly challenge a more-or-less unified leadership, such as has existed until now (though the cracks are growing). Formally, therefore, all are for *perestroika*. But hostility is never far below the surface. At the 19th Party Congress Gorbachev was met with a stormy ovation when he berated the press for dwelling on shortcomings, but his comment that criticism could not be stifled drew stony silence from the majority. A year later at the Congress of People's Deputies, the whole country witnessed the bitter hostility of the majority of delegates towards the liberals from Moscow and the Baltic republics. At party meetings, high level regional functionaries have expressed concern that the political situation was getting out of hand. At a conference in July 1989 with first secretaries of republican and regional party organisations Gorbachev openly warned those who dreamt of a return to the good old days.

For the most part, however, opposition expresses itself in inconsistent or toothless laws and half-measures and in active and passive resistance to the reform. For example, the long-awaited law of 1987 permitting legal suits against officials who violate civil rights effectively rules out action on matters of importance to citizens, since most of these are decided by collegial bodies which the law protects from legal action. This prompted one law professor to call it 'a toy for the bureaucrats'. Almost all of the economic reform measures reflect the unresolved struggle between partisans of the market and those who want to retain the essential elements of the 'command system'. Although the new Law on the State Enterprise appeared to give enterprises their autonomy, ministries continue to dictate through 'state orders' that can cover up to 100 per cent of output. In practice these state orders cannot be refused, and in any case most managers accept them happily as there is still no market in machinery and raw materials, while the ministry guarantees the supplies for its orders. It is promised that these inconsistencies will progressively be corrected. But time is running out on a reform that is slow in showing results.

Commenting on the year gone by in the trade union paper *Trud* at the end of 1988, Gavriil Popov, a leading pro-market economist, admitted:

> I was unable to imagine to what degree the apparatus is incapable of carrying out even its own version of *perestroika*. The devotion of the conservative forces of the apparatus to the past, the desire to preserve at any price their old methods of work (and themselves, as the bearers of these methods) surpassed all my expectations.

Examples of this at all levels of management abound in the Soviet press. Enterprise democracy is making slow headway against managerial resistance, and trade union officials generally remain on the side of management or else passive in conflicts. Meetings are called to decide on a choice of 'cost-accounting regime' at which the workers are informed of the choice already made. Directors have themselves elected chairpersons of the organs of self-management, which then meet only to rubberstamp the directors' decisions. Easy profits are made by unjustifiably jacking up prices and concentrating on production of expensive brands of goods, thereby causing scarcity of affordable brands. A wage reform that seeks to raise basic wages through internal economies is rammed through by arbitrarily demoting all the workers to lower skill levels, reducing bonuses and then raising the wages of the various grades.

There are also numerous reports of fictitious staff reductions in the apparatus. Ministries that are praised for their foresight in ending new hiring early and reducing staff through natural attrition are found upon closer inspection to have included the staff of subordinate enterprises in their calculations. The personnel of the State Committee on Supply actually grew by 4,000. In other cases, organisations liquidate themselves only to reappear under a new name. A report of the government–union working group on employment from May 1989 stated that inflated managerial staff in the enterprises is being paid for by reductions in worker personnel. Experience to date makes it difficult to avoid the conclusion that the reform will continue to flounder as long as it is entrusted to the bureaucracy.

The Workers

Soviet social scientists and journalists frequently attribute workers' mistrust of the economic reform to their alleged penchant for an easy life. In fact, according to the All-Union Trade Union Council, real wages have stagnated over the past 18 years. Health and safety conditions in industry are terrible. Production cadences wreak havoc with workers' lives, alternating periods of enforced idleness with 'storming' that requires massive overtime, including frequently weekends and holidays. Trade unions are the tools of management, and, in the last analysis, workers have no sure recourse against arbitrary decisions of the administration. And last but not least, workers experience daily in their factories the terrible waste and irrationality of a system that deprives them even of the satisfaction of doing good work when they want to.

It is not reform itself, but what is being proposed that makes workers uneasy. They are being told that social guarantees and egalitarian tendencies discourage productivity. If workers want a better life, they must give up certain guarantees, allow the others to be weakened, and accept as legitimate a greater measure of socioeconomic inequality. This is worrying to workers not only because it conflicts with basic values and attitudes, but also because the decisions are being made and applied in the absence of genuine democracy at either the state or enterprise level.

Soviet workers tend to look on the October revolution of 1917 as a good thing that went sour and needs to be restored to its original ideals. Most do not see the market reform as doing this. On the contrary, it threatens even those mediocre social guarantees that they already enjoy, offering in return the mere promise of a higher level of consumption. One of these guarantees is job security. Together with the chronic labour shortage that the 'command economy' constantly reproduced, it gave workers a certain bargaining power *vis-à-vis* management, even in the absence of democratic trade unions: if workers were dissatisfied with wages or conditions, they could always 'vote with their feet', that is seek work elsewhere. Managers, on the other hand, had little incentive to economise on labour costs and tried to give the workers a relatively higher wage within the limits at their discretion.

Under the 'command economy' relations between workers and managers were characterised by a sort of collusion to conceal productivity reserves and, when necessary, violate the spirit and even the letter of the law in order to meet plan targets. Workers could depend on a relatively stable, if still mediocre, wage that was only loosely related to the actual work performed or to the performance of the enterprise. In return they would make management's job easier by tolerating legal violations and substandard conditions. The tendency within enterprises and branches was toward wage levelling. The incentive role of the individual wage was further reduced by the increasingly large part of workers' income that came from social funds, that is free or subsidised services and goods that bore no direct relation to work. (This official policy was portrayed as part of the transition to the higher phase of socialism, where each person would receive according to his or her need, regardless of that person's contribution to the economy.)

While these characteristics of Soviet labour relations have existed in some degree since the 1930s, this system attained its fullest expression under Brezhnev. It is important to note that this was the direct consequence of the Brezhnev regime's refusal to reform the economy, a refusal dictated by the corporate interests of its bureaucratic base as well as by a more general fear of the popular forces that structural reform might unleash. For this reason many Soviet workers now feel that they are being blamed for the sins of others.

The reform would eliminate the workers' *de facto* job security. Subjected to market discipline, enterprises would be forced to shed excess manpower, and some would go bankrupt. Unemployment allocations have been restored for the first time since the 1920s. But the director of Gosplan's research institute has complained that 'people have a simplistic understanding of guarantees: to keep the same job, in the same profession, in the same enterprise'. Few would deny that Soviet enterprises are overstaffed and that a certain redistribution of the labour force is economically justified. But in the absence of democratic trade unions or real self-management abuses are already widespread. Dismissals proceed without consultation with the worker collectives, as required by law, and the first to be fired are pensioners, older workers, and women with small children, that is workers who through no fault of their own are less productive – and also, of course, 'trouble-makers' who refuse to accept management's violations of the law.

More generally, the ending of job security and the threat of unemployment radically change the correlation of forces in the enterprise, giving management effective new means to enforce its will. Even if the Soviet Union will continue to suffer from a general labour shortage for some time the threat of being made redundant will be deeply felt, since most jobs will be in unattractive sectors and regions. In addition many social benefits, for example one's place in the queue for housing, are related to length of service at the enterprise. In the course of the illegal demotions related to the wage reform managers have simply told workers to sign the reclassification decision or look for work elsewhere. Despite official denials, some economists are quite frank about the utility of 'a small reserve army of labour' for enforcing discipline. And if this army is to play its role well, life within its ranks cannot be too comfortable. The slowness with which the government has been moving to establish the promised job-placement and retraining system speaks loudly of the low priority assigned to so important an issue for workers.

The market reform would also eliminate income guarantees, since its aim is to link incomes more closely to 'the results of labour'. In particular, wages will strongly depend on the market performance of the enterprise, something that will lead to increased inequality between enterprises and sectors. There is also the intention to reduce the relative size of the social wage in incomes. Originally this was to be achieved through a price reform that would reduce or eliminate subsidies on basic goods and services and be compensated for by higher individual wages. But this project, essential to any market reform, has had to be shelved for the present in the face of intensely hostile public reaction. 'Are you trying to say that social funds are unnecessary and free benefits corrupt?' retorted a textile worker during a roundtable discussion on social justice. 'They are our pride, our hard-won right, our guarantees of social protection. The problem is that they have not been distributed justly.'

Workers tend to identify socialism with the guarantee of a decent income for anyone who works conscientiously or who is unable to work. This should not depend upon such 'accidental' factors as the situation of the individual or the enterprise in the market. Nor should workers be penalised for the 'sins of others' – i.e. the failure in the past of their ministry or director to invest in up-to-date technology. These were decisions over which the workers had no control. Yet although most workers hold strong egalitarian values, they are not 'levellers'. They believe that dangerous, onerous and generally unattractive work merits higher material compensation. They also agree that talent and initiative, contributions by specialists to economic productivity and more productive work by workers, when they are responsible for the results, should be rewarded. But these incentives should not lead to qualitative social inequality that divides society into hostile groups. Nor should people, who through no fault of their own cannot be as productive as the best, be penalised by a less-than-decent living standard.

The conflict between workers' sense of justice and market criteria of rationality emerges clearly in the following worker's letter that appeared in the summer of 1989 in the daily paper *Sotsialisticheskaya industriya*:

Lately I have been doing a lot of thinking about the formula: 'From each according to his abilities; to each according to his labour'. Does that mean that a young member of a cooperative, a football player or a rock musician should receive truckloads of money, while I, who have lived through war, cold and hunger and have worked 44 years should get crumbs?

But why talk about me and them? One factory grows rich under the new economic model by jacking up prices. A mechanic in this factory earns well, even excellently, since his wage depends upon the profits. The factory managed to have its state order lowered to cover only the more expensive goods, leaving the cheap goods to freely exchange for meat and building materials for housing. The other factory makes only inexpensive goods, though very much needed by the economy. The authorities won't let it change. And you can't exchange these goods for anything, since these are parts used only in industry. The factory is poor, and the mechanic, who repairs exactly the same kind of machinery as his counterpart at the first factory, is also poor, without meat and housing. Equal work – different lives.

I heard on the radio that we have 40 million poor. What will the figure be in the future? Will not our state be divided into a class of rich and a class of poor?

Some workers, of course, are enthusiastic about the reform. They welcome the market as giving them more initiative and autonomy and allowing them to earn high wages. These are especially highly skilled workers, in great demand, who do not fear the risks of competition in an unfettered market. However, the harsh discipline and the sweatshop-like pace in much of the cooperative sector have cooled the ardour of many of these. Even in the state sector many of the miraculous recoveries of failing enterprises that have been leased out to the workers have been found to be due to massive overtime. Another source of working class support for the reform is in enterprises that have benefited from investments in modern technology and/or produce goods that put them in a favourable position in the market, especially the world market. But even here there is disenchantment with the absence of genuine self-management and enterprise autonomy, as ministries continue to dictate and redistribute earnings among enterprises.

In the coalminers' strike in the summer of 1989, Soviet leaders and the media were at pains to explain – one could almost hear the sigh of relief – that the workers' protest movement was really in support of *perestroika*. They based this assertion upon the workers' demand for enterprise autonomy, for the right to sell above-plan coal at contractual prices and to decide on their own how to use this income. It was emphasised over and over that this was the strike's central demand, a claim that is difficult to judge given the virtual media monopoly of the pro-market position as well as the role of the government commission in formulating the final version of the workers' demands and the settlement. But there is little doubt that workers' basic grievance was that they were not benefitting from the wealth they produced, which was being fully appropriated by the central government only seemingly to disappear thereafter. In the existing political and ideological context, the demand for decentralised control of at least some part of this wealth through increased enterprise autonomy is a logical one (though there were a few reports of strike leaders demanding a national conference of miners collectively to discuss the situation of the industry – this is the path being taken, for example, by workers in the fishing industry). But this is certainly not a sufficient basis to affirm that the workers have embraced the market reform as such, with the social and economic consequences described above.

In the very midst of the miners' strike Gorbachev made the following comment: 'Of late the growth of significant social strata under the influence of radical leftist positions has become evident. Populist ideas, leftist speculation on demands for social justice in the spirit of universal equalising circulate broadly'. Virtually ignored by the media was the Donbass miners' demand to close down food, medical and processing cooperatives, market enclaves in the still basically administrative system. Popular hostility to what are considered the unjustly high, unearned incomes of these cooperators is fierce; a referendum would certainly yield a majority in favour of their severe restriction, if not complete outlawing. But when Gorbachev did make a passing reference to this demand at a conference of first party secretaries in 1989, it was only to dismiss it as an easy but unwise solution, saying that their activity should be regulated by local authorities. Another demand that was given short shrift was the ending of bureaucratic privilege.

The miners' strike, probably the most massive collective labour protest since the October revolution, has made very clear the workers' potential to make or break the economic reform. Gorbachev moved quickly to try to coopt this movement to his cause. But he cannot credibly pursue this strategy without also responding to the workers' political aspirations – also made very clear during the strike – for genuine democracy and for their own independent political and economic organisation. If our analysis is correct, this strategy is fundamentally flawed, since the economic reform as presently conceived is ultimately incompatible with the workers' interests and aspirations. In any case it would require a genuine commitment to democracy, something that Gorbachev has not been able to make.

The Intelligentsia

Support for Gorbachev's project is strongest and most widespread among the intelligentsia. This group includes artists, writers, performers, and 'specialists' – i.e. people with diplomas of higher education in non-management positions. The latter numbered 9.6 million in 1985. This is a very heterogenous group, whose interests are less determinate than other groups in society. One should, therefore, be more wary of generalisations concerning the intelligentsia than of even those about functionaries and workers.

Most of the intelligentsia felt particularly abused under the Brezhnev regime. Intellectual freedom, a professional as well as human interest for this group, was reduced to its narrowest limits. Those who wielded power rarely sought or took into account the opinions of representatives of the intelligentsia. The relative (and, towards the end, absolute) material situation of the intelligentsia declined over that period, so that when Brezhnev died, specialists in industry were earning on the average slightly less than workers. Those outside of industry generally earned even less.

For these people, *perestroika* is restoring justice and rationality. They are delighted at the liberalisation and reassured by the controlled nature of 'democratisation' – contempt and fear of the workers run deep in the intelligentsia. At the same time, the political status, though not necessarily real power, of the intelligentsia has sharply risen. Prominent members of the intelligentsia now dominate public debates and have become leading parliamentarians. A sign of the times is the appointment of academician Abalkin, a popular figure among the intelligentsia, to be Vice-Chairman of the Council of Ministers and Chairman of the state commission on economic reform. In nominating him, the prime minister insisted that Abalkin retain his post as head of the Economics Institute of the Academy of Sciences, that is that he maintain his ties with the intelligentsia, and stressed the need to bring into government work the best intellectual forces. Social scientists are calling for massive expansion of their fields as a requisite of any modern society.

The intelligentsia appears to be broadly supportive of the market reform, which they see as a move away from ideology and towards rationality. The increased socio-economic inequality that will result is expected to benefit the highly skilled. Impatient and envious glances are being cast at the incomes of artists and professionals in the Western market economies. The cooperative (really private) sector, which has made very high incomes possible for some, is hiring mainly the very skilled. Publicists are exhorting readers to shed old stereotypes and accept the huge incomes that people with skills that are in demand on the world market can expect to make. One senior engineer expressed his satisfaction in this way: 'I have been working for twenty years at a scientific institute but only now am I beginning to understand the social significance of my work. The cost-accounting and self-financing regimes have destroyed unproductive economic levelling. As project manager I earned 1,500 rubles last month. Before, my salary was never over three hundred'. In 1988, with the market reform still far from implemented, average wages of workers rose by 10 per cent; salaries of scientific-technical and managerial personnel rose by 20–30 per cent. This trend became more accentuated in the first half of 1989.

There are important differences in the outlook of pro-*perestroika* intellectuals. Many would readily subscribe to the witticism that 'socialism is the shortest route between capitalism and capitalism'. They identify the bureaucratic system with socialism and see its experience as proof of the latter's utopian and harmful nature. These people often espouse extreme neo-liberal positions, arguing that any government intervention in the activity of enterprises is by its very nature undemocratic – whether that government is itself democratic or not seems not to matter – and counterproductive. Calling for the fullest autonomy for enterprises, for leasing them to the workers, for the promotion of cooperative and private enterprise, they note that under centralised planning there was an absence of initiative and responsibility because property belonged to everyone and so to no one. (In fact, the centralised economy was fully controlled by the bureaucracy and in no real sense 'everyone's'.) The implication is that social forms of property are contrary to human nature and inherently unproductive. They also call to drastically reduce or even eliminate free and subsidised social services, to marketise them, since redistribution by the state makes labour 'unfree' and violates the principle of 'payment according to labour'. They are strongly seconded in these views by the members of the burgeoning cooperative sector.

These more extreme proponents of the market – it is difficult to say what proportion they are, but it is significant – tend, logically, to be cautious in their support for democracy, given attitudes within the working class toward the measures they espouse. Characteristically, they mythologise the mixed economy of the 1920s as Soviet Russia's golden age, gliding over the fact that its political regime, though certainly more liberal than Stalin's, was far from democratic. They often limit their advocacy of democracy to enterprise autonomy and the reduction of state economic regulation. One economist, summing up the results of discussions at a conference of social scientists in Novosibirsk in 1988, wrote that workers were either hostile to or suspicious of the economic reform. Apparently they had some reason to be since, according to the author, the reform could not be at once 'soft and deep'; sometimes 'harsh and unpopular measures' would be required. He concluded by expressing the conference's doubts about whether the people were ready for 'responsible democracy'.

Other pro-market intellectuals, including many in the 'informal' movement, see the market reform rather as a way of making socialism work. They argue that since the reform will demand sacrifices, popular support depends upon maintaining social guarantees as well as on genuine democratisation as the only real insurance that this reform, unlike those in the past, will ultimately benefit the people. They emphasise that the reform has no chance of succeeding against bureaucratic resistance unless it can win popular support. But, like Gorbachev's response to the miners' strike, this position poses serious questions. Can a consistent market reform win the support of a majority of the people? In other words, is a viable market reform compatible with the kind and extent of guarantees that the people want? And even if some solution could be found, is the current political leadership prepared to allow the kind of political changes, that is genuine democracy, that are required to overcome the workers' scepticism?

A third intellectual current tries to address itself to these questions. It finds its support among Marxist elements in the 'informal' movement and in the social sciences, as well as among a section of the specialists in industry whose work and social situation place them in close daily contact with workers. Their voice is rarely heard in the mass media, but they represent a minority that attributes the failures of the Soviet system not to socialism but to its absence. They agree with the marketeers that the problem is the absence of a genuine owner, whose economic wellbeing depends on how efficiently his or her wealth is managed. But this owner is a collective one, the Soviet people, whose power over economic planning and management has been usurped by the bureaucracy. Yet the bureaucrats themselves are not owners. Their socioeconomic situation depends not on how much they increase national wealth but on how well they please their bureaucratic superiors. Soviet experience shows that not only are these not the same thing, but they are often in conflict.

These intellectuals see in *perestroika* an attempt by the bureaucracy's leaders to save their system. It is unacceptable to the majority of the people. The solution to the crisis that the majority will accept – and, therefore, the only one that has a chance politically – is not to abolish central planning in favour of small-group and individual ownership, but to democratise economic decision-making so that the people become real, not just formal collective owners. For these intellectuals democracy is not simply a political condition for successful economic reform: it is the very essence of economic reform. Democratisation of the economic system at all levels, especially the centre, where the most important decisions are taken, and not only that of the enterprise, creates the social basis for unalienated labour, that is labour that is no longer fundamentally coerced and driven principally by motivation external to itself. This would allow the release of the tremendous productive reserves that workers possess which are presently concealed and suppressed or cannot find application. In this view, democratic planning and management create the conditions for overcoming the contradiction between economic efficiency and social guarantees, so central to the argument of the marketeers. (In any case, according to this current, even in a regime of alienated labour this contradiction is at best a relative one. In particular, the relationship between income differentiation and economic performance is by no means as self-evident as the marketeers claim.)

A somewhat extreme expression of this position is the following letter by an economist responding to an article advocating 'socialist commodity production':

> There is generalised disenchantment with social property: we have not succeeded in building a flourishing society on its basis. . . . Our theoreticians believe that the moving force in the economy can be either coercion or the ruble. And they prefer the latter. But genuine Marxism sees the moving force of socialism in emancipated labour, which is foreign to coercion as well as to stimulation by the long ruble.
>
> The genuine transformation of production relations on a Marxist platform requires a change not in the forms of ownership but in how they are used. What is happening now is a scattering of social property among private-corporatist clans. In these conditions there is no place for the basic principles of socialism for which the toilers mounted their revolutionary assault on private property. Long live free labour on the basis of scientific norms of management and equivalent remuneration!

Most supporters of this current do not reject the market in principle. But they insist that its use be subordinated to the collective choices of the population as to what type of social development is desirable, rather than, as the marketeers would have it, the market imposing its by no means neutral criteria of rationality on society's development. Once this fundamental social issue has been resolved through consistent democratisation, the correct balance between central planning and regulation and decentralised control and management, whether, by what means and how much to use the market, remain important, but essentially technical questions that can be put to the test of practice.

Another oppositional intellectual current, whose public voice is much louder than the preceding, rejects *perestroika* from reactionary positions. There are two major sub-groups: the 'Stalinists' and the Great-Russian chauvinists. They are grouped around the chauvinistic *Pamyat'* movement and such journals as *Nash sovremennik* and *Molodaya gvardiya*. The 'Stalinists' defend 'socialism', which they identify with the traditional bureaucratic regime and the 'command economy'. They deplore the decline of ideology and discipline and the departure from 'socialist' principles under the reform. The 'chauvinists', on the other hand, are 'patriots', who stress the decline of the Great-Russian culture and people. They trace this to the revolution, portrayed as a Jewish plot, which broke the essential continuity of Russian history. Stalin's crimes and contemporary difficulties are also attributed to the Jews.

These reactionary movements draw support from elements of the intelligentsia who prospered under the old system and/or who feel they lack the talent and skills to succeed under *perestroika*, as well from diehard party stalwarts who have given their lives to public activism and find it difficult to reorient themselves in the new conditions. There is ample evidence of toleration and support of these movements within the bureaucracy. *Pamyat''s* propaganda in particular violates the Soviet Constitution and criminal codes, which categorically forbid the spreading of national hatred.

Perspectives

The working class, because of its numbers, its strategic position in the economy, and its potential for concerted action based upon a relatively homogeneous social situation that pits it uncompromisingly against bureaucratic rule, is the only social basis upon which a qualitative restructuring of the Soviet economy can succeed against bureaucratic resistance in the Soviet context. Many analysts express concern that unless *perestroika* brings concrete improvement to workers' lives soon, they will be attracted by reactionary demagoguery and form an anti-*perestroika* alliance with the conservative elements of the bureaucracy. This is unlikely – election results and the miners' strike confirm that – except perhaps among the most socially marginal, unstable working class elements. Workers were fed up with the Brezhnev's rule, and these reactionary movements have no positive programmes. (Popular alliances with local bureaucracies have occurred in the Baltic countries and Armenia on the basis of national demands, but in these cases the apparatus has been running to keep up with a mobilised people in order not to be swept aside.) As for anti-semitism, in Russia proper it has always drawn its force from state policy rather than popular culture. Workers remain attached to the revolution, and its description as a Zionist plot is a bad joke to them.

A more serious problem is the virtual absence from public debate of an alternative to the market reform. One can find in the positions of Boris Yel'tsin, in his stress on equality and justice, as well as from time to time in the trade union press, elements of a left critique of the market reform, but these do not add up to a programme. In large part, this situation reflects pressures from the bureaucratic leadership – Gorbachev has repeatedly condemned 'leftist' positions and specifically warned the press to be more supportive of *perestroika* – but also the interests and attitudes of editors, publicists and the majority of the intelligentsia, who support the market reform. When the choice is presented as either market or bureaucracy – both of which are unattractive – this can have a certain demobilising effect on workers.

On the other hand, even without their own programme of economic reform, workers have no difficulty understanding that their fundamental interests lie with the struggle for democracy. This too was made very clear in the political demands put forward during the coalminers' strike. The workers' relative slowness in mobilising compared to intellectuals was in large part due to their scepticism about the official reform and the reality and permanence of the liberalisation. But this is changing quickly. Besides the rising tide of strikes, involving for the first time in many decades the concerted action of many enterprises (though they have so far evaded the largest cities), workers are participating in ever larger numbers in demonstrations that put forth democratic demands and are forming citywide clubs and associations (a first nationwide conference of these took place in July 1989) with such goals as the democratisation of trade unions, lower prices, shorter hours, equal conditions for the development of all children regardless of parents' social situation – demands that do not necessarily fit with 'responsible' reform. The coalminers, on returning to work, decided not to disband their strike committees but to turn them into workers' committees, which may be the embryo of an independent mass workers' organisation.

The future of this movement depends on its ability to elaborate its own social and economic programme. This would be greatly facilitated by the development of organic links with those members of the intelligentsia who support a 'third way'. This is a fundamental question, because in the absence of an alternative vision the logic of the market reform encourages the division of the workers along ethnic, regional and even enterprise lines as they fight – sometimes together with the local bureaucracy – to wrest a greater degree of autonomy from the central bureaucratic authorities. Whether this happens depends also on how far the regime is prepared to tolerate even a fragmented labour movement.

What is certain is that when the inevitable confrontation arrives – either within the bureaucracy over Gorbachev's *perestroika* or between the bureaucracy and society over the issue of democracy – the decisive element in the correlation of forces will be the relative strength or weakness of the working class. It alone can defeat the bureaucracy.

14

Gorbachev: Bolshevik or Menshevik?

KEN JOWITT

The relative status of party cadre and Soviet citizen, the definition of political membership, more generally the 'constitution' of the Soviet polity, is the key issue of Gorbachev's rule. Under Gorbachev's leadership, can the Soviet regime recast the until now categoric status, the 'non-biodegradable' quality of the party *apparat* and cadre? The central question in the Soviet Union today is political, not economic, technological, or military. It is whether 'the party of a new type', one of professional revolutionaries, can be converted into a party of politicians. This is the significance and implication, if not the motivation, of Gorbachev's reforms. If Lenin's most famous book was *What is to be Done?*, the title of Gorbachev's next book should be *What is to be Undone!*

The historic quality of Gorbachev's political design is his effort both to relativise the place of the apparatus in the party, and the party's place in the Soviet Union. The risk for a Leninist is that should the efforts succeed it will be at the expense of the party's Bolshevik or Leninist identity. On the assumption that those who support Gorbachev are more or less aware of these risks, why do they entertain them?

Developmental Stages and Phases

Leninist regimes typically confront three (sequentially phased) developmental tasks: Transformation, Consolidation, and Inclusion (see Jowitt 1974, 1975, 1978, 1983 and 1987 for further discussion of these terms). Each task has an identifiable and different political imperative, the party's response to which creates distinguishable regime profiles.

Leninist Transformation regimes are relatively decentralised in response to the imperative of coping with the turbulent environment created by the party's effort to destroy its opposition's political and military power.

These regimes have a 'war camp' profile, vividly captured by the image of Trotsky's armoured train. By way of direct contrast, Leninist Consolidation regimes are exceptionally centralised in response to the imperative of minimising access to the new regime by what the party leadership sees as a socio-culturally unreconstructed and contaminating society. Regimes of this order – Stalinist regimes – have a *castle and moat* profile. During this stage (often referred to as totalitarian) Stalin's observation that 'the party has become in all respects like a fortress, the gates of which are opened only to those who have been tested', forcefully expresses the tenor and organisation of Leninism.

Leninist Inclusion regimes reject this overriding fear of socio-cultural contamination, with its hysterical emphasis on class war and anxious search for 'enemies of the people', with an ambivalent but substantial attempt at political reconciliation with society. In response to the emergence of socially articulate audiences and incipient publics on the one hand, and the party's 'genetic' imperative to maintain a monopoly of political organisation and membership on the other, most Leninist regimes have rejected their castle and moat profile with its emphasis on ideological difference, political distance, and violent dominance of society. In its place Inclusion regimes with a *court profile* have developed; regimes still centralised in organisation and concentrated in power, but less violent and more accessible. Established between 1954 and 1961 in the Soviet Union, and in most other Leninist regimes by the end of the 1960s (in China between 1978 and 1980), the central dilemma for Leninist Inclusion regimes is to establish their political legitimacy – not simply sustain their punitive power and intimidating authority – without sacrificing the party's political exclusiveness.

Since Khrushchev, all Soviet leaderships have oriented themselves primarily to the task of Inclusion. For some thirty years the CPSU's major political task has been to ensure that the social products of its developmental efforts identify themselves and act in terms that are consistent with the party's ideological and organisational self-conception. Once it ideologically disabled itself with the announcement that the class enemy had been replaced by the 'state of the whole people', the threat to the regime has been that the growing range of articulate social audiences in Soviet society might express itself as an articulated plurality of political and ideological publics. Since the 20th, 21st and 22nd Party Congresses the CPSU has been faced with the reality that Soviet socio-cultural developments threaten the emergence of a new political frame of reference that jeopardises the party's status as THE political membership organisation in the Soviet Union.

However, while all post-Stalin Soviet leaderships have been predominantly Inclusive in orientation, their particular features have varied substantially and consequentially. All have rejected a 'sultanist' leader's direct control of a police apparatus terrorising a society feared as a threatening source of inner party contamination. But each – Khrushchev, Brezhnev, Andropov, Chernenko, and now Gorbachev – has made the 'Inclusive word flesh' in his own political fashion.

Clearly, there is much more to this than the personal idiosyncracies of particular Soviet leaders, which of course play a role. But not the determining one; each developmental stage in the history of the Soviet (and other Leninist) regimes can be analysed in terms of charismatic, traditional, and modern phases. During its initial Transformation *stage* the Soviet regime moved from the Red Army – civil war charismatic *phase* of heroic confrontations, to NEP with its mixture of modern economic relations and growing traditional peasant social influence in local party organisations (something the Smolensk party records, captured by the Germans at the start of the Second World War, demonstrate quite clearly).

Similarly since 1956 one can detect quite clear contrasts in the several Inclusive Soviet leaderships that have succeeded one another in power. Khrushchev, the so-called 'hare-brained schemer', 'adventurist', and 'voluntarist', erratically and ineffectually attempted charismatic (not simply populist) modes of organising and acting, as in his Virgin Lands campaign of the late 1950s. While undoubtedly a reflection of his personal predilections, Khrushchev's attempted *charismatic* variant of Inclusion was more a political assault on an embedded Stalinist Consolidation regime than a manifestation of political neurosis.

Khrushchev's attack on the party organisation in 1962, his attempted elevation of the party 'laity', the *obshchestvenniki*, or activists, and his ideological emphasis on 'state and party of the whole people' were traumatic challenges to the party apparat's interpretation of Inclusion; namely, symbolic ideological enfranchisement of Soviet society, and its own exclusive political enfranchisement.

The Brezhnev leadership accepted the post-Stalin Inclusive argument that political membership must not be absolutised in the person of a patrimonial or 'sultanist' leader like Stalin, but rejected Khrushchev's plebiscitarian argument that party citizenship should be generalised to the entire party. Brezhnev's rule absolutised *appa-rat*/cadre citizenship and answered Hough (1971) who in the light of the party apparat's internal differentiation and complexity asked: 'On what questions are the first secretaries dogmatically agreed on the nature of the answers?' The answer is: on their superior and exclusive political status. The consequence of Brezhnev's rule was the creation of a *neotraditional* form of Leninist Inclusion regime consisting of a booty economy, parasitical party, and scavenger society.

The Brezhnev Legacy

The remarkable thing about the Soviet economy is how pre-modern it is. All too often form is confused with content, and a country that produces sputniks, missiles and steel 'must' have a powerful modern economy. In fact it has three relatively unintegrated areas of economic action: military, consumer, and 'black market'. More importantly the Soviets have a neotraditional *political* economy, one radically different from those that currently impress political scientists. In crucial respects the Soviet economy resembles an ancient Greek *oikos* more than a modern economy – i.e. a social configuration in which the social, political, and economic arenas of society are not institutionally or conceptually delineated in private/-public terms. While not literally organised as a 'household', the Soviet political economy does formally approximate an *oikos*. As Katsenelinboigen (1976) has noted, the Soviet leadership and even many Soviet economists have looked upon the economy 'as a bazaar'. The Soviet approach to planning has, in Grossman's words, 'done little by way of consciously steering the economy's develop-ment or finding efficient patterns of resource allocation' (Grossman, 1977). And, perhaps most important, the economy has been approached by both Soviet cadres and subjects as a source of 'booty' and plunder. Lacking any sense of ownership or attachment to social goods, Soviet subjects have viewed them as free goods to be appropriated whenever possible. For their part, Soviet cadres regu-larly exact economic tribute from all areas under their rule and understand economic development in gross arithmetical not econ-omical terms. Gorbachev's startling observation that without vodka and oil the Soviet economy would not have experienced any real growth during the Brezhnev years is somewhat less surprising in the context of this peculiar 'political economy'.

However, it has been in the political and social realms, and the relation between the two, that the most serious developments occurred during Brezhnev's rule. Under his aegis, 'trust in the cadres' led to the emergence of a parasitical communist party: not subject to effective central discipline, not able to distinguish between the particular interests of its elite members and the general interests of the party or country, and insensitive to the distasteful social ethos and threatening political climate it was creating in the Soviet Union.

At the 27th Party Congress in 1986 Gorbachev pointed out that 'at some stage individual republics, *krais*, *oblasts* and cities have been removed from the sphere of criticism; in places this has led to the appearance of untouchable raions, collective and state farms, industrial enterprises, and so forth. From all this one must draw a hard conclusion: in the party there are not and must not be organisations outside control'. But obviously there were! In fact by the early 1980s, the CPSU had degenerated from a Bolshevik combat party to what Hirschman (1970) writing about economic firms once referred to as a 'lazy monopoly', 'a little noticed type of monopoly tyranny . . . an oppression of the weak by the incompetent, an exploitation of the poor by the lazy'.

Gorbachev inherited a Leninist party riddled with acts of individual corruption; cities like Moscow controlled by Grishin Mafias; and entire republics like Uzbekistan run by party leaderships who confused party rule with rule by persons drawn from their ethnic clan.

Rather than being unique, Romania, which I have characterised as 'socialism in one family', was simply an extreme example of the party familiarisation occurring in a number of Leninist regimes from North Korea, to Vietnam, Bulgaria and the Soviet Union. By 1985, when Gorbachev was selected general secretary, he might well have wondered how Lenin's 'party of a new type' had come to resemble a Mafia of 'the old type'.

But from a Leninist point of view there was no humour in any of this. Yel'tsin's frustration at the scope and depth of political and personal corruption in the Moscow party reminds one of the letter St Boniface wrote in the 8th century, in which he informed the Archbishop of York that he was compelled to restore adulterous priests to their positions 'because if all the guilty ones were punished as the canons demanded there would be no one to administer baptism and perform other rites of the church' (Sperry, 1905, p. 18).

The greatest irony in all this was that by the end of Brezhnev's rule the CPSU, more than any 19th century Western polity, approximated Marx's depiction in 'On the Jewish Question' of capitalist civil society. Only in this instance civil society, as conceived by Marx, was located *inside the communist party*. Soviet party cadres placed their egoistic interests, their personally selfish and private familial commitments above and even equated them with the party's general interest. As for the mass of party members, they were relegated to the political impotence Marx postulated for the mass of citizens in bourgeois polities. All of this may suggest that Soviet political development is more subject to the ironical than to the dialectical. Regardless of which, this development has been of enormous consequence not only to the political and organisational integrity of the Soviet party but to the type of society that emerged under its auspices, a 'scavenger society'.

One of the most misleading characterisations of the Brezhnev period has been the notion of a 'social contract', a relationship between the regime and society (in the Soviet Union, or in Gierek's Poland or Husak's Czechoslovakia) presumably based on an implicit trade-off: personal and social security for the subject, political control by the party elite, or what has been called the authoritarian welfare state (Breslauer, 1978). In fact none of these terms are apt. The only authoritarian Leninist regime has been the Polish because only there does a powerful autonomous and autocephalous institution, the Church, exist. Second, a politically distinctive feature of Leninist polities is the party's denial of independent political stature to the state. In fact the creation of state political autonomy is one of Gorbachev's major and most difficult tasks. And finally, the notions of welfare and welfare state mean radically opposed, not simply different things in a regime of subjects and a regime of citizens.

Most serious of all, the notion of social contract focused only on the instrumental nexus between the Soviet regime and society, and failed to grasp the expressive dimension of this relationship. Language does matter, and my use of the terms parasitical (party) and scavenger (society) are quite deliberate. They are intended to dramatise the ethos and tenor of the relationship between regime and society, to sensitise the reader to these critical but typically unexamined dimensions of social and political life in the Soviet and other Leninist regimes.

Far from a social contract, the nexus between the Brezhnev regime and Soviet society was that of a *protection racket*. Members of Soviet society were rewarded for, and punished for not, acting like scavengers. Under Brezhnev, while the CPSU lost its ability (and perhaps willingness) to locate and strategically define a social combat task, and consequently its ability to discipline its agents and prevent them from becoming what in pre-industrial societies are known as 'big men', that same party enforced its monopoly over political membership, social privilege, and ideological insight into what was historically and absolutely 'correct'. The effect on Soviet society was neither neutral nor 'contractual'; it was invidious.

Members of this society were forced to act in morally debilitating and personally insulting ways. Brezhnev's rule saw the degeneration of the party, and the party's denigration of society. Shoddy work, bribery, recourse to the 'second economy', nepotism, hypocrisy and servility were imperatives in the Brezhnev neotraditional polity. If not 'role models', those who found scavenging agreeable were materially successful. For those members of Soviet society who were more educated, urban, skilled *but above all* more individuated, articulate, and ethical this reality was embarrassing, alienating and offensive; the source of increasing resentment, anger, and potentially of political rage.

Catalysts for Change

The political sociology of the Brezhnev neotraditional era consisted of a civil society (*à la* Marx) *within the CPSU* exacting political and economic tribute from a society forced to act like scavengers. This was Gorbachev's inheritance, next to which a 'mess of pottage' might look appealing. However, the increasing urgency and sense of emergency that characterise his actions arise in no small measure from the stimulus-threat that appeared in a regime whose neotraditional features directly approximated that of the Soviet. The regime was Poland, the threat, Solidarity!

As suggested earlier, during the Leninist stage of Inclusion the major imperative is to ensure that the new more socially articulate audiences who appear in the context of industrialisation, migration, education and urbanisation adopt a definition of their political status and role consistent with the ideological preferences and political exclusivity of the party. The failure of the Polish party in 1980 must have been traumatic AND predictable for Soviet leaders like Gorbachev. Solidarity was *not* the emergence of civil society in Poland. It was the creation of what in another context Weber once called a *national citizen class* – in my terms, a public that reordered the strictly hierarchical relation between rulers and ruled with the integrative role and domain of citizenship. Solidarity was the *de facto* emergence of a liberal definition and framework of political membership and organisation. The dual power that appeared in Poland was stark and prophetic: citizen versus cadre.

While Solidarity was the central political catalyst for an increasingly forceful rejection of Brezhnev neotraditionalism, it was not the only one. The American SDI initiative, the frustrating and embarrassing Soviet failure to keep up in the technological revolution, the ending of the Sino–Soviet conflict and the appearance of radical reforms in what was once again seen as a *bona fide* Leninist regime: all were important catalysts. Others were equally important including, I suspect, a growing concern within part of the Soviet elite over the international fragmentation of the Leninist world into increasingly unrelated and unrecognisable components.

By the early 1980s some Soviet leaders could and did see the appearance in the 'Third World' of self-designated Leninist or 'scientific socialist' regimes and movements. At best they were 'façade Leninist regimes' *à la* Benin and South Yemen, at the worst Fanonist Movements of Rage like the Khalq in Afghanistan, the Khmer Rouge in Kampuchea and Sendero Luminoso in Peru. These were (are) regimes and movements that find their *raison d'être* more in Fanon's book *The Wretched of the Earth* than in Lenin's *What is to be Done?*

In Western Europe, if Eurocommunism had very little impact on political life in Italy, France, and Spain it very probably made a substantial and specific impression on certain members of the Soviet elite including Gorbachev. Eurocommunism's message was that West European communist parties found the Soviet neotraditional polity irrelevant, and more likely to converge with the 'Third World' than the 'First'.

Finally, in East Europe the emergence of full-blown 'socialism in one Romanian family' and incipient 'socialism in one Bulgarian family' in the 1970s was supplemented by less extreme but no more viable (and even less stable) forms of neotraditionalism in Poland and Czechoslovakia.

In the course of half a century 'Moscow "Centre"' (Jowitt, 1987) had exchanged minimal military power and maximum political and ideological status (in the Leninist world) for maximum military power and near pedestrian status. This could hardly have been viewed neutrally by the entire Soviet leadership.

More importantly, by the end of Brezhnev's rule there was a growing degree of impatience and frustration directed at what some Soviet leaders must consider a curse; namely the regime's apparent inability to develop a political format that can sustain social support, economic growth and the party's political integrity. This syndrome of impatience, frustration and concern had a political locus in what one of Gorbachev's assistants has called the 'daughters of the 20th Congress'. In this connection I.T. Frolov, who became editor of *Pravda* in 1989, has described how a number of cadres who now support and assist Gorbachev worked together in Prague on the editorial board of the international communist journal *Problems of Peace and Socialism* under Aleksei Rumyantsev, who even in the early 1960s voiced his sharp dissatisfaction with the decay in the Soviet regime. Frolov's vignette has far-reaching significance. He is describing a *core site*, a setting in which a leader of stature in control of an organisational base gathers a group of political 'companions' with whom he engages in political discussion, criticism and preparation.

One particularly decisive 'site' emerged: its leader, Andropov; its base, the KGB; and a set of 'companions' including Vorotnikov, Ryzhkov, and perhaps Gorbachev. These 'sites' were *perestroika's* nuclei.

From Neotraditional to Semi-Modern Leninism

Gorbachev's programme of *perestroika* is an effort to create an Inclusion regime in the Soviet Union whose modern elements match in strength and status the traditional and charismatic components of a Leninist regime. A modern society is one in which the dominant institutions are procedural, the dominant actor is the individual, and the dominant ethos is empirical. The thrust of Gorbachev's reforms consists of an effort to upgrade the role of the *individual* party member in opposition to the *corporate* stratum of *apparatchiki*, to upgrade the role of *impersonal* procedure in opposition to the *personal* arbitrary discretion of (former) party 'big men' like the Ukrainian leader Shcherbitsky, and to upgrade the status of critical analysis (*glasnost'*) in opposition to regime secrecy and ritual.

Whether one looks at the central place accorded election procedures, the notion of a 'rule-of-law state' (see Chapter 6), the introduction of economic practices in place of administrative command, or the remarkable ideological emphasis now placed on the individual, one is witnessing an extraordinary effort to recast the Soviet regime in a modern direction. My use of the term *semi-*modern in describing Gorbachev's reforms has two bases. To begin with, I take seriously Gorbachev's assertion (despite the abandonment of Article 6) that he will not voluntarily sacrifice the principle of party dominance. Second, while Gorbachev's conception of the party's leading role differs radically from any seen in the Soviet

Union since the early 1920s, it still implicitly assumes an identity of political preference on the part of Soviet society and the communist party. Far from being corroborated, Gorbachev's assumption has been and will continue to be seriously challenged by many constituent elements in Soviet society. At some point the likely response to these challenges will be a reaffirmation by the party leadership of its 'Bolshevik' credentials in an effort to retain political dominance not mere governance. Any such 'Bolshevik' reaffirmation would neither eliminate many of the modern practices currently being upgraded nor allow them to set the political and economic terms of Soviet life; thus the term semi-modern.

Gorbachev's Novelty

The novelty of Gorbachev's intended reforms seems so obvious that one doesn't have to spend a great deal of time making the point. There is the demand that 'party practice must become thoroughly democratic'; a demand backed up with a forceful observation about the party apparatus which 'should be helping the party, [but] not infrequently puts itself between the party masses and party leaders and still further increases the alienation of the leaders from them'. There is the acute criticism that 'some comrades think people can only be checked up on from above, [which] is not true. There is still another kind of verification, the check up from below in which . . . subordinates verify the leaders'. In the same vein the party's general secretary has emphasised that 'rank and file members verify their leaders at meetings by criticising defects, and . . . by electing or not comrades to leading party organs'. There are admonitions to the effect that every communist 'must change his very approach to the non-party person. For this purpose the Communist must treat the non-party person as an equal'. At the centre of all these observations and critiques is the hallmark demand for *glasnost'*: 'in the Soviet Union and the CPSU Communists must honestly and openly admit their mistakes, honestly and openly indicate the way of correcting them. Not many of our comrades undertake this business with satisfaction. But they must!' Finally, one is struck by the Soviet leader's political sensitivity to socio-cultural change in Soviet society, to the 'failure to understand that the workers now have a higher sense of dignity and a sense of being the ruling class [and] will not tolerate a bureaucratic attitude on the part of the party'.

The difficulty with these novel statements is that they are Stalin's, Molotov's, Zhdanov's and Yaroslavsky's, and that they were made in 1925 *and 1937* (see Getty, 1985, pp. 92, 134, 142, 146, 155, and Stalin, 1925, pp. 158–215).

Gorbachev is not a Stalinist. Quite the contrary! While terminological similarities exist in Stalin and Gorbachev's political language, their meanings radically oppose one another. The tenor of their pronouncements has nothing in common. Stalin's language in the 1930s has a decidedly hysterical tone, while Gorbachev's is sober and procedural. The intent behind their formally similar language is equally dissimilar. Stalin's call is for a political purge of the party; Gorbachev's for a psychological recasting of the party members' attitudes. Most important, Stalin wanted to strengthen the party as an exclusive Bolshevik political 'fortress'. According to Stalin, the Menshevik Martov wanted the party to be more a banquet than a fortress; so does Gorbachev.

Absolutisation, Generalisation and Relativisation

The novelty and difficulty of Gorbachev's semi-modern efforts to recast the party's role in the Soviet Union, and analogously the Soviet Union's role in international politics, can be understood in these terms.

Khrushchev restored the party's organisational integrity with his de-Stalinisation speech and actions. At the 20th, 21st and 22nd Congresses he attacked the absolutisation of the party's political identity in the person of its *vozhd'* or leader. Khrushchev made the point bluntly in his 'secret speech' in 1956: 'After Stalin's death, the Central Committee of the party began to implement a policy of explaining concisely and consistently that it is impermissible and foreign to the spirit of Marxism–Leninism to elevate one person, to transform him into a superman possessing supernatural characteristics akin to those of a god'.

Khrushchev's Leninist Magna Carta at the 20th Congress consisted of a covenant within the party never to select a leader who might act 'rudely' like Stalin. In effect, Khrushchev's party platform was 'don't kill the cadres'. For him it was the party that should be absolutised, not its leader, no matter how much the latter's power should be augmented in an effort to dynamise both society and party.

Quite quickly and consistently (for a 'hare-brained adventurist') Khrushchev tried to *generalise* the party's politically effective membership beyond the confines of the *apparatchiki* to include the *obshchestvenniki* – i.e. the active party members who were not part of the apparatus. Khrushchev attempted to create a form of plebiscitarian leadership in place of Stalin's patrimonial one. And all of Khrushchev's plebiscitarian efforts had the same rationale: to prevent the coagulation of power, initiative (or lack of it), and status within the confines of the now unfrightened *apparatchiki*. In this regard Khrushchev was a 'Leninist Luther' with too few powerful 'German princes' behind him. In fact they surrounded, opposed, and deposed him.

In contrast to particular policy conflicts, the political issue behind Brezhnev's opposition to Khrushchev was over how inclusive, or generalised, the definition of party 'citizenship' was to be. Khrushchev quite clearly wished to upgrade the role and influence of the *obshchestvenniki*, the party 'laity', in relation to the *apparat*. His attempt to 'dilute' the Central Committee's membership by inviting technical experts to its meetings; his bifurcation of the party organisation in 1962; his sponsorship of concepts like 'state and party of the whole people' were all challenges to the party cadre and *apparat* – and recognised as such.

If Khrushchev's 'electoral platform' was 'don't kill the cadres', then surely Brezhnev's was 'don't fire the cadres'. Almost all students of the Soviet Union have noted the remarkable stability of cadre assignment during Brezhnev's tenure. The slogan 'respect for the cadres' became in practice the absolutisation of cadre power, the conflation of *apparat* and party. Between 1953 and 1982 – i.e. Stalin and Brezhnev's death – party power had been generalised to the party apparatus, and then absolutised in its hands. Functional, central–peripheral and personal conflicts in the party were on full display during this period, but Brezhnev's political genius lay in his ability to mediate such and preserve the *apparat's* corporate monopoly and privilege within the party regime.

The intent behind Gorbachev's actions is to terminate the conflation of *apparat* and party rule. In doing so some of his actions are, like Khrushchev's, 'Lutheran'. The Protestant-like encouragement of initiative from all communists captured in the phrase, 'every communist is a leader', the Protestant-like activation of the party 'laity' in elections within the party and for the Congress of People's Deputies, and the critical comments about the arrogance and command style of the apparatus are all reminiscent of Khrushchev, but not identical. Khrushchev's *modus operandi* was mobilisational; Gorbachev's preference is procedural. He repeatedly warns against the temptation to substitute campaigns for sober procedural action. In fact, the measure of Gorbachev's novelty and risk as a Soviet leader is the centrality of 'Madisonian' features in his vision of the Soviet party and polity.

His effort to create viable, electorally based soviets, a 'rule-of-law state', and his introduction of a new form of state Presidency are vivid critiques of Stalin's patrimonial rule, Khrushchev's plebiscitarian rule, and Brezhnev's patriarchal rule in favour of one that is more procedural. Gorbachev proposes to rule not through Gulag terror and purges; not through Virgin Lands campaigns, or through corrupt largesse, but through a proposed pattern of internal checks and balances within the party regime.

Question: what explains this radical effort, one that implicitly calls for a return to the pre-10th Congress (1921) *de facto* tolerance of factions in the party?

Answer: Gorbachev and other 'daughters of the 20th Congress' have become aware of the fact that throughout its seventy year reign the Communist Party of the Soviet Union has regularly succumbed to internal political corruption with all its negative social and economic consequences, and just as regularly has adopted correctives that pose an equal threat to the party's integrity in the short run, and prove ineffectual in the long run.

An example: by the late 1920s party organisation in various parts of the Soviet Union was riddled with corruption, venal and political. While recent studies by Getty (1985) and Gill (1987) exaggerate the degree to which central control was threatened (largely because they equate central with regular bureaucratic control, thereby missing the importance of intermittent but authoritative plenipotentiary power from Moscow), their evidence, along with that provided earlier by Fainsod (1958) does establish the *de facto* autonomy enjoyed by many regional and local party secretaries. Evidence also exists of party corruption on the eve of collectivisation. Fainsod's recounting of a scandal in Smolensk in 1928 includes one witness's observation that the '*guberniya* party conferences were just one big drinking party' (1958, p. 49).

However, Stalin's correctives posed an equal if different threat to the party's integrity. Stalin's initial answer to the syndrome of inadequate central control and pervasive peripheral corruption was to purge the party. Having concluded by the early 1930s that the tendency towards corrupt routinisation in the party was intrinsic not structural, he then attempted in the late 1930s to maintain the party's combat integrity by terrorising it. Still, even Stalin recognised that one cannot continually employ an extraordinary measure like wholescale terror to a ruling elite without paralysing it. Consequently, by the early 1950s one sees renewed signs in the party of local elites creating autonomous patronage cliques, becoming 'big men' in their own right, and confusing their personal and their families' wellbeing with that of the party. In his classic work *Power and Policy in the USSR*, Conquest (1961) describes the situation in

Georgia in precisely these terms. In explaining this recurrence of party corruption Conquest quite plausibly notes that 'even Stalin could not fully control the emergence of local power groups without a definite effort, so long as instructions went through the leaders of the group itself, and reports came back, in the main from them too'. Conquest goes on to make a persuasive case that just prior to his death Stalin was preparing to respond to party corruption as he had in the 1930s, with terror.

With his death, and the developmental shift to Inclusion, efforts were made to eliminate the possibility of any future Stalinist 'corrective'. The result: a party 'Magna Carta' that for over thirty years has placed substantial political and ideological limits on any single leader's power. The ideological rejection of class struggle as the party's central ideological orientation, the party's recasting of Soviet society as a socially benign though not politically equal entity, has removed the strategic rationale for concentrating power in the hands of a single leader charged with preventing the infiltration of the party by an unreconstructed and hostile society. The political limit is less explicit, but I think equally clear: only a party leader who has convinced elite colleagues that he does not possess the (murderous) 'rudeness' Lenin noted in Stalin can be selected general secretary.

But if the party has succeeded in removing the purge and terror 'correctives', no post-Stalin general secretary has been successful in preventing the growth of personal and organisational corruption in the party. Khrushchev's various attempts at reform: in education, in his attempted reorganisation of the ministries, and in his effort to create a powerful party–state Control Commission, all failed, a testimony to the *apparat's* power to protect its exclusive interests. Brezhnev's novelty seems to have been to take the party's organisational corruption and elevate it to the status of an organisational principle. The result by the early 1980s was organised corruption throughout the party regime.

Gorbachev and his allies have come to power determined to end the dilemma of either party corruption or party terror. It would appear that during their tenure under Brezhnev, and association with Andropov, they argued about and worked out a radical response to this primordial feature of Leninist regimes.

Party-state versus Nation-state

Gorbachev's political vision rejects Stalin's understanding of the party's leading role – and in radical respects the post-Stalinist understanding as well. In fact should Gorbachev succeed in 'democratising' the party, the major *unintended* consequence will be to undo the Bolshevik–Leninist meaning of the party's leading role.

Gorbachev has reached the conclusion that only by relativising the place of the *apparat* in the party AND relativising the place of the party in the Soviet Union can the syndrome of party corruption, party purge and social alienation be broken through. This is a momentous political conclusion. If we recall Easton's approach to a polity in which he distinguishes three possible entities – government, regime, and community – we can develop this argument (see Easton, 1965).

Stalin was the Soviet polity. Louis XIV's political aspiration was Stalin's achievement. If during the Consolidation stage the Soviet Union incarnated revolutionary socialism, and the party incarnated the Soviet Union, then Stalin incarnated the party. Stalin absolutised government, regime and community in his person.

With de-Stalinisation Khrushchev attempted politically to generalise party leadership of the Soviet Union from the government, represented by an absolute general secretary, to a regime comprised of party cadre and activists. Khrushchev tried to generalise the boundaries of the Soviet polity to include the party *as a whole*. The party in all its diversity was to become government, regime and community. (In fact with his ideological slogans of 'state and party of the whole people' he even introduced a symbolic base for a Soviet political community beyond the party's organisational confines.) Khrushchev was overthrown by a (Brezhnev-led) *apparat* who successfully equated the generalisation of political power within a party regime with its own absolute power.

Gorbachev and his supporters have concluded that to ensure the stable generalisation of political membership and power throughout the party regime, and prevent their absolutisation in the hands of one leader or one party sector, it is necessary to relativise the power of each apparatus within the party. This can be accomplished only by relativising the party's power *per se* in an extended and empowered Soviet political community. Gorbachev is arguing and striving for a new Soviet and party 'constitution'; one in which the relativisation of *apparat* power in the party, and party power in society, creates a multidimensional polity with discernible, complementary and mutually checking features at the level of the government, regime and community. He has every right to declare what he is doing revolutionary. It is a revolution in the conception of the Leninist party and polity. And he can expect opposition that in intensity matches the scope of his intended revisions.

We already have two ideologically dramatic and politically expanding expressions of Gorbachev's political vision. In Hungary a government spokesman announced in 1989 that the time had come to substitute the Hungarian coat of arms for the red star – i.e. to relativise the party regime's political status *vis-à-vis* the national community. Other efforts at political reform in Hungary point in the same direction. The intended polity is to be the Hungarian (presumably socialist) national community, not the party. In Poland the suggestion has been made (and formally approved in late 1989) to remove the formal provision in the Polish constitution assigning the party a leading role. Exactly the same point; exactly the same significance. At its core, and wherever acted on, the Gorbachevian Reform is an effort to relativise the party's political position. Gorbachev's argument is that the party must and can do so. It must, in order to break the cycle of party corruption, social alienation and economic decay. It can, because 'socialism' has for a long time been secure from internal and external enemies, but has failed to act on those realities.

Gorbachev's analysis is as follows: the CPSU has succeeded in creating more than a Soviet party regime; it has created a potential Soviet political community embracing regular and non-party members who accept the basic features of a Leninist regime. However, by absolutising the Soviet polity in either the hands of a particular leader, or a particular sector of the party, the party has denied itself political viability, social legitimacy and economic productivity.

The Gorbachevian Reform rests on an attempted relocation of charismatic 'correctness' from the party to an enlarged and differentiated Soviet polity. When Vadim Medvedev, the ideological secretary, says in March 1989 that 'the party does not lay claim to a monopoly in seeking the best paths of social progress; it does not believe that it possesses the ultimate truth. But Communists have something to defend firmly and adamantly. Namely our socialist values, our socialist choice', he is giving the Stalinist notion of 'socialism in one country' a radically new political meaning. The 'ultimate truth' has been generalised to the Soviet Union as a political community in which the party's role is central but relative. The import of the relocation of charismatic correctness is that the party is to be assigned a complementary not a dominant place *vis-à-vis* the nation. Put differently, the implication if not motivation of Gorbachev's 'restructuring' is to provide political substance to the notion of Soviet citizenship at the expense of party membership. But is a Menshevik-like reform of that order compatible with the CPSU's Bolshevik organisation and tradition?

There are three elements in Gorbachev's attempted reform that if implemented will mean the end of Leninist regimes as we have known them. First, the rejection at the 20th Congress of domestic class struggle – the political rationale for polarising and juxtaposing the party polity to Soviet society. Second, the recent efforts to replace the party's 'correct line' with the idea of a politically correct Soviet society. Which, third, finds its institutional expression in an ideally revived Soviet system led by a president whose political constituency is not exclusively the party. To the extent that Gorbachev's vision of the presidency becomes a political achievement, not simply a political aspiration, the general secretary's and the party's status become politically relative.

One thing should be clear: Gorbachev is out to revitalise, not destroy, the Bolshevik tradition. He may well be the last Leninist romantic, one who believes that relativising the party's power will allow a vital Soviet polity to emerge in which the party's power and legitimacy will be secure. But the difference, even opposition, between the intentions and consequences of his actions should also be clear.

Political Concern and Opposition

If one looks closely, there have been three Gorbachev leaderships in five years: the Gorbachev who favoured acceleration, then *glasnost'*, and now 'democratisation' (which I interpret to mean the relativisation of the *apparat* in the party, and a comparable relativisation of the party in a newly emergent Soviet polity). Gorbachev's ability to pursue increasingly radical reform reflects the catastrophes (from corruption to Chernobyl) connected with Brezhnevian neotraditionalism, the short-lived quality of Andropov's efforts, and the unavailability *to date* of an acceptable alternative to his semi-modern revision of the party polity.

Opposition to Gorbachev exists, but characterising it requires nuance. When Ligachev denies that he opposes Gorbachev and says that all members of the Politburo agree with the charter for change announced in April 1985, I accept his claim, *and* remind myself that Li Peng and Zhao Ziyang agreed on the need for the Four Modernisations in China. Political conflict develops within a coalition as differing interpretations of generally agreed reforms manifest themselves. As the political implications of Gorbachev's interpretation of *perestroika*, and particularly 'democratisation', become apparent, one can predict that political interpretations and positions divergent from, opposed to, and even mutually exclusive with his will appear in the Politburo.

Evidence of politically divergent elite interpretations of *perestroika* already exists. One major expression occurred in November

1987 at the time of the October Revolution's 70th anniversary. In the speech he delivered Gorbachev presented the most positive public appraisal of Stalin heard in years. Most (liberal) Sovietologists honed in on his blunt accusation: 'the guilt of Stalin and his immediate entourage before the party and the people for the wholesale repressive measures and acts of lawlessness is enormous and unforgiveable'. But there was more, including the recognition that 'a factor in the achievement of victory was the tremendous political will, purposefulness and persistence, ability to organise and discipline people displayed in the war years by Joseph Stalin'; and the need to recognise Stalin's incontestable contribution to the struggle for socialism, to remember that after Lenin's death it was Stalin who headed the party's leading nucleus and 'safeguarded Leninism in an ideological struggle'.

A major question arises in connection with this speech: whose position was Gorbachev expressing, his own or that of Politburo colleagues? The analysis I have presented suggests that Gorbachev was compelled to act as spokesman for positions he opposed. The full measure of opposition to Gorbachev came out in the speech's vituperative references to Trotsky 'who always vacillated and cheated'; Trotsky who denied Stalin's charter concept, the possibility of 'socialism in one country'; and of course Trotsky who criticised the political monopoly of the *apparat* in the party. I would argue strongly that Trotsky's, not Bukharin's, rehabilitation is central to Gorbachev's efforts to relativise the role of the *apparat* within the party, and recast the Soviet Union's role in international politics.

More than anything else 'New Thinking' in Soviet foreign policy means rejecting the Stalinist notion of 'socialism in one country'. No-one did that more clearly than Trotsky, who emphatically argued the need to include Russia, economically *and* culturally, in Europe. In a prophetic manner he noted that 'the conditions for the arising of a dictatorship of the proletariat and the conditions for the creation of a socialist society are not identical, . . . [they are] in certain respects antagonistic . . . Economic construction in an isolated workers' state, however important in itself will remain abridged, limited, contradictory: it cannot reach the heights of a new harmonious society . . . The world wide division of labour stands over the dictatorship of the proletariat in a separate country and dictates its further road' (Trotsky, 1960). The visceral excoriation of Trotsky in the November speech was an attack on Gorbachev's incipient efforts to relativise the party in the Soviet Union, *and* the Soviet Union in international relations (certainly not an attack on any preference by Gorbachev for 'permanent revolution' domestically or internationally).

Since 1987 there have been significant but so far indecisive signs of Trotsky's 'reentry' into Soviet political life. However, nothing would relativise Lenin more than to reintroduce and legitimate Trotsky's critical and integral association with him. If Stalin dealt a decisive blow to his opponents by murdering Kirov, Gorbachev would do the same to his by rehabilitating Trotsky.

More recently, the party plenum in July 1989 revealed acute concern over Gorbachev's conception of *perestroika*. Many Western observers of the plenum too readily and indiscriminately interpreted statements by Politburo members as attacks on Gorbachev. It would be more accurate to say that the major thrust was one of acute concern over the party's status and role, pointedly illustrated by Ryzhkov's worried queries about the 'party's leading role in society's life', and the doubts about 'its role as society's political core'. Ideological secretary Medvedev captured the spirit of concern by declaring: 'Most of us are in the grip of complex and contradictory reflections, experiences and doubts: Are we going in the right direction . . . are we not weakening the very foundations of our socialist development?'

But the political concern of Ryzhkov and Medvedev became in Ligachev's hands a political criticism and attack on Gorbachev. Ligachev focused precisely and accurately on the 'deviant' elements in Gorbachev's intended radical recasting of the party. Ligachev declared that 'it must be borne in mind that the CPSU is above all the party of the working class, and any restriction on it signifies a belittling and weakening of (its) role. A correct decision has been made to convene a workers' congress in the very near future'. One can find comparable statements by East European leaders who are concerned with, or adamantly oppose the type of party reform Gorbachev espouses. At the 1989 Hungarian party congress Karoly Grosz, while endorsing a range of radical changes in the party's ideological and organisational format, warned against the party's 'ignoring the working class and the values and ideals of communism'. And in an interview given to *Pravda* in 1989 before his ouster Ceauşescu emphasised the Romanian party's working class character and the professional revolutionary quality of its leaders.

This ideological emphasis on the working class character of the party is a direct political challenge to the creation of a national polity in which the party will play a relative not absolute role. And in presenting this challenge Ligachev is not speaking as a Stalinist but as a Bolshevik–Leninist, for whom the party is THE polity. Ligachev made his Bolshevik position crystal clear when in the same speech he pointedly asserted: 'there can be an increase in the soviets' role in society only if the party is strengthened, and not at the expense of its weakening, as certain people propose'. Ligachev can quite justifiably cry Menshevism, not Bolshevism, when Miklos Nemeth commenting on the Hungarian party's reorganisation says, 'We don't want members, we want voters'. Gorbachev's reforms in the Soviet Union have not approached that point but have the same implication: not the removal of the party *per se*, but rather its Menshevik-like reconstruction as a party of individual members acting through several regime institutions each with relative, but none with absolute influence.

Gorbachev had defenders like Zaikov and Nazarbayev at the July 1989 plenum; and he defended himself by reminding his colleagues that they had all agreed to the unsettling and 'revolutionary' implications of *perestroika*. Remaining true to his conception of party 'democratisation', he renewed his call for less central control and greater initiative and autonomy on the part of primary party organisations. But this is precisely the issue generating political concern from leaders like RSFSR president Vorotnikov who until now have critically supported him.

Regime Analogies

In the midst of great uncertainty historical analogies can help make sense of events in the Soviet Union (as well as Eastern Europe, and China). In the past I have used the analogy of the Ottoman Empire and, unlike some others, still find it valuable because the Soviet and Ottoman cases are analogous, not identical.

The Soviet elite, like its historical Ottoman counterpart, characteristically favours a combat task and ethos – more social, less military, in the Soviet case – to sustain its integrity as a ruling organisation. However, since Khrushchev it has been unwilling and unable to find a combat task that subordinates the particular interests of its cadres to the party's general interests. In Ottoman history one periodically finds the same phenomenon and in both cases the result is political, social and economic crisis. The Soviet and Ottoman responses to this condition are also analogous.

Nativists confront Westernisers: in the Soviet case those for 'socialism in one country' confront those with a more ecumenical understanding of the Soviet Union's place in international politics. Proponents of plenipotentiary reform confront proponents of procedural reform: in the Soviet case this takes the form of opposition between those who prefer the KGB (as the least corrupt, best informed party sector) and those who favour elections to soviets and party committees as the central mechanism for reform. Finally, those with a more civic vision of the Soviet polity confront those with a more ethnic vision.

One can go a long way towards making sense of the historically remarkable events in the Soviet Union (and Eastern Europe) with a civic–ethnic framework. Analytically distinct, these orientations merge and conflict politically. One must be aware of their possible complementarity and polarity, of their respective weighting within an elite, and each of its members. Coincidentally, a former part of the Ottoman Empire, Yugoslavia, currently offers a telling contrast and conflict between a primarily civic oriented Slovenian party and a more ethnic oriented Serbian party.

In speculating about political outcomes in the Soviet Union three regime types are conceivable; one is probable. Least likely is a semi-modern civic regime that remains in some identifiable sense Leninist or Bolshevik. This is Gorbachev's intention. However, as noted earlier, intentions and implications are quite different things; and the implication of his reforms are Menshevik not Bolshevik. One has only to look at Hungary. A more likely outcome is the emergence of an ethnically oriented Soviet regime. This could be relatively benign should a member of the current leadership become a Russian Atatürk (to extend the Ottoman analogy); or dangerous should a Ligachev become the leader of a nativist xenophobic Soviet regime. Recent charges by the party head of a Jewish *oblast* in the Soviet Union about Ligachev's possible support of anti-semitic statements in the media indicate fears of such an outcome. However, more likely than either of these decisive outcomes is a Soviet polity marked for a prolonged period of time by political turbulence and instability; one in which Nativists confront Westernisers, Andropovites confront Gorbachevites, 'civics' confront 'ethnics', and neither the *apparat* nor terror provide the regime with its political lynchpin.

A number of years ago, Melvin Croan (1970) asked whether Mexico might not be the future of Eastern Europe. One could also look at Argentina, a regime and country split for decades between two forces – a nativist, xenophobic Peronist elite with ambivalent military and passionate working class nationalist support, and a more civic oriented political leadership more internationally oriented and supported by an urban professional middle class – who turbulently alternate in power. Argentina is a nation with a consistently unrealised economic potential; a European society unable to create a West European political culture; and a polity with sustained and largely contained political instability. The point is not that

Argentina or Mexico is the Soviet future. We should have learned long ago from Marx's mistake not to posit any regime's present as any other's future. The point is to dramatise the contours of the emerging polity in the Soviet Union (and Eastern Europe), and emphasise the international predominance of regimes whose primary political feature is contained instability.

The conflict within the CPSU between proponents of a semimodern and proponents of a neotraditional organisation of the party will be exacerbated by the conflict within and outside the party between 'civics' and 'ethnics'; between those who support a polity in which the critically articulate and active individual citizen is the more valued actor, and those who support a polity in which the corporate and solidarity cultural group is the more valued actor.

The most likely response (not solution) to these conflicts will be the emergence of a strong, not absolute, 'Giolittian' president and presidency. It will be this office and person who will carry the political weight of relativising the party's role without eliminating it; of addressing the Soviet Union's ethnic groups and demands without completely accepting ethnic sovereignty or xenophobia. At least one factor favours this outcome – its alternative, political chaos.

Guide to Further Reading

General

All the chapters in this volume are based, to varying extents, on the contemporary Soviet press and other sources. A substantial selection of these sources is available in translation in the *Current Digest of the Soviet Press* (Columbus, Ohio, weekly) and in daily monitoring services such as the American-based *Foreign Broadcast Information Service* and the *BBC Summary of World Broadcasts*. Detailed commentaries on current developments are available in the research reports issued by Radio Liberty and Radio Free Europe in Munich. More extended scholarly commentaries are available in the journals that specialise in Soviet affairs, among them *Soviet Studies* (Glasgow, quarterly), *Slavic Review* (Austin, Texas, quarterly), *Problems of Communism* (Washington DC, bimonthly), *Soviet Economy* (Silver Springs, Md, quarterly), *Survey* (London, quarterly) and the *Journal of Communist Studies* (London, quarterly).

An extensive commentary, from the Soviet point of view, is available in *Soviet Weekly* (London) and in *Moscow News* (Moscow, published weekly in Russian and foreign languages). *Soviet News*, issued weekly by the Soviet Embassy in London, contains official and other statements. Important speeches and other documents are frequently issued in pamphlet form by the Novosti Press Agency. Gorbachev's own speeches and articles are available in a number of collections, among them *Selected Speeches and Articles*, 2nd edn (Moscow: Progress, 1987); *Socialism, Peace and Democracy: Writings, Speeches and Reports by Mikhail Gorbachev* (London and Atlantic Highlands, NJ: Zwan, 1987); *Speeches and Writings*, 2 vols (Oxford and New York: Pergamon, 1986 and 1987). Gorbachev's bestselling book *Perestroika: New Thinking for Our Country and the World* (London: Collins, 1987) is available in numerous editions.

Chapter 1   A New Soviet Politics?

For an early assessment of Gorbachev's accession and the prospects as they appeared at that time see Brown (1985). The best biography of Gorbachev is Medvedev (1988); see also Schmidt-Hauer (1986). For the development of the Gorbachev reforms more generally see McCauley (1987), an early but still useful collection. Lewin (1988) is an interpretive essay; Bloomfield (1989) is a sympathetic but not uncritical symposium. Joyce *et al.* (1989), a symposium by British and American scholars, covers domestic and international developments; Brown (1989a) covers developments in theory as well as political practice. Hill and Dellenbrant (1989) is a British and Scandinavian symposium. White (1990a) provides a detailed and analytic account of the Gorbachev administration to date.

Chapter 2 Rethinking Soviet Socialism

A thorough introduction to the changes in official ideology that have occurred from the Khrushchev period up to the adoption of a new Party Programme in 1986 is available in White and Pravda (1988). The Party Programme itself is conveniently available together with a detailed introduction in White (1989). On the notion of 'developed socialism' see Evans (1977); on more recent changes see Evans (1986). A provocative discussion of the role of ideology in Soviet political practice is available in Walker (1989). For Soviet Marxism more generally see Scanlan (1985).

Chapter 3 The Political Leadership

There is at present no single authoritative text which analyses all the post-1985 changes in the Soviet leadership. Gustafson and Mann (1986, 1987) and Tatu (1988), however, provide at least partial accounts of recent changes, and Brown (1989b) is a more comprehensive discussion by several authors. Lowenhardt (1982) deals with the Politburo as an institution, and Voslensky (1984) with officialdom as a social group. Hough and Fainsod (1979) provide a thorough review of the Soviet leadership prior to the Gorbachev period, and Breslauer (1982) deals with the Khrushchev and Brezhnev periods. There is also a discussion of Soviet elite change and its consequences in Bialer (1980) and Breslauer (1984). Among numerous pieces devoted to the succession and regime formation processes, the Bunce–Roeder exchange (1986) is especially lively and revealing. Bunce (1981) and Roeder (1985) may also be consulted. A wide range of issues involving Soviet elite politics are treated in Lane (1988).

Chapter 4 The Party

For a general account oriented towards a student readership see Hill and Frank (1987). Two standard histories of party development are Rigby (1968) and Schapiro (1970). The Party Programme and Rules, as adopted in 1986, are conveniently available in White (1989); for the Rules since their adoption see Gill (1988). Several recently published volumes contain chapters dealing with the CPSU: see for instance Smith (1988), Sakwa (1989), Hill (1989), and Hammer (1986). For a selection of more research-oriented studies see for instance Potichnyj (1988) and Rigby (1989), which expertly examines a number of the issues central to the CPSU, its role and performance. The work of John H. Miller merits attention: see for instance his two chapters in Miller *et al.* (1987). Gorbachev's impact on the CPSU is considered in Hill (1988).

Chapter 5   The Soviet State

The Soviet state system was thoroughly overhauled in the wake of the 1988 Party Conference; amendments to the Constitution were adopted in December 1988, and further legislation on local government and other matters was still outstanding at the end of 1989. For current developments, accordingly, it is essential to consult the periodical literature. Not everything changed, however, and even where changes have taken place they need to be seen in the context of what preceded them. The theory of the state in Soviet society received attention in Harding (1984). Constitutional change up to the adoption of the 1977 Constitution is considered in Unger (1981), which includes the relevant texts. The workings of the old-style state institutions at the national level are considered in Vanneman (1977) and Siegler (1982). For the local elections that incorporated an 'experimental' element of choice see White (1988) and Hahn (1988a). For a discussion of the introduction of political reform in late 1988 see Hahn (1989) and White (1990b); a fuller account is in Urban (1990). A full account of the March 1989 national elections is available in White (forthcoming).

Chapter 6   The Rule of Law and the Legal System

The basic English-language account of the Soviet legal system is Butler (1988). For encyclopedic coverage see Feldbrugge (1985). A comprehensive 'casebook' is Hazard *et al.* (1984). Current all-union, republican and departmental legislation is translated and updated as amended in a looseleaf service published by Oceana Publications since 1979, *Collected Legislation of the USSR and Constituent Union Republics*, edited by W.E. Butler. Selected enactments appear in a Soviet publication, *Legislative Acts of the USSR* (Moscow, since 1981) and in translation in *Soviet Statutes and Decisions* (White Plains, NY, quarterly). For scholarly discussion of these and other matters see the *Review of Socialist Law* (Dordrecht, quarterly) and the *Yearbook on Socialist Legal Systems* (Dobbs Ferry, since 1986).

Chapter 7   Patterns of Participation

A good study of participation in the Brezhnev period is Friedgut (1979); the more recent period is considered in Hahn (1988b). The significance of uncontested elections is well discussed in Zaslavsky and Brym (1978). On the uses of the Soviet petitioning mechanism see Lampert (1985). Hague and Harrop (1987) provide a useful comparative perspective on participation in liberal democratic, communist and Third World societies. The results of a major survey of Soviet emigres, including their political attitudes, are reported in Millar (1987). Popular attitudes to official values can be gleaned from Soviet public opinion surveys of the 1970s, interestingly analysed in Shlapentokh (1982, 1989). On informal associations, see Brovkin (forthcoming). On the media and *glasnost'* see for instance Mickiewicz (1988), Remington (1988) and Benn (1989). For the changes in electoral and other arrangements, see Chapter 5 above.

Chapter 8   The Nationalities

There is a large general literature on the national question in the USSR. See for instance Katz (1975); Carrère d'Encausse (1979); Connor (1984), a study that includes other communist-ruled systems; and Wixman (1984), an ethnographic handbook. Karklins (1986) uses interviews with Soviet German emigres to provide a perspective 'from below'; Motyl (1987) is principally concerned with Ukraine. Kozlov (1988) provides an informed Soviet perspective. For recent developments see Nahajlo and Swoboda (1990) and current periodicals; a particularly helpful symposium, focussing on Russia and the Baltic republics, appeared in *Problems of Communism*, July–August 1989.

Chapter 9   Economic Management and Reform

Given the rapid pace of development in recent years, the best sources are journals such as *Soviet Studies* and *Soviet Economy* and the commentaries provided in the Radio Liberty research reports. The best monographs are Hewett (1988), which concentrates upon the longer-term background to current changes, and Aslund (1989), which provides a thorough and critical discussion of the Gorbachev reform programme. The Soviet viewpoint is set out in Aganbegyan (1988). Also useful are the weighty reports issued every two years by the United States Congress Joint Economic Committee, the most recent of which is *Gorbachev's Economic Plans* (1987).

Chapter 10   Social Policies and New Social Issues

Current Soviet arguments about *perestroika*, social policy and 'socialist social justice' can be found in Gorbachev (1987), Mchedlov (1987) and Zaslavskaya (1988). A more propagandistic but nonetheless informative tract on how socialism is supposed to increase the people's wellbeing is provided by Klavdienko (1986). Smith (1988), Chapter 11, offers an up-to-date introductory account of the Soviet welfare state. A more detailed discussion is provided by George and Manning (1980). Employment policies are examined by McAuley (1979) and Lane (1987). Echols (1986) gives a succinct comparative analysis of earnings in East and West. On housing, see Andrusz (1984) and Morton (1974). On healthcare, see for instance Ryan (1978), Hyde (1974) and Navarro (1977). Davis and Feshbach look particularly at infant mortality (1980). On youth, see Wilson and Bachkatov (1988) and Riordan (1989).

Chapter 11   The Politics of Foreign and Security Policy

An accessible introductory text is Nogee and Donaldson (1988). Useful edited volumes include Laird (1987) and Laird and Hoffman (1987). The standard history is Ulam (1974) and its continuation Ulam (1983). The Brezhnev years are covered in Edmonds (1983) and Steele (1985). On domestic aspects, consult Bialer (1981). On security the best recent study is Dibb (1988). The changing Soviet theory of international relations, up to and including Gorbachev's 'new thinking', is considered in Light (1988).

Chapter 12   Perfecting the Political System of Socialism

For an important statement of a broadly reformist position on Soviet political development see Afanas'ev (1988), in which an earlier version of Chapter 12 appeared. Discussions of this kind are best followed through the Soviet press and scholarly journals, some of which are translated or otherwise made available to an English-speaking readership (see above). Among other contributors to this debate so far as the political system is concerned, Fedor Burlatsky and Boris Kurashvili have been particularly influential. On these writings and the discussions from which they emerge see for instance Brown (1984) and Nove (1989), Chapter 7.

Chapter 13   The Social Basis of *Perestroika*

This chapter is based upon the Soviet central press as well as popular and more specialised social science periodicals. Many of these appear in the translated sources noted at the start of this section, and additionally in *Soviet Sociology*, *Soviet Studies in Philosophy*, *Soviet Review*, and *Soviet Studies in History* (all published in Armonk, NY, by M.E. Sharpe). See also *Labour Focus on Eastern Europe* (London) and *Critique* (Glasgow) for a critical perspective on these issues. A useful interpretive essay is Lewin (1988). A more detailed account of some of the points treated in this chapter, with full citations, is available in Mandel (1988) and (1989).

Chapter 14   Gorbachev, Bolshevik or Menshevik?

The theoretical approach to Soviet politics that is developed in this chapter is set out in Jowitt (1974, 1975, 1978, 1983 and 1987). Other accounts that have been drawn upon in preparing this chapter include Breslauer (1978), Mann (1986), Rigby (1979) and Croan (1970) in addition to the sources that are directly cited.

Bibliography

This bibliography contains full details of items cited in the chapters or in the Guide to Further Reading section, together with a number of other items that students may be expected to find useful.

Afanas'ev, Yu. (ed.) (1988) *Inogo ne dano*, Moscow: Progress.

Aganbegyan, Abel (1988) *The Challenge: Economics of Perestroika*, London: Hutchinson.

Andrusz, Gregory D. (1984) *Housing and Urban Development in the USSR*, London: Macmillan.

Aslund, Anders (1989) *Gorbachev's Struggle for Economic Reform*, Ithaca: Cornell University Press.

Bahry, Donna (1987) *Outside Moscow: Power, Politics and Budgetary Policy in the Soviet Republics*, New York: Columbia University Press.

Benn, David Wedgwood (1989) *Persuasion and Soviet Politics*, Oxford: Blackwell.

Bialer, Seweryn (1980) *Stalin's Successors*, New York: Cambridge University Press.

Bialer, Seweryn (ed.) (1981) *The Domestic Context of Soviet Foreign Policy*, London: Croom Helm.

Bloomfield, Jon (ed.) (1989) *The Soviet Revolution. Perestroika and the Remaking of Socialism*, London: Lawrence & Wishart.

Breslauer, George (1978) 'On the Adaptability of Soviet Welfare-state Authoritarianism', in Karl W. Ryavec (ed.) *Soviet Society and the Communist Party*, Amherst: University of Massachusetts Press.

Breslauer, George (1980) 'Political Succession and the Soviet Policy Agenda', *Problems of Communism*, vol. 29, no. 3 (May–June) pp. 34–52.

Breslauer, George (1982) *Khrushchev and Brezhnev as Leaders: Building Authority in Soviet Politics*, London: Allen & Unwin.

Breslauer, George (1984) 'Is There a Generation Gap in the Soviet Political Establishment? Demand Articulation by RSFSR Provincial Party First Secretaries', *Soviet Studies*, vol. 36, no. 1 (January) pp. 1–25.

Brovkin, Vladimir (forthcoming) 'Informal Political Associations in Russia, 1988–1989', *Soviet Studies*.

Brown, Archie (1984) 'Political Science in the Soviet Union: A New Stage of Development', *Soviet Studies*, vol. 36, no. 3 (July) pp. 317–44.

Brown, Archie (1985) 'Gorbachev: New Man in the Kremlin', *Problems of Communism*, vol. 34, no. 3 (May–June) pp. 1–23.

298

Brown, Archie (1989a) 'Political Change in the Soviet Union', *World Policy Journal*, vol. 6, no. 3 (Summer) pp. 469–501.

Brown, Archie (ed.) (1989b) *Political Leadership in the Soviet Union*, London: Macmillan.

Bunce, Valerie (1981) *Do New Leaders Make a Difference? Executive Succession and Public Policy under Capitalism and Socialism*, Princeton, NJ: Princeton University Press.

Bunce, Valerie and Echols, John M. (1980) 'Soviet Politics in the Brezhnev Era: "Pluralism" or "Corporatism"?', in Donald Kelley (ed.) *Soviet Politics in the Brezhnev Era*, New York: Praeger.

Bunce, Valerie and Roeder, Philip G. (1986) 'The Effects of Leadership Succession in the Soviet Union', *American Political Science Review*, vol. 80, no. 1 (March), pp. 215–240.

Butler, William E. (1988) *Soviet Law*, 2nd edn, London: Butterworths.

Carrère d'Encausse, Helene (1979) *An Empire in Decline*, New York: Newsweek.

Cohen, Stephen F. (1985) *Rethinking the Soviet Experience*, New York: Oxford University Press.

Connor, Walker (1984) *The National Question in Marxist–Leninist Theory and Practice*, Princeton, NJ: Princeton University Press.

Conquest, Robert (1961) *Power and Policy in the USSR*, New York: Macmillan.

Croan, Melvin (1970) 'Is Mexico the Future of East Europe?: Institutional Adaptability and Political Change in Comparative Perspective', in Samuel P. Huntingdon and Clement H. Moore (eds.) *Authoritarian Politics in Modern Society*, New York: Basic Books.

Davis, Christopher and Feshbach, Murray (1980) *Rising Infant Mortality in the USSR in the 1980s*, Washington DC: Bureau of the Census.

Dibb, Paul (1988) *The Soviet Union: The Incomplete Superpower*, 2nd edn, London: Macmillan.

DiFranciesco, Wayne and Gitelman, Zvi (1985) 'Soviet Political Culture and "Covert Participation" in Policy Implementation', *American Political Science Review*, vol. 78, no. 3 (September) pp. 603–21.

Easton, David (1965) *A Systems Analysis of Political Life*, New York: Wiley.

Echols, John M. (1986) 'Does Socialism Mean Greater Equality? A Comparison of East and West along Several Major Dimensions', in Stephen White and Daniel N. Nelson, (eds.) *Communist Politics: A Reader*, London: Macmillan.

Edmonds, Robin (1983) *Soviet Foreign Policy: The Brezhnev Years*, Oxford, Oxford University Press.

Evans, Alfred B. (1977) 'Developed Socialism in Soviet Ideology', *Soviet Studies*, vol. 29, no. 3 (July), pp. 409–28.

Evans, Alfred B. (1986) 'The Decline of Developed Socialism? Some Trends in Recent Soviet Ideology', *Soviet Studies*, vol. 38, no. 1 (January) pp. 1–23.

Fainsod, Merle (1958) *Smolensk under Soviet Rule*, Cambridge Mass.: Harvard University Press.

Feldbrugge, F.J.M. (ed.) (1985) *Encyclopedia of Soviet Law*, Dordrecht: Martinus Nijhoff.

Friedgut, Theodore (1979) *Political Participation in the USSR*, Princeton NJ: Princeton University Press.

George, Vic and Manning, Nick (1980) *Socialism, Social Welfare and the Soviet Union*, London: Routledge.

Getty, J. Arch (1985) *The Origins of the Great Purges. The Soviet Communist Party Reconsidered, 1933–1938*, New York: Cambridge University Press.

Gill, Graeme (1987) 'The Single Party as an Agent of Development: Lessons from the Soviet Experience', *World Politics*, vol. 39, no. 4 (July) pp. 566–78.

Gill, Graeme (1988) *The Rules of the Communist Party of the Soviet Union*, London: Macmillan.

Golubeva, V. (1980) 'The Other Side of the Medal', in Women in Eastern Europe Group, *Women and Russia: First Feminist Samizdat*, London: Sheba.

Gorbachev, Mikhail (1987) *Perestroika: New Thinking for Our Country and the World*, London: Collins.

Grossman, Gregory (1977) 'The "Second Economy" of the USSR', *Problems of Communism*, vol. 26, no. 5 (September–October) pp. 25–40.

Gustafson, Thane and Mann, Dawn (1986) 'Gorbachev's First Year: Building Power and Authority', *Problems of Communism*, vol. 35, no. 3 (May–June) pp. 1–19.

Gustafson, Thane and Mann, Dawn (1987) 'Gorbachev's Gamble', *Problems of Communism*, vol. 36, no. 4 (July–August) pp. 1–20.

Hague, Rod and Harrop, Martin (1987) *Comparative Government and Politics*, 2nd edn, London: Macmillan.

Hahn, Jeffrey W. (1988a) 'An Experiment in Competition: The 1987 Elections to the Local Soviets', *Slavic Review*, vol. 47, no. 2 (Fall) pp. 434–47.

Hahn, Jeffrey W. (1988b) *Soviet Grassroots: Citizen Participation in Local Soviet Government*, Princeton, NJ: Princeton University Press.

Hahn, Jeffrey W. (1989) 'Power to the Soviets?', *Problems of Communism*, vol. 38, no. 1 (January–February) pp. 34–46.

Hammer, Darrell P. (1986) *USSR: The Politics of Oligarchy*, 2nd edn, Boulder, Col.: Westview.

Harasymiw, Bohdan (1984) *Political Elite Recruitment in the Soviet Union*, London: Macmillan.

Harding, Neil (ed.) (1984) *The State in Socialist Society*, London: Macmillan.

Hazard, John, *et al.* (eds.) (1984) *The Soviet Legal System: The Law in the 1980s*, Dobbs Ferry: Oceana.

Hewett, Ed A. (1988) *Reforming the Soviet Economy*, Washington DC: Brookings.

Hill, Ronald J. (1988) 'Gorbachev and the CPSU', *Journal of Communist Studies*, vol. 4, no. 4 (December) pp. 18–34.

Hill, Ronald J. (1989) *The Soviet Union: Politics, Economics and Society*, 2nd edn, London: Pinter.

Hill, Ronald J. and Dellenbrant, Jan Ake (eds.) (1989) *Gorbachev and Perestroika*, Aldershot: Edward Elgar.

Hill, Ronald J. and Frank, Peter (1987) *The Soviet Communist Party*, 3rd edn, London: Allen & Unwin.

Hirschman, Albert (1970) *Exit, Voice and Loyalty*, Cambridge Mass: Harvard University Press.

Hough, Jerry F. (1971) 'The *Apparatchiki*', in H.G. Skilling and Franklyn Griffiths (eds.) *Interest Groups in Soviet Politics*, Princeton, NJ: Princeton University Press.

Hough, Jerry F. and Fainsod, Merle (1979) *How the Soviet Union is Governed*, Cambridge Mass: Harvard University Press.

Hyde, Gordon (1974) *The Soviet Health Service*, London: Lawrence and Wishart.

Jones, Ellen (1986) *Red Army and Society. A Sociology of the Soviet Military*, paperback edn, London: Allen & Unwin.

Jowitt, Kenneth (1974) 'An Organisational Approach to the Study of Political Culture in Marxist–Leninist Systems', *American Political Science Review*, vol. 68, no. 3 (September) pp. 1171–91.

Jowitt, Kenneth (1975) 'Inclusion and Mobilization in European Leninist Regimes', *World Politics*, vol. 28, no. 1 (October) pp. 69–96.

Jowitt, Kenneth (1978) *The Leninist Response to National Dependency*, Berkeley: Institute of International Studies.

Jowitt, Kenneth (1983) 'Soviet Neotraditionalism: the Political Corruption of a Leninist Regime', *Soviet Studies*, vol. 35, no. 3 (July) pp. 275–97.

Jowitt, Kenneth (1987) 'Moscow "Centre"', *East European Politics and Society*, vol. 1, no. 3 (Autumn) pp. 296–348.

Joyce, Walter, *et al.* (eds.) (1989) *Gorbachev and Gorbachevism*, London: Cass.

Karklins, Rasma (1986) *Ethnic Relations in the USSR. The Perspective from Below*, Boston: Allen & Unwin.

Katsenelinboigen, Aron (1976) 'Conflicting Trends in Soviet Economics in the Post-Stalin Era', *Russian Review*, vol. 35, no. 4 (October) pp. 373–99.

Katz, Zev (ed.) (1975) *A Handbook of Major Soviet Nationalities*, New York: Free Press.

Klavdienko, V (1986) *People's Wellbeing in Socialist Society*, Moscow: Progress.

Knight, Amy W. (1988) *The KGB. Police and Politics in the Soviet Union*, Boston: Unwin Hyman.

Kornai, Janos (1980) *Economics of Shortage*, Amsterdam: North-Holland.

Kozlov, V.I. (1988) *The Peoples of the Soviet Union*, London: Hutchinson.

Laird, Robbin F. (ed.) (1987) *Soviet Foreign Policy*, New York: Academy of Political Science.

Laird, Robbin F. and Hoffman, Erik P. (eds.) (1987) *Soviet Foreign Policy in a Changing World*, New York: Aldine.

Lampert, Nicholas (1985) *Whistleblowing in the Soviet Union. Complaints and Abuses under State Socialism*, London: Macmillan.

Lane, David (1987) *Soviet Labour and the Ethnic of Communism. Full Employment and the Labour Process in the USSR*, Brighton: Harvester.

Lane, David (ed.) (1988) *Elites and Political Power in the USSR*, Aldershot: Edward Elgar.

Lewin, Moshe (1988) *The Gorbachev Phenomenon*, Berkeley: University of California Press.

Light, Margot (1988) *The Soviet Theory of International Relations*, Brighton: Wheatsheaf.

Lowenhardt, John (1982) *The Soviet Politburo*, Edinburgh: Canongate.

McAuley, Alastair (1979) *Economic Welfare in the Soviet Union*, London: Allen & Unwin.

McCauley, Martin (ed.) (1987) *The Soviet Union under Gorbachev*, London: Macmillan.

Mandel, David (1988) 'Economic Reform and Democracy in the Soviet Union', in Ralph Miliband *et al.* (eds.) *The Socialist Register 1988*, London: Merlin Press.

Mandel, David (1989) '"Revolutionary Reform" in Soviet Factories', in Ralph Miliband *et al.* (eds.) *The Socialist Register 1989*, London: Merlin Press.

Mann, Michael (1986) *A History of Power from the Beginning to A.D. 1760*, New York: Cambridge University Press.

Mchedlov, M.P. (1987) *Socialist Society: its Social Justice*, Moscow: Progress.

Medvedev, Zhores (1988) *Gorbachev*, rev. edn, Oxford: Blackwell.

Mickiewicz, Ellen (1988) *Split Signals. Television and Politics in the Soviet Union*, New York: Oxford University Press.

Millar, James R. (ed.) (1987) *Politics, Work, and Daily Life in the USSR. A Survey of Former Citizens*, New York: Cambridge University Press.

Miller, John H. *et al.* (eds.) (1987) *Gorbachev at the Helm: A New Era in Soviet Politics?*, London: Croom Helm.

Morton, Henry W. (1974) 'What Have the Soviet Leaders Done about the Housing Crisis?', in Henry W. Morton and Rudolf L. Tokes, (eds.) *Soviet Politics and Society in the 1970s*, New York: Free Press.

Motyl, Alexander J. (1987) *Will the Non-Russians Rebel?*, Ithaca: Cornell University Press.

Nahajlo, Bohdan and Swoboda, Victor (1990) *Soviet Disunion. A History of the Nationalities Problem in the USSR*, London: Hamish Hamilton.

Navarro, Vincente (1977) *Social Security and Medicine in the USSR*, Lexington: Lexington Books.

Nelson, Daniel N. (1988) *Elite–Mass Relations in Communist Systems*, London: Macmillan.

Nogee, Joseph L. and Donaldson, Robert H. (1988) *Soviet Foreign Policy since World War II*, 3rd edn, Oxford and New York: Pergamon.

Nove, Alec (1989) *Glasnost' in Action*, Boston: Unwin Hyman.

Potichnyj, Peter J. (ed.) (1988) *The Soviet Union: Party and Society*, New York: Cambridge University Press.

Remington, Thomas F. (1988) *The Truth of Authority. Ideology and Com-*

munication in the Soviet Union, Pittsburgh: University of Pittsburgh Press.

Rigby, T.H. (1968) *Communist Party Membership in the Soviet Union, 1917–1967*, Princeton, NJ: Princeton University Press.

Rigby, T.H. (1979) *Lenin's Government: Sovnarkom 1917–1922*, New York: Cambridge University Press.

Rigby, T.H. (1989) *Political Elites in the USSR: Central Leaders and Local Cadres from Lenin to Gorbachev*, Aldershot: Edward Elgar.

Riordan, James (ed.) (1989) *Soviet Youth Culture*, London: Macmillan.

Roeder, Philip G. (1985) 'Do New Soviet Leaders Really Make a Difference? Rethinking the "Succession Connection"', *American Political Science Review*, vol. 79, no. 4 (December) pp. 958–76.

Ryan, Michael (1978) *The Organisation of Soviet Medical Care*, Oxford: Blackwell.

Sakharov, A.D. (1974) *Sakharov Speaks*, (ed.) Harrison Salisbury, New York: Knopf.

Sakwa, Richard (1989) *Soviet Politics: An Introduction*, London: Routledge.

Scanlan, James P. (1985) *Marxism in the USSR. A Critical Survey of Current Soviet Thought*, Ithaca: Cornell University Press.

Schapiro, Leonard B. (1970) *The Communist Party of the Soviet Union*, 2nd edn, London: Eyre & Spottiswoode.

Schmidt-Hauer, Christian (1986) *Gorbachev: The Road to Power*, London: Tauris.

Shlapentokh, Vladimir (1982) 'The Study of Values as a Social Phenomenon: the Soviet Case', *Social Forces*, vol. 61, no. 2 (December) pp. 403–17.

Shlapentokh, Vladimir (1989) *Public and Private Lives of the Soviet People: Changing Values in Post-Stalin Russia*, New York: Oxford University Press.

Siegler, Robert W. (1982) *The Standing Commissions of the Supreme Soviet*, New York: Praeger.

Smith, Gordon B. (1988) *Soviet Politics: Continuity and Contradiction*, London: Macmillan.

Sperry, Earl E. (1905) *An Outline of the History of Clerical Celibacy in Western Europe to the Council of Trent*, Syracuse: Syracuse University Press.

Stalin, Joseph (1925) 'Questions and Answers' (Speech delivered at the Sverdlov University), in Stalin, *Works*, vol. 7, Moscow: Foreign Languages Publishing House, 1954.

Steele, Jonathan (1985) *The Limits of Soviet Power*, Harmondsworth: Penguin.

Tatu, Michel (1988) 'The 19th Party Conference', *Problems of Communism*, vol. 38, nos 3–4 (May–August) pp. 1–15.

Trotsky, Leon (1960) *The History of the Russian Revolution*, trans. Max Eastman, Ann Arbor: University of Michigan Press.

Ulam, Adam (1974) *Expansion and Coexistence. Soviet Foreign Policy, 1917–1973*, 2nd edn, New York: Praeger.

Ulam, Adam (1983) *Dangerous Relations. The Soviet Union in World Politics, 1970–1982*, New York: Oxford University Press.

Unger, Aryeh L. (1981) *Constitutional Development in the USSR*, London: Methuen.

Urban, Michael E. (1985) 'Conceptualising Political Power in the USSR: Patterns of Binding and Bonding', *Studies in Comparative Communism*, vol. 18, no. 4 (Winter) pp. 207–26.

Urban, Michael E. (1990) *More Power to the Soviets*, Aldershot: Edward Elgar.

Vanneman, Peter (1977) *The Supreme Soviet: Politics and the Legislative Process in the Soviet Political System*, Durham, Md: Duke University Press.

Voslensky, Michael (1984) *Nomenklatura: The Soviet Ruling Class*, Garden City: Doubleday.

Walker, Rachel (1989) 'Marxism–Leninism as Discourse: the Politics of the Empty Signifier and the Double Bind', *British Journal of Political Science*, vol. 19, no. 2 (April) pp. 161–90.

White, Stephen (1988) 'Reforming the Electoral System', *Journal of Communist Studies*, vol. 4, no. 4 (December) pp. 1–17.

White, Stephen (1989) *Soviet Communism: Programme and Rules*, London: Routledge.

White, Stephen (1990a) *Gorbachev in Power*, Cambridge and New York: Cambridge University Press.

White, Stephen (1990b) '"Democratisation" in the USSR', *Soviet Studies*, vol. 42, no. 1 (January) pp. XX–XXX.

White, Stephen (forthcoming) 'From Acclamation to Limited Choice: the Soviet Elections of March 1989', *Slavic Review*.

White, Stephen and Pravda, Alex (eds.) (1988) *Ideology and Soviet Politics*, London: Macmillan.

Willerton, John P., Jr. (1987) 'Patronage Networks and Coalition Building in the Brezhnev Era', *Soviet Studies*, vol. 39, no. 2 (April) pp. 175–204.

Wilson, Andrew and Bachkatov, Nina (1988) *Living with Glasnost. Youth and Society in a Changing Russia*, Harmondsworth: Penquin.

Wixman, Ronald (1984) *The Peoples of the USSR: An Ethnographic Handbook*, Armonk NY: Sharpe.

Zaslavskaya, Tat'yana (1988) 'The Human Factor in the Development of the Economy and Social Justice', in Vladimir Gordon, trans., *Big Changes in the USSR*, Moscow: Progress.

Zaslavsky, Victor and Brym, Robert J. (1978) 'The Functions of Elections in the USSR', *Soviet Studies*, vol. 30, no. 3 (July) pp. 362–71.

Index